Supported Housing and the Law

Sue Baxter is policy and implementation officer at Sitra. She is responsible for providing training and consultancy on a range of housing management and support issues. Sue is an experienced housing practitioner with work experience ranging from a project co-ordinator with Women's Aid, as a finance officer for an alcohol agency, a fundraiser for a day centre; a principal supported housing officer and an area manager for a number of Registered Social Landlords. Sue carries out training in all areas of housing law, housing management and support, and anti-social behaviour. She is author of Sitra's publication *DIY Possession.*

Helen Carr is a solicitor and academic who has specialised in housing and social welfare law for over 20 years. She has worked at Bradford Law Centre, London Metropolitan University and the Law Commission. She is currently a senior lecturer with Kent Law School, sits as a part-time Chair with the Residential Property Tribunal and is legal adviser to the Independent Review Service for the Social Fund. She has published widely and is co-author of *The Housing Act 2004: a practical guide* (Jordans, 2005) and *Law for Social Workers* (OUP, 2005).

This book has been funded by a Housing Corporation Innovation and Good Practice Grant. The Housing Corporation is the government agency that funds new affordable homes and regulates housing associations in England.

Housing Corporation
Maple House
149 Tottenham Court Road
London W1T 7BN

0845 230 7000
www.housingcorp.gov.uk

**HOUSING
CORPORATION**

The Legal Action Group is a national, independent charity which promotes equal access to justice for all members of society who are socially, economically or otherwise disadvantaged. To this end, it seeks to improve law and practice, the administration of justice and legal services.

Supported Housing and the Law

Sue Baxter and Helen Carr

 Legal Action Group
2007

 sitra policy, training & consultancy
for housing with care and support

This edition published in Great Britain 2007
by LAG Education and Service Trust Limited
242 Pentonville Road, London N1 9UN
www.lag.org.uk

British Library Cataloguing in Publication Data
a CIP catalogue record for this book is available from the British
Library.

ISBN 978 1 903307 51 9

Printed and typeset by Hobbs the Printers, Totton, Hampshire SO40 3WX

Foreword

Having been involved in the housing sector for the majority of my professional life, I warmly welcome *Supported Housing and the Law* as a much needed publication dedicated to clarifying the notoriously complex legal and regulatory framework around supported housing.

We are experiencing unprecedented transition in the sector, but how successfully policy will translate into practice remains an open question. Here I endeavour to outline some thoughts on both key challenges we face and on how success could be meaningfully measured. The promise of reform offers an opportunity for us to reflect on housing in a wider context, through the lens of its effect on community sustainability and regeneration.

There are indicators that we may be at the starting point of new times and practices. The Lyons enquiry into Local Government and the Hills report *The Future of Social Housing* supported the exploration of alternative policy frameworks. The Cave Review has recommended a new regulatory framework more amenable to new organisational forms, new providers and partnerships, and innovative thinking in social housing. It positions the tenant at the centre of reform.

The merger of the Housing Corporation and English Partnerships into the new homes agency – as it is presently dubbed – gives us another opening to look afresh at the future. It provides a potentially unique opportunity to widen the role and remit of housing associations and other supported housing providers as community regeneration agencies by making better use of land, development solutions and partnerships for neighbourhood-based change. Housing associations are just one side of a complex equation which entails myriad partnerships of variable quality, including with non-registered providers of *Supporting People* services. While ensuring standards are met, it is essential to support a range of diverse relationships existing within the sector in order to take full advantage of current opportunities.

With such opportunities come parallel threats and challenges. This is a subject which will loom large on the Government's agenda for the foreseeable future, in part owing to the urgency of need for mainstream affordable housing. However, I have long been convinced that this renewed pressure on mass unit building could act as a distraction from developing community centred approaches which will have a lasting positive effect in our most disadvantaged areas.

People are also demanding more from services. They expect better value for people as well as value for money: manifested in a greater sense of client satisfaction, less movement between services and measurable, customer-focused outcomes.

The future of *Supporting People* will look ever more complex and challenging as demand increases, and the suppliers of services and housing struggle to keep pace. This will have an effect on the shape of the market in terms of which organisations survive and whether the needs of particular client groups, including the most socially excluded, are met. The introduction of *Supporting People* was, as stated in Chapter 11, the biggest change in funding arrangements the supported housing sector has ever seen. It has continued to evolve almost constantly since its introduction. Whether the programme is sufficiently robust to support the weight of change will become clearer over time.

Supported housing has traditionally suffered from a lack of clear operational boundaries and a framework for measuring performance and setting standards. *Supporting People* as the key framework for financial and operational assessment has led to some organisations increasing their operational capabilities. Yet, the greatest challenge for many organisations remains providing a service for those with complex needs.

The potential of supported housing providers in community regeneration is not to be underestimated. Registered Social Landlords, for example, have the will and ability to work with the most deprived, socially excluded communities, with people who may have multiple social care challenges and are often the hardest to reach.

At Turning Point we have developed Connected Care, a model for service delivery which takes a comprehensive audit of community social care need with input from that community and designs a service specification on this basis. The majority of clients that access Turning Point services are people who may require a housing service, but this area of need interfaces with multiple other social care barriers, such as mental health and substance misuse challenges. Connected Care is one model which is able to cope with this complexity of need: need which includes housing – but is not defined by it.

I would argue that emphasis must remain on these kinds of models. The time is right to look at new institutional forms, relationships, purpose, finance and regulation. Housing associations and other supported housing providers have access to communities that are some of the most vulnerable and excluded in society. We have the opportunity to engage with these communities. We have the resources to strive for vibrant and attractive communities that create customer driven environments and where funding and regulatory institutions hold organisations to account.

This publication gives us a comprehensive and accessible tool for understanding the legal issues of supported housing as they currently stand. It is also necessarily a forward looking document which forces us to question our future position in the legal framework and then reflect on possibilities of reform. The authors are to be congratulated on their exceptional clarity and skill in articulating a complex situation which has, until now, lacked a definitive navigator of relevant legal structures.

Lord Victor Adebowale CBE
Chief Executive of Turning Point
August 2007

Preface

This book started life following meetings at the Law Commission in connection with the particular legal needs of supported housing providers. This then led to e-mail conversations between us about the 'right' legal answers to real life practical problems facing the providers of supported housing. Neither of us found reaching the answers easy, but eventually we felt we made some progress, and we thought that others might find our thinking through of problems useful. Eventually Sitra, on our behalf, applied to the Housing Corporation for funding to support the publication of a book, and approached Legal Action Group (LAG) to see if they would be interested in such a venture. We are really grateful for the funding from the Housing Corporation and the support that the project received from them. James Berrington and Julia Murray have been particularly enthusiastic and well informed throughout. We are also very grateful to Eileen McMullan (policy manager) at Sitra who has supported the project from the beginning and without whom several chapters would have been much poorer and Esther Pilger, our publisher at LAG, who has always been positive and sensitive to what we were trying to achieve.

Unfortunately the law in connection with supported housing is particularly complex – it is a matter of regret for both of us that the government has given no sign that it intends to implement the Law Commission proposals to simplify tenure and set up a legal framework which is specifically designed for supported housing. One major aim of the book proposal was to produce something which was user friendly despite the complexity of the law and the range of topics which have to be covered. In order to achieve this we have been very lucky to have the services of a reader panel. We would like to thank Ian Molland and Wendi Turner for their hard work and their helpful comments during the writing of this book. There are a large number of other people who have assisted us in our work. Deserving special thanks is Carl Chapple, homelessness policy and campaigns officer at Cymorth Cymru, who shared his expertise on drug use in hostels, and Caroline Hunter, who has been very helpful whenever we have needed a third opinion on contentious matters. Thanks are also due to Ruth Ohlsen, who took valuable time away from her PhD to share her expertise on mental health. As you can see, we have done our best to share responsibility as widely as possible, but the mistakes within the book remain ours and ours alone. The law is up to date to the end of May 2007. Any new developments – and we know the law and the regulatory framework keep changing – will be featured in Sitra bulletins. We look forward to hearing the government's response to the House of Lord's decision in *YL v Birmingham City Council*.

Helen would like to thank her family for letting her spend time writing which might otherwise (but not necessarily) have been devoted to them. She would also like to thank Sue, who has responded brilliantly to the challenge of writing a book for the first time in circumstances which, because of the time frame imposed by the Housing Corporation funding regime, have been pretty fraught.

Similarly, Sue would like to thank Jack and Rosa, who have managed seven months with limited access to both mother and computer, Simon for being resigned to being at the back of the queue for the computer, and her wonderful friends who have kept her sane. She would also like to thank Helen for her support in writing this book, her infinite patience with a fumbling novice writer, and especially her tolerance in explaining legal principles to one who should have known.

Both Helen and Sue would like to dedicate this book to two women who have provided housing, support and love to many people over the years – Helen's mother, Jean Carr and Sue's mother, Margaret Ambler.

Last but not least we have drawn heavily on material drafted by Sitra. We would like to thank those authors who will doubtless recognise their contribution to the text.

Sue Baxter
Helen Carr
June 2007

Contents

APPENDICES 533

Introduction

This book is designed to provide the providers of supported housing, their advisers and service users with a straightforward introduction to the legal and regulatory framework which governs supported housing. The contents are orientated to supported housing rather than general needs housing or care homes because it is in this area of work that there is a lack of published information. Nonetheless, we anticipate that those who work in general needs housing and care homes will find parts of the book useful.

We have no expectation that readers will read the book through from beginning to end, but assume they will dip into it, using different chapters as and when necessary. We have endeavoured to make it a practical and user-friendly book by using case studies to illustrate the types of dilemmas which face providers, frequently asked questions where helpful, and text boxes to explain key points and to summarise the law. We also refer readers to useful websites and further reading where we think this would be helpful. We have drawn from a range of materials in writing the book, including information provided by Sitra from relevant training courses and briefings.

We begin the book by describing the evolution of supported housing, and the fact that its ad hoc development means that the law, particularly in relation to tenure, has failed to recognise its distinctive nature. The first part of the book outlines the legal foundations of housing law which embraces a number of specialist areas of law, including contract, tenure, homelessness and human rights. All these areas are pertinent to the supported housing sector in different ways. We start by explaining the different sources of law including statute and common law, before discussing areas like equity and European regulations. We conclude this part of the book with a discussion of when you should seek expert legal advice. In many ways you can treat this part as a reference section which you can turn to when you need to. Nonetheless, we hope that readers will find our descriptions of, for instance, the legal characteristics of contracts and the operation of human rights, useful in their own right, as well as helpful in understanding later parts of the book.

Part two of the book concentrates on the regulatory framework which impacts upon the day-to-day provision of supported housing in a myriad of ways. In the main, the forces of the private market do not provide checks on supported housing. Service users as consumers have little choice as to their landlord or support provider and cannot obtain these products from another provider when dissatisfied. External and internal regulation is designed to safeguard quality and help improve provision. We look at the regulatory role of the Housing Corporation, the inspection regime of the Audit Commission, and the continually changing face of the Supporting People programme. We also look briefly at the work of the Care Standards Commission, which regulates care homes. Lastly, we examine how organisations are managed and their internal frameworks for ensuring that services are delivered to a high standard.

In part three the book turns to the day-to-day problems of managing supported housing provision. This part of the book is an opportunity to see how law operates in practice, building on the first part, which sets out those areas of law that apply to supported housing. We focus on practical problems, many of which have been raised regularly with Sitra on its advice line, and suggest ways in which you can approach these problems in accordance with the legal and regulatory requirements. We cover the responsibilities involved in drafting and managing occupancy agreements, terminating agreements, and the legal dimensions of raising rents. We look at how behaviour can be managed when working with vulnerable people and your responsibilities towards vulnerable occupiers. We provide advice on difficult areas such as confidentiality and managing information. We do not suggest that your task is easy or that we can provide all the answers; the law is complex and the demands upon provision can be intense. However, we do suggest that, being informed about the law and regulatory requirements and approaching your work in an organised and ethical way which anticipates and provides for problems, will make your work easier.

In part four we provide information that will support you in the procedural processes involved in going to court. So, for instance, we look at the procedures involved in obtaining injunctions, issuing possession proceedings and obtaining warrants for possession. We also consider the alternatives to courts, both going to the tribunal and using alternative dispute resolution procedures, both of which we anticipate will become increasingly mainstream.

We have used the appendices for a whole host of useful information; policy checklists, statutory materials, extracts from regulatory documents and some pro-forma letters.

It is our intention that this book will assist you in your tasks of improving provision and increasing the professionalisation of the supported housing sector. We would be pleased to hear from you regarding the strengths and weaknesses of the book, and what you would like to see in any future edition.

What is supported housing?

Objectives

1.1 By the end of this chapter you will:

- Understand the diverse history of supported housing and its role in tackling social exclusion
- Appreciate the extent to which funding has shaped the provision of housing and support
- Understand what is meant by supported housing
- Appreciate who supported housing is provided for, and who it is provided by
- Understand the different types of supported housing and the difference between accommodation-based and non-accommodation-based services
- Be familiar with the services (housing management, support and care) provided in supported housing

Overview

1.2 Supported housing is an umbrella term which is applied to a whole range of housing-based solutions for vulnerable people. These solutions have emerged over time and in response to pressing social needs to accommodate those who required support and care services, either to remain in the community or to overcome particular problems such as domestic violence.

1.3 This makes the definition of supported housing problematic. It has been defined in many different ways depending on who regulates, commissions, provides or uses the services. This chapter identifies some common strands of supported housing provision. We provide you with an idea of the scope of the sector and the range of provision, from privately or voluntary sector-managed schemes for people with learning disabilities through to local authority-managed floating support schemes. We begin the chapter by giving you a brief history of the sector. We consider the ways in which the need for, and availability of, funding and the changing philosophies on how best to provide for those with support needs influenced its development. We then consider the definition of supported housing, and describe the groups of people who require supported housing and the different ways in which it is provided. The chapter ends with an overview of the services that can be provided in supported housing.

History of the sector

1.4   What is surprising is the limited attention that historians and social policy analysts have paid to the growth of supported housing. To some extent this may be because, although it plays a significant role in working with marginalised groups across the welfare state, the sums invested in the sector are relatively small compared with mainstream health and social care services.

Pre 1900

1.5   The first recorded example of supported housing was Lady Edith Bisset of Wiggold, who in 1235 endowed a charity which provided housing for 'two female lepers' in Cirencester, and the oldest charity still in existence is thought to be the Hospital of St Oswald in Worcester, founded in around 990. Although many of those who currently provide housing with support can trace their roots back to the 19th century and the Victorian age (1837–1901), the focus at that time was to provide general needs housing for the labouring classes. Philanthropy (defined as practical benevolence, especially through large-scale charitable works) was prevalent in this era, and some current providers can trace their own links back to the 1800s. For example, the Peabody Trust, founded by George Peabody, and the Guinness Trust, founded by Sir Edward Guinness, still both provide general needs housing today. The purpose of housing provision at the time was to maintain a healthy, hardworking and, more importantly, disciplined workforce. Organisations did not provide housing for the masses, or support and care for those unable to provide for themselves.

1.6   Provision for those unable to care for themselves came from charitable or religious institutions. Provision was in large institutions such as asylums in which the 'mad' were locked up, workhouses for those unable to support themselves and homes for 'fallen women' (who became pregnant outside of marriage). The result was that those who were not able to stay in the community were subject to strict discipline and surveillance in specially designed institutions. This explains the fear and loathing with which many regarded such institutions.

The 20th century

1.7   The 20th century saw great changes in the provision of social welfare, including housing and support, although the development of social housing did not fully embrace those with support needs until the latter part of the century. At the start of the century there was increased pressure on the state to provide social housing with the slogan 'homes *fit for heroes*'. This resulted in the first major piece of social housing legislation – the Housing and Town Planning Act 1919 (Addison Act). Local authorities were given a statutory duty to provide housing, with a central subsidy provided by central government. As the years went by, subsidies were either increased or cut, reflecting the housing policy of the time.

1.8   Housing associations continued to play an important role in housing, including housing for homeless people, the elderly and people with disabilities, although their contribution was small. Most housing associations were based in local communities, providing for very local needs. The increase in the number of housing associations resulted in the creation of the National Federation of Housing Societies in 1935 (now the National Housing Federation – NHF), a membership organisation that acts as a trade body for housing associations and promotes good practice in the provision of social housing. The Housing Act 1957 allowed local authorities to give mortgages to housing associations and the Housing Corporation was set up in 1964 to make loans to 'housing societies'.

1.9   For the majority of those who required support, institutional care continued, although an increase in state provision of such care followed the Beveridge Report in 1942 (*Social Insurance and Allied Services* Cmd 6404, HMSO), which laid the foundations of the welfare state. This introduced the idea that there would be state support for those who needed it 'from the cradle to the grave'.

The 1970s and 1980s

1.10   The significant increase in housing association provision in the 1970s was preceded by the 1966 TV docu-drama 'Cathy Come Home', which highlighted the plight of a homeless young mother. A number of large housing associations developed as a response to this, for example, Notting Hill Housing Trust. The Housing Act 1974 lead to two significant changes in the provision of social and supported housing:

1   The framework of the housing association grant was created, enabling housing associations to apply capital funding to provide housing.
2   Housing associations were enabled to develop hostel schemes and

central government revenue funding for hostels became available through a grant called the hostel deficit grant (HDG).

1.11 The move away from institutional care to what has become known as community care had already begun for those with mental health problems, and in 1975 two government white papers were published – *Better Services for the Mentally Handicapped* and *Better Services for the Mentally Ill* – which cemented the shift from institutions to community-based support. This, along with the government's 1981 Hostels Initiative, which replaced large homeless institutions ('spikes') with smaller community-based services, led to a growth in the number of shared supported housing services available to a range of client groups. In Box 1.1 we outline the key facts that contributed to the growth of supported housing.

Box 1.1 Key facts

Supported housing expanded considerably during the 1980s, mainly due to policy changes in two key areas:

- the closure of large institutions for people with mental health problems and learning disabilities; and
- government initiatives around housing homeless people.

1.12 The underlying philosophy of supported housing provision at that time was that services should be provided in small community settings rather than in large institutional settings. The belief remained that those with support needs were best accommodated in shared housing and that this provision was easier to manage with assumptions about efficient service delivery and concerns about allowing vulnerable people security of tenure. This was reinforced by the financial incentives or bias within the housing association and social security funding systems; funding from the Housing Corporation was only available for shared housing and welfare benefit entitlement meant that social service departments had a financial incentive to place people in private residential care.

The 1990s

1.13 The most significant piece of legislation in the 1990s was the NHS and Community Care Act 1990, implementing the government's white paper *Caring for People*, which followed recommendations by Sir Roy Griffiths. As well as saving money, the principles behind the Act were about enabling people to live as normal a life as possible in their own homes or in a homely environment in the community. The Act changed the revenue funding system for registered care homes, and from April 1993 local authority social services departments became responsible for organising and purchasing individual placements in residential care from a cash-limited budget.

1.14   In 1991, the funding framework for housing association supported housing changed and the hostel deficit grant was replaced by the special needs management allowance (SNMA). For the first time this grant was payable on self-contained as well as shared accommodation. Subsequently, SNMA was replaced by the supported housing management grant (SHMG) in 1995.

1.15   Attitudes also changed; self-contained housing was seen as a positive option for people with support needs. Schemes that were developed in the late 1990s were mainly self-contained and floating support schemes. Support was offered to those in their own homes and withdrawn when no longer required.

The 21st century

1.16   The fragmented and complex funding arrangements for supported housing were causing unease to the government. An Audit Commission report in 1998 on the role of housing in community care, *Home Alone*, identified at least 25 streams of funding being paid by four government departments. Developments outlined earlier in the chapter had happened in a piecemeal way, simply adding to the framework without comprehensive review. *Home Alone* also revealed that regulation was patchy, so public money was not adequately safeguarded and service users were not satisfied with the services they received. Around the same time there was concern about public protection following a series of high-profile incidents such as Christopher Clunis's fatal attack on Jonathon Zito. The results of the inquiry suggested that community solutions for people with mental health problems were not working.

1.17   The disquiet about funding became a crisis when a series of court decisions ruled that housing benefit should not pay for support within supported housing rents, potentially removing a much-needed stream of funding.

1.18   All of this culminated in a review of funding for the sector. The beginning of significant change began with a consultation paper, *Supporting People*, published by the Department of Social Security in November 1998. The resulting *Supporting People* programme introduced in April 2003 introduced a number of changes. It:

1 separated the funding for housing and support;
2 joined up a number of separate funding streams;
3 gave local authorities, through a joint commissioning body, control over the planning, funding and review of services; and
4 linked up *Supporting People* plans to wider community plans and other strategic priorities.

1.19   The programme has decoupled funding for housing costs from funding for support costs, so, in principle, there is no longer a tie between the kind of accommodation and type of tenure someone holds and their access to support services. Local authorities now administer the single 'pot' of monies that encompassed previous 'legacy' funding and monitor local services through the agreement with the service provider.

1.20   Although *Supporting People* enables the provision of support to people in their own homes (allowing for those with support needs to live in self-contained accommodation), shared housing has not disappeared. There is a legacy of provision developed in the 1980s and early 1990s still in use, and this model of provision may well be appropriate in some circumstances. It is important to maintain a range of housing and support solutions to meet the diverse needs of a range of client groups who find they need accommodation and support in many different circumstances; for example, temporary crisis accommodation in a women's refuge may more appropriately be provided in shared accommodation. (Chapter 11 will discuss the *Supporting People* programme in more detail.)

1.21   We have suggested in this brief history that there has been a transition from a provision of supported housing funded by philanthropy and charity to one primarily funded by the state. This has been accompanied by a move from a paternalistic to an empowering philosophy of supported housing provision. The increased involvement of the state has brought increased regulation, and providers are expected to demonstrate that their outcomes promote independence and do not encourage service users' dependence. The intensification of state attention has also lead to reliance on the sector to deliver strategic functions. On 20 May 2006 Prime Minister Tony Blair wrote in a letter to Hilary Armstrong:

> ... In many areas of public service delivery, the third sector [an umbrella term for charities, voluntary and not for profit organisations] has the potential for better user focus, better reach and better outcomes than the state, both in terms of service quality for users and value for money for the taxpayer. [see www.number10.gov.uk]

We point you towards the Homelessness Code of Guidance for Local Authorities which guides local authorities on exercising their homelessness function. The code is an example of how the broad social role supported housing now plays in delivering a government strategic objective of social inclusion. The importance of the role of support providers in preventing and tackling homelessness is explicit in the code. Housing authorities are expected to *consider all the current activities that contribute to the provision of support for people in the district ... the range of providers ... are likely to embrace the public, private and voluntary sectors* (emphasis added).

Towards a definition

1.22   There is no generally agreed definition of supported housing. If you asked, say, five support workers for a definition, they would probably each give you a different one, which would reflect the environment within which they work. Generally, supported housing has been described as any housing scheme where housing, support and sometimes care services are provided as an integrated package. However, we feel that this is a limited definition because as it misses the essence of what the sector, its providers and its staff aim to achieve. We would add the following important elements:

1   Supported housing is a finite resource which is not generally available but limited to those who are vulnerable.
2   The purpose of support is to enable service users to live as independently as possible within their community.
3   Service users are empowered to become socially included in the wider sense of community participation.
4   The support provided varies and relates to the nature of the accommodation. For instance, women living in a refuge may receive support onsite by support workers, whereas people living in their own home may receive floating support within their own homes to enable them to sustain their accommodation

1.23   One problem within the supported housing sector is that there is no common language. Many terms appear to be interchangeable, and the way one provider uses a term may be different from another. This is not designed to shroud the sector with mystery, but is as a result of the somewhat disparate the way the sector has developed. We have attempted to use the most common understanding of terms, but it is always useful for practitioners to check other parties' understanding of a term when it is used. In Box 1.2 we offer our brief definition of terms associated with supported housing.

Box 1.2 Explanation of terms

Service user – an individual who receives a supported housing service.

Client groups – a generic term which describes groups of people with certain types of support need who may be eligible for supported housing.

Provider – an organisation or individual who provides a supported housing service.

Support worker – our generic term for a member of staff who directly provides a support (and in some cases housing management) function to a service user.

Social housing – housing managed/developed by the local authority or not for profit organisation, usually housing associations for those in housing need, generally those on a low or limited income.

General needs housing – social housing which is not designed for a specific group requiring support. It represents the bulk of social housing.

Links with social housing

1.24 Many people associate supported housing with social housing, which is housing provided by local authorities, housing associations, voluntary agencies and charities. Supported housing is distinct from general needs social housing because:

1 There are higher staff levels than other forms of social housing because support and care services are provided in addition to housing management.
2 It is commonly arranged through partnerships between different organisations, including statutory sector bodies and voluntary sector organisations.
3 It is not confined to the 'not for profit' sector; companies and individuals manage schemes for those with support needs on a commercial basis.

Who is supported housing for?

1.25   Supported housing caters for a wide range of client groups with diverse needs, who require different levels of support in a range of accommodation models. If you have experience in the sector, you will know that service users do not neatly fall into categories, which in most cases are determined by funding requirements. Service users often have complex or multiple needs; for example, some people with mental health problems may also have substance misuse issues and may be homeless. In Box 1.3 we identify a range of service users who may require support.

Box 1.3 Groups of people who may require support

1   Older people with support needs.
2   Older people with mental health problems/dementia.
3   Frail elderly people.
4   People with mental health problems.
5   People with learning disabilities.
6   People with a physical or sensory disability.
7   Single homeless people with support needs.
8   People with alcohol problems.
9   People with drug problems.
10 Offenders or people at risk of offending.
11 Mentally disordered offenders.
13 Young people at risk.
14 Young people leaving care.
14 Women at risk of domestic violence.
15 People with HIV/AIDS.
16 Homeless families with support needs.
17 Refugees.
18 Teenage parents.
19 Rough sleepers.
20 Travellers.

This is an indication of the variety of needs met and not a definitive list. It is taken from definitions used in the *Supporting People* programme. The *Supporting People* programme is examined in more detail in chapter 11.

Types of supported housing

1.26 Changes in funding have led to an increased variety of housing provision as the sector has responded to different government initiatives. Whilst some types of provision can be used to accommodate groups with different needs, others are 'client group' specific. For example, hostels can specialise in the accommodation of young people, people with substance misuse issues or those at risk of offending, whereas women's refuges will only accommodate women escaping domestic violence.

1.27 Supported housing is commonly divided into two basic types of provision:

1 accommodation-based projects where vulnerable people live in a specifically designated property to receive support services; and
2 non-accommodation-based projects where vulnerable people can receive the necessary support services irrespective of where they are living.

1.28 Another important distinction between types of supported housing is that it can be permanent or temporary. Funding requirements usually mean providers have to designate schemes as either permanent or long stay or temporary stay.

1.29 Accommodation-based services can either be permanent or temporary.

1.30 Temporary simply means that there is no intention that the accommodation and/or support will be provided on a permanent basis. Funding requirements usually mean that the service user can be supported for up to two years. If permanent, the service user can be housed and supported for the longer term.

1.31 In non-accommodation-based services, the accommodation may be permanent, but the support can be provided on a temporary basis.

Accommodation based

1.32 There are several different types of accommodation-based projects:

1 Shared supported housing – a term commonly used in the sector to describe a temporary or permanent scheme where service users have their own room but share bathroom, kitchen and other communal areas with other service users. Support is delivered by staff who may have an office in the property or visit on a regular basis.

2 Self-contained supported housing – in which service users have their own flat or house. Sometimes it is sited in a block or cluster of the same type of provision and sometimes it is dispersed within a locality. Support is provided by staff who may have an office in the block or offer a visiting service.

3 Hostel – accommodation where a larger number of service users have their own rooms and share communal areas with other service users. Staffing is often provided on a 24-hour basis, seven days a week and in some cases meals are provided.

4 Bed and breakfast – temporary accommodation that is usually shared and provided by the local authority or on its behalf. The accommodation is provided for homeless people awaiting a decision as to whether the local authority will offer to house them under its statutory homeless duties. Support is not always provided, but it has become increasingly common.

5 Women's refuge – temporary accommodation for women (and their children) who have experienced domestic violence. Women often share a room with their children and share other communal areas with other women and their families. Support is provided by workers, sometimes 24 hours a day, seven days a week.

6 Adult placements – long and short term accommodation with care/support provided for the service user in the personal (usually family) home of a provider. This term can also be used to describe non-accommodation based services such as day services, befriending or support in the community.

7 Housing for older people (sometimes called sheltered) – accommodation that is specifically for older people, usually over 55, and predominately in self-contained houses or flats. The support is provided by a warden, who may live on the site, or support staff who visit the property. Some schemes are designated 'extra care' where meals and care may be provided in addition to support.

8 Residential care home – can be temporary or permanent accommodation registered under the Care Standards Act 2000 to provide accommodation, support and personal care to service users. Service users usually have their own room and share communal areas; however, some newer homes have private as well as communal cooking and washing facilities. Support and care are provided by workers 24 hours a day, seven days a week.

9 Foyer for Young People – temporary accommodation for young people (usually aged 17–25 years) with support and access to employment training and education. The accommodation may be

shared or self-contained. Support is provided by staff, who have usually have an office on site and may be available 24 hours a day, seven days a week.

10 Teenage parent accommodation – temporary accommodation specifically for young people (usually aged 17–21 years) who have become, or are about to become, parents. Service users often share a room with their babies and share kitchen, bathroom and communal areas with other service users. Support is provided by support workers who have an office on site.

11 Almshouses – permanent, usually self-contained, accommodation often targeted at the older poor of a locality or those from certain categories of employment. The accommodation is generally managed by a charity or the trustees of a bequest.

12 Shared ownership (now Homebuy) schemes – permanent self-contained accommodation where the service user buys part of the equity of the property (for example, 70 per cent). Leasehold schemes for the elderly (LSE) may provide support when the service user requires it and the support worker will be located in an office nearby.

13 Supported lodgings – similar to adult placements. An individual rents out rooms in their home and provides support to a service user with support needs; commonly used to house young people. The service user will have their own room but share bathroom, kitchen and other communal areas with the lodgings provider, who also provides the support.

Non-accommodation based

1.33 The following arrangements exist when the accommodation may not be designated as supported housing. Housing-related support will be provided, so they fall under the umbrella of supported housing:

1 Floating support services – support that is provided, usually on a temporary basis, to service users by a visiting support worker to enable the service user to sustain their tenancy and remain in their home.

2 Resettlement services – support services that enable people who have lived in supported or temporary accommodation to effect a successful transition to a permanent home and sustain their accommodation.

3 Outreach services – usually an accommodation-based scheme

providing support services to service users in the community. This service is usually on a less formal basis than floating support running advice session or surgeries.

4 Community/alarm services – usually associated with older people, where an alarm is provided for emergency use in the service users' home. Support services are thus provided when needed to enable service users to stay in their own home.

5 Home improvement services – schemes that are designed to support service users in acquiring the aids and adaptation they require to stay in their own home.

Who provides supported housing?

1.34 In order to understand the 'make up' of the sector it is useful to describe the types of organisations and individuals providing supported housing.

1 Housing associations – are 'not for profit' bodies governed by a voluntary board that provide low cost housing for people in housing need. Housing associations fall into two groups; those registered with the Housing Corporation and usually funded by it (referred to as registered social landlords or RSLs) and those that are not registered. Those who remain unregistered are either part of the voluntary sector or profit-making bodies. RSLs manage the majority of supported housing, either directly or via partnerships with voluntary and statutory agencies. RSLs provide a wide range of provision including hostels, shared or self-contained supported housing, leasehold schemes for the elderly, home improvements, floating support and in some circumstances registered care homes. The majority of RSLs manage general needs housing and supported housing. There are a small number of specialist housing associations that only provide supported housing, for example, Centrepoint is an RSL that provides housing and support services for young homeless people.

2 Local authorities – provide supported housing in their locality either directly or in partnership with a voluntary agency or RSL. Local authorities are the second largest provider of supported housing due to the number of schemes they manage for people with learning disabilities and older people. They provide a wide range of supported housing, including hostels, supported housing and a large number of sheltered schemes. Local authorities also provide bed and break-

fast accommodation or temporary housing associated with their duties to homeless people.

3 Voluntary agencies/organisations – not for profit organisations that provide services for the public good. Their activities are governed by a board or committee of volunteers. Voluntary organisations manage a wide range of supported housing, including hostels, supported housing, women's refuges, teenage parents and foyers, often in partnership with RSLs and local authorities.

4 Charities – are voluntary 'not for profit' organisations that provide services for the public good. Most charities are registered with the Charity Commission and the majority of RSLs and voluntary organisations are also registered charities. Charities are also called voluntary agencies, although some organisations prefer to refer to themselves as charities, for example, almshouses managed by the charitable trustees of a bequest.

5 Private companies – are organisations set up to make a profit out of their activities. Private companies manage bed and breakfast, registered care homes, hostels and supported housing.

6 Private individuals – are members of the public who are paid to provide supported housing. It is usually one person or a family who provide support services by managing an adult placement or supported lodgings.

7 National Health Service – the NHS as a government department works in partnership with or funds RSLs, agencies and private companies and individuals to provide supported housing. Health trusts as local agencies responsible for health services also work in partnership with these bodies and manage provision directly. Their provision includes supported housing and care homes, where care is provided as one of the services.

1.35 Collectively RSLs, voluntary organisations and charities are referred to, particularly by government, as the 'third sector', the first sector being the state and the second sector being the private sector. The increasing importance of 'third sector' organisations has been recognised by government, which launched the Office of the Third Sector in May 2006. In Box 1.4 we outline the role of the Office of the Third Sector.

Box 1.4 Office of the Third Sector

The Office of the Third Sector was set up to formalise the government's role in supporting voluntary and community organisations and charities, amongst others. It works as an advocate for

the third sector and works across government with departments, for example, the Department of Communities and Local Government. The Office of the Third Sector conducted a review of the third sector to inform the 2007 spending review.
See www.cabinetoffice.gov.uk/third_sector.

What services are provided?

1.36   Supported housing is characterised by the provision of support and, in some circumstances, care, as well as accommodation and housing management services. There are no clear boundaries between these services, and this can present difficulties where those who fund a particular activity want to ensure that workers are not delivering services that should be paid for by another funding body. Support workers can find this confusing, as unsustainable distinctions are drawn up between care and support or other services. In many parts of the country, commissioners are moving towards aligning different funding streams and jointly commissioning services to deliver agreed outcomes. The next section offers a broad outline of the different categories of service based on the expected outcome, and examples of the activities required to achieve them.

Housing management

1.37   The aim of housing management services is to ensure that the property is safe, maintained and well managed. Housing management activities take place in both supported and general needs accommodation. These activities include carrying out repairs, ensuring that the property conforms to health and safety requirements, collecting rent, dealing with rent arrears, neighbour disputes and tenant participation, managing voids and lettings and taking legal action if a user does not keep to the terms of their occupancy agreement. In general needs social housing the staff responsible for housing management are usually called housing officers. A number of RSLs and local authorities have separated some housing management functions, creating income recovery officers who collect rent arrears and community involvement officers who ensure tenant participation. Most local authorities and RSLs have a separate maintenance function, although in some cases the first point of contact may be the housing officer.

Support

1.38   Support services are provided to enable a service user to live independently or sustain their capacity to do so. Support services can include assistance with budgeting and welfare benefits, enabling access to training, education or employment, development of living skills, support to manage a tenancy or licence agreement, giving general emotional support and empowering the user to access leisure activities, social networks and achieve social inclusion. Front line staff who provide these services are generally described as support workers, support officers, project workers or key workers.

1.39   It is common for support and housing management to be provided by the same organisation, although, since the introduction of the *Supporting People* funding regime, separate delivery of the two services has increased. This change is often prompted by the decisions of those who commission services or business decisions about the best way to deliver these services.

1.40   This has led to two main models of service delivery:

1   The same member of staff provides both services – staff can be referred to as supported housing officers, but also key workers, support workers, support officers or project workers.
2   The housing management and support functions are split between two members of staff, who are sometimes located in different teams/departments within the same organisation or different organisations. Commonly the housing management service is delivered by a housing officer or supported housing officer and the support service by the support worker, key worker, tenancy sustainment worker or even floating support worker.

1.41   There is a debate in the sector as to whether it is better for housing management and support to be provided by the same or different workers. One view is that a worker expected to provide both services experiences a conflict of interest. One moment they wear the 'landlord's hat', serving a warning letter for rent arrears, and the next they wear the 'support worker hat', aiming to support the user to manage the arrears. The concern is that the relationship of trust built up by providing support is negated by enforcing the landlord role. This is why some landlords have separated housing management and support into different teams or departments. The opposite viewpoint is that providing both services enables workers to take a 'holistic' view of the service user, understanding, for example, that they have fallen into rent arrears due to their substance misuse issues. It is sometimes very difficult to separate housing management and support services in some services, for example, women's refuges and hostels. The separation of housing management and support relies on good communication between the two workers.

1.42   In some cases the housing management and support are delivered by different organisations. For example, in a young persons' scheme, the building may be owned and managed by a housing association and the housing management function provided by their general needs housing officers. The support is provided by a voluntary agency which specialises in working with young people, and staff may be called support workers or key workers.

1.43   In floating support schemes, people living in general needs housing requiring support may receive services delivered by a floating support worker or a tenancy sustainment worker, and the housing management function continues to be provided separately by the landlord. Floating support workers will work with a service user for a period of time, which is defined by the service user's needs. When support is no longer required the support service 'floats off' to support another service user in another property.

Care

1.44   Care services are usually associated with health or social care; for example, the prevention, treatment and management of physical and mental illness and the preservation of mental and physical wellbeing. In the context of supported housing, it includes social care duties that fall within the remit of social services. Care services include assistance with personal care to the user, for example, washing, feeding and taking them to the toilet, administering medication, changing dressings and cooking and shopping for them. In supported housing a member of staff who provides care services is usually called a care worker.

1.45   It is not uncommon for a scheme to provide housing management, support and care with one worker providing all three services and known as a support worker, key worker, project worker or scheme worker. The current funding regime means that such a scheme would attract separate funding streams to provide all three services.

Summary

1.46   The chapter provides you with an understanding of the term supported housing and how provision has developed over time. We believe that by understanding the history of the sector you will appreciate current provision and the potential tensions in that provision. We have provided you with key themes to enable you to come to your own understanding of supported housing. It may be useful for you to look up some of the sector's definitions. We discuss the Housing Corporation definition of supported housing in chapter 10 and the *Supporting People* definition of support which we consider in chapter 11. Whilst considering the range of people who benefit from the provision of supported housing, we have tried to acknowledge that service users do not fall into neat categories or boxes. We have outlined the main types of accommodation and non-accommodation-based services and furnished you with details of the most common type of provider. Lastly, we have attempted to explore the housing management, support and care services that can make up supported housing services. We hope you are able to identify your own scheme within our account and understand that the work you do contributes to a much wider sector.

PART I

CHAPTER 2

Sources of law

Objectives

2.1   By the end of this chapter you will:

- Be familiar with some of the basic principles of English law
- Have been introduced to cases and statutes
- Have an understanding of the structure of the English legal system

Introduction

2.2   This chapter provides an introduction to those aspects of the English legal system with which you need some familiarity in order to understand the rest of the book and the legal environment in which you operate. We start by describing some of the basic principles which underpin our legal system, and then spend some time discussing statute law and case-law. Finally, we provide you with a brief description of the court structure in England and Wales.

Some basic principles

The rule of law

2.3   The rule of law, in simple terms, means that no matter how much any individual may dislike a law, whilst they remain a member of this particular society, they are bound to obey it. So, for instance, you may think it nonsensical that the law requires you to grant a service user a tenancy when you consider that it would be better if he or she was issued with a licence. You can hold that opinion, but you are bound to follow the law.

2.4   The rule of law is fundamental to democracy. We are governed by our elected political representatives in parliament, who can pass or repeal whatever laws they see fit, and we, the citizens, have to obey those laws. Our redress against politicians is the ballot box. Of course, there are all sorts of problems with this. Elections are unlikely to be fought on the legal status of the residents of supported housing. Nonetheless, imperfect though our system may be, we have to conform to its requirements.

2.5   The rule of law also means that the courts' function is to interpret the will of parliament expressed in statute and not to make the law up, unless there is a 'gap' in the statute – and even then there are principles which they are obliged to follow.

2.6   Parliament has to a certain extent constrained its actions via the Human Rights Act 1998 and through European Community law. We will consider the Human Rights Act in more detail in chapter 7, and you will see the impact of European Community law when we look at procurement rules in connection with *Supporting People* in chapter 11 and when we describe the law on discrimination in chapter 6.

The distinction between private and public law

2.7   There is an important distinction to be drawn between public and private law. Public law cases are cases brought by or against public authorities, such as the social services departments of local authorities. Private law cases are cases brought by private individuals. Public law proceedings, because they involve public authorities interfering with the way individuals live their lives, are required to conform to certain standards. Those standards are achieved through the operation of the law. The particular area of the law that performs this function is administrative law, which we will discuss below.

2.8   In contrast, an example of private law would be a dispute between a car owner and a garage over the quality of a repair to the car. If the owner refuses to pay the bill because of dissatisfaction with the quality of the repair, the garage may sue the car owner in the county court. How the dispute is to be resolved by the court is set out in the law of contract and the rules of court. The outcome of the case, though, is not of interest to society as a whole, only to the parties to the dispute.

2.9   Supported housing is at the interface between public and private law. Most supported housing is not provided by public authorities, since case-law under the Human Rights Act 1998 has found that registered social landlords are not public bodies, unless they are carrying out public functions – and the provision of accommodation to the vulnerable is not in itself a public function. Therefore, principles of administrative law, at least for the moment, are not directly applicable. However, providers receive their funding from the state and carry out functions on behalf of the state. This has two consequences. First, administrative law principles apply to the decisions of the local authority *Supporting People* team and providers will have rights of redress if those principles are breached. Secondly, the definition of public authority may change in the future to embrace organisations which are funded by the state to provide welfare services. That may mean that providers will have administrative law principles imposed upon them. There are particular concerns about the lack of protection given to the residents of private care homes. The argument is that because some residents' care is funded by public money then the private establishment is in effect a public body. You can see that if the law changed to treat private care homes as public bodies, in some circumstances this would have certain consequences for supported housing provision. We discuss this more fully in chapter 7 when we look at the Human Rights Act 1998.

Administrative law

2.10   The state is very powerful and well resourced in comparison with an individual. Administrative law attempts to ensure that justice is done between the state and the individual by embracing particular principles that operate to restrain arbitrary or wrong decision making by the state. These principles are openness (often described as transparency in cases), fairness, rationality (including giving reasons for decisions), impartiality (which means that decision takers should be independent), accountability, the control of discretion, consistency, participation, efficiency, equity and equal treatment. These principles can be collectively described as the requirements necessary for fairness, and are often referred to as the requirements of 'natural justice'. Sometimes these principles conflict, and then the decision maker must weigh up the various principles and make the best decision he or she can in the circumstances. You may feel that these legal standards, even though you are not required to uphold them, are appropriate standards for organisations providing social services to vulnerable people. They are certainly principles which inform good practice.

Judicial review

2.11   The mechanism available for people who believe that they have not been treated fairly by the state is to apply for judicial review. Judicial review is the process by which the courts oversee decisions made by public officials and ensure that they have been made fairly. So if a provider's funding was cut and proper procedures were not followed, perhaps because relevant information was not taken into account in the decision-making process, then judicial review may be an appropriate way to challenge the decision.

2.12   In judicial review cases judges do not substitute their decision for the public official's decision. What concerns the court is the process of decision making, because natural justice requires that decisions are made following the correct procedures. If, after judicial review, the courts consider that procedures have not been followed appropriately, they can quash the decision of the public body and order that the decision is made again following proper procedures. The Human Rights Act 1998 has added an additional requirement to the principles of good decision making – decisions must be proportionate to the outcome which is sought. We discuss this in full in chapter 7.

The difference between the common law, equity and statute law

2.13   The general understanding of common law is law which is established by the courts and developed from precedents. This is quite distinct from statute law, which is law that has been passed by parliament. The term common law is also used to distinguish legal rules from the operation of equity. Equity is the umbrella term for the principles which were developed by the Courts of Chancery and designed to mitigate the harshness of the common law. Typical areas in which equity operates today are in connection with trusts, with equitable interests in property and with particular remedies. You will come across the impact of equity in your work, for instance, when you are involved in granting tenancies to those aged under 18, or when seeking injunctions, which are equitable remedies. We explain the implications of the operation of equity when we discuss these particular areas.

2.14   The role of the courts is not limited to the development of the common law and equity. They have a vital role in interpreting the meaning of statutes, in making findings of fact and in managing the practice of litigation. As society becomes more complicated, the role of common law diminishes, since more and more statutes are passed dealing with more and more areas of behaviour within society. But common law is not wholly extinct: murder is not a statutory offence; it is a common law offence. This means that you cannot look in an Act of parliament for a definition of murder; rather, you have to look at decisions of courts in the past as to what defines murder. However, the penalty that must be imposed for murder is set out in a statute. Similarly, a tenancy is a creation of common law. It has not been statutorily defined, and we rely on cases to understand the legal status of a tenant. However, much of the work carried out within supported housing is governed by statute, and the next part of this chapter describes in more detail this very important source of law.

> **Box 2.1 Frequently asked questions**
>
> **We want to stop a service user's ex-partner from coming to our scheme for young women and our solicitor suggested applying for an injunction. She described this as an equitable remedy – what does this mean? And does it have the same weight as breaking the law?**
>
> Injunctions are equitable remedies; this means that they are available on a discretionary basis and not automatically. The court will decide whether in all the circumstances of the case it is appropriate and just for the scheme to have the benefit of an injunction. Once the court grants an injunction, then, if the ex-partner breaches it, he or she is in contempt of court, and may be liable to imprisonment.

Statutes

2.15　Statutes – Acts of parliament – start life as bills. These may be bills sponsored by government ministers or private members' bills. Private members' bills are, as the name suggests, bills sponsored by ordinary backbench members of parliament. Most bills are government bills, but within the field of supported housing there have been some very significant Acts which started life as private members' bills, for instance, the Homeless Persons Act 1977 and the Disabled Persons (Services, Consultation and Representation) Act 1986.

2.16　Often the subject matter of a bill is discussed extensively before it gets to parliament. Sometimes the government may publish a green paper which will set out a number of proposals to change the law and ask for comments. Green papers got their name because in the past they were published with green covers. Following this consultation process the government may set out its revised policy objectives in a white paper. White papers were originally published with white covers. A relatively recent innovation is the draft bill procedure whereby the government publishes a bill in draft form, before it is introduced in parliament as a formal bill. This enables consultation and pre-legislative scrutiny before it is issued formally. The Mental Capacity Act 2004 is an example of a piece of legislation which was originally published as a draft bill and was extensively debated prior to its introduction to parliament.

2.17　The formal parliamentary process starts when a bill is presented to parliament, generally by the minister responsible for it. There are a series of readings, scrutiny and debates on the bill. Eventually the bill receives the royal assent and crystallises into its final form – the Act of parliament. However, there is often a long delay before particular sections are brought into effect. We will discuss this further when we look at the example of the Housing Act 2004.

Delegated legislation

2.18   In most Acts of parliament there is a power for delegated legislation. Delegated legislation, as its name implies, gives the power to some person or body to pass legislation that has the same effect as if it had been passed by parliament through its normal process of legislation. For the delegated legislation to come into force, normally it must be 'laid before parliament'. This requires a copy of the proposed delegated legislation to be placed (or laid) in the House of Commons and the House of Lords for a specified number of days. After that, the legislation comes into force. It may require a vote without a debate or the alternative form is when it comes into effect by 'negative resolution'. This means that it will come into force unless sufficient members of parliament require a vote to be taken.

2.19   Delegated legislation is also known as secondary legislation, or statutory instruments. Statutory instruments come in two forms: regulations and orders. It is not important to distinguish between these.

Guidance

2.20   Guidance is provided by the state to help public bodies exercise their powers, particularly when the statute imposes statutory duties in connection with vulnerable people. In your area of work, the most significant example is the Code of Guidance on Homelessness published by the Department of Communities and Local Government. While statutory instruments have the full force of a statute, the role of guidance is not so clear-cut. Basically, public bodies are required to follow government guidance unless there is a well-articulated reason for them to deviate from that guidance. However, even if guidance is followed by a public body, it cannot be guaranteed that it is acting within the law. Guidance issued by a government department will always only amount to a view of what the department thinks the law is. It is, however, the function of the courts to decide what the legislation means, and guidance cannot usurp that function.

Good practice

2.21 One purpose of this book is to promote good practice and through-out we try to give you useful examples. However, one word of warning: our views of good practice are simply opinions based upon the ideals of how support provision should function. They are not statute law or common law, and therefore good practice must always give way to the requirements of statute, regulations, and guidance, if the require-ments conflict.

The Housing Act 2004

2.22 One way we can illustrate important features of a statute is to look in a little more detail at the most recent major piece of legislation that the government has passed on housing – the Housing Act 2004.The date 2004 is the year that the Act received Royal Assent. It is not necessar-ily the year when the whole of the statute comes into force, although some provisions did come into force immediately. The Housing Act 2004, like many statutes, contains complex provisions which required additional work. The delegated legislation was published after the Act received royal assent. In the case of a complex piece of legislation like the Housing Act 2004, different parts of the Act have different com-mencement dates. The implementation schedule is published on the Department of Communities and Local Government website (www.communities.gov.uk).

2.23 The front cover of the statute has the royal coat of arms, the name of the statute and the words Chapter 00. What this refers to is that it is the statute of that parliamentary session. There is also a note to say that explanatory notes have been produced to assist in the understanding of the Act and are available separately. This is a recent innovation. If an Act is one which you will frequently use, the explanatory notes provide a really useful source of information about its provisions.

The contents of the statute

2.24 Turning the page you will see the contents of the statute. You will see that this particular Act is divided into seven parts, it has 270 sections and 16 schedules.

Sections and subsections

2.25 If we look at one of those sections, say section 212, we can see the typical layout for a section of an Act. The section has a heading, in this case 'Tenancy deposit schemes'. It is then divided into nine subsections, which are numbered in brackets. If you want to refer to a particular subsection then you would say section 212 subsection 1. If you are referring to this subsection in writing you would write section 212(1).

Schedules

2.26 Not everything is contained in the body of the statute. Most Acts have schedules attached which contain further material, usually of a more detailed kind. The Housing Act 2004 has 16 schedules. They are listed beneath the contents of the Act. Schedules are set out slightly differently from the main body of the Act. If you turn to Schedule 1 you will see its title, 'Procedure and Appeals relating to improvement notices'. In small script to the right of the title there is a section number, section 18. This is the section in the Act which gives effect to the schedule. The schedule is then set out in paragraphs and subparagraphs. If you wish to refer to a paragraph within a schedule then you refer to it as paragraph 1(2) of Schedule 1 to the Act. We say 'to' the Act rather than 'of' the Act because the Schedule is attached to the Act.

Amendments

2.27 Frequently, statutes contain provisions which amend the provisions of earlier statutes. The Housing Act 2004 is no exception. So, for instance, section 181 of the Act provides:

> (1) In Schedule 5 to the Housing Act 1985 (exceptions to the right to buy) paragraph 11 (single dwelling-house particularly suitable for elderly persons) is amended as follows.
> (2) In sub-paragraph (4) (questions arising under paragraph 11 to be determined by the Secretary of State), for 'the Secretary of State' (in both places) substitute 'the appropriate tribunal or authority'.

2.28 What this means is that from the commencement date of this provision of the 2004 Act, that particular paragraph of Schedule 5 to the Housing Act 1985 has to be read in the new way.

2.29 Acts can do more than amend particular sections. They can introduce whole new sections into other Acts. In the Housing Act 2004, new provisions in relation to the exercise of the right to buy are

introduced into the Housing Act 1985. The new sections are introduced by section 183 of the Housing Act 2004, but they will become sections 138A–138C of the Housing Act 1985. You will always recognise
sections of legislation which have been introduced by subsequent legislation because of the use of the capital letter.

Reading statutes – statutory interpretation

2.30   Despite the expertise of parliamentary draftsman, and the extensive
scrutiny of the parliamentary process, there will inevitably be some
uncertainties about what particular provisions of statutes mean when
practically applied. It is the function of the courts to resolve the dilemmas which arise through the process known as statutory interpretation.

2.31   Statutory interpretation has evolved over centuries. When courts
have had to decide what a statute says, there has developed a series
of so-called 'rules' that guide the courts. Their effect is to set out the
approach that should be adopted by the courts. There are three main
'rules': first, the 'literal rule', which says that the words in a statute
are taken to have their literal meaning unless such an interpretation
produces a nonsensical result. In that case the 'golden rule' applies,
which says that if the literal meaning produces an absurd result, then
you look at it in the overall context of the statute. If these two rules
do not help, then the 'mischief rule' is applied. This rule states that you
interpret the meaning of the word in the light of what the problem or
mischief was that the statute was passed to deal with. The Human
Rights Act 1998 has an impact on statutory interpretation, in that it provides that courts must strive to interpret legislation in a way which is
compatible with convention rights and the intention of parliament.
When it is not possible to interpret the legislation in this way, the
courts may strike down delegated legislation, but not primary legislation (although they may make a declaration of incompatibility, which
should prompt government action).

Cases

2.32   Throughout the book we refer to cases. These references may be in
connection with interpretations of statutory provisions or to illustrate
particular common law terms, such as the meaning of tenancy. All
you need to know about cases at this point is that they have authority

in deciding what the law is, and that the higher the court that makes the decision, the more authoritative the decision is. If the decision we are talking about is made by the House of Lords then it binds lower courts and provides an extremely authoritative statement of the law. Cases, once you have some familiarity with them, are not particularly difficult to read. Sometimes the details that surround them can seem quite mysterious, particularly, for instance, their names and the references to law reports. If you want to know more about reading cases, we suggest that you look at a good legal method book such as *Holland and Webb* (James Holland and Julian Webb, *Learning legal rules: a student's guide to legal method and reasoning*, 6th edn, Oxford University Press, 2006).

The court hierarchy

2.33   Our brief review of the sources of law will have demonstrated that:

- Decisions made by judges are essential to our understanding of what the law actually is on a particular topic.
- There is a hierarchy of courts and the more senior the court, the more authoritative is the decision made by it.

2.34   The diagram set out in Box 2.2 overleaf illustrates the court system.

Summary

2.35   This chapter is inevitably a simplified explanation of the operations of the English legal system. We elaborate where necessary in the chapters which follow. However, we hope that it provides you with a sufficient introduction so that you can begin to develop your familiarity with the legal environment within which you operate.

Box 2.2 The courts system

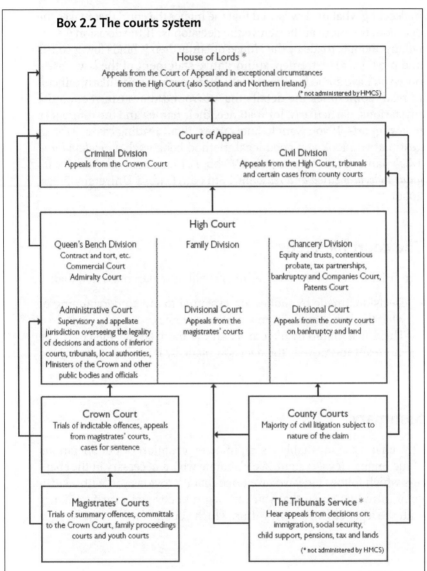

House of Lords *

Appeals from the Court of Appeal and in exceptional circumstances
from the High Court (also Scotland and Northern Ireland)

(* not administered by HMCS)

Court of Appeal

Criminal Division
Appeals from the Crown Court

Civil Division
Appeals from the High Court, tribunals
and certain cases from county courts

High Court

Queen's Bench Division
Contract and tort, etc.
Commercial Court
Admiralty Court

Family Division

Chancery Division
Equity and trusts, contentious
probate, tax partnerships,
bankruptcy and Companies Court,
Patents Court

Administrative Court
Supervisory and appellate
jurisdiction overseeing the legality
of decisions and actions of inferior
courts, tribunals, local authorities,
Ministers of the Crown and other
public bodies and officials

Divisional Court
Appeals from the
magistrates' courts

Divisional Court
Appeals from the county courts
on bankruptcy and land

Crown Court
Trials of indictable offences, appeals
from magistrates' courts,
cases for sentence

County Courts
Majority of civil litigation subject to
nature of the claim

Magistrates' Courts
Trials of summary offences, committals
to the Crown Court, family proceedings
courts and youth courts

The Tribunals Service *
Hear appeals from decisions on:
immigration, social security,
child support, pensions, tax and lands

(* not administered by HMCS)

© Crown Copyright. Reproduced from HMCS at www.hmcourts-service.gov.uk.

The diagram makes the hierarchy of the courts clear. It also illustrates the system of appeals. We will discuss the practicalities of the courts and tribunal hearings you are likely to attend in Part 4 of this book.

An introduction to the law of contract

Objectives

3.1   By the end of this chapter you will:

- Be familiar with the necessary components of a contract
- Understand the impact of the Unfair Terms in Consumer Contract Regulations 1999 (SI 1999 No 2083) on the terms of a contract
- Have an outline knowledge of the consequences of breach of contract
- Have considered the limitations on contractual capacity of minors and mentally incapacitated persons

Overview

3.2   Contract is the legal medium through which we conduct the vast majority of our everyday transactions, from buying a bus ticket to buying a mobile phone. Contracts obviously vary tremendously in their complexity and some, such as employment contracts and occupation contracts, are subject to specialist regulation through statute. Later in the book we spend a lot of time looking at the particular rules which govern the contractual relationship between a landlord and an occupier of housing. However, at this point we are going to consider the general principles of the law of contract. This is for three reasons:

- The general principles also apply to specialist contracts, although sometimes in a modified form.
- There is a multiplicity of contracts that support providers are potentially involved in, not just with service users but also with local authorities and registered social landlords, and it is important to recognise the specific legal qualities of those contractual relationships.
- Some agreements that are important to the smooth running of supported housing are not contractual agreements, but protocols or conventions. Therefore, different legal consequences follow when these agreements are not followed. This chapter aims to enable you to distinguish between contractual and non-contractual agreements.

3.3   The chapter begins by describing in simple terms the prerequisites of a contract. It then considers the importance of the Unfair Terms in Consumer Contract Regulations, which have a particular impact upon terms of occupation contracts. The chapter then considers the legal consequences of breach of the terms of the contract. The final section of the chapter outlines the impact of reduced legal capacity of one party, either because he or she is a minor or because he or she is incapacitated.

The essential elements of a contract

3.4 A contract is an agreement between two or more parties that is legally enforceable because of the element of exchange of something of value between the parties. This exchange of value is known as 'consideration'. So, to take an everyday example, you enter into a contract with the bus company when you buy a bus ticket in exchange for the journey on the bus provided by the company from bus stop A to bus stop B. If the bus company fails to deliver its side of the bargain, then you are entitled to damages – the return of your fare and the cost of the alternative means of getting to your destination.

3.5 Of course, this is a grossly simplified version of contract law. Each element can be unpicked and debated. We will concentrate here on two aspects, agreements and consideration.

Agreements

3.6 As we have already pointed out, an agreement is a prerequisite of a contract. Whether an agreement has been reached is generally an objective decision – would someone external to the process of bargaining consider that the parties had reached an agreement? The courts prefer the objective approach because it allows for certainty in the identification of enforceable bargains.

3.7 Agreement is reached when an offer by one party is accepted by the other. An offer is a statement of a willingness to enter into a contract on particular terms. An acceptance happens when the party to whom the offer is addressed communicates acceptance of those terms. Contract text books spend some time distinguishing between 'invitations to treat' – such as displays of goods in shops and advertisements – and offers. The distinction is important because parties have to know when they are bound. So, for instance, if a supported housing provider advertised its service stating that it had rooms available for single young substance abusers, that would not be an offer which could be accepted by someone fitting the category, but an invitation to treat.

The offer would only be made following an application in response to this advert, perhaps following an interview. The parties would only be bound once the young person had accepted the offer.

Consideration

3.8   English law does not distinguish between those agreements which are enforceable through the courts and those that are not by insisting on particular formalities. An oral agreement is as binding as a written one. This has particular consequences in housing – a landlord can be bound by an oral statement its agent makes when showing a prospective tenant around a room, perhaps promising to replace the broken hand basin. And, of course, tenancies and licences can be oral. The distinction between enforceability and unenforceability lies in consideration. In everyday speech, consideration can be translated as price paid for a benefit. If a price is to be paid, or has been paid, by one party to gain a benefit from the other, then it is likely that there is an enforceable contract. It is the notion of consideration which distinguishes the protocols you enter into with other providers or your administering authority from contracts. The price paid has to represent some value, but the law does not inquire into its adequacy. So, for instance, doing something in return for love and affection does not constitute consideration. This also means that the courts will not rewrite the terms of the contract for you to make it fair. If you contract with your local authority to provide support services at an unrealistic price, that is your problem. However, in some circumstances the Unfair Terms in Consumer Contract Regulations will apply, so the harshness of the rule may be mitigated for some terms, although the regulations do not cover the price agreed between the parties.

3.9   Closely related to consideration is the requirement that there must be an intention to create legal relations between the parties before a contract can be enforceable. The courts presume that agreements made in domestic and social situations are not intended to create legal relations. So if you promise your child £10 if he or she does the washing up for a week, that will probably not be a contract despite the fact that there has been an agreement between you and consideration – he or she washes up in exchange for the money. However, the presumption can be rebutted. For instance, you may run a café, your child may be an adult looking for work and gave up other work to carry out his or her commitment to you. Moreover, some promises could not be contractual but, by their nature, can only be aspirational. So when an organisation sets itself the aim of treating all its residents with dignity and respect, this is unlikely to be incorporated into a contract between it and its residents; its nature is aspirational.

Box 3.1 Frequently asked questions

One of our residents who has a one-year fixed term assured shorthold tenancy wants to leave before the end of the year. We want her to pay us compensation for breach of her tenancy agreement. We have a long waiting list for our properties.

Your resident entered into a contract with you. One term of the contract was that the contract would last for a fixed period of one year. Clearly, if she leaves early, she will have breached her contract and be liable for damages which equal the loss of rent to you for the remaining period. You are, however, under a duty to mitigate your loss. It is likely that you could fill the vacancy quickly. If the resident gives you one month's notice of her decision to leave, it is unlikely that you would be able to claim any further compensation. During that time you could interview potential applicants and select someone to move into the vacated flat.

Terms

3.10   The contents of a contract are set out in the terms that have been agreed between the parties. If a term is not performed then the contract is breached. We consider the consequences of breach below. In general, a person is bound by a document setting out those terms that he or she signs, whether or not it has been read, except where the signature was achieved as a result of fraud or misrepresentation.

3.11   However, it can be a bit more difficult than this to work out the precise terms of the contract:

- Not everything which is said or written between the parties prior to the formation of the contract will become a term of the contract.
- Statements of opinion, such as 'this is the best room in the house', will have no legal effect, and representations, although they may be persuasive in leading you to enter into the contract and may have legal consequences, will not become terms.
- Certain terms will be implied into the contract, either by statute, by custom or by the common law. In housing, terms relating to the

standard of repair in tenancies are implied by statute – section 11 of the Landlord and Tenant Act 1985 – and by common law. We will discuss these implied terms more fully in connection with disrepair in chapter 16.

3.12   There are particular terms of contracts that are known as exclusion clauses that are used to limit the liability of one party in the event of failure to perform. Whilst in some circumstances exclusion clauses may be reasonable, they can operate detrimentally, particularly where one party to the contract is much more commercially powerful than the other. The Unfair Contract Terms Act 1977 restricts the operation of exclusion clauses. Attempts to exclude or restrict liability for negligence causing death or personal injury are void under the statute. Exclusion clauses relating to other loss or damage caused by negligence are only valid if they are held to be reasonable. Where one party deals as consumer or on the other's written standard terms of business, the other party cannot exclude or restrict liability for his own breach of contract or claim to be entitled to render a contractual performance substantially different from that which was reasonably expected of him or render no performance at all, except in so far as the contract term satisfies the requirement of reasonableness.

3.13   Perhaps a more relevant method of policing the terms of the contract for supported housing providers is the Unfair Terms in Consumer Contracts Regulations.

Unfair Terms in Consumer Contracts Regulations 1999

3.14   The Unfair Terms in Consumer Contracts Regulations 1999 (SI 1999 No 2083) were enacted into English law in order to implement an EC Directive on Unfair Terms in Consumer Contracts. Unlike the Unfair Contract Terms Act 1977, which controls exclusion clauses, the regulations can bite on any term of the contract and the contracts which are regulated include contracts relating to land.

3.15   The aim of the regulations is to regulate unfair terms in contracts between a seller or supplier and a consumer. An unfair term is defined in regulation 5(1):

> A contractual term which has not been individually negotiated shall be regarded as unfair if, contrary to the requirement of good faith, it causes a significant imbalance in the parties' rights and obligations under the contract, to the detriment of the consumer.

3.16   Moreover, all terms (including core terms – see below) must be written in plain and intelligible language.

3.17   Important points to note are that:

- The regulations do not apply to terms that are individually negoti-ated. They apply when the supplier uses a standard form of contract. Your normal occupation agreement is likely to be a standard form of contract.
- The regulations provide some examples of terms that may be con-sidered to be unfair. These include terms which attempt to make dis-proportionately high sums payable by the consumer in the event of breach (penalty clauses), clauses which enable the supplier to alter the terms of the contract unilaterally without a valid reason set out in the contract and clauses which have the effect of binding the consumer to terms with which he or she had no real opportunity of becoming actuated before the conclusion of the contract. Time spent explaining the meaning of an occupation contract to a prospec-tive occupier is therefore obviously time well spent!
- Good faith is the key to fairness. Factors which the court will take into account in assessing good faith will include:
  - the relative strengths of the bargaining positions of the parties;
  - the extent to which the supplier has dealt fairly and equitably with the consumer; and
  - whether the consumer had an inducement to agree to the term.

3.18   Because there is a shortage of accommodation, organisations provid-ing it must be very careful not to exploit their bargaining position when drafting their standard occupancy contracts. It will not be ade-quate to say, 'well if they don't like it, they will just have to go else-where'!

Core terms

3.19   The test of fairness will not be applied to terms which define the main subject matter of the contract or which concern the adequacy of the price or remuneration. This is best explained by seeing the purpose of the regulations as preventing unfair surprises being sprung on the consumer, whilst at the same time preserving both parties' freedom to contract for the bargain they want. What it means is that the regulations will not interrogate the appropriateness of the price that is being demanded/paid by the parties. However, this distinction is not easy, and undoubtedly the courts will be involved in disputes over whether terms are or are not core terms. The Office of Fair Trading has indicated that terms in occupation agreements relating to the description of the premises and the rent payable are core terms.

Enforcement

3.20   Any term held to be unfair will not bind the consumer, but the rest of the contract will continue to bind the consumer if it is capable of continuing without the unfair term. It is not primarily the courts that oversee the operation of the regulations. The Office of Fair Trading (OFT) takes primary responsibility, alongside trading standards departments, the Consumers' Association and a number of other regulators.

Box 3.2 Frequently asked questions

If we have a term in our occupancy agreement that a service user thinks is unfair, what can they do?

Anyone can refer standard form contracts to the Office of Fair Trading or other regulators, including Trading Standards and the Consumers' Association. These bodies will consider complaints and take the necessary action, including injunctions to restrain the use of apparently unfair terms. The service user may also refuse to adhere to the term because they believe it is unfair. If you choose to enforce the term in court by initiating possession proceedings, the court may scrutinise the term for any apparent unfairness.

Guidance on unfair terms in tenancy agreements

3.21   As we have already pointed out, the regulations apply to contracts relating to land. The OFT has done extensive work in relation to such contracts and has published guidance on unfair terms in tenancy agreements. It was revised in September 2005 and is available on the internet at www.oft.gov.uk – you are strongly advised to read it when you revise your terms and conditions. The guidance deals primarily with potential unfairness in assured and assured shorthold tenancy agreements in England and Wales. It also refers briefly to public sector and social housing agreements and to the pre-tenancy agreements that can precede an assured shorthold tenancy. The guidance does not apply to lodging arrangements. The OFT explains that the guidance is designed to help landlords, letting agents and suppliers of standard or model terms to meet the requirements of the regulations and to assist housing advisers. The OFT expects those using, or recommending, standard pre-formulated tenancy agreements to review their terms and conditions in light of the guidance and amend or remove any unfair terms from their contracts.

3.22   The OFT gives some strong indications of its approach to enforcement of the regulations. This makes it a mine of useful information. You should read the entire document, but some flavour of the impact of the regulations is contained in the following paragraphs:

> 2.6 In assessing fairness, we take note of how a term could be used. A term is open to challenge if it is drafted so widely that it could be relied on in a way to harm consumers. It may be considered unfair if it could have an unfair effect, even if it is not at present being used unfairly in practice and there is no intention to use it unfairly. In such cases landlords could achieve fairness by redrafting the term more precisely, so that it reflects their practice and intentions.
>
> 2.7 Transparency is also fundamental to fairness. Regulation 7 introduces a further requirement that standard terms must use plain and intelligible language. Terms should not just be clear for legal purposes. When we assess fairness, we also have to consider what a consumer is likely to understand by the wording of a clause. Even if a clause would be clear to a lawyer, we will probably conclude that it is potentially unfair if it is likely to mislead, or be unintelligible to consumers. Contracts should be in language that is plain and intelligible to ordinary people. Consumers should also have the chance to read all the terms before agreeing to the contract.

3.23   In relation to support providers who are subcontractors the following is relevant:

> 3.9 We regard disclaimers covering problems caused by a landlord's agents or sub-contractors in the same way as those covering loss or damage caused directly by the landlord's own actions. A tenant is likely to have had no choice about the agent or sub-contractors used, and has no contractual rights against them. The landlord has chosen to enter into agreements with them, and therefore should not seek to disclaim any legal liability that they have for the defaults of their agents or contractors.

3.24   Finally, it is worth alerting providers to this paragraph:

> 3.32 We would object to a provision giving the landlord an excessive right to enter the rented property. Under any kind of lease or tenancy, a landlord is required by common law to allow his tenants 'exclusive possession' and 'quiet enjoyment' of the premises during the tenancy. In other words, tenants must be free from unwarranted intrusion by anyone, including the landlord. Landlords are unfairly disregarding that basic obligation if they reserve a right to enter the property without giving reasonable notice or getting the tenant's consent, except for good reason.

3.25   The guidance also provides some examples of terms which are potentially unfair. Again the whole document is invaluable, but the following may give you an indication of terms which may be unacceptable:

Obligation	OFT view
Against keeping any inflammable materials	The term should be narrowed so that it does not include small items for domestic use, such as boxes of matches.
Against moving furniture	This should be narrowed so it does not preclude tenants from moving furniture such as chairs.
Against having guests overnight	This is normal use and enjoyment of the property on an occasional basis.
Against keeping any pets	Our objection is to blanket exclusions of pets without consideration of all the circumstances. Such a term has been considered unfair under comparable legislation in another EU member state because it could prevent a tenant keeping a goldfish. We are unlikely to object to a term prohibiting the keeping of pets that could harm the property, affect subsequent tenants or be a nuisance to other residents.
Against changing the phone or utility supplier	The tenant should have the choice of supplier although he may be required to keep the landlord informed of any change and to return the account to the original supplier at the end of the tenancy.
Against the display of any notices	This should be narrowed to the type of notice that is precluded, eg potentially offensive notices.
Against making any noise that can be heard outside the property	This should be narrowed to preclude excessive noise that may cause a disturbance.

Breach of contract and damages

3.26   A breach of contract occurs when one party to the contract fails or refuses to perform a term of the contract, or performs the term defectively. The failure must be without lawful excuse. The normal remedy for breach of contract is damages. Damages are compensation to the claimant for the loss that he or she has suffered as a result of the defendant's breach of contract. Compensation is calculated with the aim of putting the claimant in the position that he or she would have been in had the contract been performed according to its terms. Compensation is only paid for loss that the claimant can prove arose as a result of the defendant's breach of contract. A claimant must take steps to mitigate his or her loss, which means that he or she must take all reasonable steps to minimise the loss arising from the breach. Damages cannot be recovered when the loss which the claimant has suffered is too distant from the defendant's breach of contract. Generally, the rule is that compensation is only payable for losses which were in the contemplation of the parties at the commencement of the contract.

Capacity

3.27   The law assumes that adults enter into contractual bargains on equal terms and will not interfere to protect them from the consequences of their personal weaknesses. In formal terms, this is explained as adults of sound mind having full contractual capacity. However, the law does interfere to protect minors – young people under the age of 18 – and the mentally incapacitated from being inappropriately bound by contracts they are deemed not to have the capacity to enter into freely. At the same time, the law is concerned to protect people who in good faith enter into contracts with minors and the mentally incapacitated. The reconciliation of these two positions leads to terribly complicated rules, which in themselves are not particularly coherent. What we describe below is a simplified and practical approach to the difficulties posed by legal incapacity.

Minors

3.28   The general rule is that a minor is not bound by a contract that he or she enters into during his or her minority. However, there are three exceptions to this:

- A contract to supply a minor with 'necessaries' is binding upon the minor where the contract as a whole is for the benefit of the minor and its terms are not harsh or onerous. The cases indicate that a 'necessary' is widely defined, although the meaning depends upon the status of the minor – the richer he or she is, the more goods will fall into the definition.

- A minor is bound by a contract of employment if that contract is generally for his or her benefit.
- Certain contracts with minors are valid and binding upon the minor unless he or she repudiates liability (rejects the burdens of the contract) before reaching the age of 18. Only the minor can repudiate; the adult is bound. Examples of such contracts are contracts to acquire an interest in land or shares in a company.

3.29   One crucial thing to remember is that the incapacity of minors can only be used as a defence to a claim and not as the basis for a claim. We look at the practical ramifications of this when we consider tenancies and minors in chapter 4.

Mental incapacity

3.30   The law is not so generous to individuals suffering from mental incapacity. Mental incapacity is not a ground for the setting aside of a contract or for the return of benefits conferred under a contract, unless the incapacity is known to the other party to the contract. This may have harsh consequences in certain circumstances when vulnerable people enter into contracts they cannot afford. However, providers must not treat people who are mentally incapacitated as having no rights. For instance, the covenant of quiet enjoyment applies to tenancies, as we discuss in chapter 4. Providers cannot therefore move a carer into the rented home of a mentally incapacitated person without the permission of that person.

Summary

3.31   What makes a contract a contract as opposed to a promise or a protocol is the element of 'consideration'. As soon as a price is paid for something or something else of value is exchanged, then the law of contract comes into play. We have tried to show in this chapter how you can recognise the range of contractual relationships you have entered into as part of your work as a provider of supported housing. You are likely to have contractual relationships with your administering authority, with your workers and with your service users. However, we have pointed out that not all the commitments you enter into will have contractual force.

3.32   Most contracts are regulated to a greater or lesser extent by the law. Contracts in connection with housing have attracted particular attention from parliament over the years, so that terms are implied by statute into contracts in connection with repairs and, most recently, the contractual relationship between landlords and tenants has been modified by the tenancy deposit scheme. In this chapter we have concentrated on the regulation of contracts by the Unfair Terms in Consumer Contract Regulations and suggested that you should pay particular attention to the drafting of terms within your occupancy contracts. In other chapters in this book, we will look at the way in which landlord and tenant law impacts upon occupancy contracts and the impact of anti-discrimination legislation. Finally, in this chapter we have drawn your attention to the means by which certain people, to a greater or lesser extent, are protected by law from the full implications of the contracts they have entered into.

CHAPTER 4

Tenure and protection from eviction

Objectives

4.1   By the end of this chapter you will:

- Understand the general legal principles underpinning the distinction between a tenancy and a licence
- Be able to apply those principles to particular facts
- Be able to understand the consequences of the distinction in the context of supported housing
- Have a basic understanding of the statutory protection of tenants
- Understand the key features of the assured and the assured shorthold tenancy
- Understand the operation of the legal safety net of the Protection from Eviction Act 1977

Introduction

4.2   The history of the development of legal protections for tenants and other occupiers of rented housing has been long, complex and politically fraught. The result is a system of detailed and overlapping statutory schemes that do not necessarily fit contemporary purposes and are not always understood by legal advisers or judges. Supported housing provides a good example of this. Housing law does not treat the providers or occupiers of supported housing as a special case, nor does it provide a coherent legal framework that enables providers to recognise with any certainty the legal status of their occupiers. This chapter is in three parts. It begins by considering the lease/licence distinction and outlines its application within supported housing. In the second part it briefly describes the current system of statutory protection of tenants, with further detail provided on the operation of the assured tenancy regime. The final part of the chapter considers the Protection from Eviction Act 1977, which provides a safety net of legal protections for some licensees and tenants.

The significance of the lease/licence distinction

4.3   The most important aspect of legal status is whether an occupier has a lease (a tenancy) or a licence. There are two main advantages to an occupier in being a tenant as opposed to a licensee. First, it is generally harder for the landlord to recover possession of the premises, because the protection provided by the Housing Act 1988 extends to tenants only. We shall examine this protection below. Secondly, the landlord must repair premises let on a tenancy (see below). This obligation does not apply with a licence, unless the landlord has actually agreed to repair, which would mean that he or she had a contractual obligation to repair.

4.4   One way to understand the basis of the lease/licence distinction is to consider it in the context of the history of statutory protection. The most significant case in relation to the lease/licence distinction is the decision in *Street v Mountford* [1985] AC 809, which we discuss more fully below. It was decided when the Rent Act 1977 provided very strong protections for tenants that landlords were keen to avoid. In *Street v Mountford* the House of Lords overruled a long line of decisions that privileged the intentions of the parties to the contract of letting over the legal effects of the contract itself. The House of Lords considered that this was allowing landlords to take advantage of their strong market position to defeat the legal protections that tenants had been given in the Rent Acts. Therefore, you could explain *Street v Mountford* as an attempt to ensure that occupiers of rental housing receive the (then) very strong protections available to tenants in as many circumstances as possible, regardless of the intentions of the parties to the contract of letting.

4.5   The context of supported housing is a long way away from the practices of private sector landlords 30 years ago. It can be difficult for providers to understand why the courts do not recognise their expertise and their concerns with the behaviour of residents, the safety of workers and other residents and the need for residents to take up move-on accommodation when it is available. Whilst providers may think these matters should be important in deciding the status of a residential occupier, the courts are bound by the decision in *Street v Mountford*. However, *Street v Mountford* does not provide a clear rule which can be applied in all circumstances; what it does is to point judges to the crucial characteristics of a tenancy. Before we consider these, we outline the legal significance of a licence.

The status of licensees

4.6   Typical examples of licensees in the residential context are guests in your home or a grown-up child living with you. Such occupiers are in the premises by permission of the occupier and their right to continue there can be withdrawn. The licence can be a bare licence, which is just a simple permission such as you would give to someone dropping in for a cup of tea, or it can be contractual, so you could be paid money by your adult children towards their board and lodgings, or indeed you could have a lodger sharing your house. With a bare licence permission can be withdrawn after reasonable notice, and with a contractual licence you are bound by the terms of the contract. With a lodger, for instance, you may have agreed to give one week's notice on either side. It is important to note that many licensees who have a contract, like most tenants, cannot be evicted without a court order, because of the Protection from Eviction Act 1977, which we discuss below. If a former licensee remains in the premises after termination of their permission to do so, they become a trespasser. Clearly, for those providing housing, there are a lot of attractions to letting on licences. They are relatively informal, rooms can be relet with the minimum of fuss and minimum loss of income and rules can be enforced to the benefit of everyone living in a project. However, not only are there ethical problems in controlling the behaviour of residents through insecurity of tenure, the courts are likely to find that anyone occupying their own room even in a shared property is likely to have the benefits of a tenancy.

The requirements of a tenancy

4.7 Most people who pay money (rent) to live in someone else's property are tenants. The word 'tenant' has legal significance. It describes a particular type of arrangement which gives particular rights to the occupier and imposes particular responsibilities upon the landlord. The decision in *Street v Mountford* means that if someone is a tenant, the person or persons renting is entitled to three things:

1 exclusive possession – the right to exclude others, including the landlord, from the property;
2 of identifiable premises;
3 for a known period (such as a weekly period).

4.8 However, the decision in *Street v Mountford* also means that if you have these things, then regardless of whether your agreement calls itself a tenancy or whether you or your landlord are aware of your status, you are a tenant.

4.9 A tenant is able to say that under the contract (that is, the verbal or written agreement of letting), while the tenancy continues, he or she is entitled to live there and to exclude anyone else from being there. Moreover, the status of tenant gives rise to particular statutory protections. So most people who are now tenants have the benefits of the

protections of the Housing Act 1988, which means that particular formalities have to be complied with, and notice periods given, before
the tenant can be evicted.

4.10   The problem is that often tenants and even landlords do not realise
that the arrangement is a tenancy. This is because of the elusive nature
of exclusive possession. For instance, the landlord may tell an occupier
that the landlord will let him/herself into the room when it is convenient to do so, or, in the context of supported housing, move
someone in to share the room. This may lead the occupier to think
that they do not have the right to exclude the landlord and therefore they
are a licensee. If, in fact, the agreement grants the occupier exclusive
possession, the landlord is behaving illegally – in breach of the covenant
of quiet enjoyment which we discuss later. In addition, a landlord may
try to describe a letting as a licence, when in fact it is a tenancy. The
House of Lords in *Street v Mountford* said it does not matter what the
letting is called; what matters is what the person actually gets from
the landlord under that agreement.

4.11   So, if landlords and tenants cannot look at the name of the agreement or at the intentions of the parties under the agreement, how can
they tell the legal status of the rental agreement? *Street v Mountford*
directs judges to scrutinise the factual situation of the provision. The
facts of provision are likely to be different in every case, another reason
why it is impossible to give providers the clear guidance they would like.

4.12   The crucial fact is that there must be exclusive possession. However,
the law does not provide clarity on what facts are necessary to prove the
existence of exclusive possession, and indeed the cases suggest that the
intentions of the parties are to an extent part of the facts of exclusive
possession. So the courts have responded to the requirement to balance
the rights of occupiers for security of tenure and the needs of providers
for straightforward eviction in an ad hoc way, utilising the flexibility of
the lease/licence distinction and relying on the presence or absence of
the elusive exclusive possession to determine the respective rights
and responsibilities of landlords and occupiers. We are sure this is
not what you want to hear; if you want clarity, however, our best advice
is to assume that the occupier is a tenant unless there are strong factual indications in your provision to suggest the contrary.

Shared accommodation

4.13   One way in which to understand judicial reasoning when distinguishing between a lease and a licence is to consider cases in connection with occupiers who share accommodation. These multiple

occupancy agreements were discussed by the House of Lords in *Antoniades v Villiers* [1990] AC 417 and *AG Securities v Vaughan* [1988] 3 WLR 1205. In the *Antoniades* case, a young couple were looking for accommodation together. They each signed a separate agreement, described as a licence agreement, to share a one-bedroom flat. Each agreement provided that the 'licensor' also had the right to occupy the premises and that he or she might license others to share occupation with the licensees. The House of Lords held that the arrangement was clearly a lease and that the young couple were joint tenants of the flat even though they had signed separate agreements. The terms allowing occupation by the landlord or others were clearly shams, not intended to be used in reality. This contrasts with the other case that the House of Lords heard at the same time, *AG Securities*. Here the premises comprised a flat which had four bedrooms, plus bathroom and kitchen. The flat was occupied by four people who were selected by the owner and who did not previously know one another. Each had arrived at a different time and each paid a different amount for the use of the flat. The individuals were not given exclusive possession of any part of the flat. There were no locks on bedroom doors and in no sense were the occupiers given the impression that any room was theirs. It was a typical student-type house-sharing agreement. The House of Lords was clear that these were genuine licences.

4.14   What we can learn from the flat-sharing cases is that the status of occupiers should be understood in the light of all the circumstances – the relationship between the sharers, the negotiations which led up to the agreement, the nature and the extent of the accommodation and the intended and actual way in which the accommodation was used. Do not be swayed by what the landlord or the occupiers *think* the arrangements are. What matters is the objective reality of the situation.

Hostel accommodation

4.15   There are cases which are much closer to the current context of supported housing. The difficulty which has arisen concerns the nature of exclusive possession in the context of hostel accommodation provided by either local authority or housing association landlords. In *Westminster City Council v Clarke* [1992] 2 AC 288, the local authority had retained extensive control over the hostel it ran to rehouse single men through the insertion of a mobility clause into the rental agreement. The House of Lords decided that the occupiers did not have exclusive possession. The effect of the agreement was that the landlord had retained possession of all of the rooms of the hostel in order to supervise and control the activities of the occupiers. This would suggest that in many cases providers are not granting exclusive possession. It was generally understood that where social landlords provided bed-sitters for the vulnerable homeless in hostels and maintained strict controls over the management of the residents and the hostels, licences as opposed to leases were created. This allows a social landlord to optimise short-term provision of accommodation without granting security of tenure. However, the House of Lords stated that the decision was limited to the particular facts of the case, and it may be that a successful argument could be advanced to restrict the decision to local authority provision.

4.16   More importantly, in the decision of the House of Lords in *Bruton (AP) v London and Quadrant Housing Trust* (1999) 31 HLR 902, in relatively similar factual circumstances, the judges returned to a very straightforward interpretation of the lease/licence distinction. As Mr Bruton had exclusive possession for an identifiable period (here, for a weekly term) at a rent of a room in the housing trust's hostel, he was found to have a tenancy. This was despite the fact that the trust itself only had the premises on licence and that Mr Bruton had understood that he only had a licence. What this means is that, in most circumstances, residents who are paying rent for the exclusive use of accommodation will have tenancies, even if this causes difficulties for social landlords attempting to accommodate some very vulnerable people in short-term accommodation. The reason Mr Bruton took his case to court was to get his landlord to carry out repairs. He needed a tenancy so that there would be a legal obligation to repair his accommodation.

4.17   Some hostel accommodation provided by local authority landlords and housing association landlords is excluded from the Protection from Eviction Act 1977. This means that the occupier has no security of tenure at all and can be evicted without a court order. We discuss the provisions of the Protection from Eviction Act 1977 later in this chapter. However, we now turn to discuss some of the specific responsibilities which arise from the granting of a tenancy.

Legal implications of tenancies

4.18   Unfortunately, even when you have solved the initial problem of tenancy or licence, the law governing tenancies is complex, and rights vary depending upon the statutory regime that the tenant falls under. Before we start to unravel those matters, however, we should consider some basic principles which apply to all tenancies.

Information requirements

4.19   There are certain matters that the law requires of a landlord which are important to mention here. First, if the rent is payable weekly, the landlord must supply the tenant with a rent book (Landlord and Tenant Act 1985, ss4–7). Failure to do so is a criminal offence. However, the requirement only applies when the rent is payable weekly. Most rents in private accommodation are now payable monthly, so it is of limited use. Secondly, there is an obligation (under section 48 of the Landlord and Tenant Act 1985) on landlords to provide tenants with an address in England and Wales at which notices, including notices relating to legal proceedings, may be served on them by tenants. Failure to comply with this requirement renders any rent or service charge not due until the requirements have been satisfied. It does not mean that the tenant will not be required to pay the arrears of rent once the section 48 notice has been provided. Finally, any tenant who has an assured shorthold tenancy which began after 27 February 1997 who does not have a written tenancy is entitled to a written statement from the landlord of certain key provisions of the tenancy (section 20A of the Housing Act 1988). If the landlord fails to provide this, he or she commits a criminal offence. The requirements are met if the information is provided in the tenancy agreement.

Other legal characteristics of a tenancy

4.20   Tenancies have other characteristics. First, what is called the covenant of quiet enjoyment is implied by law into every tenancy. What this means is that the landlord makes a legally binding promise that the tenant's lawful possession of land will not be substantially interfered with by the landlord. In practical terms, therefore, the landlord cannot go into the tenant's home without permission, send the tenant threatening letters or stop the tenant using the premises as he or she wishes. The covenant is particularly useful in the context of harassment and illegal eviction. The second characteristic about which it is useful to know is the tenant's obligation to behave in a 'tenant-like' manner. This means that the tenant should look after the property, carry out minor repairs and not let damage occur through carelessness. If the tenant does not do so, then he or she may be liable to the landlord for damages. It is unfortunate that such significant terms are not self-explanatory. They reflect the medieval origins of landlord and tenant law.

Tenants terminating agreements

4.21   Tenants can surrender their tenancies as long as they do so consistently with the terms of their agreement. We discuss this more fully in our chapter on contracts. Tenants may also simply abandon the tenancy. What is important is to be sure that the tenant really does want to give up possession of the property. Landlords have been caught out in the past by courts interpreting events as something other than surrenders or abandonment, and finding that the agreement continues. You should always endeavour to get the tenant to sign a surrender so you have evidence. If the tenant simply disappears, the best advice is to get a court order. Only in that way can you be sure of your legal position.

Young people and tenancies

4.22   There are two obstacles to young people becoming tenants. First, you have to be 18 or over to acquire a 'legal interest in land', which is what a tenancy is. Secondly, contracts with young people under 18 are enforceable against the young person only if they are 'contracts for necessities'. We discuss what is called the 'contractual incapacity' of young people in chapter 3. This may theoretically make it difficult for the landlord to recover unpaid rent from a young person. However, these hurdles can be overcome. In most circumstances a contract to rent accommodation would be considered by the courts to be a contract for necessities. Even if landlords cannot grant legal tenancies to under-18s, they can grant 'equitable leases'. Equitable leases are in very simple terms leases which do not comply with all the legal formalities but the courts consider should be treated as if they do. Such agreements attract the normal provisions of security of tenure. Unfortunately, many landlords do not understand the law and, if they are prepared to rent accommodation at all to young people, may try to do so on a variety of arrangements which are less favourable to the young person. This is not necessary. We suggest that if you rent to under-18s you use your standard form of tenancy agreement. The only thing you need to do is to issue a new tenancy agreement once the young person reaches the age of 18. This is to avoid any legal uncertainty. Another reason why many landlords are reluctant to grant a tenancy to a person under the age of 18 is that they consider that it will be difficult to recover rent arrears accrued whilst the person is under 18. We expand upon this explanation in Box 4.2.

4.23 Some providers have been trying to guard against difficulties in collecting arrears from a legal tenant who is over 18 which were accrued whilst the tenant was under 18 and holding an equitable tenancy. One device which has been used is to get the young person to sign two agreements: one is the equitable tenancy; the other is the legal tenancy which is dated for the young person's 18th birthday. The idea is that the arrears will be accrued during the period of the legal tenancy and therefore the young person can be evicted even when he or she has reached 18 for previous arrears. This seems to us to be legally incoherent. A post-dated lease operates as a contract for a lease which becomes an equitable tenancy when the young person goes into possession. It cannot be a legal lease waiting to happen at the date of the 18th birthday. We are firmly of the view that the way forward in dealing with the problem of arrears is to use a term of the legal lease as described above. This does not avoid all potential legal problems, as we discuss below. In Box 4.1 we set out a suggested term for the agreement.

Box 4.1

It is a term of this tenancy agreement that the tenant repays arrears of £xxx accrued during the previous tenancy of this property. The arrears shall be repaid at the rate of £x per month which is payable at the same time and in the same manner as the rent.

4.24 If the tenant fails to pay the accrued arrears then he or she can be evicted under ground 12 of the Housing Act 1988 for breach of a term of the tenancy agreement. This ground is a discretionary ground, and therefore you cannot be certain of gaining possession. There is the possibility that the judge may consider that this is a device to gain possession on money grounds other than rent. However, it still seems to us the best way forward, and should make sense to most judges. Further information is available from Shelter, which publishes a good practice guide on tenancies and minors.

4.25 The most important consequence of the grant of a tenancy is the statutory protections it gives rise to, in particular security of tenure, rent protection and succession rights. It is to these matters that we now turn.

Box 4.2 Legal options for housing agreements with persons under 18

Type of arrangement	Legal meaning	Difficulties	Comment
Licence agreements	Licences are contracts – therefore there are no difficulties in a person under 18 signing a licence. The principles of 'contracts for necessities' means that the rent is very likely to be enforceable.	If the agreement grants exclusive possession (and most agreements granting exclusive occupation will grant exclusive possession) courts are likely to find that the agreement is a lease. Because a person aged under 18 cannot hold a legal estate in land, the lease will be equitable – see below.	There are real difficulties in offering under-18s licences because the courts may well find that the arrangement is a lease and not a licence. Moreover Housing Corporation guidance is that you should offer as much security as you are able to. In addition, you should not discriminate against someone simply on the grounds of their age. If most of your occupancies are tenancies then why offer those under 18 licences?
Lease signed by person under 18	There is nothing to stop a person aged under 18 signing a lease. However, it will not be a legal lease but an equitable lease. This means that there is a trust, and the legal estate vests in the	The law is quite uncertain about where the trust vests. More practically, there may be difficulties in recovering arrears of rent accrued during the equitable lease after the legal	We would suggest that if the young person is in arrears at the time of the grant of the legal lease, you put a clause in the new tenancy agreement requiring the tenant to pay off the arrears at a certain amount each week or month.

	trustee, which is likely to be the landlord. The trustee has a legal responsibility to grant the equitable tenant a legal lease as soon as he or she reaches 18. Equitable tenants have the same statutory protection as legal tenants. Equitable tenants can be evicted for non-payment of rent.	lease has been granted. The legal lease is a new lease and you cannot evict someone for rent arrears from a previous tenancy.	If the tenant breaches that term then you can issue possession proceedings for breach of tenancy agreement. The court will oversee this – it will only grant possession if the facts are made out and a possession order would be reasonable.
Lease signed on behalf of the young person by someone else	Here the young person has an equitable tenancy and the other person, frequently the Director of Housing or the Director of Social Services, holds the legal title as trustee. That person has an obligation to grant the young person a legal lease when he or she reaches 18.		

The occupation agreement as a contract

4.26   Do not forget that an occupation agreement is a contract. Its terms – as long as they are fair – are binding on both parties. Any fixed term that is agreed between the parties is a term, so that the landlord is obliged to provide the room or flat for the period, and the occupier is obliged to remain there. Breach of contract leads to claims for damages, although any claim is subject to the duty to mitigate your loss. For further details on the legal effects of contract, see chapter 5.

Recognising the relevant statutory framework – a summary

4.27   As we have already indicated, a variety of statutes have been enacted over the last 100 years providing specific protections for tenants. However, depending upon the political climate, the extent of those rights, and the conditions under which they have been exercised, have varied enormously. The Rent Act 1977 could be described as the high water mark of tenants' rights. The assured shorthold tenancy framework following the implementation of the Housing Act 1996 provides a much more limited set of rights to tenants. In order to understand tenants' rights you need to be able to recognise the relevant statutory regime. To do this you need the answers to two key questions:

- Who is the landlord?
- When did the tenancy commence?

4.28   The potential landlords are local authorities, housing associations and private landlords, who can be individuals or companies. The most significant date is 15 January 1989, the date of the commencement of the Housing Act 1988, after which date no new Rent Act tenancies could be created. However, the commencement date of the relevant sections of the Housing Act 1996 – 28 February 1997 – is also important.

4.29   In simple terms, all private tenancies created on or after 15 January 1989 are governed by the Housing Act 1988 and must be either assured tenancies or assured shorthold tenancies. All private tenancies created before that time are governed by the Rent Act 1977 and are regulated tenancies. When the local authority is the landlord then the Housing Act 1985 is the relevant piece of legislation, and local authority tenants generally have secure tenancies regardless of the commencement date. However, there are two exceptions to this. Some local authorities use introductory tenancies for the first year of the tenancy. Introductory tenancies are governed by the provisions of the

Housing Act 1996. Local authorities also have the power to apply to court to demote a secure tenancy to a demoted tenancy.

4.30 Housing association tenancies are slightly more complex, in that the legislation treated them in different ways depending on whether the government of the day saw housing associations as part of the private or public sector. Pre-January 1989, the housing association tenant was seen as part of the public sector, with the rent governed by the fair rent provisions of the Rent Act 1977 and the other terms determined by the Housing Act 1985. New tenancies created on or after that date by housing association landlords are governed by the Housing Act 1988 and are generally assured tenancies, although some housing associations are using assured shortholds for probationary periods. Housing associations can also apply to court to demote assured tenancies. The demotion process creates an assured shorthold tenancy.

4.31 The Housing Act 1996 added a final twist from its commencement on 28 February 1997. Prior to that date, a private sector landlord had to comply with rigorous technical procedures to create an assured shorthold tenancy. From that date, all new tenancies created are assured shorthold tenancies unless the landlord informs the tenant that the agreement is for an assured tenancy. These complex provisions have real significance, particularly in relation to the tenant's right to remain in the property.

Exclusions

4.32 Note, however, that not all tenancies are covered by statutory regimes, either because the tenancy is one which is specifically excluded from protection by the statute or because the tenancy agreement itself falls outside the scope of the statute. So, for instance, consider a tenant of a private landlord who started living in the property in July 1990. On the face of it, that means that the relevant statute is the Housing Act 1988. However, the tenant also owns a property where she lives five days a week. Section 1 of the Housing Act 1988 requires that, for the tenant to receive the protection of the statute, she must occupy the property as her only or principal home. Clearly this tenant does not, so she will not be protected by the Act. What protection would such a tenant have? She would be a common law tenant whose tenancy can be ended by a notice to quit. Her only (and limited) protection would be via the Protection from Eviction Act 1977, which we will discuss later.

4.33 Our second example relates to those tenancies which are excluded from statutory protection. The same basic facts apply – a tenant moved into the property in July 1990. This time, however, it turns out that she has a resident landlord. Such an agreement is excluded from the Housing Act 1988 on the basis that a landlord should not be obliged by statute to allow a tenant to continue to live in his own house when that relationship has broken down. Again, what the tenant has is a common law tenancy with only the Protection from Eviction Act 1977 for protection. If the tenant shares living accommodation, that is more than a hall or stairway, with the landlord, she will receive no protection.

4.34   We have provided a summary of the main statutory regimes in Box 4.3.

4.35   We will not cover the details of all of the various statutory regimes in this chapter. If you want to know more you should use one of the specialist books which we recommend at the end of the chapter. However, it is important that you understand something of the operation of the Housing Act 1988 and the two forms of tenancy that you are most likely to come across, the assured tenancy and the assured shorthold tenancy. We elaborate on these below

---

Box 4.3 The main statutory framework – a summary

Rent Act 1977	*Regulated tenancies* Strong security of tenure. 'Fair' rents (including Housing Association tenancies created prior to the commencement of Housing Act 1988). Strong succession rights.	Private residential tenancies. Created prior to 15 January 1989.
Housing Act 1985	*Secure tenancies* Strong security of tenure. Including Housing Association tenancies created prior to commencement of Housing Act 1988.	Local authority and Housing Action Trust tenancies whenever created which comply with the landlord and tenant conditions set out in the statute.

	Demoted tenancies	Very limited security. Created by the Anti-Social Behaviour Act 2003. Last for one year and require a court order.
Housing Act 1988	*Assured tenancies* Strong security of tenure. Market rent.	Private residential tenancies.
	Assured shorthold tenancies which comply with statutory criteria. Housing Associations can demote assured tenancies to assured shorthold for one year following court order. Market rents. Very limited security of tenure.	Created on or after 15 January 1989.
Housing Act 1996	Presumption that a tenancy is assured shorthold. Unless notice to contrary.	Private residential tenancies created on or after 8 February 1997. *Introductory tenancies* Probationary tenancies for first year of tenancy.

Assured tenancies under the Housing Act 1988

4.36   The Housing Act 1988, as amended by the Housing Act 1996, governs private sector and housing association tenancy agreements commencing from 15 January 1989 to date. It creates the assured tenancy and the assured shorthold tenancy.

4.37   All assured and assured shorthold tenants must occupy the property as their only or principal home. The important exclusions from the assured tenancy regime are those tenancies covered by other statutory frameworks and tenancies where the landlord resides in the same property as the tenant. Succession provisions in the 1988 Act are limited. There can be only one succession, and only the spouse or partner of the tenant can succeed.

Rent control

4.38   The rent regime is a market system. The tenant is taken to have freely agreed the original rent with the landlord and therefore cannot legally challenge it. If he or she has agreed rent review clauses then he or she is similarly bound. If there are no provisions for rent increases, the landlord may increase the rent annually via a notice procedure. The tenant can challenge the increase, but the Rent Assessment Committee will intervene only if the rent has been raised above the market rent level. As the committee can raise the rent as well as lower it, the tenant has to be very sure before challenging any increase.

Security of tenure – evicting the assured tenant

4.39   Security of tenure is the extent to which the tenant has the right to remain in the property after the landlord has decided he or she no longer wants to let to the tenant. In general, the assured tenant has extensive security of tenure. In order to evict the tenant, the landlord must serve a notice called a notice of seeking possession, often referred to as a 'NoSP'. The notice must specify the grounds for possession and set out the period of time before which court proceedings cannot be issued. The ground for possession is the reason that the landlord gives for wanting to evict the tenant. The landlord is allowed to use only those reasons which the statute allows. A summary of the grounds for possession – the legally acceptable reasons – in the assured tenancy regime are set out in Box 4.4

4.40   You will notice that there are two different types of ground. One is described as mandatory. This means that if the facts of that ground are made out, then the court has no alternative but to evict the tenant. The other type of ground is discretionary. This means that even if the landlord makes out the facts of the case, the court will grant a possession order only if it is reasonable to do so.

Eviction for rent arrears

4.41   The biggest difference between the assured tenancy regime and the secure tenancy regime, which is the regime which local authority tenants benefit from, relates to eviction for rent arrears. There is a particular ground for eviction, ground 8, which is available to the landlords of assured tenants when there are two months' arrears of rent outstanding both at the date of the notice of seeking possession and at the date of the eviction. This ground is mandatory. This means that if the facts are made out the court has no option but to grant the possession order. The rent could be in arrears because of housing benefit delays or because of problems within the family. The reasons for the non-payment of rent are irrelevant. The court must order possession. Many housing association landlords choose not to use ground 8. However, since November 2006 evictions for rent arrears must follow the rent arrears protocol. This requires social landlords to take extensive steps to resolve rent disputes prior to court proceedings. In particular the landlord must contact the tenant as soon as the tenant falls into arrears, to make contact after the service of statutory notices and to consider alternative dispute resolution. We discuss the pre-action protocol in full in chapter 17, and elaborate further on legal problems arising when a tenant falls into arrears with rent.

Box 4.4 Housing Act 1988 Sch 2 – grounds for possession of dwelling houses let on assured tenancies

Part I: Grounds on which court must order possession – the mandatory grounds

	Ground	NSP
Landlord's former/future principal home – notice prior to tenancy or just & equitable to dispense with notice	Grd 1	2 mths or just and equitable to dispense with notice
Mortgagee repossessing – notice prior to tenancy or just & equitable to dispense with notice	Grd 2	2 mths or just and equitable to dispense with notice
Former holiday let, now fixed term 8 or less months – notice prior to tenancy	Grd 3	2 wks
Former student let, now fixed term 12 or less months – notice prior to tenancy	Grd 4	2 wks
Required for minister of religion – notice prior to tenancy	Grd 5	2 mths

Demolition/reconstruction/ substantial works by original landlord, requiring possession	Grd 6	2 mths
Inherited periodic tenancy, 12 or less months after death	Grd 7	2 mths
Rent arrears – 8 weeks at NSP and hearing	Grd 8	2 wks

Part II: Grounds on which court may order possession – the discretionary grounds

Suitable alternative accommodation available	Grd 9	2 mths
Rent arrears (any) – at NSP and issue	Grd 10	2 wks
Rent arrears – persistent delay, even if none now	Grd 11	2 wks
Breach of tenancy agreement	Grd 12	2 wks
Waste/neglect by tenant/ resident causing deterioration of dwelling	Grd 13	2 wks
Nuisance or conviction for immoral/illegal use or conviction for arrestable offence in locality	Grd 14	instant
Domestic violence and leaver unlikely to return – RSL landlord only	Grd 14A	2 wks
Ill-treatment of furniture by tenant/resident causing deterioration	Grd 15	2 wks
Ex-employee of landlord	Grd 16	2 mths
False statement to obtain tenancy	Grd 17	2 wks

Assured shorthold tenancies under the Housing Act 1988

4.42   Assured shorthold tenancies (ASTs) are a particular type of assured tenancy which give very limited security of tenure. They now provide the normal form of tenure within the private rented sector. The rules set out in paras 4.37 and 4.38, which cover the scope of the assured tenancy regime and the exclusions from it, apply equally to the assured shorthold tenancy. The distinguishing feature of the assured short-hold tenancy is that tenants can be evicted from the tenancy with two months' notice once the first six months have expired. When the Housing Act 1988 was originally passed, there were some procedural requirements which needed to be conformed with before an AST could be validly created. The tenant had to be given notice that the tenancy was an AST and there had to be a fixed term of a minimum of six months. However, landlords seemed to have difficulty complying with the requirements of the Act, so the Housing Act 1996 abolished the requirements. All tenancy agreements created on or after 28 February 1997 are automatically ASTs unless the landlord serves notice otherwise. Housing association landlords usually serve a notice on the tenant saying that the tenancy is to be an assured tenancy. Private landlords do not serve such a notice. Therefore, all tenancies in the private sector which commenced after 27 February 1997 are likely to be assured shorthold tenancies.

Rent control

4.43   The rent control provisions for ASTs are more rigorous than for assured tenancies. However, the provisions give very little real benefit to the tenant of an AST. The tenant is allowed to challenge the initial rent during the first six months, but only if the rent is significantly higher than the market rent. It is also extremely unlikely that any tenant with such limited security is going to risk his or her future in the property by commencing such a challenge.

Evicting the assured shorthold tenant

4.44   During the initial six months of an AST the landlord can recover possession only by obtaining a possession order from the court based upon a limited range of grounds (which, however, includes all of the rent grounds). After the initial six months, a specific procedure for recovering possession is open to the landlord, who can give notice of not less than two months stating that he or she requires possession. The notice – known as a section 21 notice after the section in the Act which gives this power – may be given before the expiry of the six months, although no order for possession can be applied for before the six-month period is complete. The court must make an order for possession and has no discretion at all, as long as it is satisfied that the correct notice has been served. No matter how long a tenant has been in the property, the two-month notice period is legally sufficient.

Box 4.5 Frequently asked questions

We have a tenant on an assured shorthold tenancy who refuses to co-operate with our support workers. Can we evict them?

In strictly legal terms there is no problem here. However, Good Practice on Tenure, which we discuss in chapter 10, requires a provider to review the situation and to consider exactly what the problem is with the support provision. If it turns out that the tenant has withdrawn from support, or not engaged with support, or that the tenant's support needs are too high or too low for the project, then the provider/landlord can issue a section 21 notice. Good practice would also suggest that the tenant should be given a right of appeal against the notice and if the appeal is upheld the notice should be withdrawn. All decisions to serve a section 21 notice should be ratified by a senior member of staff and action should be monitored by the management board. Tenants served with a section 21 notice should be helped to find alternative accommodation to prevent them from becoming homeless.

The accelerated possession procedure

4.45   Not all possession cases have to go to a full court hearing. If a landlord wishes to evict an assured shorthold tenant, he or she can use a paper-only procedure called the accelerated possession procedure. The landlord has to have given the tenant a written agreement and written notice to benefit from this much cheaper court procedure. If he or she is able to apply to use the accelerated possession procedure, the tenant has only 14 days within which to respond. If the tenant has any doubt about his or her status, then it is critical to get good legal advice. Note that the accelerated possession procedure is also available for some grounds which can be used to evict the assured tenant. The disadvantage to the landlord is that he or she cannot use the accelerated possession procedure to get an order for rent arrears. If the landlord wants to get a court order against the tenant for rent, then he or she must use the full court procedure or sue the tenant separately for a rent judgment.

4.46   If an occupier is not covered by the Housing Act 1988, or one of the other statutory regimes we have mentioned, the Rent Act 1977 or the Housing Act 1985, they may still be entitled to protection under the

Protection from Eviction Act 1977. The third part of this chapter considers the legal safety net provided by this Act.

Box 4.6 Frequently asked questions

In 1994 we issued full assured tenancy agreements to two separate residents within one of our services. The accommodation used to be run as a registered care home but is now supported living. In 2003, for some reason, a new tenancy was issued which was an assured shorthold tenancy. The property is a two-bedroomed house and the two tenants have their own individual bedrooms but share the rest of the facilities. How can we sort out this mess?

Here the agreement between each tenant and the provider is clearly a tenancy. There is exclusive possession of the bedroom; there is no need for there to be exclusive possession of the whole of the property. Once the assured tenancy was granted it could not be terminated unless the tenant surrendered the tenancy or on grounds set out in the Housing Act 1988. As far as we know the tenancy has not been terminated; it therefore continues to exist. The assured shorthold tenancy has no validity whatsoever. You should write to the tenants explaining that the second agreement was a mistake, and that they occupy the property on an assured tenancy basis.

Protection from eviction

4.47   The Protection from Eviction Act 1977 provides the answers to two important questions. First, what security is offered to tenants and other occupiers who do not fall within the standard protections of the Rent Act 1977, the Housing Act 1985 or the Housing Act 1988? Secondly, what happens if the landlord does not follow the procedures set out in the statutory regimes, that is, illegally evicts the tenants? The Act provides civil and criminal remedies for illegal eviction and harassment and sets out procedures which provide a minimum of protection for all residential occupiers – except those who are specifically excluded from its provisions.

Criminal offences

4.48   Illegal eviction and harassment of residential occupiers are criminal offences. Section 1(2) of the Protection from Eviction Act 1977 states:

> If any person unlawfully deprives a residential occupier of any premises of his occupation of the premises or any part thereof, or attempts to do so, he shall be guilty of an offence unless he proves that he believed, and had reasonable cause to believe, that the residential occupier had ceased to reside in the premises.

4.49   The key word is 'unlawfully': the landlord cannot change the locks or throw out the tenant's possessions; he or she must obtain possession, if at all, by way of court order and the court bailiff.

4.50   Section 1(3) also makes it an offence to harass the occupier knowing that this is likely to make him or her leave, or to prevent him or her from exercising a right connected with the occupancy. Cutting off services is a prime example of such harassment, and is specifically provided for within section 1(3). Providers must be very careful not to take action which could lead to such offences being committed.

4.51   Illegal eviction or harassment is a criminal offence even if the landlord has cast-iron grounds in law for possession, and even if the tenancy was granted for a fixed period which has now expired. Nor is it necessary that the occupier is a tenant. Note that the statutory provision relates to residential occupiers which includes licensees.

4.52   The local authority can prosecute a landlord who unlawfully evicts or harasses an occupier in breach of the Act. There are wide differences in the willingness of authorities to take criminal proceedings against offending landlords. However, it is probably unlikely that a provider would be prosecuted. More practical difficulties could arise in connection with renewal of support contracts or in requiring staff to commit criminal offences. Moreover, quite properly, the Housing Corporation requires that RSLs operate within the law.

Excluded occupiers

4.53   The Act does not protect all residential occupiers. Lettings made on or after 15 January 1989 which are holiday lets, temporary lettings to squatters where the landlord is a resident landlord, who shares living accommodation with the tenant, or is hostel accommodation provided by a social landlord are excluded from the Protection from Eviction Act 1977 by section 3A of the Act. Therefore, the landlord can recover possession without court proceedings, so long as reasonable notice is given, which will usually be four weeks, or contractual notice, which could be as short as a week. The exclusion of hostel accommodation from the requirements of the Protection from Eviction Act 1977 is probably narrower than you would think. The accommodation must not be self-contained and must be provided by the local authority, a registered social landlord or a charitable housing trust.

4.54   There is another exception that has been recognised in case-law. The Court of Appeal in *Mohamed v Manek and Kensington and Chelsea RLBC* (1995) 27 HLR 439 excluded certain licensees of bed and breakfast accommodation from protection under the Act where the accommodation was provided on a temporary basis pending inquiries under the homeless provisions which were at that time set out in Part III of the Housing Act 1985. Again, this would suggest that providers are able to argue that their provision is temporary and therefore out of the scope of the Act. This argument may well succeed in the case of night shelters and other very short-term provisions or where the landlord is the local authority. For instance, the Court of Appeal in *Desnousse v Newham LBC* [2006] EWCA Civ 547 decided that once a local authority has taken a decision that no duties are owed under homelessness legislation to a person placed in temporary accommodation for the period of its investigations of intentionality there was no need for the local authority to issue court proceedings if that person refuses to vacate the accommodation. The reasoning of the court was, however, limited to local authorities. It considered that local authorities could be trusted to act lawfully and responsibly. You should not assume that the courts will take the same approach to housing associations that do not have public law obligations.

Box 4.7 Frequently asked questions

We manage an alcohol scheme and one of our service users has disappeared from the service after starting drinking again. Can we change the locks and relet his room as we have lots of people waiting to come into the service?

We do not advise providers to change the locks in any circumstances without giving notice to the service user and securing vacant possession. The notice given would depend on whether the occupancy agreement was excluded from the benefits of the Protection from Eviction Act 1977. If occupancy agreement is excluded, you would still be expected to give reasonable notice before changing the locks. We look at abandonment more fully in chapter 15.

Civil remedies for illegal eviction

4.55   Tenants and licensees may themselves bring a civil case for damages for harassment or unlawful eviction, and should be advised that, if they wish to regain possession or prevent further harassment, they should apply to the county court for an injunction. Such proceedings can be taken whether or not the local authority has decided to prosecute or even if the landlord was acquitted. Subject to satisfying the means test, the tenant can usually obtain legal assistance, and in an emergency this can be granted very quickly (see chapter 9). Tenants can sue for trespass, breach of the covenant of quiet enjoyment and breach of contract. They can also sue for breach of the statutory duty in section 3 of the Protection from Eviction Act and under a specific statutory tort under sections 27 and 28 of the Housing Act 1988. Licensees can sue for breach of contract.

4.56   Harassment can lead to very large awards of compensation in the civil courts. In *Tagro v Cafane* [1991] 2 All ER 235, the Court of Appeal upheld an award of £46,538 against a landlord who ransacked the tenant's bedsit. Some £30,000 of this represented the increase in value of the property to the landlord once the tenant had left. Lord Donaldson described the case as 'a cautionary tale for landlords'! Injunctions stopping further harassment or ordering the landlord to let the residential occupier back into the property are probably just as useful to the residential occupier. He or she is unlikely to want to stay in the property for much longer, if the relationship with the landlord has broken down to such an extent, but getting back in can provide a breathing space enabling the residential occupier to look for alternative accommodation.

Procedural requirements

4.57   The other important provisions of the Protection from Eviction Act 1977 are procedural protections for licensees and tenants who are not covered by the Rent Act 1977 or the Housing Act 1985 or 1988, but are not excluded from the Protection from Eviction Act 1977 – see above. So long as the property is rented as a home, both landlord and tenant have to give at least four weeks' notice before ending the tenancy, whatever the agreement may say to the contrary (section 5(1)). The notice must contain prescribed information. Section 3 of the Protection from Eviction Act 1977 requires the landlord to obtain a court order to recover possession of the premises.

4.58   A summary of the legal protections against harassment and illegal eviction is set out in Box 4.8.

Box 4.8 Summary of the legal protections against harassment and illegal eviction for non-excluded residential occupiers

Protection	Legal authority	Comment
Criminal offences of illegal eviction	PfEA 1977 s1	Dependent on local authority willingness to prosecute.
Criminal offences of harassment	PfEA 1977 s1	
Civil actions for statutory torts	PfEA 1977 s3	Injunctions can be obtained to stop harassment or to enable the occupier to re-enter the premises.
	HA 1988 ss27, 28	Damages can also be obtained. Damages for breach of HA 1988 s27 calculated by a statutory formula.
Civil actions for breach of contract and tort	Common law	Injunctions can be obtained to stop harassment or to enable the occupier to re-enter the premises. Damages can also be obtained.
Procedural protections	Either requirements of notice (grounds) court order under HA 1988 s85 or s88 or requirements of notice and court order under PfEA 1977 s3 and s5	

The Housing Corporation

4.59   We discuss the role of the Housing Corporation in chapter 10. The Housing Corporation provides guidance on tenure in a good practice publication on tenure, which will support you in navigating the series of decisions you must make in connection with tenure. You will find this extremely helpful in the absence of legislation specific to supported housing. It is available from www.housingcorp.gov.uk.

Summary

4.60   This has been a long chapter. However, it is necessary that you understand the legal framework relating to tenure and protection from eviction before we consider its application in the type of situations which providers face in running supported housing provision. We have remarked upon the lack of fit between the law on tenure and the needs of both the users and providers of supported housing. In particular, the law almost always insists that occupancies are tenancies rather than licences and therefore residents are entitled to full notice. The provisions of the Protection from Eviction Act 1977 mean that by failing to adhere to the law providers could be committing criminal offences. The Law Commission's draft bill on rented homes considers the ways in which the legal framework could be adapted to more appropriate protections for residents and avoid the legal quagmire of the lease/licence distinction. The draft bill also recommends legislating specifically for the supported housing sector. We would like to see government take the needs of supported housing seriously enough to provide the clarity necessary for effective legal regulation and implementation of the report. In the meantime, you must understand the principles of the current law and understand how they impact upon your practices and procedures. We hope to help you with this task throughout the rest of the book.

We have not been able to give full details of the complexity of tenure within this chapter. We recommend the following further reading:

- A Arden and C Hunter, *Manual of Housing Law* (8th edn, Sweet & Maxwell, 2007);

- D Astin, *Housing Law: an adviser's handbook* (Legal Action Group, forthcoming 2008);
- D Hughes, M Davis, V Matthews, and A Jones, *Text and Materials on Housing Law* (Oxford University Press, 2004);
- D Roberts and G Robson, *A Practical Approach to Housing Law* (Routledge Cavendish, 2005).

Homelessness

Objectives

5.1   By the end of this chapter you should:

- Understand the framework of homelessness law
- Be able to advise residents of their basic rights under homelessness law and know how they can access further advice if necessary
- Understand the interface between homelessness law and supported housing and, in particular, be aware of the consequences of a resident becoming homeless from a supported housing project

Overview

5.2   People who work in housing understand how easy it is to become homeless and the difficulties homeless people face in accessing secure and affordable housing. The law does not provide accommodation for every homeless person via homelessness legislation. Only those people who are homeless through no fault of their own and are in priority need as defined by the law are entitled to housing. The law is complex and subject to frequent challenge, and in the short space allocated to this chapter we cannot provide detailed explanations. We begin by setting out where the law is stated, then outline the operation of the law. Finally, we suggest additional reading and sources of advice.

Information on the law

5.3   The statutory framework of homelessness law is found in Part VII of the Housing Act 1996, and references to sections within the chapter are to that Act unless otherwise stated. Important amendments to the Housing Act 1996 have been made by the Homelessness Act 2002, which imposes strategic responsibilities for homelessness on local housing authorities. The Homelessness (Priority Need for Accommodation) (England) Order 2002 (SI 2002 No 2051) and the Welsh equivalent, the Homeless Persons (Priority Need) (Wales) Order 2001 (SI 2001 No 607 (W30)) make important additions to the classes of people who should be considered to be in priority need of accommodation. District and borough councils must also take into account the Homelessness Code of Guidance for Local Authorities, the latest edition of which was published by the Department of Communities and Local Government in July 2006. The code is a very useful source of information about how housing authorities should respond to homelessness applications and is worth quoting to your local homeless persons unit when it is proving difficult to persuade it that a service user has rights. However, you should also note that where the code and the Act are in conflict, the statutory provisions prevail.

Summary of the duties in Part VII of the Housing Act 1996

5.4 The statutory obligation placed upon local authorities is to make available suitable accommodation for a person who meets the four criteria of the Housing Act 1996 ('the Act'). The person must be:

- eligible for assistance;
- homeless;
- in priority need of accommodation; and
- not intentionally homeless.

5.5 The duty is also subject to the local connection provisions of the Act. Once someone applies to the housing authority as homeless, then the local housing authority has a duty to investigate their application.

Eligibility for assistance – the first key inquiry

People from abroad

5.6 No duty is owed by the housing department to anyone, however dire their situation, if the legislation and the regulations taken together make them ineligible for assistance (section 185). The philosophy behind this is to remove the right to emergency housing assistance for anyone whose immigration status is restricted. The eligibility rules are set out in the Allocation of Housing and Homelessness (Eligibility) (England) Regulations 2006 (SI No 1294), which came into force on 1 June 2006. The explanatory memorandum published on the Office of Public Sector Information website provides a very useful summary of the changes – see www.opsi.gov.uk/si/em2006. This is a complicated area of law and if you need to know more about the eligibility for housing assistance of someone from abroad you should seek specialist advice.

Homelessness – the second key inquiry

5.7   It is not necessary to have no roof over your head before you are considered homeless. A person is homeless if he or she, together with any person he or she can reasonably be expected to live with, has no accommodation which they are entitled to occupy and which it would be reasonable for them to continue to occupy (section 175). Accommodation includes accommodation overseas. A person does not have to be actually homeless to qualify under the Act, if he or she is likely to become homeless within the next 28 days. Many local authorities try to avoid duties arising as a result of threatened homelessness. For instance, an authority may decide that, despite the landlord having served notice on a tenant and there being no defence to the proceedings, that person is not threatened with homelessness. The Code of Guidance states at paragraph 8.14:

> ... with certain exceptions a person who has been occupying accommodation as a tenant and who has received a valid notice to quit, or notice that the landlord requires possession of the accommodation, would have the right to remain in occupation until a warrant for possession was executed (following the granting of an order for possession by the court). The exceptions are tenants with resident landlords and certain other tenants who do not benefit from the Protection from eviction Act 1977. *However authorities should note that the fact that a tenant has a right to remain in occupation does not necessarily mean that he or she is not homeless.* In assessing whether an applicant is homeless in cases where he or she is a tenant who has a right to remain in occupation pending execution of a warrant for possession, the housing authority will also need to consider whether it would be reasonable for him or her to continue to occupy the accommodation in the circumstances. (emphasis in original.)

5.8   The sentence we have italicised is highlighted in bold text within the code. If your local authority does not accept that someone in this position is homeless, you should refer the applicant(s) to a good housing lawyer.

5.9   A person is entitled to occupy a place he or she owns, or has a tenancy or licence of, or has a right to occupy by marriage. A cohabitee living in his or her partner's premises has an entitlement to occupy as a licensee, unless that right is withdrawn on relationship breakdown.

5.10   The applicant may have rights which he or she cannot exercise. For instance, the landlord has changed the lock or the applicant has nowhere to park his or her caravan. People in these circumstances are usually treated as homeless.

5.11   An informal licence which a person has by virtue of living with relatives or friends may be terminated at any moment; it nevertheless constitutes a right to occupy, so a person is homeless 'intentionally', with all the disastrous consequences that follow from this label, if he or she gives this up for no valid reason. But if the hosts genuinely want that person to leave, and are not colluding to get him or her a home with the local authority, that person is threatened with unintentional homelessness. Young people aged 16 and 17 have informal licences with their parents which can be terminated.

5.12   The Act gives some indication of when it would not be reasonable to continue to occupy accommodation. For example, under section 177, it will not be reasonable: 'if it is probable that this will lead to domestic violence or other violence or threats of violence against the applicant or against someone else who normally lives with him or her, or might be expected to live with him or her'. Other factors that may make it unreasonable to continue to occupy accommodation include the physical conditions in the property, overcrowding, and the affordability of the accommodation.

Box 5.1 Frequently asked questions

We have a scheme to accommodate women fleeing domestic violence who are referred by the homeless persons unit for up to six months. Can the local authority say they are no longer homeless?

Your type of accommodation provides very short-term accommodation. The local authority should not regard crisis accommodation such as women's refuges or direct access hostels as suitable for occupation in the medium or longer term. The local authority should treat the women as homeless – thus overcoming the first legal barrier to any finding that they are owed duties under the homelessness legislation. However, it will also look at the other criteria outlined in this chapter – eligibility, priority need, intentionality and local connection – before making a decision.

Priority need – the third key inquiry

5.13   Once the authority has decided that someone is eligible for assistance and is homeless then it has to decide whether the applicant, or someone who can be expected to live with the applicant, is in priority need.

Section 189(1) sets out that the following are in priority need:

(a) a pregnant woman or someone with whom she resides or may reasonably be expected to reside;

(b) a person with whom dependant children reside or may be expected to reside (including a child who could reasonably be expected to if the applicant had a home);

(c) a person who is vulnerable as a result of old age, mental illness or handicap, or physical disability, or who has some other special reason for being vulnerable or with whom such a person resides or may reasonably be expected to reside;

(d) a person whose homelessness, or threatened homelessness, results from flood, fire, or similar emergency or disaster.

5.14   The Homelessness (Priority Need for Accommodation) (England) Order (SI 2002 No 2051) sets out six further categories of applicants with priority need. The additional categories reflect the vulnerability of these particular groups to homelessness. The categories are:

(a) a person aged 16 or 17 who is not a relevant child or a child in need to whom a local authority owes a duty under section 20 of the Children Act 1989;

(b) a person under 21 who was (but is no longer) looked after, accommodated or fostered between the ages of 16 and 18 (except a person who is a 'relevant student');

(c) a person aged 21 or more who is vulnerable as a result of having been looked after, accommodated or fostered (except a person who is a 'relevant student');

(d) a person who is vulnerable as a result of having been a member of Her Majesty's regular naval, military or air forces;

(e) a person who is vulnerable as a result of:
    (i)   having served a custodial sentence;
    (ii) having been committed for contempt of court or any other kindred offence; or
    (iii) having been remanded in custody;

(f) a person who is vulnerable as a result of ceasing to occupy accommodation because of violence from another person or threats of violence from another person which are likely to be carried out.

5.15   The Code of Guidance provides useful amplification of these categories. Particularly useful is chapter 12 of the code, which provides guidance on specific duties towards 16- and 17-year-olds.

5.16   The Welsh Assembly similarly extended the categories of priority need. Unlike the regulations in England, there is no requirement for an applicant to establish that they are vulnerable as a result of fleeing violence, leaving the armed forces or being released from custody. However, those leaving custody will be in priority need only if they have a local connection with the local housing authority they have approached. The Welsh categories are set out in the Homeless Persons (Priority Need) (Wales) Order 2001 (SI 2001 No 607 (W30)).

5.17   The legal meaning of vulnerability in the context of homelessness is restrictive. In *R (on the application of Pereira) v Camden* (1998) 31 HLR 317, it was decided that a drug addict was vulnerable only if his condition made him less able to obtain and keep a home than other homeless people. Despite various challenges, that interpretation has been supported by the courts. The current Code of Guidance states:

> When determining whether an applicant ... is vulnerable the Local Authority should consider whether, when homeless the applicant would be less able to fend for him/herself than an ordinary homeless person so that he or she would suffer injury or detriment, in circumstances where a less vulnerable person would be able to cope without harmful effects ... The applicant's vulnerability must be assessed on the basis that he or she is or will become homeless and not on his or her ability to fend for him- or herself while still housed.

Intentionality – the fourth key inquiry

5.18   The housing authority now has to decide whether the applicant became homeless intentionally (section 184), which means that the applicant has to have had accommodation which it would be reasonable to continue to occupy, and by some deliberate act loses it (section 191). The same criteria apply to threatened homelessness (section 196).

5.19   There are several important points to note here. First, there has to be a deliberate act which leads to the homelessness. So, according to the code, a person in rent or mortgage arrears through careless financial management whose property is repossessed is homeless intentionally, whereas the person whose arrears arose from genuine difficulties will be unintentionally homeless. It is the housing department, subject to review and appeals procedures, which makes the decisions. Secondly, the deliberate act must be that of the applicant. Finally, you cannot intentionally become homeless from accommodation which it is not reasonable to continue to occupy.

So if an applicant has left home as a result of their stepfather's violence, this cannot be intentional homelessness because it was not reasonable to continue to occupy the accommodation.

Box 5.2 Frequently asked questions

We have a service user who was evicted from her previous accommodation as she did not pay her rent when she became mentally unwell. She has done really well in our scheme and is ready to move on to independent accommodation. If we refer her to the local authority, will she still be treated as intentionally homeless? She has been with us for 18 months on an assured shorthold tenancy.

Applicants who are found to be intentionally homeless must obtain accommodation for themselves for a settled period in order to break the chain of causation between an act causing homelessness and the current homelessness. Whether accommodation is settled is a question of fact. The relevant factors will be security of tenure and length of residence. An assured shorthold tenancy is capable of constituting settled accommodation. A period in a short-term supported housing project is probably not settled accommodation. If people become homeless from settled accommodation unintentionally, they can then apply to the local authority and their application will not be tainted by their former intentionality.

Local connection

5.20   Under the statute, local connection means being normally resident in the area, or employed there or having family ties. There is no requirement on an applicant to apply to the local authority with which he or she has a local connection; an applicant can apply anywhere, and to as many authorities as he or she chooses. However, once an applicant has been accepted as being in priority need and not intentionally homeless, there can occasionally be a problem identifying which local housing department has the duty of providing accommodation. If neither the applicant nor a person who would reasonably be expected to live with them has a local connection, but does have a local connection with another local authority's area, the housing authority can pass the responsibility to that other authority. However, local authorities cannot transfer the responsibilities if an applicant has a good reason to leave the area where she had a connection, nor if to return there would be to return to the probability of violence, including domestic violence. It is the first authority approached which must provide temporary accommodation until accommodation is available in the area where the local connection applies. Chapter 18 of the Code of Guidance provides extensive information on the operation of local connection provisions.

Box 5.3 Summary of housing duties and powers

Decision of housing authority	*Housing Act 1996*	→ Duties → *Powers*
Unintentionally homeless and have a priority need	s193	→ Duty to secure accommodation
Unintentionally homeless and no priority need	s192	→ Duty to provide advice and assistance → *Power to secure accommodation*
Unintentionally threatened with homelessness and have priority need	s195(2)	→ Duty to take reasonable steps to ensure that accommodation does not cease to be available
Unintentionally threatened with homelessness and do not have a priority need	s195(5)	→ Duty to provide advice and assistance → *Power to take reasonable steps to ensure that accommodation does not cease to be available*
Intentionally homeless and have a priority need	s190(2)	→ Duty to provide advice and assistance and secure accommodation for such period as will give applicant a reasonable period to secure accommodation for him/herself

---

Intentionally homeless and no priority need	s190(3)	→ Duty to provide advice and assistance
Threatened with homelessness intentionally and have a priority need	s195(5)	→ Duty to provide advice and assistance
Threatened with homelessness intentionally and no priority need	s195(5)	→ Duty to provide advice and assistance

Securing suitable accommodation

5.21   Local housing authorities may discharge their duty to secure that accommodation is provided for the applicant either by providing accommodation themselves for the applicant, by ensuring that some other person provides it or by giving such advice and assistance as will enable the applicant to secure accommodation. The housing authority can discharge its duty by offering an allocation of permanent accommodation under Part VI of the Act if the applicant meets its own waiting list criteria. Otherwise, permanent accommodation may be provided by a housing association or a private sector landlord.

5.22   The accommodation offered must be suitable for the applicant and his or her household. The Code of Guidance gives some indication of suitability. For instance, in paragraph 17.41 it states:

> The location of the accommodation will be relevant to suitability and the suitability of the location for all the members of the household will have to be considered ... The Secretary of State recommends that local authorities take into account the need to minimize disruption to the education of young people, particularly at critical points in time such as close to taking GCSE examination.

> **Box 5.4 Frequently asked questions**
>
> **We work with young people who are referred by the local author-
> ity which has a statutory duty to house them. The young people
> live in our scheme for six months and the local authority finds
> them a flat when they are ready to move on. One of the young
> people has been causing a nuisance and we want to evict her.
> Does the local authority have to find her a flat if we evict her?**
>
> Once the local authority has found that it has a duty towards
> someone, it can only discharge that duty with the provision of
> permanent accommodation. If your accommodation was pro-
> vided on the basis that it was a temporary solution pending a
> permanent solution, then eviction from your accommodation
> should not affect the homeless status of the young person.

5.23   Refusal of an offer of suitable accommodation will discharge the duty
of the housing authority. An applicant must be very clear of the consequences of refusal. Refusing a suitable offer would mean that any future
applications would run the risk of failure because of intentionality.

5.24   The accommodation that the local housing authority makes available to eligible applicants under Part VII of the Housing Act 1996
must be suitable – section 206.

5.25   An offer of an assured shorthold tenancy may be suitable accommodation in certain circumstances.

5.26   Applicants may ask for a review of the suitability of the accommodation that is offered to them regardless of whether or not they accept
the accommodation.

5.27   The right of review does not apply to duties to accommodate on
an interim basis. We discuss the review process below.

Reviews of local authority decisions

5.28   Section 202 of the Housing Act 1996 creates a right to a review by the
housing department of certain decisions on homelessness, followed by
a right to appeal to the county court. The review must be requested
within 21 days of the authority's decision. Decisions which may be
reviewed are those relating to:

- eligibility for assistance;
- the nature and extent of any duty owed under sections 190, 191,
  192, 193 and 195;

- local connection decisions;
- suitability.

5.29   An applicant should use the review procedure to explain why they are challenging the housing authority's decision and to set out any new information which would be relevant to the decision. The applicant can provide written or oral representations. He or she can be represented, although it is hard to find an experienced housing advisor to do this. Housing authorities have the power to accommodate the applicant pending a review. Decisions whether to provide accommodation in these circumstances should be made reasonably.

Appeals to the county court

5.30   Section 204 of the Housing Act 1996 provides a right of appeal on a point of law to the county court where the applicant is dissatisfied with the decision on review or the applicant is not notified of the decision on the review within a prescribed time period. Legal advice should be obtained urgently if the decision of the internal review is unfavourable. The appeal must be brought within 21 days of the decision. The court may give permission for an appeal to be brought after 21 days, but only where it is satisfied that there is good reason for the applicant's delay. The county court can confirm, quash or vary the decision of the housing authority. The county court can also hear appeals from decisions of housing authorities not to accommodate the applicant pending the appeal.

5.31   An applicant has the right to complain to the local government ombudsman if he or she believes that there has been maladministration (see chapter 27).

Summary

5.32   In supported housing there is a considerable provision of temporary accommodation. Service users are expected to move on to more independent accommodation when they no longer need the support of the scheme. The ideal is that service users will be able to access social housing, as this presents the most secure form of accommodation. To be eligible for local authority housing the service user will have to be regarded as statutorily homeless. Providers must be careful not to make decisions which jeopardise the rights of service users to permanent housing. Housing associations usually have arrangements with the local authority to house applicants who are nominated by the local authority. As we have demonstrated, the law relating to homelessness is complicated and you are advised to seek specialist support for service users in this area. There will, however, be other service users that are not considered statutorily homeless and you will be expected to explore other avenues for them, for example, finding them private rented accommodation which you could help them to access by using a local rent deposit scheme.

5.33   This chapter has sought to provide you with a succinct and simplified overview of the law relating to homelessness. It is likely that your local authority will disagree with some of our interpretations of the legislation. If you are not able to persuade them by using the Code of Guidance, and you are concerned about the consequences of decisions upon your service users, you should seek legal advice.

Discrimination and the law

Objectives

6.1 By the end of this chapter you will have:

- Been introduced to the regulatory and legal framework of discrimination law
- Understood the basic requirements of the law preventing discrimination on the grounds of race, sex, age, disability, religious belief and gender reassignment
- Considered the implications of the requirements of discrimination law relating to the selling, letting or managing of property
- Understood the regulatory framework in connection with discrimination
- Appreciated the need for equality and diversity policies and procedures which reflect the legal requirements and good practice and are kept under review

Overview

6.2 The purpose of discrimination law is to eliminate unjustifiable discrimination on legally specified grounds in particular fields of social activities. Discrimination law is neither coherent nor complete; it has grown in response to public awareness of the damage caused to individuals as a result of discrimination, to European Community requirements and to human rights law. What this means is, first, that the law is scattered over a number of statutes and embellished by a multiplicity of statutory instruments. Secondly, the law is subject to constant change. We discuss human rights law in the next chapter. What you will learn there, however, applies equally to discrimination law. Our understandings of what law can achieve and of what is culturally and socially acceptable constantly evolves. You can expect the field of discrimination law to develop and for new legal requirements to be imposed upon service providers. Moreover, observation of minimum legal standards is unlikely to be sufficient for the provision of an excellent service. If service users are to maximise their potential then policies need to be put in place to demonstrate that providers recognise diverse needs and to embrace positively cultural diversity. The involvement of service users is likely to produce the most effective policies. Providers have equivalent responsibilities to their employees.

6.3 It is not possible in a general guide to provide the details of this complex and specialised area of law. What we offer is an introductory outline and suggestions of useful sources of further information. Any individual suffering problems relating to discrimination should seek expert legal advice.

6.4   The chapter begins by describing some basic concepts within discrimination law and then outlines the current statutory framework for race, sex, disability, religious belief and age discrimination. We then consider in more detail the requirements placed on individuals and organisations that sell, let or manage property, particularly in connection with the requirements of race and disability discrimination legislation. The final part of the chapter considers the regulatory requirements imposed by *Supporting People* (which we discuss more fully in chapter 11) and the regulatory requirements of the Housing Corporation (its more general regulatory role is discussed in chapter 10). We conclude by considering the need for carefully drafted and constantly reviewed policies and procedures in connection with the elimination of discrimination.

The statutory framework of discrimination law

6.5   We have set out the statutes which provide the basis of UK discrimination law in Box 6.1. Once you see the range of statutory provisions you will understand why there is a powerful lobby of lawyers and activists seeking a single Equality Act.

Box 6.1 The statutory framework of discrimination law	
Statute	*Comment*
Equal Pay Acts 1970 and 1983	• Prohibits discrimination on grounds of sex which relates to pay and contract terms.
Sex Discrimination Act 1975	• Prohibits discrimination on the basis of sex or marital status. • Applies equally to discrimination against men and women. • Also prohibits discrimination against a person on the basis of gender reassignment.

Race Relations Act 1976	• Prohibits discrimination on the basis of race, colour, nationality (including citizenship), national or ethnic origin
Disability Discrimination Acts 1995 and 2005	• Prohibits discrimination against a disabled person – ie someone who has a disability as defined in section 1 of and Schedule 1 to the DDA. • From December 2006 all public authorities have a duty to promote disability equality.
The Race Relations (Amendment) Act 2000	• Places a duty on public authorities in carrying out their functions to have due regard to the need to eliminate unlawful discrimination and to promote equality of opportunity and good relations between persons of different racial groups.
Employment Equality (Sexual Orientation) Regulations 2003 (SI 2003 No 1661)	• Prohibits discrimination on grounds of sexual orientation. • The definition covers lesbians and gay men, heterosexuals and bisexuals. • Can include discrimination based on perception of a person's sexual orientation or association with individuals of a particular sexual orientation.
Employment Equality (Religion or Belief) Regulations 2003 (SI 2003 No 1660)	• Prohibits discrimination on the grounds of religion or belief. • No definition of religion or belief, although the explanatory note to the regulations states that 'courts and tribunals may consider a number of factors when deciding what is a 'religion or belief' (for example, collective worship, clear

	belief system, profound belief affecting way of life or view of the world).
The Employment Equality (Age) Regulations 2006 (SI 2006 No 1031)	• Prohibits discrimination on grounds of age. • It is irrelevant whether the discrimination is because you are young or old.

The Equality and Human Rights Commission

6.6   Government has always recognised that it is difficult for individuals to navigate their way around discrimination law. In October 2007 it created the Equality and Human Rights Commission (EHRC) which unifies and extends the work of the Equal Opportunities Commission, the Commission for Racial Equality and the Disability Rights Commission. The website of the EHRC is www.equalityhumanrights.com. Box 6.2 explains the purpose of the Commission.

Box 6.2
The Equality and Human Rights Commission champions equality and human rights for all, working to eliminate discrimination, reduce inequality, protect human rights and to build good relations, ensuring that everyone has a fair chance to participate in society.

6.7   The Commission's website contains extensive information on the legal responsibilities of employers and service providers.

6.8   Other helpful guidance on discrimination is available from:

- Age Concern: www.ageconcern.org.uk;
- Discrimination Law Association: www.discrimination-law.org.uk; and
- Department for Business Enterprise and Regulatory Reform: www.berr.gov.uk/employment.

Legal Action Group publishes two comprehensive and accessible guides to discrimination law: Palmer et al, *Discrimination Law Handbook* (2nd edn, 2007) and O'Dempsey, Jolly and Harrop, *Age Discrimination Handbook* (2006).

Key concepts in discrimination law

6.9 There are some basic approaches which are common throughout discrimination law. There are three types of discrimination which are unlawful: direct discrimination, indirect discrimination and victimisation. We provide you with outline definitions of these and give examples to illustrate these important legal concepts. Harassment is also prohibited within the legislative framework, so we include a definition of harassment.

Direct discrimination

6.10 Direct discrimination occurs when someone is treated less favourably than someone else in similar circumstances on the grounds of their gender/race/disability/age and the treatment was detrimental.

> **Examples**
> Racially offensive graffiti appears on a tenant's property. The tenant complains to the landlord, but nothing is done to remove it. If the landlord normally takes prompt action to deal with complaints about other types of anti-social behaviour, the tenant could successfully argue that the landlord has not provided housing management services on a fair and equal basis and has directly discriminated against her.
>
> A provider refuses to employ someone simply because they are over 50.
>
> A provider refuses to let a room to someone with a guide dog because of its 'no pets' policy.

Indirect discrimination

6.11 Indirect discrimination occurs when a condition or requirement is applied equally to everyone, but in practice:

- the proportion of one race or gender who can comply is considerably smaller than other groups; and
- an employee or potential employee is unable to comply because of their race or gender; and
- the employer cannot show the condition or requirement is objectively justifiable.

6.12   Note that it is lawful to discriminate indirectly if the condition or requirement imposed is objectively justifiable.

> **Examples**
> A housing co-operative relies on its members to spread information about vacant properties by word of mouth. As its members are predominantly from one racial group, people from other racial groups would be very unlikely to hear about housing vacancies. Unless the co-operative is able to justify its practice as a reasonable and proportionate way of letting properties, the practice would amount to unlawful indirect discrimination.
>
> A firm restricts recruitment to recent graduates – fewer older people would be able to meet this requirement and if the employer could not justify the requirement then it would be unlawful.

Victimisation

6.13   A person is victimised if he or she is treated detrimentally because they have made a complaint or allegation or have given evidence against someone else in relation to a complaint of discrimination.

> **Example**
> An estate agency dismisses a temporary worker who has informed the EHRC that a manager instructed staff not to show properties to inquirers of east European origin, because they were 'all time wasters and not serious about purchasing properties'.

Harassment

6.14   Harassment occurs when someone is subjected to harassment by their employer or by someone for whom the employer is responsible on the basis of their sex/race/disability/age.

> **Examples**
> A tenant brings a complaint of racial harassment against his landlady when she persists in making racially offensive remarks to him despite his attempts to explain his unhappiness.

Someone has a partner who is significantly younger than them and this is the basis of repeated comments and jokes from colleagues. This could be unlawful if the person finds it humiliating or offensive.

Scope of discrimination law

6.15 Each ground of unlawful discrimination has a different scope, by which we mean that the areas of life affected by the law differs depending upon the basis of the discrimination. This is confusing and adds to the complexity of discrimination law. It also suggests that we, as a society, are more concerned about some grounds of discrimination than others. We have set out in Box 6.3 the different fields in which discrimination law bites.

Box 6.3 The scope of discrimination law

Field of practice	*Basis of discrimination*
Employment	
• Covers selection procedures, offers, promotion and benefits, dismissal or other detriments.	Race Sex Disability
• Also covers other relationships such as contract workers, members of the police force, barristers, trade unions, etc.	Sexual orientation Religion Age
Further and higher education	
• Discrimination in schools or other educational establishments prohibited on grounds of race and sex.	Race Sex Disability Sexual orientation
• The Special Educational Needs and Disability Act 2001 prohibits discrimination against disabled pupils and requires schools to ensure that disabled pupils are not substantially disadvantaged.	Religion Age

---

Provision of goods and services to the public

Race
Sex (including gender
reassignment)
Disability

Selling, letting or managing property
• Covers landlords, estate agents,　　Race
managing agents and managers　　Sex
of residential accommodation.　　Disability

Functions of public authority to eliminate discrimination
• The duty on public authorities to　　Race
have due regard to the need to　　Disability
eliminate unlawful discrimination
and to promote equality of
opportunity and good relations
between persons of different racial
groups was brought in by the Race
Relations (Amendment) Act 2000 in
response to a recommendation by
the McPherson Report.
• The Disability Discrimination Act
2005 amended the Disability
Discrimination Act 1995 to place a
duty on all public sector authorities
to promote disability equality.

Selling, letting or managing property

6.16　Whilst providers have obligations not to discriminate in a variety of areas of their work, especially in relation to their employment practices, it is the field of selling, letting or managing property which is particularly pertinent to this book. In this section of the chapter we will examine in more detail the implications of discrimination legislation upon landlords and managing agents. We begin by considering the impact of the Disability Discrimination Act 1995 and discuss the *Romano* case, where some of the difficulties inherent in the protections given to disabled people were examined by the courts.

The meaning of disability

6.17   The impact of the Disability Discrimination Act 1995 ('the Act') is making itself felt in the social housing world. The critical definition of disability in the Act is set out in Box 6.4

> **Box 6.4 Section 1 of the Disability Discrimination Act 1995**
>
> 1. (1) Subject to the provisions of Schedule 1, a person has a disability for the purposes of this Act if he has a physical or mental impairment which has a substantial and long-term adverse effect on his ability to carry out normal day-to-day activities.
>   (2) In this Act 'disabled person' means a person who has a disability.

6.18   Certain essential questions arise from this statutory definition

What counts as a physical or mental impairment?

6.19   The Act does not define 'physical or mental impairment'. It is mental impairment which has caused landlords the most difficulty. Paragraph 1(1) of Schedule 1 to the Act provides that 'mental impairment' includes an impairment resulting from or consisting of a mental illness only if the illness is a 'clinically well-recognised illness', and paragraph 1(2) provides that regulations may make provision for conditions of a pre-scribed description to be treated as amounting to impairments, or as not amounting to impairments, for the purposes of the Act. Regulations have prescribed that the following are not to be regarded as 'impair-ments' for the purposes of the Act:

(a) a tendency to set fires;
(b) a tendency to steal;
(c) a tendency to physical or sexual abuse of other persons;
(d) exhibitionism; and
(e) voyeurism.

Box 6.5 Frequently asked questions

Would a service user with an addiction to alcohol or drugs be protected by the Disability Discrimination Act?

An addiction (which includes a dependency) to alcohol, nicotine or any other substance is to be treated as not amounting to an impairment for the purposes of the Disability Discrimination Act unless the addiction was originally the result of administration of medically prescribed drugs or other medical treatment.

What are 'long-term' effects?

6.20   Schedule 1 to the Act contains assistance on the meaning of the phrases 'long-term effect' and 'effect on ability to carry out normal day-to-day activities', which are found in section 1(1). Paragraph 2(1) of the Schedule provides that the effect of an impairment is a long-term effect if:

(a) it has lasted at least 12 months;
(b) the period for which it lasts is likely to be at least 12 months; or
(c) it is likely to last for the rest of the life of the person affected.

What does effect on ability to carry out day-to-day activities mean?

6.21   Paragraph 4(1) of Schedule 1 provides that an impairment is to be taken to affect the ability of the person concerned to carry out 'normal day-to-day activities' if it affects one of the following:

(a) mobility;
(b) manual dexterity;
(c) physical co-ordination;
(d) continence;
(e) ability to lift, carry or otherwise move everyday objects;
(f) speech, hearing or eyesight;
(g) memory or ability to concentrate, learn or understand; or
(h) perception of the risk of physical danger.

Discriminating against disabled occupiers

6.22   Section 22(3) protects a disabled person in occupation of premises from discrimination on the grounds of their disability. We have set out its provisions in Box 6.6.

> **Box 6.6 Section 22(3) of the Disability Discrimination Act 1995**
>
> It is unlawful for a person managing any premises to discriminate against a disabled person occupying those premises –
>
> (a) in the way he permits the disabled person to make use of any benefits or facilities;
> (b) by refusing or deliberately omitting to permit the disabled person to make use of any benefits or facilities; or
> (c) by evicting the disabled person, or subjecting him to any other detriment.

Justification

6.23 Discriminatory treatment may be justified if the discriminator can demonstrate justification under section 24(2)–(5). We have set out the provisions in Box 6.7.

> **Box 6.7 Section 24(2)–(5) of the Disability Discrimination Act 1995**
>
> (2) For the purposes of this section, treatment is justified only if –
>   (a) in A's opinion, one or more of the conditions mentioned in subsection (3) are satisfied; and
>   (b) it is reasonable, in all the circumstances of the case, for him to hold that opinion.
> (3) The conditions are that –
>   (a) in any case, the treatment is necessary in order not to endanger the health or safety of any person (which may include that of the disabled person);
>   ...
> (4) Regulations may make provision, for purposes of this section, as to circumstances in which–
>   (a) it is reasonable for a person to hold the opinion mentioned in subsection 2(a);
>   (b) it is not reasonable for a person to hold that opinion.
> (5) Regulations may make provision, for purposes of this section, as to circumstances (other than those mentioned in subsection (3)) in which treatment is to be taken to be justified.

The *Romano* case

6.24   *Manchester City Council v Romano, Samari* [2004] EWCA Civ 834 explored the meaning of these provisions in the context of the eviction of secure disabled tenants. In *North Devon Homes Ltd v Brazier* [2003] EWHC 574, [2003] HLR 59, QB, the implications of which shocked social landlords, the High Court made it clear that when considering whether it is reasonable to make an order for possession against a tenant who suffers from a mental impairment, the possible effect of the 1995 Act must be taken into consideration by the court.

6.25   The judgment in the *Romano* case elaborated upon this. The Court of Appeal made it clear that the effect of the 1995 Act is to state that if a tenant is disabled and the reason why the landlord is seeking possession relates to the tenant's disability, then the landlord must believe that he is justified in taking this action on section 24(3) grounds and that his justification must be objectively reasonable. So landlords cannot ignore the connection between disability and eviction when seeking possession. The Code of Practice to the Act helps providers understand what this means.

The Code of Practice

6.26   The Code of Practice to the Disability Discrimination Act contains relevant information for landlords. First, and very importantly, paragraphs 3.11–3.13 of the Code of Practice make it clear that a discriminatory act may have occurred even though the relevant service provider did not know that the person in question was disabled. Paragraph 3.13 sets out the following information:

> Service providers seeking to avoid discrimination, therefore, should instruct their staff that their obligations under the Act extend to everyone who falls within the definition of 'disability' and not just to those who appear to be disabled. They may also decide that it would be prudent to instruct their staff not to attempt to make a fine judgment as to whether a particular individual falls within the statutory definition, but that they should focus instead on meeting the needs of each customer.

6.27   Paragraph 9.26 of the Code of Practice is headed 'Eviction' and states that:

> It is unlawful for a person managing any premises to discriminate against a disabled person occupying those premises by evicting the disabled person. This prohibition does not prevent the eviction of a disabled tenant where the law allows it, for example, where he or she is in arrears of rent

or has breached other terms of the tenancy, and where the reason for the eviction is not related to disability. However, in each case, appropriate court action needs to be taken to obtain an eviction order.

6.28 What is most significant about the *Romano* case is that, in answering the question as to whether discrimination was justified under the Act, the interpretation of justification in the context of the protection of health and safety of others is to be a broad one. The court adopted the World Health Organization's definition of health: 'Health is a state of complete physical, mental and social well-being and not merely the absence of disease and infirmity.'

6.29 Ms Romano's next door neighbour, who had been suffering as a result of her behaviour, gave evidence that he was:

> ... going to work tired because my sleep has been disturbed. This makes my work difficult as I have explained. I am a Driving Examiner and need to be fully aware of what is going on around me ... I have been to the courts to obtain some peace and rest ... The stress this has caused me in my marriage and in my work is unmeasurable.

6.30 The court decided that therefore he was suffering harm, using the World Health Organization definition and that eviction was justified.

6.31 The judgment gave advice to social landlords about the interface of the Disability Discrimination Act 1995 and the Housing Act 1985 at paragraphs 117–119, which is very important. We have set this out in Box 6.8.

Box 6.8 Advice from the Court of Appeal in the *Romano* case

This judgment shows that landlords whose tenants hold secure or assured tenancies must consider the position carefully before they decide to serve a notice seeking possession or to embark on possession proceedings against a tenant who is or might be mentally impaired. This is likely to compel a local housing authority to liaise more closely with the local social services authority at an earlier stage of their consideration of a problem that might lead to an eviction than appears to be the case with many authorities, to judge from some of the papers the DRC placed before the court. To remove someone from their home may be a traumatic thing to do in the case of many who are not mentally impaired. It may be even more traumatic for the mentally impaired.

To send a warning letter to a tenant about his conduct is not to subject him to a detriment within the meaning of the Act, but it may well be that at such a stage it might be wise for a local

> housing authority to start considering whether it would be able in due course to hold in good faith an opinion of one of the kinds mentioned in section 24(3) of the Act and to set about obtaining the necessary evidence for that purpose. Such evidence will not simply involve obtaining evidence about the mental condition of the tenant. If the council believes that the tenant suffers or may be suffering from a mental impairment of the type described in section 1 of the Act ..., then it will be prudent for it to obtain evidence of the effect of the tenant's behaviour on the health or safety of one or more of the complainants (for which see paragraphs 60–75 of the 1995 Act) if section 24(3)(a) of the 1995 Act is to be relied upon. In the first instance a statement by that complainant supported by a short letter from the complainant's GP or other medical adviser is likely to suffice. The importance of taking these steps in a careful manner is buttressed by research evidence which shows the significant proportion of sufferers with mental health problems among those who are guilty of anti-social behaviour. Paragraph 53 of this judgment draws attention to the fact that a landlord may perform a discriminatory act even if it does not know that the person in question is disabled: hence the need for a careful appraisal.

6.32   If we distil the court's advice into key points, then what we learn is that providers should:

- ensure that the potential for disability discrimination is recognised in eviction policies;
- be aware of the link between mental impairment and anti-social behaviour;
- have procedures available which identify the possibility that a mental impairment is contributing to the issue of possession proceedings at a very early stage;
- get medical evidence of harm from any complainant;
- liaise with social services as soon as any issue of disability discrimination becomes apparent.

Race and housing

6.33   Under section 21 of the Race Relations Act, it is unlawful for all landlords, private or social, including landlords of long leasehold properties, to discriminate against a person, or harass them, on racial grounds, in either the management or letting of premises, except where the premises are small and, even then, only in very limited circumstances. The definition of 'premises' includes hostels, bed and breakfast outlets, student accommodation and temporary accommodation secured for people who have a right to be housed by the local authority under the homelessness legislation.

6.34 Landlords must not discriminate against, or harass, an applicant or tenant, on racial grounds:

- by refusing to rent premises;
- in the terms, including the proposed rent, on which they offer premises;
- in the way they treat someone, compared with others who need such premises;
- in the way they make benefits or facilities available to tenants or by refusing to provide those benefits and facilities (including repairs, maintenance, car parking and dealing with complaints of racial harassment or discrimination); and
- by evicting tenants or occupiers, or subjecting them to any other detriment (other detriments may include requiring entry to the premises to inspect the accommodation).

Code of Practice on racial equality in housing

6.35 The Commission for Racial Equality published a Code of Practice in connection with racial equality in housing in October 2006. As the commission points out, following the code's recommendations should enable anyone with responsibility for the activities and decisions of a housing organisation, including those involving direct letting, to defend themselves better in any case of alleged racial discrimination brought against the organisation. The code is written in an accessible way, with lots of examples and very good advice. We cannot recommend it too highly; however, here we have space only to outline some of its contents. It is available to download from www.equalityhuman-rights.com/en/publicationsandresources/race/pages/services.aspx.

Box 6.9 Frequently asked questions

Are supported housing providers legally obliged to follow the code?

The code is a statutory code. This means it has been approved by the secretary of state and laid before parliament. If a provider is

---

> taken to court in a case brought under the Race Relations Act, the courts are required to take its recommendations into account, if the code is introduced into evidence, and the recommendations appear relevant to any question arising during the proceedings. As we pointed out in chapter 2, a code of guidance is not an authoritative statement of the law; this can only be provided by the courts.

The benefits of the code

6.36   The Commission for Racial Equality (now EHRC) suggests a number of benefits from adhering to the Code of Practice. We have set these out for you in Box 6.10.

Box 6.10 The benefits of the Code of Practice

This code should help housing organisations and agencies, including individual landlords, to:

- understand and meet their legal obligations under the RRA;
- adopt and put into practice effective policies, designed to prevent unlawful racial discrimination or harassment, and promote equal opportunities and good race relations;
- make sure users of housing services are treated equally, and that their needs are taken into account, wherever possible, and reflected in the services the organisation provides;
- improve satisfaction with the services they provide;
- reduce the risk of legal liability, costly and time-consuming disputes and potential damage to an organisation's reputation; and
- be regarded as an organisation that does what it says, and provides a fair and useful service for everyone in the area it serves.

The code should also help those who use housing services to know their rights under the RRA, and to be aware of what constitutes good practice in the field of housing and race relations.

6.37   Very usefully, the Commission for Racial Equality suggests the most useful way to approach the development of effective race equality strategies. We have set these out in Box 6.11.

Box 6.11 Effective race equality strategies

- Racial equality, and equality more generally, should be one of the organisation's core values and should be reflected in any mission statement it might adopt.
- The organisation's functions and policies should be audited and reviewed, to make sure they cover all housing needs in the area served, and the information used to develop a racial equality strategy and action plan.
- The organisation should consult staff and local communities, including recent arrivals and traditionally excluded groups, such as Gypsies and Irish Travellers, in developing its racial equality strategy and action plan.
- Leadership and commitment from the board, councillors and senior managers should be secured at all stages of the racial equality strategy, from development to realisation.
- The organisation's housing plans and arrangements should be based on up-to-date information about the housing needs and requirements of people from all backgrounds in the community it serves.
- The organisation should make sure information about its services and its racial equality strategy reaches people from all racial groups.
- The organisation's staff should be trained to provide an equal service to all customers, regardless of their racial group.
- The organisation should keep its racial equality strategy and action plan under regular review, and revise it, as needed.
- The organisation's progress in achieving racial equality should be monitored and evaluated against the work and achievements of other housing organisations, and good practice promoted as widely as possible.

6.38   The code provides a huge amount of practical advice on the management of housing. For instance, it raises the following questions in connection with supported housing: Have housing initiatives and programmes taken full account of the needs and preferences of people from all racial groups? Are programmes being developed fairly and equitably? It suggests the following operating principles in connection with *Supporting People* (discussed in chapter 11):

- Service providers should be explicitly and actively committed to making services equally available to all.
- Services should meet the religious, language, dietary and cultural needs of those who use, or might use, them.
- All staff should be trained, and all agencies associated with a *Supporting People*, initiative, should have robust policies and procedures on racial equality, and on dealing with racial harassment.
- Providers of services must have arrangements for collecting and analysing data on racial groups, and using the information to tackle any shortfalls in services.
- Providers of services should consider how they might use section 35 of the Race Relations Act to provide supported housing for people from ethnic minorities. Section 35 allows housing organisations, including ethnic minority housing associations, to make special provision for certain groups; for example, by developing temporary hostel accommodation catering especially for newly arrived Somali refugees, who may have needs arising from shared traumatic experiences. To take advantage of this exception, the housing or service provider must have objective evidence of the special need they wish to meet, and must demonstrate that the special provision is proportionate.

6.39   The code makes the link between racial harassment and anti-social behaviour and provides good advice on the development of anti-social behaviour policies, which we will look at in more detail in chapter 20. Finally, the code reminds its readers of the importance of training, monitoring and racial impact assessments.

Regulatory requirements

6.40   Both the Housing Corporation and *Supporting People* impose requirements on providers who receive funding from them in connection with discrimination.

Housing Corporation

6.41   We discuss the role of the Housing Corporation in chapter 10. As part of the registration process, as registered social landlords, housing associations are required to demonstrate, when carrying out all their functions, their commitments to equal opportunity. They must work towards the elimination of discrimination and demonstrate an equitable approach to the rights and responsibilities of all individuals. They must promote good relations between people of different racial groups. It is clear that the Commission for Racial Equality Code of Practice will be very useful in enabling registered social landlords to meet the Housing Corporation requirements.

6.42   More specifically, any provider registered with the Housing Corporation must demonstrate that:

- it is fair in its dealings with the people, communities and organisations with which it has relationships, and takes into account the diverse nature of their cultures and backgrounds;
- its governing body has adopted an equalities and diversity policy that covers all aspects of equalities, including race, religion, gender, marital status, sexual orientation, disability or age;
- in relation to black and minority ethnic (BME) people, the policy incorporates targets in the following areas:

  1 Future lettings: are proportionate to BME housing need.
  2 Tenant satisfaction: is at least as high as for non-BME tenants.
  3 Dealing effectively with racial harassment: the applicant establishes targets for reporting, victim support and satisfaction, and action taken against perpetrators.
  4 Governing body membership: the number of BME new appointments and re-appointments to the governing body is proportionate to BME housing need.
  5 Staffing: new appointments and promotions achieve the same levels of representation, at all levels of the organisations.
  6 Representation in tenants/residents associations: reflects the ethnic mix of the applicant's tenants in the relevant area.
  7 Employment performance of suppliers, contractors and consultants: as a criterion for award of work or contracts and a condition of doing business, the applicant should set for its consultants, contractors and suppliers the same requirements that it has to meet itself in respect of staffing, customer satisfaction and dealing with racial harassment.

Supporting People

6.43   Local authorities, who administer *Supporting People*, are public authorities for the purposes of the Race Discrimination (Amendment) Act 2000, and are therefore under a duty to have due regard to the need to eliminate unlawful discrimination and to promote equality of opportunity and good relations between persons of different racial groups.

The Quality Assessment Framework, which is used to ensure that *Supporting People* programmes reach minimum standards (see chapter 11), has a requirement that particular equal opportunity standards are achieved. Providers will therefore have to demonstrate that their provision provides for fair access, diversity and inclusion. Providers therefore must ensure that services are committed to the values of diversity and inclusion and to the practice of equal opportunity (including accessibility in its widest sense) and that the needs of black and minority ethnic service users are appropriately met.

Policies

6.44   This chapter demonstrates that a good equal opportunities policy which is constantly reviewed and is collectively owned by management staff and service users is absolutely essential. It enables providers to keep within the law, which as we have seen is constantly developing; and is likely to be a regulatory requirement from funders, either the Housing Corporation or the state via its *Supporting People* programme. However, the real need for a policy should not be because of fear of legal or regulatory failure, but because a policy is a prerequisite of the type of service providers wish to provide, one which addresses needs effectively and appropriately. We have included some guidelines to developing an equal opportunities policy in the appendices.

Summary

6.45   In this chapter we have looked at the basic structure of discrimination law, and the way in which problems are recognised and responded to with the aim of producing fair and appropriate access to limited resources. We have also considered in more detail the particular legal demands placed upon landlords in the context of disability discrimination and race discrimination. Finally, we discussed the regulatory demands placed upon organisations and the need for robust and carefully considered policies which really interrogate what it means to be an equal opportunities organisation. In the next chapter we discuss human rights. It may well provide a more fruitful approach to discrimination. Article 14 of the European Convention on Human Rights focuses on non-discrimination. It provides that:

The enjoyment of the rights and freedoms set forth in this Convention shall be secured without discrimination on any ground such as sex, race, colour, language, religion, political or other opinion, national or social origin, association with a national minority, property, birth or other status.

6.46 You will note that it applies to any ground for discrimination, and the examples it provides are far wider than the prohibitions of UK discrimination law. This alerts us to a different approach. Instead of thinking about those areas where the law forbids us to discriminate, human rights has a more positive ethos, to treat individuals with dignity and respect. If these can be the drivers of your equalities policies and procedures, then you are unlikely to be caught out by changes in legal or policy requirements.

CHAPTER 7

Human rights

Objectives

7.1   By the end of this chapter you will have some familiarity with:

- The origins of European Convention on Human Rights
- The extent of convention rights
- The impact of human rights upon your organisation
- The legal mechanisms for enforcing human rights

Overview

7.2   The purpose of this chapter is to introduce you to the legal culture of human rights and to provide you with some understanding of what it means to provide public services to fellow citizens within the framework of human rights. Lord Falconer, formerly Secretary of State for Constitutional Affairs, in the introduction to the third edition of the government's *Guide to the Human Rights Act 1998*, states that:

> We all benefit from living in a society in which all public authorities deliver their services with human rights in mind. In doing that they need to balance the rights of the individual with the rights of wider society. They get the overwhelming majority of those decisions right. Those that are thought to be wrong can be tested and where necessary our courts will deal with disputes.

7.3   We think this provides a useful pointer to the significance of human rights. It provides an ethical basis for actions of the state and agents of the state in relation to individual citizens. As the law currently stands very few supported housing providers are likely to be public bodies within the meaning of public law. This may well change. We discuss the meaning and implications of 'public bodies' later in the chapter. Nonetheless, this does not mean that human rights are not relevant. First, public bodies have obligations towards people based upon their human rights and, secondly, the ethos of human rights should permeate all public services, even when the actions of the organisation providing by the service cannot be challenged in the courts.

7.4   The chapter is structured as follows: we begin with a brief history of human rights, which is a useful aid in understanding the framework and preoccupations of the European Convention on Human Rights; we then turn to consider the key human rights in relation to supported housing and illustrate these with some brief case details; and in the third part of the chapter we consider the workings of the Human Rights Act 1998.

The origins of human rights

7.5   There is a multitude of philosophical, historical and political drivers to human rights. However, the most significant force behind the European Convention on Human Rights 1950 (the European Convention) was the Second World War and its aftermath. The convention is framed to prevent a repeat of the rise of fascism and totalitarianism, of oppression of individual rights in the name of the state and in the name of the majority. As Lord Justice Sedley put it in his lecture for the Legal Action Group in 2003:

> The Convention is a child of its time – the post-war years when the states of western Europe tried to set their faces both against the devastation of the recent past and against any new form of totalitarianism. So the Convention says many important things about due process, personal integrity and free speech and ideas; but nothing directly about the most elementary of all human needs, a right to enough food and shelter to keep body and soul together. (Lord Justice Sedley, December 2003 *Legal Action* 19.)

7.6   British lawyers were actively involved in the drafting of the convention, which was designed to give legal force within Europe to the principles set out in the United Nations Declaration of Human Rights of 1948. The UK signed the European Convention in 1951 and the convention became binding upon its signatories in 1953. However, the UK for many years refused to incorporate the convention into its domestic law. Therefore, prior to the implementation of the Human Rights Act 1998, enforcement of its provisions was via the European Court of Human Rights in Strasbourg and not through the domestic courts. Because the convention was not part of the normal course of business in the courts, British lawyers were in general not familiar with convention rights, and finding a specialist lawyer who was prepared to take a case to Strasbourg was both difficult and expensive.

7.7   The Human Rights Act 1998 was one of the first pieces of legislation enacted by the incoming Labour government in 1997, and was implemented on 2 October 2000 after a two-year period for the training of the judiciary and public authorities. Its primary purpose is to enable individual convention rights to be enforced through the UK courts, and to provide a check on the activities of parliament and public bodies.

7.8   Opinions differ about the appropriateness of a human rights culture at the beginning of the 21st century. In particular, concerns are expressed that human rights cannot work in the context of the so-called war on terror. So Melanie Phillips argues:

At a time of such a grave threat to national security, we can no longer afford to allow the judges to compromise our security. Human rights law should be repealed, or at very least we must derogate from those parts of it that prevent us from safeguarding this country's interests. (See www.melaniephillips.com/articles/archive/001373).

7.9 On the other hand, it can be argued that it is in times of political conflict that the fundamental freedoms of human rights are most significant. Lord Steyn (a law lord), for instance, explains:

> A constitutional democracy must protect fundamental rights. It is morally right that the state and all who act on its behalf in a broad functional sense, should respect the fundamental rights of individuals. Without such a moral compass the state is bound to treat individual arbitrarily and unjustly. Moreover, the best way of encouraging multi-culturalism and tolerance in Europe is by creating societies in which human rights are protected. By the Human Rights Act Parliament transformed our country into a rights based democracy. By the 1998 Act Parliament made the judiciary the guardians of the ethical values of our bill of rights. ([2005] 4 EHRLR 349 at 350.)

7.10 It is important not to limit your appreciation of human rights to the rights of those suspected of terrorism or involved in acts of violence. Perhaps the most significant impact of the Act has been its effects on the ordinary lives of ordinary people. One example from a recent case will illustrate this. In *R (Bernard) v Enfield LBC* [2002] EWHC 2282, the High Court considered the application of Mrs Bernard, a severely disabled, wheelchairbound woman who lived with her family in inappropriate local authority accommodation. Despite the social services department having assessed her needs and recommending special adaptations, so that, for instance, Mrs Bernard could access the bathroom, the local authority failed to respond to the family's needs. The High Court found that the local authority had positive obligations to enable the family to live as normal a life as possible and to secure Mrs Bernard's physical integrity and human dignity. The lack of action by the local authority was a breach of Mrs Bernard's right to respect for family life, under article 8 of the European Convention.

The extent of convention rights

7.11 In this part of the chapter we will consider some key concepts which underpin the workings of the European Convention and then go on to discuss the contents of particular convention articles.

Victims

7.12   The first key point is that it is only victims of breaches of convention rights who can bring proceedings under the Human Rights Act. So only the person who has been affected by an act or decision of a public authority can take action, in relation to that act or decision. The restriction of action to victims means that the scope of the Human Rights Act is more limited than judicial review, which we discussed in chapter 2.

Public authorities

7.13   While the courts have to consider the convention rights in all cases even if they do not involve a public authority, a victim can bring a case under the Act only if the act or decision in question is one of a public authority. A public authority is a broader concept than you might think. It is best understood as a body carrying out a governmental or public function. Local authorities are public bodies. Other examples include schools, departments of central government (such as the Home Office), hospitals and prisons. Private companies that exercise public functions, such as organisations that run private prisons, are also public authorities under the Act. Some bodies have mixed public and private functions – for purposes of the Human Rights Act they are described as 'hybrid' authorities. However, the question of which bodies are 'hybrid' has proved to be complex. Many housing associations, for instance, carry out functions which courts may decide are public functions. However, other functions would clearly be private functions. It is difficult to provide clear guidelines on whether a housing association is or is not a public authority. In an important case, *Donaghue v Poplar Housing and Regeneration* [2002] EWHC 2559, the court decided that because the housing association concerned had a particularly close relationship with, and was performing very similar functions to, a local authority, then it was a public authority. However, in *Heather v Leonard Cheshire Foundation* [2002] 2 All ER 936, the Leonard Cheshire Foundation, a charity providing residential care, was held not to be a public authority. The case-law is still developing in this area. What is certain is that the courts are not going to allow public authorities to evade their responsibilities under the Act by delegating public functions to private bodies. On the other hand, the courts have a particular responsibility to ensure that the scope of the Human Rights Act is not extended beyond what was intended by parliament. We set out in Box 7.1 some details of the most recent case, *YL v Birmingham City*

Council, in which the House of Lords considered the meaning of public body in the context of the private provision of publicly funded care.

Box 7.1 *YL v Birmingham City Council* [2007] UKHL 27

An 84-year-old person with Alzheimer's disease was threatened with eviction from the private care home where she was living because of what was said to be the bad behaviour of her family when they visited her. Medical opinion was that the person would be put at considerable risk if she was moved. Lawyers for the woman, known as YL to protect her privacy, issued proceedings arguing that it was a breach of YL's human rights (article 8 – see below) if she was evicted. They argued in the House of Lords that the private care home was exercising the functions of a public body because the local authority had funded YL's placement thereafter assessing that she was in need of care because of her condition. The private care home argued that it was not carrying out public functions but was a private body, and they said that the funding source of any individual service user is irrelevant.

The House of Lords decided by a majority of 3:2 that the provision of care services by a private body did not engage the provisions of the Human Rights Act 1998, even in circumstances where a public body was paying the fees of the service user.

Living instrument

7.14   This point highlights another important feature of the convention. It is a living instrument, designed to be interpreted in the light of prevailing social and cultural conditions, and not frozen in the 1950s when it was drafted. So the fact that a challenge under the convention has failed in the past does not mean that it will not succeed in the future.

Margin of appreciation

7.15   This is a technical term which has lost some clarity in its translation from French. What it means is that the European Court of Human Rights will allow domestic courts some space to make decisions which reflect their national domestic concerns, rather than impose its interpretation on the way the articles should operate. This is particularly relevant when the courts have to weigh up competing priorities, for instance, individual liberty and national security. Of course, the margin of appreciation can only go so far; the European Court of Human Rights does ensure some consistency in the interpretation of the European Convention.

Rights can be absolute, limited or qualified

7.16 Rights are formulated in different ways under the European Convention. Some rights are so fundamental that they are absolute. These rights include the right to protection from torture, inhuman and degrading treatment and the prohibition on slavery. Others, such as the right to liberty, are limited under explicit and finite circumstances that are set out in the convention itself. Finally, certain rights are qualified, which means that interference with these rights is permissible only if the interference is:

- justified in law;
- done with a permissible aim set out in the Convention; and
- necessary in a democratic society, which means that it must fulfil a pressing social need, pursue a legitimate aim and be proportionate to the aims being pursued.

7.17 Proportionality is a particularly important requirement. Interference with rights is not justified if the means used to justify the aim are disproportionate.

7.18 Examples of qualified rights are the right to respect for private and family life and the right to freedom of expression.

Box 7.2 Frequently asked questions

What happens when one person's right conflicts with another person exercising their rights? One of our residents wants to display a BNP poster in his room. He says it is his human right to do so. Other residents find this offensive.

It is often difficult to decide whose rights are to prevail in situations of conflict. The first point to note is that if your organisation is not a public body then the obligation upon you to uphold his rights is unenforceable. However, if you are going to follow a human rights-based approach to solving such problems, you would ask yourself whether your interference with his right to freedom of expression is justified, necessary and proportionate.

> Freedom of expression is protected within article 10 of the convention, which we set out below. It is a qualified article, so you are entitled to take into account the rights of others, public safety considerations, etc. As the poster is in his room, you may decide that he is entitled to display it; on the other hand, if your project is explicitly committed to anti-racism you may consider that it is in breach of the ethos of the project.

The articles of the convention

7.19   This book is not the place to provide a full explanation of the articles of the European Convention. We will explain those articles which are most likely to be relevant to your work and then suggest further reading which you may find interesting.

Article 2 – the right to life

1. Everyone's right to life shall be protected by law. No one shall be deprived of his life intentionally save in the execution of a sentence of a court following his conviction of a crime for which this penalty is provided by law.
2. Deprivation of life shall not be regarded as inflicted in contravention of this Article when it results from the use of force which is no more than absolutely necessary:
   (a) in defence of any person from unlawful violence;
   (b) in order to effect a lawful arrest or to prevent the escape of a person lawfully detained;
   (c) in action lawfully taken for the purpose of quelling a riot or insurrection.

7.20   The article protects citizens' rights by:

- preventing the state from taking life;
- ensuring that the state investigates deaths in which the state may have had some responsibility; and
- imposing positive obligations upon the state to protect life, so, for instance, deportation from the UK to states where there is a real possibility that the deportee's life may be endangered is a breach of article 2.

7.21   Article 2 does not include the right to take your own life.

Article 3 – *freedom from torture or inhuman or degrading treatment*

No one shall be subjected to torture or to inhuman or degrading treatment or punishment.

7.22   Not only must the state not torture its citizens. It has a positive obligation to protect individuals from breaches of the article by other individuals. The article was breached, for instance, when the state failed to protect children from abuse by their parents.

Article 6 – *right to a fair trial*

1. In the determination of his civil rights and obligations or of any criminal charge against him, everyone is entitled to a fair and public hearing within a reasonable time, by an independent and impartial tribunal established by law. Judgment shall be pronounced publicly but the press and public may be excluded from all or part of the trial in the interests of morals, public order or national security in a democratic society, where the interests of juveniles or the protection of the private life of the parties so require, or to the extent strictly necessary in the opinion of the court in special circumstances where publicity would prejudice the interests of justice.
2. Everyone charged with a criminal offence shall be presumed innocent until proved guilty according to law.
3. Everyone charged with a criminal offence has the following minimum rights:
   (a) to be informed promptly, in a language which he understands and in detail, of the nature and cause of the accusation against him;
   (b) to have adequate time and facilities for the preparation of his defence;
   (c) to defend himself in person or through legal assistance of his own choosing or, if he has not sufficient means to pay for legal assistance, to be given it free when the interests of justice so require;
   (d) to examine or have examined witnesses against him and to obtain the attendance and examination of witnesses on his behalf under the same conditions as witnesses against him;
   (e) to have the free assistance of an interpreter if he cannot understand or speak the language used in court.

7.23   As the article makes clear, many kinds of hearing, both civil and criminal, are covered by article 6. There have been more challenges to the UK government based on article 6 than any other article. One particular impact of article 6 is an increase in rights to appeal decisions made by the state.

Box 7.3 Frequently asked questions

We have a service user who is alleged to have broken the law whilst visiting her family abroad. She claims she will not get a fair trial if she is extradited to that country. Will it be contravening her human rights in this country to send her back to another country where these rights may not be respected?

This is a question which the courts have tackled in connection with the deportation of foreign nationals who are suspected of having terrorist connections. The courts have decided that the UK would be in breach of its obligations under the European Convention if it deported foreign nationals to a country where there is a serious risk that those rights will not be respected. It is irrelevant that that particular country is not a signatory to the convention.

Article 8 – the right to respect for private and family life

1. Everyone has the right to respect for his private and family life, his home and his correspondence.
2. There shall be no interference by a public authority with the exercise of this right except such as is in accordance with the law and is necessary in a democratic society in the interests of national security, public safety or the economic well-being of the country, for the prevention of disorder or crime, for the protection of health or morals, or for the protection of the rights and freedoms of others.

7.24   The right includes, for instance:

* freedom to choose sexual identity; and
* freedom of dress and appearance.

7.25   If you are a public body and you prevent your service users from expressing their sexual identity without justification and disproportionately, you may have breached your service users' article 8 rights. As we illustrated when we discussed the case of *R (Bernard) v Enfield* above, problems with housing have led to a number of challenges under article 8. On the face of it, for instance, any decision to terminate someone's occupation of their home can form the basis of an article 8 case. However, a number of points need to be made here. First of all, article 8 does not give someone the right to a home, but the right to respect for private and family life. Secondly, the article is a qualified right. Therefore, a breach of the article may be acceptable as long as the breach is founded in law, is legitimately pursued and is a proportionate response to the problem that is being addressed. So eviction for non-payment of rent through the courts does not trigger an article 8 case. The courts have had more difficulty in responding to evictions without court supervision, for instance, the eviction of someone who has no legal right to be in the property, but the property is in many senses their home; or when someone is evicted from an introductory tenancy when there is no court interrogation of the eviction, simply a review of the process. After some potentially conflicting decisions, the courts have not extended the protections of the article to occupiers in these circumstances. Instead, they view housing legislation as providing the necessary balance between landlords and tenants, and therefore evictions where no court proceedings are necessary will comply with article 8 in most circumstances because they are democratically legitimate. There may be cases where this does not apply, but such cases will be rare and victims will have to make their case to the courts.

Article 10 – freedom of expression

1. Everyone has the right to freedom of expression. This right shall include freedom to hold opinions and to receive and impart information and ideas without interference by public authority and regardless of frontiers. This Article shall not prevent states from requiring the licensing of broadcasting, television or cinema enterprises.
2. The exercise of these freedoms, since it carries with it duties and responsibilities, may be subject to such formalities, conditions, restrictions or penalties as are prescribed by law and are necessary in a democratic society, in the interests of national security, territorial integrity or public safety, for the prevention of disorder or crime, for the protection of health or morals, for the protection of the reputation or rights of others, for preventing the disclosure of information received in confidence, or for maintaining the authority and impartiality of the judiciary.

Article 14 – the right not to be discriminated against

The enjoyment of the rights and freedoms set forth in this Convention shall be secured without discrimination on any ground such as sex, race, colour, language, religion, political or other opinion, national or social origin, association with a national minority, property, birth or other status.

7.26   This article is a little different from the other articles of the convention. It comes into operation only once one of the other articles has been breached. However, discrimination in connection with housing is almost always going to involve non-compliance with article 8. Article 14 is probably the least litigated part of the convention. We think that article 14 has a great deal of potential within housing. For instance, discriminating against allocation someone housing on the grounds of mental capacity or race may well be found to be discriminatory if there is no justification for doing so.

What relevance does the Human Rights Act have for you?

7.27   Even if your organisation is not a public body for the purposes of the Human Rights Act, we would like to suggest that it has relevance. What it does is to enact an ethical framework that is particularly valuable for governing the conduct of any organisation that deals with vulnerable individuals. It may only bind public bodies, but it is useful guidance for other organisations. It is sometimes easy to forget, in the urge to act in what we think are individuals' best interests, that they have the right to self-determination and privacy. For instance, providers may feel uncomfortable about a service user visiting a prostitute. The Human Rights Act provides a useful way of considering any decision to interfere with his or her freedom. Have you any right to prevent your service user's action? Is your interference proportionate to the harm you are seeking to address? Something else that is important to bear in mind is that the Act is not just about legal cases, but is seeking to enhance democracy by building a culture that is aware of and committed to fundamental values designed to ensure that everyone is treated with fairness and respect.

7.28   Of course, you may also be aware that a public body is acting in breach of one of your service user's rights, or even your own rights. The next part of this chapter explains the mechanisms for enforcing human rights.

The legal mechanisms for enforcing human rights

7.29   Generally, when someone has been the victim of a potential breach of their convention rights, the appropriate legal action will be judicial review of the public body's action by the High Court. Such cases usually have to be taken within one year of the action complained of. When the court considers the human rights issue raised, it will review the law to see if the public authority had any choice about the action it took. It will try to interpret the legislative basis of the public authority's action to see if it can be interpreted in a way which is compatible with convention rights. If the legislation can be interpreted compatibly and the public authority is found to have acted in breach, then the court can remedy that breach using its usual powers. The Human Rights Act also extended the powers of the courts to grant damages for breach of convention rights. However, the courts are reluctant to do this and, where they have, levels of damages have been quite small. If the legislation cannot be interpreted compatibly, the courts' powers depend upon the type of legislation that forms the basis of the public authority's action. If the legislation was secondary legislation, then the court may quash or disapply that legislation. If the breach arises out of primary legislation – Acts of parliament – then the court cannot quash the legislation. This is because the Human Rights Act maintains the supremacy of parliament which must be recognised by the courts. Instead, what the courts can do is to make a declaration of incompatibility. Such a declaration will not make that Act invalid and the public authority involved will not be acting unlawfully in applying the legislation. However, it makes it clear to the government that there is a problem with the legislation and provides support for the victim in taking their challenge to Strasbourg.

7.30   There is another mechanism built into the Human Rights Act which is designed to ensure that all new legislation takes the European Convention into account. A minister who is introducing a bill into parliament has to make a statement as to whether or not the bill is compatible with convention rights, and to highlight those provisions of the bill which are relevant. All bills are scrutinised by the Joint Parliamentary Committee on Human Rights, which has considerable expertise in human rights law and is able to make proposals as to how a bill can be made more compatible with convention rights.

Summary

7.31   The Ministry of Justice (formerly Department of Constitutional Affairs) published *A Guide to the Human Rights Act* in October 2006 (available at www.justice.gov.uk/docs/act-studyguide.pdf). We would recommend this as an excellent and informative explanation of the workings of the Act. The flowchart in Box 7.4 is reproduced from this guide. We try to raise issues of human rights throughout the book, and provide examples of non-compliance with the convention. Do not forget that this area of the law is constantly changing and you should ensure that you read briefings on the latest developments.

Further reading

7.32   There is extensive further information on the implications of the Human Rights Act 1998. We recommend the following books from Legal Action Group (LAG):

Keir Starmer QC, *European Human Rights Law* (2nd edition forthcoming, 2008)

Jenny Watson and Mitchell Woolf, *Human Rights Act Toolkit* (2nd edition, 2008)

Box 7.4 Human Rights Act flowchart

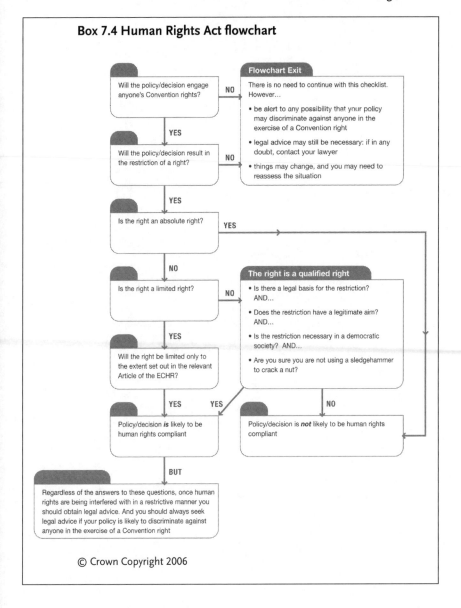

Will the policy/decision engage anyone's Convention rights? — NO

Flowchart Exit

There is no need to continue with this checklist. However...

- be alert to any possibility that your policy may discriminate against anyone in the exercise of a Convention right

- legal advice may still be necessary: if in any doubt, contact your lawyer

- things may change, and you may need to reassess the situation

YES

Will the policy/decision result in the restriction of a right? — NO

YES

Is the right an absolute right? — YES

NO

Is the right a limited right? — NO

The right is a qualified right

- Is there a legal basis for the restriction? AND...

- Does the restriction have a legitimate aim? AND...

- Is the restriction necessary in a democratic society? AND...

- Are you sure you are not using a sledgehammer to crack a nut?

YES

Will the right be limited only to the extent set out in the relevant Article of the ECHR?

YES   YES   NO

Policy/decision *is* likely to be human rights compliant

Policy/decision is *not* likely to be human rights compliant

BUT

Regardless of the answers to these questions, once human rights are being interfered with in a restrictive manner you should obtain legal advice. And you should always seek legal advice if your policy is likely to discriminate against anyone in the exercise of a Convention right

© Crown Copyright 2006

Anti-social behaviour

Objectives

8.1   By the end of this chapter you will be familiar with:

- The tools available to landlords to manage residents' behaviour and protect residents from harm
- The responsibilities of social landlords to respond to anti-social behaviour
- The anti-social behaviour order (ASBO) and the Crime and Disorder Act 1998

Overview

8.2   Housing and conflict between occupiers sometimes seem to be inextricably linked, so it is not surprising that issues relating to the management of inappropriate behaviour arise in supported housing. Both providers and service users are likely to be concerned, either because:

- a service user is a victim of anti-social behaviour; or
- a service user is or is alleged to be a perpetrator.

8.3   There is an extensive range of legal tools available to tackle anti-social behaviour; some of these result from recent developments to landlord and tenant law, others are more akin to criminal law and have been designed to address general concerns about behaviour in our communities. Decisions to invoke the law as a tool for controlling anti-social behaviour have to be carefully considered. Providers must resolve the tension between the need to address behaviour via speedy and effective remedies and the need to respect due process and the legal rights of the alleged perpetrators. Deciding to deprive someone of their home, in particular, must be done carefully and should be proportionate to the harm that the behaviour is causing. Moreover, evictions for anti-social behaviour may have an impact upon local authority decisions to allocate housing to an alleged perpetrator.

8.4   In this chapter we concentrate on describing two types of legal controls on anti-social behaviour. The first involves powers that tackle individual behaviour, either through housing law or by utilising the anti-social behaviour order available under the Crime and Disorder Act 1998. The second type of control is concerned with strategic responses to anti-social behaviour. In chapter 20 we look more carefully at the good practice in managing individual service users' behaviour and at drafting anti-social behaviour policies.

Evicting the anti-social occupier

8.5 As we have already discussed in chapter 4, the occupation agreement between the landlord and the residential occupier sets out respective rights and responsibilities. Many social landlords in recent years have extended the terms of their agreements to ban a wide range of unacceptable behaviour, from racial harassment to drug misuse. The occupier is given responsibility for the behaviour of visitors and children. The presence of such clauses enables the landlord to evict for breach of terms of the agreement (see chapter 4) and is limited only by statutory requirements that arise from the legal status of the occupation agreement. So evictions of anti-social secure (local authority) tenants must be upon specified grounds, notice must be given and it must be reasonable to evict. While there are some mandatory grounds available for evicting the assured tenant, evictions based upon allegations of behaviour must be reasonable and the ground that is used must be proved. It is easier to evict the assured shorthold tenant who is allegedly responsible for anti-social behaviour through use of the section 21 notice procedure. The eviction of common law tenants and licencees needs only to conform to the requirements of the Protection from Eviction Act 1977. (See chapters 4 and 23 for further information on termination of residential occupancies.) Remember that the terms in tenancy and licence agreements must be fair. Fairness includes transparency. A vague term prohibiting anti-social behaviour without definition or limits could well fall foul of the Unfair Terms in Consumer Contract Regulations 1999 (SI 1999 No 2083), which we have discussed in chapter 3. However, recently, some of the more long-standing protections of secure and assured tenants have been dismantled when there are allegations of anti-social behaviour.

Quicker evictions

8.6 Speed is of the essence in dealing with anti-social behaviour. It is self-defeating if someone who is behaving in an intimidatory way is able to remain in the property for a substantial period of time pending a court hearing. Possession proceedings against secure and assured tenants on nuisance grounds can be commenced immediately upon service of the notice of proceedings rather than giving a minimum of four weeks' notice that all other grounds require. However, eviction of the assured shorthold tenant through the section 21 procedure requires a two-month notice period. It may be more appropriate to consider injunctions, which we discuss below, to restrain difficult behaviour.

Reasonableness

8.7 The requirement of reasonableness provides a judicial restraint on arbitrary eviction by social landlords. However, the courts have responded to anti-social behaviour by requiring judges to give proper weight to the landlord's obligations to other tenants in the locality and ensuring that, where there are serious breaches of the tenancy agreement, only in exceptional circumstances will it *not* be reasonable to make an order for possession. Moreover, statutory requirements for possession proceedings now require courts to consider the past impact of the anti-social conduct on other people, the likely continuing effect of the nuisance and the likely future effect of any repetition of the conduct, when considering whether it is reasonable to make an order for possession.

Introductory tenancies

8.8 There have been other statutory initiatives. The best known is the introductory tenancy regime, which operates as an exception to the normal security of tenure of local authority housing for a probationary period of a year. A local housing authority may elect to operate an introductory tenancy regime and, when such an election is in force, every new tenancy becomes an introductory tenancy for the first 12 months. During this period the local authority can seek a possession order from the courts, subject to certain procedural requirements but without proving grounds.

Box 8.1 Frequently asked questions

We provide tenancy sustainment services to service users who are in a variety of accommodation, including local authority. We are supporting a service user on an introductory tenancy who has been issued with a notice due to his nuisance behaviour. Is there anything we can do?

A service user who is an introductory tenant and is threatened with eviction is in a difficult position. The service user can seek a

---

review of the landlord's decision within 14 days of the service of the notice of proceedings. The procedural requirements for review are set out in the Introductory Tenants (Review) Regulations 1997 (SI 1997 No 72). If you are providing support to someone in this position you may want to help them with their review.

Demoted tenancies

8.9 Registered social landlords do not have access to the introductory tenancy regime, although it is possible to use assured shorthold tenancies for a probationary period if there is a particular need to do so. However, there is a further limitation of introductory tenancies – they apply only at the start of a tenancy agreement. Anti-social behaviour may arise later during the lifetime of a tenancy. Demoted tenancies provide an option which is available throughout the lifetime of a secure or assured tenancy. Registered social landlords, as well as local authorities, are able to apply to court for a demotion order when the tenant, or another resident or visitor to the tenant's home, has behaved in an anti-social manner. This converts secure or assured tenancies to insecure demoted tenancies for a year. The court will only make the order if it is reasonable to do so. During the demotion period the landlord may commence action to evict without proof of reasons if it feels the need to do so. The non-assured demoted tenant will have to be given four weeks' notice, with reasons for the proceedings, and will have the right to a review before the local authority can issue proceedings. The demoted assured tenant has no similar rights. The registered social landlord will be able to evict using the two-month notice only ground. If no possession proceedings are taken during the demotion period, for example, because the tenant's behaviour improves, then the tenancy is automatically promoted to secure or assured status.

Injunctions

8.10 Injunctions are court orders which generally order someone to stop doing something illegal. Injunctions arising from common law obligations have always been available to landlords to restrain occupiers from breaching their occupancy agreements. They provide a very useful alternative to evictions and for a number of policy reasons they may be a more appropriate tool for the supported housing provider.

There are limitations on the availability of common law injunctions, for instance they are only available against a party to a contract to restrain a breach of its terms. Statute has intervened to create extended injunctive powers.

8.11   The Housing Act 1996 provides strengthened powers (in section 153A) for social landlords to apply for injunctions to restrain anti-social behaviour. The level of anti-social behaviour needed to trigger an injunction is low. All that is required is conduct which is capable of causing nuisance or annoyance. However, there must be a connection between that conduct and the housing management functions (broadly defined) of the landlord. Social landlords can intervene to protect a wide range of victims, not only people who live in the landlord's properties, but also people who live in the locality of those properties, people carrying out lawful activities in the locality of the housing accommodation and people who are employed by the landlord in carrying out its housing function. The court will be able to attach an exclusion order and/or a power of arrest to the injunction where the conduct involves violence, threats of violence or a significant risk of harm. Social landlords also have powers under the Housing Act 1996 to obtain injunctions to restrain unlawful use of premises (section 153B) and breaches of tenancy agreements (section 153D). Powers of arrest and exclusion orders are available on the same basis as under the anti-social behaviour injunction.

Anti-social behaviour policies

8.12   It is clearly good practice for a provider to have developed anti-social behaviour policies. However, it is also a statutory requirement. Section 12 of the Anti-social Behaviour Act 2003 imposes a statutory duty upon social landlords to prepare, keep under review and publish anti-social behaviour policies. The duty is designed to increase social landlords' accountability to local communities and to residents. The policies and procedures feed into performance measurement by central government, as well as increasing the capacity of victims to press their case for social landlords to take action. Publication of the policies is meant to deter potential perpetrators, who will know the action they will face, and additionally should increase the sharing of good practice in managing anti-social behaviour.

The role of the local authority as housing provider

8.13 The Homelessness Act 2002 allows a housing authority to decide that an applicant for housing is ineligible for housing on the basis of unacceptable behaviour. The Act requires that housing authorities allocate housing according to need. However, the Act provides that the extent of the priority of a particular applicant may be determined (amongst other factors) by taking into account any behaviour which affects suitability to be a tenant. In addition, local authorities will not be required to give any priority to applicants who are guilty of unacceptable behaviour.

Other ways of controlling behaviour

8.14 Other behaviour management techniques – for example, approved behaviour contracts (ABCs) – are promoted by the Home Office to improve community safety. ABCs typically involve local authorities targeting disruptive young people and drawing up explicit behaviour contracts designed to improve their conduct. Providers who house young people may come across or be involved in the development of these contracts.

The Crime and Disorder Act 1998

8.15 There are a number of orders available to respond to particular instances of anti-social behaviour. We discuss below the most infamous of these, the 'anti-social behaviour order'.

Anti-social behaviour orders (ASBOs): Crime and Disorder Act 1998 s1

8.16 The anti-social behaviour order (ASBO) defines anti-social behaviour as acting in a manner that causes or is likely to cause harassment, alarm or distress. A person (child over 10 or adult) can be made subject to an ASBO if the court is satisfied that the person has caused the harassment, alarm or distress as defined in the Act, or might have done so. Although ASBOs are civil orders, the court must be satisfied to a criminal burden of proof – beyond reasonable doubt – before making an order. The use of hearsay and third party evidence is permitted in order to protect witnesses and victims.

8.17   Interim orders are available to ensure that the community is protected as soon as possible from anti-social activities.

8.18   The application for an ASBO can be made by any body defined as a responsible authority in the Act. The list includes the local authority, the police and registered social landlords. There is currently a great deal of encouragement for registered social landlords to use the powers the Act makes available. Applicants who are not the police or the local authority will have to consult the police and the local authority before making an application. Registered social landlords' and housing action trusts' powers are limited to situations in which they need to take action against their tenants or to protect their tenants. ASBOs can also be made in the magistrates' court following conviction for a criminal offence – known as 'CRASBOs'. In these circumstances there is no need for an application. The CRASBO can be suspended until completion of the sentence.

8.19   ASBOs are available to a county court where the court is already dealing with proceedings relating to anti-social behaviour, such as possession proceedings. If the potential recipient of the ASBO is not a party to the proceedings but his or her behaviour is relevant (for instance, it is the adolescent son of the tenant, who has terrified the neighbour, who is being evicted), then the landlord may apply to have that person made a party. This avoids the cost and inconvenience of issuing separate proceedings for an ASBO when the evidence would be predominantly the same. The standard criteria for making ASBOs apply.

8.20   Once a court has accepted that the defendant has behaved in 'a manner that caused or was likely to cause harassment alarm or distress' and that an order is necessary to protect local people from further acts, then the court is able to impose those prohibitions which it deems necessary to protect people from further anti-social acts.

8.21   When a court makes an ASBO it must make a parenting order at the same time, unless it does not consider that the parenting order is desirable in the interests of preventing any repetition of the kind of behaviour which led to the ASBO. Orders must last for not less than two years (section 1(7)) and can last indefinitely. Although there are provisions to vary the order, the court cannot discharge an order that has not lasted for two years, unless all parties agree.

8.22   Perhaps the most significant feature of the anti-social behaviour is the serious consequences of breach. Doing anything in breach of the order is a criminal offence. On summary conviction the court can sentence to six months in prison or a £1,000 fine. The breach can be dealt with in the Crown Court, with a maximum sentence of five years and an unlimited fine.

Strategic duties under the Crime and Disorder Act 1998

8.23 The current government has recognised that anti-social behaviour cannot be categorised simply as a matter with housing or criminal consequences for victims. The impact of anti-social behaviour can contribute to social exclusion, and local government has a key role in promoting inclusion. Section 6 of the Crime and Disorder Act 1998 imposes a duty on local authorities to create local crime and disorder reduction partnerships. These partnerships require the police, probation service, health authorities and others to work alongside the local authority to produce and implement a local strategy for the reduction of crime and disorder. Supported housing providers may well be involved in the production of these strategies. The duty in section 6 is supplemented by a less well-known duty on local authorities, contained in section 17 of the Crime and Disorder Act 1998, to consider the crime and disorder implications of their core activities. This section may provide an avenue for judicial review of local authority decision making, for instance, when a local authority cuts the funding of a support project for young people without taking into account the crime and disorder implications of such a decision.

Box 8.2 Frequently asked questions

One of our vulnerable tenants has had their property colonised by drug dealers. The local police have threatened to close down the property under their crack house closure powers. Can they do that when it isn't the tenant's fault?

Sections 1–11 of the Anti-social Behaviour Act 2003 give the police powers, in consultation with the local authorities, to close properties taken over by drug dealers or users of class A drugs. After a closure notice is served the police can apply to the magistrates' court within 48 hours for a closure notice that lasts up to three months (in some cases six months). The police can

---

serve a closure notice if they have reasonable belief that class A drugs are being used, produced or supplied on the premises and that a serious nuisance is being caused. This can take place even if the tenant is not involved and their property is simply being used. The tenancy, however, will still continue until the landlord brings it to an end. While the property is 'closed', the tenant will have to apply to the homeless persons unit, as it is a criminal offence to enter a 'closed' property. Some local authorities, for example, Camden, have developed protocols to manage crack house closures and protect vulnerable tenants: see www.respect.gov.uk.

Legal apparatus and anti-social behaviour – a summary

8.24   Box 8.3 provides a summary of the range of tools available to, and responsibilities imposed upon, social landlords in relation to anti-social behaviour. We have included references to orders other than ASBOs to familiarise you with these terms.

Box 8.3 Summary of providers' responsibilities towards controlling anti-social behaviour

Focus	Mechanism	Innovation	Comment
The landlord's role in controlling its occupiers' anti-social behaviour	Occupancy agreements	Explicit anti-social behaviour clauses added.	Providers should ensure that occupiers are familiar with the terms of their agreement. Terms must be fair.
	Grounds for possession	Extended by the Housing Act 1996.	Requirement of proportionality.
	Reasonableness requirement	Reinterpreted by the Court of Appeal. Structured discretion in cases of anti-social behaviour introduced by the Anti-social Behaviour Act 2003.	Needs of landlord and other tenants stressed.
	Injunctive powers	Statutory powers introduced by Housing Act 1996 and extended by Anti-social Behaviour Act 2003.	Use not a prerequisite to possession proceedings.

		Security of tenure	Introductory tenancies – discretionary probationer tenancies introduced by Housing Act 1996. Demoted tenancies – reduction of security of tenure for anti-social tenants introduced by Anti-Social Behaviour Act 2003.	These have been found by the courts to be Human Rights Act 1998 compliant.
Strategic responsibilities of social landlords	Policy development		Section 12 of the Anti-social Behaviour Act 2003 imposes a statutory duty upon social landlords to prepare, keep under review and publish anti-social behaviour policies.	
Local authority as housing provider	Allocation schemes		Power to exclude potential anti-social tenants from social housing.	Anti-social tenants will be forced to rely on the private rented sector and

			supported housing provision.
Action against anti-social individuals (including children)	Civil controls, criminal penalties for breach	Anti-social behaviour orders – s1; Crime and Disorder Act 1998 Parenting orders – s14; Child Safety Orders – s11.	Status of civil proceedings despite eventual criminal penalties.
Action against anti-social groups in designated areas		Section 8 of the Crime and Disorder Act 1998 local child curfew schemes. Section 30 of the Anti-social Behaviour Act 2003. Dispersal of groups and removal of young persons to their place of residence.	
Local government	Strategic and planning duties	Crime and Disorder Act 1998 s6 and s17.	Ensures local delivery of central government priorities via crime and disorder reduction partnerships.

Summary

8.25   This chapter has described the legal framework which enables providers to respond to anti-social behaviour. However there are three important points to note:

- decisions to intiate court proceedings need to be taken with care;
- you have responsibilities to both perpetrators and victims of anti-social behaviour; and
- you should bear in mind the aims and objectives of your organisation when you are making decisions about what actions to take.

8.26   We discuss the practical issues of responding to anti-social behaviour in chapter 25 of the book. We place particular emphasis on the policy process. It is better to have thought through the appropriate responses to the various problems that might arise and written these into a policy framework than to act on the spur of the moment, commencing legal proceedings which may be disproportionate or inappropriate.

CHAPTER 9

The legal profession

Objectives

9.1   At the end of the chapter you will:

- Appreciate the role of legal professionals
- Understand when it is necessary to approach a lawyer and how to find appropriate legal representation
- Appreciate how to get value from legal representation and how to complain if you feel that you are not getting an appropriate service

Overview

9.2   Our aim in this book is to provide you with the foundations for ensuring that your service provision is both lawful and conforms to the requirements for good practice. There will be times, however, when the law is not clear, or is complex, or you are expected to go to court to defend or enforce a legal right. In these circumstances you will need to seek the advice of a lawyer. This chapter aims to support you in making the decision to use the services of a lawyer and suggests ways for you to get the best out of your relationship with your lawyer.

Who are lawyers and what do they do?

9.3   The legal profession in England and Wales is made up of two types of lawyers. Lawyers can be either solicitors or barristers; they have an expertise in the practice of law and using that expertise give advice to their clients.

Box 9.1 Frequently asked questions

Who are legal executives? Are they the same as solicitors?

Legal executives are not solicitors or barristers, but are legally qualified. They specialise in a certain area of the law, for example, housing. Legal executives must pass a qualification in an area of legal practice to the same level as a solicitor in order to practice. They also have to have five years' experience working under the supervision of a solicitor. They can undertake similar day-to-day work as a solicitor in the area of work they specialise in.

Solicitors

9.4 Solicitors deal with most aspects of legal work, such as family matters, tenancy matters, criminal matters, making wills, forming companies, etc. They can work by themselves (as sole practitioners) or form partnerships with other solicitors. Usually, individual solicitors specialise in a certain area of the law. Solicitors in partnership may have individuals who specialise in different areas of work. This enables them to respond to different requests from the same user. For example, someone who wants to buy a house and make a will may see different solicitors from the same practice, one to do the conveyancing and another to draft the will. Solicitors can speak in court; however, this is restricted to certain cases and certain courts. Solicitors can appear in the county court – which is the court where possession proceedings are heard.

Barristers

9.5 A barrister's main function is to conduct a case in court and he or she may appear (have rights of audience) in all courts. Barristers also draft the legal documents that are required by the court and give 'counsel's opinion' on legal problems submitted by solicitors. You cannot approach a barrister directly; a meeting has to be arranged by a solicitor. Solicitors will arrange a meeting with a barrister if a case requires a court hearing and a barrister is necessary, or if the interpretation of law requires 'counsel's opinion'. Barristers tend to specialise in one branch of law and operate independently, although in practice they share chambers (offices) with other barristers. If the solicitor instructs (arranges for the services) of a barrister, you will have to pay two sets of fees.

When to seek the services of a solicitor

9.6 There will inevitably be occasions when either the law or the situation you are facing is complex, and you will need specialist legal advice. You should use a solicitor when:

- You are required to go to court, either to defend or pursue a legal right, and you are not able to represent yourself. For example, you are a registered social landlord (RSL) applying for an anti-social behaviour order (ASBO).
- You are required to go to court and although you could represent the organisation, the case is complex and you believe your organisation's

best interests would be best served by expert legal representation. For example, you are defending a case of disrepair – an area of law which can be complex.

- The other party to the court case has legal representation and although you could represent your organisation, you believe its best interests would be served by legal representation. For example, you are applying for a possession order for breach of tenancy and the user defending the action has legal representation and is going to raise some complex issues.

- You are unclear whether you and your organisation are operating within the framework of the law, as the law is complex and needs interpretation. For example, you are unsure whether someone who is sectioned under mental health legislation has the capacity to sign an occupancy agreement.

- You need to get legal documentation drawn up or checked. For example, you want to change the terms of your tenancy agreement.

How to choose a solicitor

9.7   It is important to find a solicitor who specialises in the area of law you require advice on. In most cases you will need a solicitor who specialises in housing law or the law relating to landlord and tenant. Unfortunately, solicitors who specialise in supported housing are few and far between. If you are seeking possession and the service user has mental health problems, try to find a practice that covers landlord and tenant and mental health or community care.

9.8   RSLs require a solicitor who has an understanding of the regulation of RSLs. This will ensure you are not only acting lawfully, but within the regulatory requirements of the Housing Corporation.

9.9   If you are taking a case to court, try to use a local solicitor who has experience of presenting cases in the local court. Local solicitors should know key court personnel and that will help you get the best outcome in your case.

How to find a solicitor

9.10   All solicitors have to be registered with the Law Society, the body that regulates and represents them. The Law Society produces a directory of solicitors and barristers which is available for purchase – see Box 9.2.

A quicker and free option, however, is visiting the Law Society website. This will enable you to find your nearest solicitor specialising in the area of law you require, for example landlord and tenant.

Box 9.2 The Law Society

Address:	113 Chancery Lane, London WC2A 1PL
Telephone:	general enquiries: 020 7242 1222
	find a solicitor: 0870 606 2555
Minicom:	0845 600 1560
Fax:	020 7831 0344
E-mail:	enquiries@lawsociety.org.uk
Website:	www.lawsociety.org.uk

9.11   If you work for an RSL or a managing agent for an RSL, the RSL may have a firm of solicitors that it uses. Alternatively, you could ask other organisations if they could recommend a solicitor.

How to get the best from a solicitor

9.12   When you first make contact with a solicitor' practice, you should check its experience in the area of law you require and also how much and how it charges for its services. It is likely that the firm will charge an hourly rate, with an additional charge for services such as writing letters, making telephone calls and issuing proceedings on your behalf. If there are several solicitors in the area you could compare costs, and in some cases ask for a quote. Solicitors' charges vary depending on experience and expertise. You will need to compare the costs with the service you are getting; you may choose a solicitor with higher costs, if they have experience of representing supported housing providers. You should ensure that you use the time you are paying for effectively both by being well prepared and checking that you are not paying your solicitor to do work you can do yourself.

First meeting

9.13   Preparation is the key to ensuring that you get the best from the solicitor you choose. Before you go to the meeting you need to write down any questions you want to ask, which could include:

- How long the meeting will last?

- How much the case is likely to cost? The solicitor should give you an estimate.
- What work can you do yourself to keep costs down? For example, you could complete the court paperwork and get the solicitor to check it rather than paying the solicitor simply to transcribe the information from your notes on to the court paperwork.
- How long the case is likely to last?
- What are the possible outcomes and what is the probability of each outcome?
- Are there any opportunities for alternative dispute resolution, for example, mediation (see chapter 27)?
- In what circumstances might you have to pay the costs of the other party involved in the action?

9.14 You will also need to make a list of questions that are pertinent to your case; for example, who will have to give evidence in a nuisance case. Take the list of questions, all the paperwork that might be relevant (see Box 9.3), a notepad and pen and a calculator (useful for calculating costs).

Box 9.3 Example of paperwork for the solicitor in a nuisance case

- a note detailing in chronological order all events and actions in connection with the case;
- occupancy agreement (tenancy or licence);
- notices;
- warning letters;
- diary logs;
- incident reports;
- witness statements;
- reports from external bodies such as the police or environmental health;
- CCTV footage.

9.15 You should be prepared to take notes during the meeting. You should also request that the solicitor puts his or her advice in writing, and ask the solicitor what will happen next. You may also want some time to think about the advice before deciding what to do next. You may, for instance, have a strong case but decide that the cost of taking the action outweighs the benefit it brings. You will need to agree a timetable with the solicitor about what will happen next.

Proceeding with the case

9.16 If you decide to take the case forward, you will need to establish the next steps. This may require another meeting, but you may be able to do this over the phone. Each time you speak to the solicitor on the phone, ensure that you make notes. It is best to make an appointment even for a phone conversation to ensure that you have had a chance to prepare. You need to ensure that you tell the solicitor of any further action and incidents. You could also have a list of questions, for example, what will happen if a witness is not available for a court hearing. You can ask the solicitor to let you know if he or she needs to do additional work as this will affect the cost of the case. If the solicitor believes it is necessary to instruct a barrister for advice or to represent you, he or she should advise you as you will have to pay for this.

Not proceeding with the case

9.17 If you decide not to proceed with the case, you may still be able to use the solicitor's advice to improve your policies and procedures. It also may be useful to publicise the advice within your organisation so all staff are aware of the legal implications of a certain action. If you do this you will need to ensure that any references to service users by name and any addresses are removed to preserve confidentiality.

Box 9.4 Frequently asked questions

We believe that we have not had a good service from our solicitor. What can we do?

If you are unhappy with your solicitor you should make a complaint. Solicitors should have a complaints policy and procedure. You could also contact the Law Society, which regulates the work of all solicitors. If you are unhappy with the response from the Law Society, you can contact the Office of Legal Services Ombudsman for England and Wales. You can only do this when you have had a formal response from the Law Society and must write to the Ombudsman within three months of that response. It will investigate the way your complaint has been handled and may order the Law Society to pay you compensation.

Legal advice for users

9.18   If you or another organisation are taking legal action against a user, or the user wants to take legal action, you should support the user in accessing legal services. You should have a list of local law centres, housing advice centres, Shelter, citizens' advice bureaux and solicitors which is available for users. Those on low incomes or benefits may be entitled to help paying for the cost of a solicitor. The Law Society has details of solicitors who provide services under the legal aid scheme and solicitors who do free or pro bono work see (Box 9.5). The Community Legal Service has also an online calculator to help determine eligibility for legal aid: see www.clsdirect.org.uk/legal-help/calculator.jsp?lang=en.

Box 9.5 Signposting to sources of free legal advice

Law Centres Federation™
For information on law centres contact LCF at:
Third Floor
293–299 Kentish Town Road
London NW5 2TJ
Tel: 020 7428 4400
Fax: 020 7428 4401
E-mail: info@lawcentres.org.uk
Website: www.lawcentres.org.uk

Citizen's Advice
For your nearest Citizens Advice Bureau visit:
www.citizensadvice.org.uk

LawWorks (operating name for the Solicitors Pro Bono Group)
LawWorks is a charity that aims to increase the delivery of free (pro bono) legal advice to individuals or communities in need. They do not give legal advice but you can make an application regarding your case. A senior solicitor will review your application, if it is suitable for pro bono work they will try and find a volunteer lawyer:
10–13 Lovat Lane
London EC3R 8DN
Tel: 020 7929 5601
Fax: 020 7929 5722
Website: www.lawworks.org.uk

9.19   If you think a service user will not understand the legal proceedings,
        you should ensure they are properly represented by someone who can
        act in their best interests. This applies even if your organisation is
        taking the action against them. The law expects those who are vul-
        nerable and unable to understand to be represented by a solicitor or a
        litigation friend. All those under 18 require a litigation friend in civil
        matters.

Summary

9.20   There will be times when you or your organisation requires profes-
        sional legal advice – for example, when you are involved in complex
        legal proceedings or when you need to draft/redraft documentation. In
        this chapter we have explained the role of lawyers and how you can
        access expert legal help. We have given you pointers to ensure that
        you get appropriate advice, and to make the best use of that advice.
        This should ensure that your organisation's money is well spent and
        that the aims of the organisation in using the law are fulfilled.

PART II

Housing Corporation

Objectives

10.1 By the end of this chapter you will:

- Understand the role of the Housing Corporation
- Appreciate the mechanisms by which the Housing Corporation maintains standards in social housing and housing management
- Understand the function of the Housing Corporation's guidance on good practice
- Appreciate the extent of Housing Corporation powers to regulate and enforce standards in registered social housing

Overview

10.2 The housing activities of housing associations are a hybrid between state and private/market provision. The extent to which the provision is characterised as private or as public has been politically contested for the last 40 or so years. So, for instance, the Housing Act 1988 transferred housing association tenancies from the legal equivalent of local authority tenancies to the assured tenancy framework, which was designed to provide a legal environment which would foster market provision. However, housing association provision is now generally regarded as quite distinct from the purely private or the purely public, belonging instead to what is described as the third or not for profit sector.

10.3 Social provision by the state is democratically accountable – if we do not like what is provided then we can vote against the national or local government that is responsible. If something is provided by the market then the 'laws' of supply and demand prevail – if we do not like what a business provides, we can take our custom elsewhere. If something is neither run by the state nor influenced by the market, there is a need for some other body to ensure:

- effective allocation of public funds;
- best value is obtained from those funds; and that
- appropriate standards are maintained.

10.4 The Housing Corporation is the national government agency which oversees registered social housing. In this chapter we consider the ways in which it achieves its aims and the relevance of Housing Corporation activities for your organisation. In the first part of the chapter we examine in some detail at the role of the Housing Corporation before discussing the variety of mechanisms available to the corporation to regulate the sector. We then look at Housing Corporation circulars, and conclude the chapter with a description of the powers available to the Housing Corporation if it believes a housing association is not meeting its standards.

The role of the Housing Corporation

10.5   Organisations and individuals who work with vulnerable people are expected by their regulators to manage their housing effectively and efficiently; this requires more than meeting basic legal minimum requirements. The Housing Corporation requires a housing association registered with it to deliver housing management services to a high standard and provides registered social landlords (RSLs) with a framework to achieve this. We describe the framework in this chapter. It is important that you understand the difference between the legal requirements imposed upon you and the – often higher – regulatory standards that the Housing Corporation requires. Solicitors will give you advice on how to operate within the law, for instance, on standards of repair or on the type of tenancy you should grant to tenants. The Housing Corporation expects that you exceed the minimum legal requirements and provide good quality housing services. It is important for those who work for RSLs or for organisations that manage on behalf of RSLs to understand the Housing Corporation's expectations.

10.6   The Housing Corporation was established by the Housing Act 1964 to fund and regulate housing associations. It is a government agency; this means that it is an independent non-profit making body with its own board of management funded by government to carry out government housing policy. The Housing Corporation has three main functions:

- Investing – it administers the National Affordable Housing Programme, which provides government funding towards building and renovating new and existing social housing.
- Regulating – it is the statutory regulator for RSLs.
- Influencing – it has a role in determining housing, community and regeneration priorities nationally, regionally and within localities.

Box 10.1 Frequently asked questions

How can an organisation register with the Housing Corporation?

The Housing Corporation sets out its registration criteria, published under section 5 of the Housing Act 1996, on its website. This sets out specific registration requirements linked to the criteria and provides guidance to organisations seeking to become RSLs.

10.7   In Box 10.2 we have set out the Housing Corporation's contact details, including regional offices which operate coterminously with government offices.

Box 10.2 Housing Corporation

National
All telephone enquiries: 0845 230 7000
Website: www.housingcorp.gov.uk

Central
Westbrook Centre
Block A Suite 1
Milton Road
Cambridge CB4 1YG
Fax: 01023 272531

Attenborough House
109/119 Charles Street
Leicester LE1 1FQ
Fax: 0116 242 4801

31 Waterloo Road
Wolverhampton WV1 4DJ
Fax: 01902 795001

London
Maple House
149 Tottenham Court Road
London W1T 7BN
Fax: 020 7393 2111

North
1 Park Lane
Leeds LS3 1EP
Fax: 0110 233 7101

4th Floor
One Piccadilly Gardens
Manchester M1 1RG
Fax: 0161 242 5901

St George's House
Kingsway
Team Valley
Gateshead NE11 0NA
Fax: 0191 482 7666

South East
Leon House
High Street
Croydon
Surrey CR9 1UH
Fax: 020 8253 1444

South West
Beaufort House
51 New North Road
Exeter EX4 4EP
Fax: 01092 428201

Funding

10.8   Generally, housing associations need to register with the Housing Corporation to receive funding for capital developments. However, since the Housing Act 2004, unregistered housing associations and private sector providers can access Housing Corporation funds for certain projects if they can provide evidence to demonstrate that they will meet the necessary regulatory standards.

10.9   Prior to the introduction of the *Supporting People* programme, the Housing Corporation funded supported housing provision in two ways: it provided both capital funding, which funded 'bricks and mortar' of the building, and revenue funding, which contributed to the annual running costs of the scheme. In April 2003, the revenue funding was transferred into the *Supporting People* programme to be administered by local authorities. However, the Housing Corporation retains its role of funding the development of new supported housing provision.

10.10   RSLs bidding for capital funding for supported housing should follow the guidance available on the Housing Corporation's website. In particular, supported housing bids should meet needs and priorities set out in the local *Supporting People* strategy, have the support of local *Supporting People* commissioners and be consistent with regional housing strategies. Further information regarding the Housing Corporation's approach to the funding and regulation of supported housing is set out in their *Housing for vulnerable people strategy statement*, available at www.housingcorp.gov.uk/server/show/conWebDoc.3724.

Regulation

10.11   One note of caution before we describe the regulatory system. Regulation of social housing was reviewed in 2007 by Professor Martin Cave, while this book was being written. We suggest that you note the government's response to the 'Cave Report', as it may choose to introduce changes to the way that RSLs and social housing are regulated (see www.communities.gov.uk).

10.12   The Housing Corporation's regulatory requirements apply to all to RSLs. Under section 36 of the Housing Act 1996, the Housing Corporation has specific powers to issue housing management guidance. This is referred to as statutory housing management guidance and RSLs must adhere to it.

10.13   RSLs are also expected to monitor the provision of housing management services that they contract out. In Box 10.3 we signpost you to the relevant Housing Corporation publication.

Box 10.3 Monitoring managing agents

The Housing Corporation has produced guidance for RSLs working with managing agents. *The Housing association and managing agents performance assessment framework* is designed to assist associations in meeting their obligations under the regulatory code and to promote good joint working with managing agents. We recommend that you read it as it will assist you in understanding the relationship between the managing agent and the owning RSL. It can be downloaded from www.housingcorp.gov.uk/server/show/conWebDoc.3214.

10.14 The regulatory documents used by the Housing Corporation are:

- the Regulatory Code and guidance;
- circulars;
- good practices notes; and
- good practice guidance.

10.15 The Housing Corporation tailors its regulatory approach to the size and type of RSL. Clearly, a small specialist RSL and a large general needs RSL will perform differently and face different operational risks. Generally, every RSL with more than 1,000 homes is assessed annually on its performance under the regulatory code and on how well it has used the Corporation funding it has been allocated. This is summarised in a Housing Corporation assessment (HCA), which gives a 'traffic light' performance summary of each RSL in key performance areas.

10.16 RSLs are expected to assess their own performance and provide the following information to the Housing Corporation:

- an annual regulatory and statistical return (RSR);
- a self-assessment compliance statement;
- financial returns; and
- a summary of its annual accounts.

10.17 Managing agents will be expected to prepare information on the schemes they manage, which will form part of the RSR. Front line staff are also expected to fill in a continuous recording form (CORE) for each letting in supported housing (accommodation). These are then collated and submitted to the Housing Corporation. The information that the Housing Corporation collects from RSLs is available to the Audit Commission, which is now responsible for inspecting RSLs. We explain the role of the Audit Commission in chapter 12.

The Regulatory Code

10.18 The Regulatory Code is the most significant part of the Housing Corporation regulatory framework. It contains the fundamental expectations and obligations of RSLs. The guidance which accompanies the Regulatory Code provides RSLs with some direction on how they can achieve the Housing Corporation's expectations. The guidance includes areas of statutory housing management guidance.

10.19 For those familiar with the *Supporting People* quality assessment framework (see section 2), the Regulatory Code has been described (albeit crudely) as offering a similar type of quality check on the housing management services provided in RSL housing. The Regulatory Code, first published in January 2002, concentrates on outcomes. This approach is designed to be flexible; it recognises that there are many processes RSLs can use to meet the standards expected by the Housing Corporation. The regulatory outcomes the Housing Corporation is seeking are that providers are *viable organisations that are well managed* (Housing Corporation Regulatory Code). The Regulatory Code is split into three areas – viability, proper governance and proper management.

10.20   1. *Viable* – RSLs must have adequate financial resources to meet their current and future commitments and must plan their business properly, including the management of business risks. The guidance expects that RSLs have a business plan, appropriate financial policies and procedures and that they have a framework for managing the risks involved with providing social housing.

10.21   2. *Properly governed* – RSLs must operate within the framework of the law, regulation and their own constitutions (a discussion of supported housing organisations' internal governance arrangements is set out in chapter 14). The governing boards of RSLs must have members with the range of skills to lead and control the organisation and protect the public investment in the housing. The Housing Corporation also expects that RSLs will promote resident participation in governance and have a commitment to equal opportunities. The housing management guidance to support both of these functions is statutory. In particular, the Housing Corporation provides detailed guidance the management of equality of opportunity and the elimination of discrimination.

10.22   Housing association households contain higher than average proportions of people who experience discrimination and other social disadvantage. In fact, direct or indirect discrimination in the housing or job market may be one of the reasons why they required the assistance of housing associations in the first place. Housing associations should ensure that their equality and diversity policies and procedures reflect emerging and developing good practice. We explain discrimination law in chapter 6.

10.23   Statutory housing management guidance governs RSLs' targets for:

- lettings;
- tenant satisfaction;
- dealing effectively with racial harassment;
- governing body membership;

- staffing;
- representation in tenants'/residents' associations; and
- the employment performance of suppliers, contractors and consultants.

10.24   *3. Properly managed* – this is the most expansive section of the Regulatory Code and will influence the quality of provision of the supported housing service. It includes the principal areas of:

- providing a housing management service;
- rent setting and rent restructuring (see below);
- tenure;
- repossession;
- maintenance and repair.

10.25   It also covers relationships between RSLs and their managing agents and the relationship between RSLs and local authorities. The Regulatory Code deals with the RSL role in assisting the local authority in housing homeless people and working with local authorities to deliver the government's *Supporting People* programme. It is useful to identify the requirements of the Regulatory Code which most impact upon your work.

10.26   RSLs are currently subject to a rent restructuring framework and must set rents at a level which works towards 'target rents'. This is part of a government strategy to align more closely rents in local authority and housing association-owned property. The framework was introduced in 2002 for general needs housing, with the option of 2003 for supported housing. The aim is to achieve a target rent over a ten-year period, calculated using formulae developed by the Housing Corporation which reflect the size, property value and local earnings. RSLs are responsible for setting rents in their agency-managed properties. Rents should be below market rents.

10.27   RSLs must use fair letting policies and exclude only applicants whose behaviour is so unacceptable that it makes them unsuitable to be a tenant. There is an expectation that RSLs will work closely with the local authority to house homeless and vulnerable people. However, in paragraphs 2.1 and 2.1a of the code, the Housing Corporation is clear that RSLs must be independent of local authorities and make their own decisions about whether to accept or reject nominations.

10.28   In paragraph 3.5.2 of the code, RSLs are expected to offer the most secure form of tenure possible compatible with the purpose of the housing and the sustainability of the community. The starting point is an expectation that occupiers will be given a full assured tenancy. If

RSLs grant anything less secure, they have to have good reasons. In supported housing provision there is a wide range of types of accommodation and services. This does mean that there may be circumstances when it would not be appropriate to grant an occupier a full assured tenancy. The Housing Corporation has published guidance on tenure for supported housing that we refer to later in this chapter. The occupation agreement should clearly set out the resident's and landlord's rights and obligations. We look in more detail at the terms of occupancy agreements in chapter 15.

10.29   The guidance on repossession is statutory guidance. RSLs should only seek to gain legal repossession of a property as a last resort. There have been a number of reports on repossession that have indicated concerns about the large numbers of residents evicted from social housing. See Box 10.4 for a reference to one such report.

Box 10.4 Signpost

'Possession action – the last resort?', published by in 2003 by Shelter and Citizens Advice, is available from www.citizensadvice.org.uk. This report had a direct impact upon the court pre-action protocol for possession actions, which we discuss in chapter 17.

10.30   RSLs are expected to have a responsive repair service that is efficient, effective and sensitive to the needs of vulnerable residents. RSLs should publish their service standards. Some RSLs have developed a system that 'flags up' the vulnerability of a particular resident when a repair is reported and sets higher service standards for those residents. For example, those who are living with Aids or HIV can expect heating or hot water repairs to be completed within 24 hours.

The Residents' Charter

10.31   The Housing Corporation produces a charter for housing applicants and residents. This is commonly referred to as the 'Corporation Charter' or 'Residents' Charter'. For ease of reference, we will refer to the Charter. The regulatory guidance is that the Charter should be provided to all applicants and residents.

10.32   The Charter lets residents know what they can expect from their RSL or managing agent and what they can do if the RSL is not honouring the Charter. Anyone applying for supported accommodation with an

RSL should be provided with a copy of the Charter, and a copy should be given to all residents when they sign their occupancy agreement. In Box 10.5 we identify good practice regarding the Charter .

10.33   The Charter was preceded by a number of charters that were specific to the type of tenure provided, so, for example, licences, assured shorthold tenancies and assured tenancy agreements each had their own charter. Some long-standing residents may have occupancy agreements that refer to the 'tenants' guarantee'; this preceded the charters and is worth mentioning as it required landlords to give residents at least 28-day notices of possession proceedings. Most RSL tenancies still include a term to this effect; this means they are contractually obliged to give a longer notice than their statutory obligations under the Housing Act 1988 for assured and assured shorthold tenancies.

Box 10.5 Good practice

- Ensure your office has a number of copies of the Charter. The Housing Corporation provides alternative formats on request, including tape, Braille, large print and translations.
- Talk through the key points of the Charter when a user signs the occupancy agreement.
- Ensure the user has a copy of the Charter if they want to make a complaint, and you should talk through with them the section on making a complaint.
- Refer to the Charter in any information handbooks you provide for your users and, when appropriate, at any meetings you have with users.
- Refer to the Charter when you are developing or revising any polices and procedures.

10.34   The Charter identifies what RSLs must do to comply with law and the Regulatory Code. However, it does not cover all legal rights; it only highlights some of the important issues that affect the relationship between a resident and his or her RSL.

10.35   The Charter covers the following matters: the way things are run; getting a new home; the relationship between the resident and the RSL; information held and shared by the RSL; consultation and user involvement requirements; and making a complaint.

10.36   The *mandatory list* for RSLs includes:

- Residents must receive a written copy of the occupancy agreement that clearly sets out their rights and responsibilities and those of the RSL, and sets out the rent and other payable charges.

- If there are shared facilities, residents must be told when these are open for use.
- Eviction must be a last resort, used only when there is no reasonable alternative. In supported housing, residents must be offered additional advice and assistance with sustaining the tenancy.
- RSL must have strategies to tackle anti-social behaviour.
- Residents must provide information about how the rent/charge is set and how it is increased and must receive a written notice of any changes to the rent/charge.
- RSLs must provide advice and information about benefits for those experiencing problems in paying their rent.
- A system for dealing with repairs that is responsive to residents' needs.
- Information held on residents must be safe and secure, up to date and deleted when no longer required.
- RSLs must consult with residents about changes to housing management or maintenance arrangements and allow residents to take a part in decision making about how services are run.
- An effective complaints and compensation policy.

Box 10.6 Frequently asked questions

Can a resident complain to the Housing Corporation if they are dissatisfied with their housing association?

Residents should always first try and resolve complaints through their housing association's complaints procedures. If they remain dissatisfied they should take their complaint to the Independent Housing Ombudsman Service:

Housing Ombudsman Service
81 Aldwych
London WC2B 4HN
Tel: 020 7241 3800
Fax: 020 7381 1942
LoCall: 0845 712 5973
Minicom: 020 7404 7092
E-mail: info@housing-ombudsman.org.uk
Website: www.ihos.org.uk

In exceptional circumstances, a resident can complain to the Housing Corporation if he or she believes that people at the RSL are acting illegally or improperly, for example, awarding

---

contracts through fraud or favouritism. The Corporation may then decide to contact the association about the allegation.

Housing Corporation
Enquiries and Complaints Team
1 Park Lane
Leeds LS3 1EP
Tel: 0845 230 7000
Fax: 0113 233 7101
E-mail: enquiries@housingcorp.gsx.gov.uk
Website: www.housingcorp.gov.uk

The Housing Corporation, along with the Department for Communities and Local Government, has produced a leaflet explaining how to complain about a housing association and what to do if you remain dissatisfied: *Complaining about a Housing Association*, which is available from the Corporation's website: www.housingcorp.gov.uk/server/show/nav.355.

Circulars

10.37　You can find circulars on the Housing Corporation website. These are documents that require RSLs to take specific action or add to or complement the Regulatory Code. The circulars set out what the Housing Corporation's expectations are and how it will assess RSLs' compliance. To best illustrate the importance of circulars, we have looked at two in detail which have particular relevance for supported housing. The first, Circular 03/04, provides definitions of housing association supported housing and housing for older people for the purposes of Housing Corporation regulation, data collection and investment systems. Supported housing is defined in the circular as either purpose built supported housing or designated supported housing. 'Purpose built' is where the housing has been designed or remodelled to enable independence where specific design features are required and support is provided by the landlord or another organisation. 'Designated' is where the housing has no design features but is provided for a specific client group that require support services for independent living.

10.38　The definition of supported housing is particularly important to providers as the Housing Corporation apply different funding criteria to the provision of supported housing.

> **Box 10.7 Frequently asked questions**
>
> **Can a tenant in a supported house buy their home?**
>
> No – supported housing is currently one of the exempt cat-
> egories of property under schemes such as Right to Acquire and
> Social Homebuy. This means that residents in this type of prop-
> erty cannot purchase it. If in any doubt the most up-to-date guid-
> ance will be available on the Corporation's website and the
> tenant's landlord should be able to advise.

10.39   The second circular 02/07, *Tenancy management: eligibility and evictions,* is relevant for all RSL provision and is not limited to supported
housing provision. It details Housing Corporation expectations of
RSLs when they assess eligibility for housing and when they are
working with residents to prevent or respond to breaches of the
occupation agreement.

Eligibility

10.40   In terms of eligibility, the circular replicates the public law requirements of natural justice that have been imposed upon local authorities
by the courts. What it does is to prevent 'blanket bans' of particular
groups or people from accessing social housing. So, for instance, an
RSL could not state in its eligibility criteria that offenders will not be
housed by the RSL. The Housing Corporation expects that each application for housing must be judged on its own merits. This prevents
applicants from being penalised for events that occurred in the past or
that they have made attempts to resolve. It enables applicants to provide explanations for the situations in which they find themselves. We
have highlighted what is expected of RSLs in determining eligibility in
Box 10.8.

> **Box 10.8 Determining eligibility for housing**
>
> - If an applicant with rent arrears has kept to an agreement to
>   pay the arrears for a reasonable period they should be eligible.
> - Decisions about anti-social behaviour should be based on
>   evidence and previous tenancy enforcement action disre-
>   garded if two or more years ago.
> - RSLs should not ask about spent convictions and pre-
>   vious convictions can only be taken into consideration if the

> applicant is likely to pose a risk to their household or the community.
>
> • Deposits (unless for furniture) or guarantors (unless the applicant is a minor) should not be requested.
>
> • RSLs should not require a local connection unless there are specific circumstances. This has presented some providers with problems where the local authority has insisted on using local connection criteria for schemes funded by *Supporting People*. For an explanation of local connection see chapter 5. If you are in this position you should bring the requirements of this circular to the attention of your *Supporting People* team.

10.41   Applicants who are rejected for housing should be able to appeal to the RSL. The appeal should be heard by adjudicators who were not involved in the original decision. Referral allocation and lettings procedures should be in writing and complied with so RSLs can demonstrate they have acted fairly and consistently.

Possession

10.42   Problems with housing benefit administration have led to confusion about whether it is appropriate to take possession action for rent arrears when the problems stemmed from the failures of housing benefit administration. The circular clarifies matters for RSLs. It makes it explicit that RSLs should not apply to court if the resident has a reasonable expectation of eligibility for housing benefit, has provided all the necessary evidence to the local authority and has paid any personal contribution. This advice has now been included in a pre-action protocol published by the Ministry of Justice – see chapter 17. The circular also clarifies when it is appropriate to use the mandatory rent arrears ground 8. The ground can be used if other reasonable alternatives have been pursued, if residents have been consulted and if the governing board has approved its use. Similarly, the circular makes clear that if a resident has perpetrated anti-social behaviour, other interventions should be pursued before eviction is considered.

10.43   RSLs, along with all other landlords, have a statutory duty to carry out an annual test of gas appliances. This, together with other health and safety requirements, is detailed in chapter 16. The circular provides suggestions as to what action should be taken by an RSL, short of eviction, if a resident does not allow access for the purposes of the annual test. RSLs should consider applying to court for an injunction, based upon enforcing the tenancy term allowing access, before seeking possession.

Support

10.44   Circular 02/07 also considers the situation where an applicant for housing will require a support package to be in place at the beginning of a tenancy. Applicants with support needs should only be excluded from housing if, despite every effort by the RSL, the necessary support is unavailable or the level of support required would undermine the RSL's ability to support other residents in the scheme. The circular reflects the tension between housing those who require support and the needs of other residents. Supported housing providers have to make difficult decisions about the ability of users to manage in the accommodation taking into account the nature of the support available. We look at this further in chapter 21 in the context of preventing emergencies.

Good practice

10.45   The Housing Corporation produces a large amount of information designed to support RSLs in improving their service delivery. This is described as 'good practice' and can be found on the Housing Corporation website.

10.46   Good practice is intended to help RSLs achieve (and exceed) the minimum standards set out in the Regulatory Code and guidance. Sometimes good practice comes with associated circulars if any elements of the good practice reflect new regulatory requirements. Advice on good practice is helpful to all supported housing providers, as it contains the key characteristics of good practice in particular problem areas, together with examples and case studies which highlight the lessons learned and improvements made. The Housing Corporation also publishes good practice guidance, if a more in-depth consideration of a particular topic is required.

10.47   The Good Practice Note on Tenure was published in November 2007. We strongly recommend that you read it, as it will guide you in your decision making about occupancy agreements and support you in managing those agreements. It covers the interface between support and occupancy in the light of the *Supporting People* programme. The code is available from the Housing Corporation (see Box 10.1) and from the Sitra website, www.sitra.org.uk.

Powers of the Housing Corporation

10.48   The Housing Corporation expects that RSLs comply with the Regulatory Code, circulars and good practice. If RSLs do not meet minimum standards and have no acceptable plans to do so, the Housing Corporation has the following regulatory tools.

10.49   *Continuing regulation* – if there are minor concerns about the performance of an RSL. An action plan is agreed between the RSL and the Housing Corporation and progress will be assessed through the monitoring of the regulatory plan.

10.50   *Supervision status* – if there are serious concerns about the performance of an RSL. The Housing Corporation will only place a Housing Association under supervision if it believes:

- it is unable or unwilling to deal with them;
- it raises matters of wider concern; or
- the risks involve the use of the Corporation's statutory powers.

10.51   An RSL's funding from the Housing Corporation can be suspended and the Housing Corporation has statutory powers under the Housing Act 1996 to make appointments on to the governing board, to direct a statutory inquiry into an RSL's affairs or to intervene where an RSL is threatened with insolvency. The Housing Corporation requires the association to inform its key stakeholders, including funders and local authority partners. The Housing Corporation will notify other bodies, including the Audit Commission and the Charity Commission. Once remedial action has been taken to the Housing Corporation's satisfaction, the housing association is removed from supervision.

Summary

10.52   Professor Martin Cave, in his review of housing regulation undertaken during 2007, pointed out that:

> Social housing is a scarce resource ... Tenants have little power to make choices about which landlord they rent their homes from, or switch to another landlord if they are dissatisfied ... there is a need for some form of

regulatory intervention to ensure social providers use resources as efficiently and effectively as possible to meet residents' needs and government objectives in relation to social housing.[1]

10.53   This highlights why it is important that supported housing providers understand the reason for, the role of and the regulatory requirements of the Housing Corporation. The Housing Corporation provides a valuable check on the activities of those housing associations that are registered with it, as well as guidance to enable services to reflect good practice and to effect continuous improvements. RSLs must adhere to the Housing Corporation requirements and are responsible for the standards of those who manage on their behalf. In the following chapters we examine the role of other bodies which regulate supported housing provision and the extent of their interface with the Housing Corporation.

1   *Every Tenant Matters:* a review of social housing regulation, 'The Cave review of Social Housing', Professor Martin Cave, June 2007, available at www.communities.gov.uk.

CHAPTER 11

Supporting People

Objectives

11.1   By the end of this chapter you should:

- Understand the aims of *Supporting People*
- Understand the range of contractual and non-contractual arrangements which are possible within the *Supporting People* framework
- Recognise the quality and monitoring tools that have been developed as an integral part of the *Supporting People* programme
- Understand the procurement and commissioning process of *Supporting People*

Introduction

11.2   *Supporting People* is the name given to the government's programme for the funding, regulation and strategic development of non-statutory housing-related support services. It was introduced in April 2003 and continues to evolve. Funding streams and quality controls are inevitably influential in shaping public services and *Supporting People* is no exception. This chapter explains *Supporting People* so that you can understand the ways in which it shapes the provision of supported housing services, and the constraints it imposes upon supported housing.

Understanding *Supporting People*

The aims of *Supporting People*

11.3   *Supporting People* is designed to fund housing-related support services which are:

1   responsive and flexible;
2   high quality;
3   economical and effective; and
4   coherently funded

11.4   It is administered by local authorities and attempts to achieve these aims through a range of tools, including strategic planning, commissioning and monitoring of provision. As you will see, the programme involves extensive jargon. We have tried to explain some of the jargon in this chapter.

11.5   It is important to bear in mind that one important feature of *Supporting People* is the separation of funding for housing and support services. Whilst the programme is about housing-related support, it treats this as distinct from the provision of housing – although in many instances the same organisation supplies both the housing and the support services.

An outline of the programme

11.6   The Communities and Local Government Department (CLG, formerly Office of the Deputy Prime Minister) receives a fund of money from the Treasury which is specifically for *Supporting People*. It allocates *Supporting People* grants from this fund to administering authorities (local authorities). It also monitors the performance of administering authorities who are responsible for implementing the programme within their local area. Administering authorities implement the programme by contracting with organisations for the provision of *Supporting People* services. They also monitor the performance of the providers of services.

11.7   A commissioning body (a partnership of local housing, social care, health and probation statutory services) forms an overview of the need for and provision of support services in the local area, and advises and approves the administering authority's *Supporting People* strategy. The priorities set out in the strategy inform the contracting and commissioning decisions of the administering authorities.

11.8   We said at the beginning of the chapter that the funding arrangements continue to evolve. The most recent proposal under the local government white paper 2006, *Strong and prosperous communities,* indicates the *Supporting People* services will be commissioned through local area agreements (LAA) from 2009. A number of area-based resources/grants will be amalgamated into an LAA grant, which will be the responsibility of local strategic partnership. For further information on LAAs, go to www.communities.gov.uk. Individual budgets are also being piloted in a number of areas, led by the Department of Health. These allow service users to decide how to use funding in a way that best suits their needs, and may include *Supporting People* funds as well as a number of other funding streams. An evaluation is due in the Spring of 2008 and this may have major implications for the funding and delivery of some *Supporting People* services. For further information, go to www.individual budgets.csip.org.uk.

History

11.9 *Supporting People* was introduced in April 2003 and was specifically designed to address the perceived failings of the old system of funding supported housing. Prior to its implementation, support services were funded by a complex and ad hoc system of grants and benefits. The provision of housing-related support services could be funded either through housing benefit, supported housing management grants from the Housing Corporation, Probation Accommodation Grants Scheme or Department of Social Security resettlement grants. Some provision was funded directly by local authority social services departments. For a number of reasons, including rapidly escalating housing benefit bills, a judicial decision restricting the scope of housing benefit, the increasing need for support services in the community as more and more people were discharged from long-stay institutions, and gaps and overlaps in the provision of support services, the incoming Labour government decided that the system needed reform.

11.10 The complexity of the funding arrangements meant that government did not know how much money was being spent on support. At the same time, it wanted to ensure that existing services were not disrupted, so, prior to the implementation of *Supporting People* in 2003, transitional housing benefit arrangements were developed to stabilise existing provision and allow the accurate calculation of the money being spent on support. Transitional housing benefit was a demand-driven benefit rather than a capped benefit. This meant that the support provided to service users in supported housing was temporarily eligible as a service charge under the housing benefit rules. Inevitably, given the combination of extensive unmet need and limited local authority funding, some providers, in partnership with local authorities, took the opportunity to increase provision. At the same time many social services authorities took the opportunity to transfer provision from social services budgets to housing benefit. The government had anticipated that the total cost of services would be £1.4 billion. In fact, the total spent on the programme was £1.8 billion for 2003/04. Subsequently, the annual budget for the programme has been reduced over time and for 2006/07 was approximately £1.7 billion. The consequences of this are still being worked through within the *Supporting People* programme. As the Audit Commission pointed out in its report, *Supporting People*, in October 2005, it has led to budget and operational uncertainty at local level which constrains long-term planning and investment by commissioners and providers. The report is available from www.auditcommission.gov.uk.

11.11   Providers of support services were given interim contracts in 2003 to cover the first three years of the programme, known as the interim period. During first three years all provision was reviewed to assess the strategic relevance, quality, efficiency and cost-effectiveness of the provision.

The organisation of *Supporting People*

11.12   Below we set out the major stakeholders in *Supporting People* and describe their roles.

Communities and Local Government Department (CLG)

11.13   This is the central government department responsible for the oversight of the *Supporting People* programme. CLG was formerly the Office of the Deputy Prime Minister. It runs the *Supporting People* website, which provides the electronic knowledge hub for the programme, at www.spkweb.org.uk. You need to read this website regularly to keep up to date on what is still an evolving programme.

The commissioning body

11.14   This is a partnership of senior representatives from social services, housing authorities, probation boards and primary care trusts. The 150 commissioning bodies have strategic responsibility for the local *Supporting People* programme. This involves the strategic assessment of needs, resources and current services and developing a strategy to make the best use of the available resources. At the end of the first three-year period of *Supporting People*, known as the interim period, some authorities have been reviewing the role of the commissioning body with the intention of merging these into local strategic partnerships.

The core strategy group

11.15   This has a broader membership than the commissioning body, potentially including all key partners, including internal and external providers. It has responsibility for ensuring the progress of the programme and for driving improvements. Its representatives are normally operational decision makers.

The administering authority

11.16   This is the local authority based on either unitary or county council structures. The administering authority has responsibility for the day-to-day administration and delivery of the *Supporting People* programme. In effect, it acts as the secretariat to the commissioning body.

11.17   It receives the grant from the CLG and then, after consulting with its commissioning body, researches and develops the *Supporting People* strategy. It reviews services to ensure that its strategic priorities are met and then delivers the programme. It issues contracts on behalf of the commissioning body for support services either to the landlord or the support provider. The fees paid by the administering authority fund the support provided to the service user by the support provider. The administering authority's *Supporting People* team is the public face of the administering authority. However, it is the wider authority which is responsible for the programme.

The service user

11.18   This is the person who is in receipt of support and therefore is at the heart of the programme. Service users who are in receipt of short-term support are not required to pay for the support they receive. Service users who are in receipt of long-term support – typically long-term sheltered housing schemes – are required to pay for support, subject to a means test.

The landlord

11.19   This is the provider of the rented accommodation in which the majority of service users live. So, for instance, the landlord may provide a hostel for the homeless, a block of sheltered housing for the elderly or self-contained accommodation for people with mental health needs. The landlord may have other identities. It may provide housing management and/or support services. It is common for the landlord to provide just the rented accommodation and rely on agents to deliver housing management services on its behalf.

Agents

11.20   An agent is a person or organisation that carries out a function on behalf of someone else. Landlords are able to contract some of their responsibilities to agents. It is common, for instance, for repairs and maintenance to be carried out by building specialists rather than the landlords themselves. This does not divest the landlord of its legal responsibilities for repair. In supported housing the provision of housing management services is frequently contracted out by the land-lord to an agent to provide these services on its behalf.

The support provider

11.21   There are over 6,000 support providers who deliver support in a multiplicity of ways to a huge variety of service users. Support providers provide services under a contract with the local administering authority, usually known as the *Supporting People* team. The types of organisation range from housing associations, voluntary organisations (some of whom might be managing agents to housing associations), local authorities and private sector providers. There is a directory of support services on the department's website at www.spdirectory.org.uk.

Contractual and other relationships

Introduction

11.22   *Supporting People* involves providers in a range of contractual relationships. Contractual relationships involve parties in important rights and responsibilities that may be enforced through the courts. In this part of the chapter, we try to disentangle those relationships. What providers need to be clear about is their status when they are contracting and the obligations inherent in these contracts. So, for instance, if you are contracting with a resident as their landlord, that has different implications from when you are contracting with a landlord to provide housing management services on its behalf. However, contract is not the only mechanism that governs relationships within the business of *Supporting People*. There are other statements of intent or protocols that can be put in place. These ensure that the various parties involved in the provision of support services are aware of and take account of the role of other agencies and develop co-operative working practices. Statements of intent or protocol arrangements are not legally binding, but they are essential to ensure that the resources employed in housing-related support services are deployed to maximum effect. We have set out the range of possible arrangements by which housing and support services may be provided and listed the contracts that arise from those arrangements in Box 11.1.

Box 11.1 The different models of supported housing provision

Model	Support contract held by	Necessary agreements	Common name
Joint provision of housing and support	Non-landlord support provider – normally a voluntary agency	• Occupancy agreement between landlord and service user. • Support contact between SP administering authority and support provider. • Management agreement between landlord and support provider acting as landlord's agent for housing management. • Joint working protocol between three parties.	Agency managed scheme
Scheme-specific separated provision; landlord does housing management at specified site, another body provides support	Non-landlord support provider	• Occupancy agreement between landlord and service user. • Support contact between SP administering authority and support provider. • Service level agreement between landlord and support provider. • Joint working protocol between three parties.	Separately managed scheme

Model	Support contract held by	Necessary agreements	Common name
Floating support – support not permanently tied to specific premises, so can be more than one landlord	Support provider (could be landlord of some properties with people with support needs)	• Occupancy agreement between landlords and service user. • Support contact between SP administering authority and support provider. • Floating support agreement or service level agreement between landlords and support provider.	Floating support
Joint provision of housing management and support by an organisation other than landlord on subcontract basis	Landlord	• Occupancy agreement between landlord and service user. • Support contact between SP commissioning body and landlord. • Management agreement for both housing and support services between landlord and support provider.	Fully subcontracted scheme

Occupancy agreements and other agreements between landlord and service user

11.23   If the service user lives in rented accommodation there will be a contract between him or her and the landlord. This is the tenancy or licence and we have discussed its terms in chapters 3 and 4. In long-term services, there may be a separate contract between the landlord/provider and the service user in connection with the provision of support.

11.24   Particular difficulties arise in two situations:

1   First, when the occupier refuses to pay for the support services provided. If the occupier is in receipt of short-term support, then the occupier/service user is not required to pay for support services and the issue will not arise. However, if the support is long-term support, such as sheltered housing, then the user may be required to pay for support. That obligation will either be in the tenancy/licence agreement or in a separate document. It is extremely unlikely that a court would order eviction for non-payment of support charges. However, providers would be able to enforce the contract and seek damages through the small claims court for any outstanding charges.

2   The second difficulty is when the occupier refuses to accept the support services on offer. If the agreement is a licence or an assured shorthold tenancy then no reasons need to be given for termination, and as long as the legally required notice is given, then the occupation agreement can be terminated. If the agreement is an assured tenancy then the situation is more difficult. The best possibility is to use ground 9 of the Housing Act 1988, which is a discretionary ground based on the availability of alternative accommodation. It will be up to the court whether possession is granted or not. We explain this further in chapter 15.

Support contracts between SP administering authorities and support providers

11.25   In short-term schemes, support is paid for by the administering authority which contracts with the provider to deliver the service. The terms of the agreement, including the costs involved, will have been agreed at the point of service review. It is absolutely crucial that this contract is properly negotiated.

Landlords and agents

11.26   If the landlord subcontracts particular responsibilities to an agent, then a management agreement or contract will set out the scope of the responsibilities subcontracted and the fee or price that is paid by the landlord to the agent for the delivery of those responsibilities. There is not a contractual relationship between the agent and the service user and the landlord remains responsible to the service user for the services even though it does not directly provide them.

11.27   There are several ways in which the relationships between the landlord and the support provider may be organised:

1   First, the scheme could be one which is fully subcontracted. What this means is that the landlord holds the support contract from the administering authority and then subcontracts the delivery of support and its own housing management service via a management agreement with the support provider. This is not a common arrangement, though developments in the commissioning and procurement of *Supporting People* services mean that this model may become more common.

2   Alternatively, the scheme could be an agency managed scheme. Here the support provider has a double status, as main contractor with the local authority for support and as the landlord's subcontractor for housing functions.

11.28   The interrelationships in agency managed schemes are particularly complex. Theoretically, both landlord and the administering authority are dependent on the other to ensure that housing management and support is provided to the service user and to commission the housing management and support provider. If the landlord decided that this provider was not competent to deliver the housing management service and decided to terminate the contract, the administering authority would be left in a difficult position. Equally, the opposite position is possible. These situations should have been anticipated in working protocols between the parties. We look at the different types of protocols and the circumstances in which they are relevant below.

11.29   A third possibility is that the landlord or another body carries out the housing management functions and a different body provides support to service users. There are arguably advantages to such a separation of functions. For instance, it is hard simultaneously to support a vulnerable individual and pursue them for rent arrears, or other breaches of their tenancy agreement.

11.30   The final possibility is that support is provided by one support provider but to a number of landlords. Floating support is commonly provided in this model. It would be impractical for the support provider to enter into detailed specific service level agreements with each of the landlords it works with, so again a non-contractual protocol is required to ensure that landlords and the support provider work together for the benefit of the service users.

Non-contractual agreements

11.31   There are three types of non-contractual agreements that you may come across in *Supporting People*.

1   Joint working protocols – these are three way agreements between administering authorities, landlords and support providers. The agreement sets out how all three parties are to deal with the commissioning of new services, monitor and review existing services, share information and respond to crises.
2   Service level agreements – these set out how support providers and landlords will work together in situations where the support provider does not carry out the housing management.
3   Floating support agreements – these cover the relationships between the variety of different landlords and the provider of the floating support. They are designed to address issues of information sharing, confidentiality and data protection and the management of risk.

11.32   Non-contractual agreements are essential, though not commonly used, because the service user is frequently not party to important contractual arrangements and because the arrangements necessary to ensure that contracts work appropriately can be complex but cannot be implemented via a contractual framework. The purposes of protocols and service level agreements are to:

1   clarify responsibility for delivering and monitoring services;
2   agree on how to deal with potential conflicts of interest;
3   have procedures to address areas of concern;
4   manage risk; and
5   ensure that all parties are acting in the interests of service users.

Monitoring and review of *Supporting People* services

Introduction

11.33   The implementation of *Supporting People* provided the government with an opportunity to move away from a rather haphazard system of provision of support services where there was little effective quality monitoring and no strategic planning. During the first three years of the programme, *Supporting People* imposed requirements on administering authorities to monitor and review services to ensure they were cost effective, of good quality and were relevant to local need – in other words, it has produced a national system of monitoring which is locally applied. However, this is a delicate and potentially dangerous exercise in culture change. Whilst quality and monitoring tools are important to ensure improvement in provision, they should not destroy other important qualities of support services, for instance, their responsiveness to local needs and to the limitations of bureaucratic provision.

11.34   This part of the chapter will summarise the following quality and monitoring tools which are integral to *Supporting People*:

1   Quality Assessment Framework.
2   Service review.
3   Accreditation of providers.
4   Performance Framework.

11.35   These tools variously focus on the quality of service provision, the strategic demand for the service, the competence of the provider and its level of performance. Taken together, they should ensure that housing-related support services are provided at an acceptable level of quality and that they are constantly improving.

11.36   The Department for Communities and Local Government (CLG) (or its predecessor, the Office of the Deputy Prime Minister) has published a number of detailed documents, which are available on the *Supporting People* website, www.spkweb.org.uk, which you need to read in order to get a complete statement of the requirements. Our description is an outline only.

The Quality Assessment Framework

11.37   This is a set of nationally defined standards which are designed to provide a standard against which administering authorities can assess the quality of support services and to enable providers, working alongside administering authorities to monitor and improve their own provision. Administering authorities are expected to use the framework flexibly, taking account of the nature of the provider and the size and scope of the service.

11.38 The Quality Assessment Framework is made up of six core objectives, which are described in Box 11.2, and 11 supplementary objectives, described in Box 11.3. The core objectives set out the minimum standards against which provision is to be measured. The supplementary objectives are additional objectives against which provision may be assessed in subsequent service reviews. Providers can choose to assess their services against some or all of the supplementary service objectives depending on internal priorities.

Box 11.2 The core objectives of the Quality Assessment Framework

Needs and risk assessment	Covering, for instance, any needs and risk assessment processes and the competence of staff to carry these out.
Support planning	Covering, for instance, the existence of individual support plans, focused on outcomes and review processes.
Security health and safety	Covering, for instance, an up-to-date health and safety policy which is regularly implemented and reviewed.
Protection from abuse	Covering, for instance, recruitment checks, induction and training, multi-agency working and whistle-blowing policies.
Fair access, diversity and Inclusion	Covering, for instance, allocations and equal opportunities policies.
Complaints	Covering, for instance, a complaints policy, and a log of action in response.

> **Box 11.3 The supplementary objectives of the Quality Assessment Framework**
>
> | | |
> |---|---|
> | Empowerment | • Informing service users. |
> | | • Consulting and involving service users. |
> | | • Empowerment and supporting independence. |
> | | • Participation in the wider community. |
> | Rights and responsibilities | • Privacy and confidentiality. |
> | | • Rights and responsibilities. |
> | The service | • The service description |
> | | • Choice, sensitivity and responsiveness. |
> | | • The living environment. |
> | Organisation and management | • Continuous improvement. |
> | | • Staff recruitment, management and development. |

11.39   For each service objective there is a set of standards against which providers assess their performance and identify which of four performance levels they meet. The performance levels are:

A   *Excellent* – demonstrates leadership in the field and incorporates mechanisms for delivering continual improvement.

B   *Good practice* – services at this level should be working towards level A.

C   *Minimum standard* – scope for improvement and a timetable for delivery of improvement towards level B should be agreed with the administering authority.

D   *Unacceptable* – the service does not meet the required minimum standard.

11.40   The objective of the framework is to provide a mechanism for continuous improvement. Providers should assess their services and then plan the strategic action required to enable the services to reach the next performance level. Improvement in quality should therefore become integrated into the management of the organisation.

Service review

11.41   During the three-year interim period, administering authorities were required to carry out a service review of all inherited provision funded by *Supporting People*. Authorities are no longer required by the CLG to undertake such reviews; instead, they are expected to introduce robust contract monitoring requirements to ensure providers deliver the service they are contracted to provide. Some administering authorities have chosen to continue with the service review as the mechanism to achieve that.

Accreditation of providers

11.42　This is a parallel process to service review. It focuses on the competence of the organisation providing the support service, rather than the quality and strategic importance of the service. However, it is equally significant in the decision to continue to fund a project – administering authorities are going to be reluctant to fund an organisation which is financially or managerially incompetent. The guidance recommends that contracts should only be awarded to accredited providers. Box 11.4 sets out the five requirements necessary for an organisation to be accredited.

Box 11.4 Requirements of the accreditation process

- Financial viability.
- Competent administrative procedures that enable the proper handling and accounting for *Supporting People* grants.
- Effective employment policies which cover:
  - staff development;
  - staff supervision; and
  - the health and safety of both staff and service users.
- Sufficiently robust management procedures to provide *Supporting People* services.
- Demonstrate a track record of competence to deliver services.

Box 11.5 Frequently asked questions

We are a housing association who are registered with the Housing Corporation and have our own internal quality assessment system. Do we still have to go through *Supporting People* accreditation?

Many providers have alternative accreditation procedures which overlap with the requirements of *Supporting People* – one example is registration with the Housing Corporation. A number of these accreditation arrangements have been considered suitable to

---

> passport providers through some or all of the accreditation requirements. Registration with the Housing Corporation passports registered social landlords through three out of five of the *Supporting People* criteria. Ultimately though, it is up to the relevant administering authority to decide whether or not it will accredit registration with the Corporation or any other recommended arrangements.

11.43   Providers who deliver services in more than one local authority area may face particular difficulties. Theoretically, accreditation by one authority permits a provider to deliver similar services to any other authority. However, as individual authorities set their own criteria for accreditation, it is possible that one authority will consider that accreditation by another is not sufficiently robust to meet its standards. The CLG suggests that groups of neighbouring authorities work together to establish common procedures and requirements, and make explicit whether they accept or refuse each other's accreditation.

Performance indicators

11.44   A national performance framework was developed with a set of seven mandatory performance indicators for *Supporting People*. These consist of three high-level national key performance indicators (KPIs) and four service performance indicators (SPIs), measuring performance at the level of individual service.

11.45   The KPIs provide information on national performance on the following areas:

- KPI1 – service users who are supported to establish and maintain independent living; or
- KPI2 – service users who have moved on in a planned way from temporary living arrangements;
- KPI3 – fair access to people who are eligible for *Supporting People* services (as measured by non-host and BME access).

11.46   The SPIs are to be used by administering authorities to monitor services and gain information for the service review. They are:

- SPI1 – Service Availability;
- SPI2 – Utilisation Levels;
- SPI3 – Staffing Levels;
- SPI4 – Throughput.

11.47 An electronic workbook was produced for collecting performance data from providers. More recently, the mandatory requirement to collect information on staffing was discarded by CLG, although a number of authorities continue to collect this.

SP client recording

11.48 A client record system was introduced to monitor access to services. It is managed by the Joint Centre for Scottish Housing Research (JCSHR), which collects and processes the information for the administering authorities the CLG. This form is available on the website www.spclientrecord.org.uk and provides information for the performance framework, including KPI3 on fair access to services.

Outcomes

11.49 In May 2007, CLG introduced a national outcomes framework for *Supporting People* services. The framework itself is based on five high-level outcomes adopted by the Department of Education (now the Department for Children, School and Families) for the *Every Child Matters* Programme. The development of the framework is an attempt to measure the impact of the programme rather than processes and outputs, and to ensure that there is well-developed set of outcome measures by the time it is integrated with local area agreements in 2009. The five high-level outcomes are:

- achieve economic well being;
- enjoy and achieve;
- be healthy;
- stay safe; and
- make a positive contribution.

11.50 A set of indicators has been developed to sit below the five outcomes and the information will be collected in an '*outcomes form*'. In short-term services this will be completed for each service user as they leave the service. For long-term services, given the numbers and impracticality of collecting information on every single service user, the idea is to sample a percentage of all service users on an annual basis

11.51 The forms will be submitted to the JCSHR, who already run the *Supporting People* client record system. It will collect and analyse the data and provide reports in much the same way as it does for client records.

Procurement and commissioning

Introduction

11.52   One of the effects of the *Supporting People* programme was to give local authorities strategic control over the planning and purchasing of *Supporting People* services. This is seen as providing a number of benefits, including widening choice for service users, improved quality of provision and greater value for money. Now that the three-year 'interim' period is over, more and more providers are finding themselves involved in exercises designed to test the market for their services (ie administering authorities will tender out services to see who can provide the same or improved services or bidding for new funds to run new projects).

11.53   We have already considered the contract between the administering authority and the provider earlier in this chapter. This section of the chapter will consider the process of contracting with the public sector.

Contracting with the public sector

11.54   Administering authorities are subject to a range of rules and procedures which govern their dealings with public money. While this may be extremely exasperating to small voluntary organisations, the rules are essential to protect the public purse. The whole process of purchase by the public sector from third parties is known as 'procurement'. It covers the purchase of goods, services and capital projects.

11.55   Administering authorities must:

1   Obtain value for money when procuring goods, services and works and fulfil their statutory duty of achieving best value (see section 3 of the Local Government Act 1999).

2   Comply with English law and European law in force in England that governs the procuring of goods, services and works. We have summarised the EU procurement rules in Box 11.6. Welfare services, including the type of services covered by *Supporting People*, are part B services under EU procurement regulation and as such are subject to a *lighter touch* in the EU rules for competitive tendering.

3   Follow their own set of internal procurement regulations which govern how they carry out procurement activities.

> **Box 11.6 EU rules on procurement**
>
> - Set out procedures for awarding contracts above certain values.
> - Aim to open up the public procurement market and to ensure the free movement of goods and services within the EU.
> - This increases opportunities for competitive suppliers, contractors and service providers.
> - They are reviewed every two years and amended if necessary on 1 January.
> - The current EU thresholds and further detailed information on the EU Procurement Directives can found at http://europa.eu.int/.

11.56 It is the internal procurement regulations which are likely to provide the biggest headaches for providers. There are a number of possibilities to deal with these regulations:

1 An 'exception' to the administering authority's standing orders could be sought. However, this may be difficult to achieve, since it may be difficult to pinpoint the difference between contracting for *Supporting People* provision and other services contracted out by the administering authority.

2 As an alternative, a provider could seek 'waiver' from the requirements. This requires the provider to apply under local standing orders for the waiver. There will be a procedure which will need to be followed, and the approval of the senior management group of the local authority will have to be given. There are possibilities that block waivers could be achieved where a number of services are affected.

3 A form of restricted tendering process may be available in the context of *Supporting People*. Some local standing orders allow for the use of 'standing lists' (lists of approved contractors/providers who are suitably qualified). This may be the most appropriate way forward for the commissioning of *Supporting People* services, since providers who are suitable will already have been identified as a result of their track record and measured competence in delivery. However, standing lists may be problematic because there needs to be criteria established for acceptance onto the list and operational formalities need to be decided.

11.57 Under *Supporting People*, the CLG stresses the unique role of voluntary organisations. As well as being seen as flexible and innovative, they are seen as having important links to hard-to-reach groups. Authorities are encouraged to nurture the third sector by holding procurement open days and provide support throughout the process. A good practice guide on procurement from the CLG suggests that authorities consult providers about the procurement process right up to the tendering exercise. Some providers will find it difficult to cope with the uncertainty that competition brings and will need to consider what they can offer in terms of added value. Local authorities have an increasing duty to value and nurture independent, community-based organisations that are close to service users. Given the difficulties faced by smaller providers having to respond to large scale bids, some are seeking to work in partnership through forming consortia or subcontractual arrangements in order to continue to be able to provide services. This is leading to a whole new set of legal arrangements between providers and the development of consortia agreements or amendments to the subcontractual model outlined in earlier in this chapter.

The Compact

11.58   The government states that it recognises the value of the third sector in the provision of high quality and effective goods and services which meet important needs. It also recognises the difficulties faced by organisations which do not necessarily have the level of infrastructure necessary to cope well with complex procurement requirements. Government has therefore set up an agreement between government – both central and local – and the voluntary and community sector in England to improve their relationship for mutual advantage. This agreement is known as The Compact and full details are available on www.thecompact.org.uk. It is relevant to *Supporting People* providers and sets out the statement of intent to work in partnership. It is supported by five codes: funding and procurement; community groups; BME groups; volunteers; and consultation. The Compact is overseen by a commissioner whose role is to improve its effectiveness. Local compacts have been agreed in most areas to cover relations between local councils, other local public sector bodies and local voluntary and community organ-isations. The national codes of good practice inform local codes. However, experience suggests that there is limited awareness of The Compact amongst those commissioning *Supporting People* contracts.

11.59   The Funding Code is the most significant code for the procurement process. It was originally published in 2000, revised and republished in 2005. You can download a copy from the Compact website. We have set out the undertakings that both providers and government agree to within The Compact in Box 11.7.

Box 11.7 Summary of Funding Code undertakings

The government undertakes to [...]
- provide whenever possible an opportunity for the voluntary and community sector to contribute to programme design;
- ask for relevant information on application forms;
- discuss risks up-front and place responsibility with the public sector body or voluntary and community organisation best able to manage them;
- respect the independence of the sector;
- recognise it is legitimate for voluntary and community organisations to include the relevant element of overhead costs in their estimates for providing a particular service;
- with public procurement, avoid seeking information about management fees and overheads;
- make payments in advance of expenditure (where appropriate and necessary) in order to achieve better value for money;
- implement longer-term funding arrangements where these represent good value for money;
- be proportionate in monitoring requirements and focus on outcomes;
- consider joining-up or standardising monitoring requirements; and
- give enough notice of the end of grant or contract arrangements where these represent good value for money.

The third sector undertakes to ...
- respect confidentiality and be clear about whom they represent and how they came to their views when consulted on programme design;
- make sure that they are eligible when applying for grants;
- have clear lines of accountability, especially with joint bids;
- agree terms of delivery at the outset and be aware of risks which they are responsible for;
- have good systems in place to manage finances and funded projects, and account for them;
- be honest and transparent in reporting; and
- plan in good time for different situations to reduce any potential negative impact on both beneficiaries and the organisation if funding ends.

11.60   Something which is of particular interest to providers will be Appendix D of the Funding Code, which sets out the government's commitment to full cost recovery for voluntary and community organisations. What this means is that it is legitimate for providers to charge overhead costs. We have reproduced some useful paragraphs from this appendix for your information in Box 11.8.

Box 11.8 Appendix D of the Funding Code

D2 All organisations in the public, private and voluntary and community sectors have indirect overhead as well as direct costs associated with the delivery of goods and services. To operate efficiently and effectively, voluntary and community organisations must be able to understand all their costs including indirect and support costs. No activity can be undertaken without the need for support functions, and funding bodies have an interest in ensuring that organisations are able to manage and administer activities properly.

D3 The key reason for the lack of 'core funding' within the voluntary and community sector is that debate has historically and typically been based on a false principle that 'core' costs are somehow unrelated to an organisation's 'real work'. Many funders have traditionally paid only for the marginal costs of the services they are seeking. But if funders follow this practice, necessary overhead costs cannot be met, or are met from donations and other sources of income which were not intended for this purpose.

D5 The methodology chosen by voluntary and community organisations to allocate relevant overhead costs should follow these principles:

- the method should be simple. Both funders and service providers should be able to calculate the amounts without disproportionate resource;
- the method should be equitable between providers where there are several funders of different services; and
- the costs should be recovered only once.

11.61   Details of the full procurement process are beyond the scope of this book, but it is an area providers must understand if they are to continue to provide *Supporting People* and other public services. Sitra runs courses which elaborate upon procurement and, in particular, on costing and pricing, which are critical if providers are going to survive in the long term.

Summary

11.62   The introduction of *Supporting People* was the biggest change in funding arrangements the supported housing sector has seen. It has transformed the relationship between provider and funder by giving local authorities strategic control over the commissioning, funding and monitoring of services. This has been a difficult transition for many providers, who, prior to the introduction of *Supporting People*, were instrumental in identifying need and developing services for a whole range of vulnerable groups that the state did not provide for. There have been successes: improvements in the quality of services, value for money and service user involvement have been highlighted by the Audit Commission as particularly noteworthy. There have also been challenges for providers, many of whom have had to cope with a succession of cuts in funding, a greater degree of bureaucracy and poor commissioning practice in some local authorities. We said earlier that *Supporting People* is still evolving and, at the time of writing, we are waiting for the publication of a *Supporting People* strategy. The challenge for providers now is to adapt to a more competitive procurement environment as commissioners decide to put services out to tender. For many, particularly smaller organisations, partnership with other providers may be the best option to continue to provide services. For the future, funding arrangements will change as services are likely to be commissioned through local area agreements from 2009 and individual budgets may become a common approach to purchasing services for some service users.

Other regulatory regimes

Objectives

12.1   By the end of this chapter you will:

- Understand the role of the Audit Commission
- Appreciate how care is regulated by the Commission for Social Care Inspectorate

Overview

12.2   In chapter 10 we explain how housing is regulated by the Housing Corporation. We then describe how support is regulated within the *Supporting People* regime in chapter 11. In this chapter we identify other regulators who may or may not be involved in inspecting your services. First, we consider the most significant of these, the Audit Commission. We then provide details of the Commission for Social Care Inspection, which regulates residential care homes and will impact upon the work of providers of residential care services. The role of the Charities Commission is considered in chapter 13.

The Audit Commission

12.3   The Audit Commission is an independent public body which has statutory responsibility for ensuring that public money is spent economically, efficiently, and effectively in the areas of local government, housing, health, criminal justice and fire and rescue services. It does this through the twin functions of audit and inspection. Its audit role works through monitoring the spending of public money, ensuring that it provides value for money, as well as ensuring that proper accounting practices are maintained. Through inspection the Audit Commission provides practical recommendations for improvements in particular service provision and disseminates best practice. The framework for inspection is known as KLOE – Key lines of enquiry – which is a set of criteria for assessment of services.

12.4   The Audit Commission has an important role in the inspection of housing services, embracing both local authority and housing association provision. Its housing inspection role impacts upon supported housing provision in two ways. First, it inspects local authorities' *Supporting People* programmes and all administering local authorities will have been inspected between 2003 and 2008, with re-inspections of those services which raise particular concerns. Box 12.1 sets out information about the inspection process. You will note that both providers and service users have a role in the inspection.

Box 12.1 Audit Commission inspections of administering local authorities' *Supporting People* **programmes**

Inspection process
The joint inspection team is generally made up of a principal inspector, housing inspectors, a tenant inspection advisor and representatives from the Commission for Social Care Inspectorate and the Probation Inspectorate. The tenant inspection advisor is a user of housing or support services.

Set-up meeting
The inspection begins with a set-up meeting between the principal inspector and key managers around 12 weeks before the on-site visit.

Information for users, providers and partners
The inspection team writes directly to primary care trusts, the Probation Service, the Commission for Social Care Inspectorate and, in two-tier areas, to district councils providing inspection information. It provides information for providers explaining the inspection process and asking them to complete and return a short questionnaire.

Self assessment
The council has to complete a three-part, self-assessment questionnaire. Part 1 is a short contextual questionnaire, Part 2 asks for information about the council based on the content of KLOE 10 and Part 3 asks for contact details for groups representing users and providing services under *Supporting People*.

Document review
The inspection team requests relevant documents up to 12 weeks in advance of the visit. These are used together with the council's self-assessment to carry out an initial review and plan the inspection visit.

Planning the inspection visit
The Audit Commission discusses with the council the names of those who should be interviewed. This will include councillors,

senior managers and representatives from partner agencies. It visits a number of services, and meets groups representing users. If possible, it also observes meetings of the *Supporting People* commissioning body and the core strategic group (or their equivalent).

Briefing
Prior to the start of the inspection visit, the inspection team meets with the council and presents a summary of its findings from the document review. This normally occurs approximately one week before the actual inspection, giving the council the opportunity to prepare feedback for the inspectors when they come on site. It also gives inspectors an opportunity to get a feel for the local area.

Inspection visit
The on-site period will last between five and eight days, dependent on the size of the area and the complexity of the *Supporting People* arrangements. Written feedback will be provided twice during the visit, usually in the middle and at the end of the process.

Inspection report
The aim is to produce a draft inspection report within four weeks of the inspection visit. The council then has ten working days to provide a written response.

Round table meeting
The final stage of the inspection is a round table meeting to discuss the council's written response to the draft report. All members of the commissioning body should be invited to the round table meeting. Following that meeting the team will produce and publish the final inspection report, taking into account the comments from the council and its partners. The council is also asked if it wishes to provide information regarding its response to the inspection report recommendations to appear alongside the report on the Audit Commission website two months following publication.

12.5   In Box 12.1 there is a reference to KLOE 10. KLOEs represent sets of questions and statements around either service or judgment-specific issues which provide consistent criteria for assessing and measuring the effectiveness and efficiency of housing services. They are designed to provide inspectors, inspected bodies and others with a framework through which to view and assess services. KLOEs include descriptors of excellent and fair services to indicate the level of service provision that the Audit Commission expects. KLOE 10 is the Audit Commission's Key Line of Enquiry (KLOE) which relates to *Supporting People* provision. The KLOE covers the areas set out in Box 12.2. There is full information about the Audit Commission's interpretation of KLOE 10 on its website, www.audit-commission.gov.uk.

Box 12.2 The *Supporting People* KLOE

This KLOE covers the following areas:

- Governance and partnerships.
- Grant compliance, strategy and needs.
- Delivery arrangements.
- Commissioning and performance.
- Value for money.
- Service user involvement.
- Access to services and information.
- Diversity.
- Outcomes for service users.

12.6   The second aspect of the Audit Commission housing role which is of significance is its role in inspecting housing association provision. Its works in inspecting registered social landlords is complementary to the Housing Corporation's regulatory role (see chapter 10). The roles of the Housing Corporation and the Audit Commission in ensuring effective social housing provision are quite distinct. Further information on their respective functions can be obtained from the Housing Corporation website. In particular, the two organisations have signed a memorandum of co-operation which sets out their different remits and explains how the information gathered from inspection by the Audit Commission informs the regulatory concerns of the Housing Corporation and vice versa. Guidance on how the Audit Commission and Housing Corporation work together can be found at www.housing-corp.gov.uk/upload/pdf/OperationalGuidanceJune2005.pdf.

12.7   The Audit Commission makes it clear that its housing inspections will conform to certain principles. It will:

- be proportionate to risk and the performance of the association;
- judge the quality of the service for service users and the value for money of the service;

- promote further improvements in the service; and
- cost no more than is necessary to safeguard the public interest.

12.8   The Audit Commission inspects registered social landlords, and not supported housing providers per se. The inspection will therefore look at a variety of housing functions and it will utilise a range of relevant KLOEs to ensure that its inspection is effective. However, when supported housing provision is the sole or one of the services provided by the registered social landlord, then supported housing will be one focus of inspection. One KLOE is particularly relevant to providers – KLOE 11. The areas covered by KLOE 11 are set out in Box 12.3.

Box 12.3 KLOE 11

The Supported Housing KLOE is intended to cover the following areas:

- access, customer care, user focus, including involvement in support plans, diversity;
- stock investment and asset management, income management, including housing and support charges;
- service user involvement;
- tenancy and estate management;
- allocations and lettings, including support planning; and
- value for money.

12.9   There is further information on the Audit Commission website about the standards it expects of registered social landlords in connection with the provision of social housing. You may also find the Audit Commission examples of best practice useful. These illustrate how particular organisations have responded to the challenges of supported housing. Examples are given, for instance, of projects to enhance service user involvement.

The Commission for Social Care Inspection

12.10   The Commission for Social Care Inspection (CSCI) registers, inspects and reports on social care services in England. It was created by the Health and Social Care (Community Health and Standards) Act 2003. It incorporates work previously done by:

- the Social Services Inspectorate (SSI);

- SSI/Audit Commission Joint Review Team; and
- the National Care Standards Commission (NCSC).

12.11 The CSCI website is at www.csci.gov.uk.

Registration

12.12 The law requires that the social care services listed in Box 12.4 have to be registered and inspected by the CSCI.

Box 12.4 The services registered and inspected by the CSCI

- care homes that provide personal care or nursing care (or both);
- adult placement schemes;
- domiciliary care agencies (often known as home care agencies); and
- nurses' agencies.

12.13 These services must be registered before they can start to operate. Registration requires that the CSCI is satisfied that:

- the people running the service are suitable; and
- the service will be run in line with the regulations and standards set by the government. The national minimum standards can be found at www.csci.org.uk/professional/care_providers/all_services/national_minimum_standards.aspx.

12.14 It is a criminal offence to run one of the social care services set out in Box 12.4 unless the CSCI has received and granted an application for registration.

Alternative Futures Ltd v CSCI

12.15 One particular difficulty that is created by the legislation is that the boundary between a care home and a service user's own home is not clear. This is significant because of the greater rigour of the regulatory regime that providers of care homes face. In addition, the funding regimes which cover care homes and supported housing are quite different. Box 12.5 sets out the main consequences of the distinction between accommodation being treated as the service user's own home rather than a care home.

> **Box 12.5 The consequences of a property being designated a care home**
>
> If accommodation is a care home then:
>
> - Standards for care, welfare and supervision of residents are legally enforceable.
> - Residents have less control over their accommodation.
> - Residents' personal income is limited and housing benefit is not payable.
> - The service is not eligible for *Supporting People* grant.

12.16   The CSCI decides whether an organisation provides a care home or support services in someone's own home. When a provider does not accept the decision of the CSCI, it has a right of appeal to the Care Standards Tribunal. We set out in Box 12.6 details of a Care Standards Tribunal decision on the distinction between a care home and a service user's own home.

> **Box 12.6 *Alternative Futures v National Care Standards Commission* [2002] 0101-0111NC**
>
> In June 2002 the Care Standards Tribunal turned down an appeal by Alternative Futures Ltd against a decision by the National Care Standards Commission (the predecessor of the CSCI) not to let them cancel the registration of 11 care homes. Alternative Futures had applied for cancellation of the registration because it felt the homes were functioning as supported housing with domiciliary care. The service users had learning disabilities and had been granted tenancies. The Care Standards Tribunal decided that the decision of the NCSC should be upheld because Alternative Futures Ltd had not done sufficient work to ensure that the residents were aware of the change of status of the accommodation. The Tribunal decided that service users are required to make a choice to accept the new proposed new arrangements and this choice should be supported by the care assessments.
>
> Two other points emerge from the decision:
>
> - The existence of tenancies for service users may be indicative but is not conclusive of the question of whether accommodation is a care home or someone's own home.
> - Providers must pay attention to the capacity of residents

> to make choices about the nature of the provision. It is not for the inspection team of the CSCI to decide whether residents have capacity. Moreover, people without capacity may have the ability to hold tenancies.

Inspections

12.17 The CSCI runs three different types of inspection of care homes – key inspections, random inspections and thematic inspections. We set out the different focuses of these inspections in Box 12.7.

Box 12.7 Different inspection regimes run by the CSCI

Key inspections
Key inspections take into account detailed information provided by the service's owner or manager, and any complaints or concerns the CSCI has received since the last inspection. The views of service users, relatives and advocates are taken into account in the inspection process. The inspection will focus on how well the service is meeting the standards set by the government and decide the future inspection mode.
These inspections will be mainly unannounced.

Random inspections
Random inspections are short, targeted inspections which focus on specific issues that have come up or check on improvements that should have been made. Random inspections are also used to investigate complaints, and sometimes are ad hoc.
Random inspections are normally unannounced and can take place at any time of the day or night.

Thematic inspections
Thematic inspections focus on a specific issue, such as medication, or a specific area or region so that the CSCI can form a view of trends in provision.

The inspection process

12.18 The CSCI describes its inspection process as having three stages: the information it collects before the inspection visit; the information collected during the inspection; and, finally, the way it reports on and responds to the information it collects. Box 12.8 elaborates upon these stages.

Box 12.8 The CSCI inspection process

Before an inspection the inspection team gathers information:

- from the people who use the services, their families and supporters (people who speak up for or advocate for the person using services);
- owners' and managers' to review the quality and effectiveness of their services;
- the staff who work for the services;
- social services and health professionals.

This informs the inspection process.

During the inspection the inspection team gathers information:

- from the people who use the service (and often to their relatives as well) to find out what they think of it;
- by looking at how the service is run to see how the staff are recruited, trained and supported, how the managers and staff treat people, how many staff there are and how they are managed;
- by looking at how well people are cared for to make sure they are treated with dignity and that their wishes are respected;
- Reviewing paperwork to check that important information is up to date.

This informs the report stage.

After the inspection the inspection team publishes a report which:

- looks at how well the service provides good outcomes for the people who use the service;
- refers to the government's National Minimum Standards which form the basis of what people should expect from care services;
- identifies what the service does well and lists any improvements it needs to make;
- sets up action plans to ensure necessary improvements happen quickly.

12.19   The CSCI has teeth – it has legal powers to ensure improvements are made, and in certain circumstances, to close down services.

Box 12.9 Frequently asked questions

What happens if a service user complains to the CSCI that they are not getting appropriate care?

The CSCI has a duty to respond to complaints by service users about care services where those complaints relate to failure to meet the regulatory standards set by government. If a complaint is made to the CSCI, it will investigate and if it finds evidence of failure it will take action to address that failure. It uses its inspection powers to obtain the necessary information to investigate complaints. It aims to complete its enquiries within 20 days of receipt of the complaint. If there is a finding of a failure to meet standards the CSCI can take action as outlined in the previous section.

Summary

12.20 Providers of supported housing may have a number of regulatory regimes to adhere to dependent on the services they offer. In this chapter and in chapters 10 and 11 we have identified the main regulatory bodies and indicated their role and their requirements. This chapter has focused on the Audit Commission and the Commission for Social Care Inspection. It can be confusing in the supported housing sector keeping abreast of legal and regulatory requirements. Throughout the chapters we have directed you to useful websites so you are able to keep your knowledge up to date.

Managing organisations

Objectives

13.1 By the end of this chapter you will:

- Understand the requirements for good internal governance
- Appreciate the role of the board of management/management committee in ensuring good internal governance
- Understand the consequences of the constitutional framework under which your organisation operates
- Understand the external legislative and regulatory requirements which shape your internal governance
- Appreciate the obligations of an organisation which employs staff to work with vulnerable people
- Appreciate your obligations as an employee

Overview

13.2 This chapter outlines how organisations should be managed to ensure they are operating within the appropriate legal and regulatory framework. It looks at the mechanisms by which they can achieve their aims and provide a good service. The ultimate responsibility for 'not for profit' organisations lies with the management committee or board of trustees, and their role is defined by law, by regulation and by the structure of that organisation. Each organisation has systems for devolving and delegating authority and responsibility. However, all individuals, particularly within small organisations, have a role to play in ensuring they are effectively and properly run. All employees are responsible for at least one part of the organisation's activities, and how they do this is defined by their contract of employment, their job description and in some cases the organisational code of conduct. Staff will need to ensure they work within the confines of their job in order to be effective and to protect service users. Moreover, staff have ethical responsibilities to ensure services are properly delivered. We consider within the chapter what action you can take if you feel that there is malpractice by an individual or the organisation.

What is governance?

13.3 In *The governance of voluntary organisations* (C J Cornforth (ed) Routledge, 2003), governance is described as 'the systems and processes concerned with ensuring the overall direction, effectiveness, supervision and accountability of an organisation'. Governance, in other words, is the structure of an organisation and the way in which 'power' is distributed amongst those within the organisation. It also includes the culture of the organisation – its values and ideals.

13.4   The way in which organisations govern their activities depends on their type, size and the number of staff. In the supported housing sector, for example, the owners of small private organisations are usually responsible for making sure the organisation is run properly. Larger 'not for profit' organisations – for example, RSLs – will have a management board, and possibly subcommittees covering different activities, for example, finance or housing. One common factor is that all organisations need structures that ensure their continued viability and accountability to their stakeholders; their own individual governance.

Types of organisations

13.5   The majority of 'not for profit' organisations will be one of the following:

- An unincorporated trust or association.
- An incorporated company limited by guarantee.
- An industrial or provident society.

13.6   The choice of organisational framework depends on that organisation's current and future purpose. In the next section we will see that smaller organisations may prefer to be unincorporated organisations as this has the advantages of less bureaucracy. Larger organisations, however, may want the reassurance of incorporation which allows the organisation to hold property and contracts in its own name. In law, the charitable status of an organisation depends on its purpose not its constitution. The Northern Ireland Council for Voluntary Action (NICVA) has produced an excellent briefing on the advantages and disadvantages of different status of organisation, available from www.nicva.org/uploads/docs/r_NotesOnLegalStructures_010704.pdf.

Unincorporated organisations

13.7   An unincorporated organisation has no separate legal existence outside of its membership. It cannot hold assets or enter into legal agreements, but it is subject to registration with the Charities Commission if it is a charity. An example of an unincorporated organisation would be a local community group that provided one house for people with mental health problems. The organisation would have the advantage of being inexpensive to run and administratively simple to manage. The disadvantage is that any assets (in this case the house) have to be held in the members' names. The members of the organisation have personal liability. This is potentially problematic if the organisation was to be sued.

Incorporated organisations

13.8   Incorporated organisations exist as legal entities separate from their membership and can, for example, enter into legal transactions under their own name. They can own or manage land, property and assets for a clearly defined purpose and for the benefit of others. Organisations that hold a number of contracts and employ a number of staff – for example, women's refuges – are likely to be incorporated organisations. The majority of housing associations are incorporated organisations. Incorporated organisations, if they are charities, are also subject to registration with the Charity Commission. The main advantage of incorporation is that the liability of members is limited to (usually) £1, that they guarantee to pay if the organisation winds up.

Box 13.1 Frequently asked questions

What is an industrial and provident society? Is it an incorporated or an unincorporated organisation?

An industrial and provident society is an organisation conducting an industry, business or trade, either as a co-operative or for the benefit of the community. It is an incorporated organisation and must be registered under the Industrial and Provident Societies Act 1965. Housing co-operatives are distinguished from other forms of housing organisation by their mutuality. Their members are the users of the housing provided by the association and are democratically involved in the running of the organisation. Any surplus made by the co-operative is usually ploughed back into the organisation to provide better services and facilities to members. Industrial and provident societies which are not co-operatives but exist for the benefit of the community are required to provide special reasons to explain why they should not be registered as companies.

Community interest companies

13.9   Community interest companies (CICs) are a specialised type of limited company designed to trade with a social purpose or carry on activities for the benefit of the community, that is, for social as opposed to private enterprise. This is achieved through three particular mechanisms:

- the 'community interest test' – all applicants for CIC status must make a community interest statement, which states their claim that their activities of will be carried on for the benefit of the community;
- the memorandum and articles of association of a CIC must comply with the relevant legislation; and
- the 'asset lock', which prevents the CIC from distributing profits and assets to its members. Its assets must be used to benefit the community.

13.10   Registration of a company as a CIC has to be approved by a regulator who is appointed by the Secretary for Trade and Industry. The regulator has a continuing monitoring and enforcement role and requires all CICs to provide an annual report.

13.11   CICs cannot be charities and therefore the tax advantages of charitable status are not available to them. However, CICs will be able to issue shares that pay a dividend to investors. The dividend will be capped in order to preserve the asset lock.

13.12   This structure would be suitable for organisations whose activities do not require them to be a charity and they are not expected to make a private profit. For example, the café in a foyer that provides employment to young people could be registered as a CIC. For more information, visit www.cicregulator.gov.uk.

Charities

13.13   Previously in law there was no statutory definition of charity. The Charities Act 2006 however has introduced a list of twelve charitable purposes. These reflect contemporary expectations of what causes should be charitable. Included is:

- relief of those in need by reason of youth,
- age,
- ill health,
- disability,
- financial hardship or
- other disadvantage

which will encompass the work of the majority of providers in the supported housing sector. There is also a general heading of 'other purposes that are currently recognised as charitable or are in the spirit of any purpose currently recognised as charitable'.

13.14   The provisions of the Charities Act 2006 are coming into effect at different stages mainly over 2007 and 2008, however some as late as 2009 to allow the Charity Commission to prepare for the changes. The Office of the third sector have produced a useful briefing on the Act: www.cabinetoffice.gov.uk.

13.15   The majority of supported housing provision falls within the definition of a charity and will be registered with the Charity Commission. Under the Charities Act 1993, all not for profit organisations with charitable objectives that have a turnover of £1,000 a year or more, have to be registered with the Charities Commission. Registering gives an organisation certain advantages, for example, most grant giving trusts, and indeed most of the public, will only give to registered charities. Charities also enjoy certain tax advantages.

Governing instruments

13.16   All organisations will have at least one governing instrument – a document defining its legal status. These documents set out what an organisation can and cannot do. The range of documents includes:

- The constitution (for associations).
- The trust deed (for trusts).
- The memorandum and articles of association (for companies limited by guarantee).
- The rules (for industrial and provident societies).

Governing structures

13.17   The governing instrument details the board or committee of people who are ultimately responsible for controlling the management and administration of the organisation. The governing structure of the organisation sets out where responsibility for decision making lies. Some organisations have a board of trustees, or a board of management or a management committee, which takes responsibility for all decision making. For ease of reference, we shall refer to the governing body as the board and its members as board members. In larger organisations (as mentioned earlier), the governing documents allow some of the powers to be delegated to subcommittees, which then have the responsibility for decisions made within the scope of their powers. The committee and any subcommittees, working parties or advisory committees must have written terms of reference setting out their delegated powers.

Box 13.2 Frequently asked questions

Can a board have a representative from the local authority or a partner housing association and what is their status?

Boards can have representatives from other organisations. Such people usually represent their stakeholders, for example, the local authority, or the probation service or housing association representative. If the representatives become members, they have a duty to act in the best interest of the organisation, even where this conflicts with the interests of their nominating company. Members who find they are having a conflict of interest should either stand down from the committee or withdraw from being involved in the particular issue. (However, they will still be liable for any decision made by the other members.) One solution is to invite such representatives onto the committee as non-voting advisors and not as members.

Branches and area committees

13.18   Unless the branches or area committees are registered in their own right as a charity or have their own constitution, they are *not* separate bodies. The decision-making powers and responsibilities rest with the main committee or branch which is registered and has a constitution. All decisions made therefore must be approved and ratified by the main branch or committee.

Company law

13.19   'Not for profit' organisations that become companies are limited by guarantee; individual members of the board or committee are only personally liable for the amount they have agreed to pay (usually £1) if the company folds. This protection will not apply if members have acted fraudulently, have continued running the organisation when it was insolvent, or have acted in breach of trust.

13.20   Even though they are not making a profit they must comply with company law and:

- Register with the Registrar of Companies.
- Make annual returns to Companies House.
- Elect a company secretary.
- Abide by company law as set out in the Companies Acts. (For charities which are also registered companies limited by guarantee, the management committee members are also the directors of the company.) This includes requirements as to the annual accounts and annual report.
- Have 'company limited by guarantee' and its company registration number on all information sent out by the company (for example, headed paper, compliments slips and annual reports).

Memorandum of association and articles of association

13.21   All companies limited by guarantee are governed by their memorandum and articles of association. In Box 13.3 we have set out the governing instruments for companies and their content. These are effectively the constitution, setting out how the company will govern itself and must be available for public scrutiny.

Box 13.3 Governing instruments for companies

The memorandum of association sets out:

- the name and address of the charity;
- the charitable aims;
- who the beneficiaries are;
- the powers of the directors (MC members);
- the amount the directors are expected to guarantee (usually £1);
- what will happen to the company's assets if it winds up;
- any special powers.

The articles of association set out:

- who and how many members the company may have;
- how directors are elected and the length of their term of office;
- the procedures for calling meetings – annual general meetings, extraordinary general meetings – who, how and

---

> when members can vote and how many members are
> required to hold a meeting that can make decisions (the
> quorum);
> - the financial procedures and procedure for appointing
>   auditors;
> - the powers it has to delegate decision making to sub-
>   committees or to staff

Charity law

13.22   As the majority of 'not for profit' organisations will be registered
charities, they must comply with the requirements of the Charities
Act 1993. The Charities Commission regulates their compliance.

13.23   The Board members are under a duty to ensure that the organisation keeps proper books and records and that annual accounts are
prepared (see 'role of the treasurer' below). In many cases the Board
members have to prepare an annual report for the stakeholders. The
accounts and content of the report must comply with the requirements of the Charities Acts 1993 and 2006, the Charities (Accounts
and Reports) Regulations 2005 SI No 572) and Reporting by Charities
– Statement of Recommended Practice (SORP) 2005. In Box 13.4 we
have signposted you to the Charity Commission for further information about charitable requirements.

Box 13.4 Signpost

The Charity Commission provides information about the legal
requirements of charities:

Website: www.charitycommission.gov.uk
Tel: 0845 300 0218
Minicom: 0845 300 0219
Fax: 0131 0703 1353

Housing Corporation requirements

13.24   Section 2 of the Housing Corporation Regulatory Code and guidance
from the Housing Corporation details the proper governance
requirements for registered social landlord s (RSLs) and their managing
agents. The Housing Corporation expects that RSLs should be headed

by an effective board with a sufficient range of expertise to give capable leadership and control. The RSL must act within the terms of its constitution and relevant legislation and maintain the highest standards of probity in all its dealings. As the conduit for the public money provided by government and invested by RSLs in their housing stock, the Housing Corporation obliges RSLs to protect this investment. In its requirements of RSLs the Housing Corporation expects more from governance than simply ensuring that board members have the requisite skills. The Corporation expects that the governing body of the organisation drives forward its requirement of an inclusive culture. This includes ensuring resident involvement and equal opportunity.

Box 13.5 Frequently asked questions

Do housing associations registered with the Housing Corporation (RSLs) who wish to have the benefits of charitable status also have to register with the Charities Commission?

RSLs can choose to be registered charities (with the Charity Commission), or to register themselves as industrial and provident societies with charitable objects. The Housing Corporation and the Charities Commission have a streamlined process for RSLs wanting to register with the Charities Commission. The Housing Corporation takes on the bulk of the pre-registration scrutiny. This is available from www.charitycommission.gov.uk/Library/supportingcharities/pdfs/housass.pdf.

RSLs who are industrial and provident societies can apply to Her Majesty's Revenue and Customs for recognition as an exempt charity (and therefore be able to take advantage of the perceived main benefits of charitable status). Although exempt charities cannot register with the Charity Commission, they are subject to Charity legislation.

Role of board members

13.25 Any person aged 18 or over can become a board member of a charity if they are of sound mind and are not disqualified by law. In Box 13.6 we identify those people who are disqualified from becoming a board member. The Charity Commissioners can grant a waiver generally or in relation to a certain charity. This could, for instance, allow a former service user to become a board member of a substance misuse organisation despite having an unspent conviction involving dishonesty. The organisation will usually have its own criteria for board membership. For example, a requirement that the person is sympathetic to the ethos of the organisation or a requirement for board members to have a range of professional skills and experience, such as personnel, legal and financial.

Box 13.6 Section 72 of the Charities Act 1993

The following people are disqualified from becoming a trustee/board member of a charity:

- those who have unspent convictions involving deception or dishonesty;
- undischarged bankrupts;
- those who have been removed from trusteeship by the Charities Commission or court because of misconduct or mismanagement;
- those disqualified from being company directors under the Company Directors Disqualification Act 1986;
- those who have failed to make payments under the county court administration orders (money judgments, etc);
- those who have made arrangements with their creditors which have not been discharged.

13.26   The board is responsible for:

- giving direction to the organisation;
- accountability to beneficiaries, funders, the public;
- ensuring the charity acts within the law and upholds its fiduciary responsibilities;
- ensuring that money, property, staff and other resources are used wholly for the charity's objects and are managed to best effect.

13.27   Most boards have 'officers' who take on particular responsibilities. These officers are commonly a chair, vice-chair, secretary and treasurer. The advantage of having named officers is that staff members have a contact between meetings and they can take a lead in certain matters. For organisations that are companies, a company secretary must be appointed.

The chair

13.28 This role provides leadership of the board and ensures it is fulfilling its responsibilities. The chair supervises the work of the director or chief executive officer. If action is required between meetings, the chair can authorise it (chair's action), for example, signing cheques over a certain amount, emergency evictions or appeals. The chair usually signs all legal documentation and represents the organisation in public and in the media.

The vice-chair

13.29 The vice-chair takes on the role of the chair if he or she is not available, and may assist in certain activities, for example, hearing appeals against eviction.

The treasurer

13.30 This role oversees the organisation's financial viability and ensures proper records, for example, annual accounts, are maintained. In very small organisations the treasurer may prepare budgets and accounts. In most organisations a member of staff performs this function and the treasurer is responsible for presenting and explaining financial information to the board. The treasurer should have the appropriate expertise to enable the board to be aware of its financial responsibilities and fulfil its legal obligations, for example, to produce audited accounts.

The secretary

13.31 In larger organisations most of the secretarial duties, for example, sending out board papers, checking that meetings will have enough members (quorate), are carried out by staff. In smaller organisations the secretary may have to take on this role. In all cases the secretary has to take minutes (a legal record) of meetings where staff are not present. The law requires that in companies the company secretary keeps the register of members, register of directors and register of charges up to date and notifies Companies House of any changes in members, prepares and files the annual return and makes sure the company documentation is kept safe. In Box 13.7 we signpost you to the Sitra website, where you can find draft job descriptions for officer posts on the board.

> **Box 13.7 Signpost**
>
> Draft job descriptions for management committee (board) members including the chair, treasurer and secretary are available on the Sitra website, www.sitra.org.uk.
>
> The board should meet on a regular basis to ensure that it can oversee the work of the organisation and inform its direction. The governing documentation will set out how often it is to meet. Most boards meet bi-monthly or quarterly. However, in small organisations where the board performs a more hands-on management role, the meetings may be monthly.

Conflicts of interest

13.32   Conflicts of interest for board members are becoming more likely as society has become more interwoven. The increased legal requirements on organisations result in board members being recruited with particular skills, for example, a local solicitor to provide legal advice. This will cause a conflict of interest if a service user is being evicted and has approached the solicitor's firm to represent him or her. Board members have to act in the best interests of the organisation, and in this case the solicitor would have to refer the service user to another practice or stand down from the board whilst the case was being heard. This becomes more complex and potentially more serious where finance is involved, for example, when a board member's relative has a building firm that wants to tender for a piece of work. In law, board members should not be placed in a position where there is a conflict between their role on the board and their own personal interest. Under company law, board members have to inform the board where they or people connected to them by family, work or membership of another organisation have any interest in a contract or transaction.

> **Box 13.8 Frequently asked questions**
>
> **One of our board members has a daughter who designs web pages. Would this be a conflict of interest if we paid her to design the web page?**
>
> First, the board should examine its policies and procedures about how work is commissioned. Work over a certain value may have to be put out to tender or need more than one quote, if this is the case, the board member should not be party to this process. If this

is not necessary and there are no rules regarding conflicts of interest, a good indicator is to imagine if decision and the connection were to be published in the local paper. Would the integrity of the board and the reputation of the organisation be damaged?

13.33 Board members should not gain any personal benefit from their position. However, they can be reimbursed for reasonable expenses, for example, childcare, travel or telephone costs. The governing documentation may allow board members with specific skills to charge; for example, an accountant could charge for preparing accounts. This needs to be within the terms of the exception outlined in the documentation, the service provided must be value for money and only a minority of board members can benefit from the exception at any one time. The NCVO provides good resources for board members to assist in these complex matters – see Box 13.9.

Box 13.9 Signpost

For further information see NCVO, *The Good Trustee Guide*:

Tel: 0800 279 8798
Minicom: 0800 018 8111
Website: www.ncvo-vol.org.uk

Standing orders

13.34 Standing orders detail the areas of responsibility in an organisation, the lines of authority and the lines of reporting. Standing orders prescribe how the day-to-day management and operations are delegated to staff. The scope of the delegation is laid down in the document, with details on how the board expects decisions to be reported to it as the body legally responsible for the organisation. The standing orders are often supplemented by policies and procedures which detail who has the authority to make decisions at different levels of the organisation and how this is fed back to the board. For example, the eviction policy and procedure may allow the director to sanction court action, but this must be reported back to the next board meeting. An eviction may be sanctioned by chair's action, but must be ratified at the next board meeting.

Employer's responsibilities

13.35   There is a wealth of legislation which regulates the management of employees. We have included some examples in Box 13.10. However, this book does not cover employment law in any detail. Within this chapter it has some importance, as we are concerned with the employer's duties to ensure that the structures exist to allow a supported housing service to be delivered. Employers must ensure that they have skilled and competent staff who can provide services within an established framework, and are supervised and supported in their work.

Box 13.10 Examples of legislation

- Equal Pay Act 1970.
- Rehabilitation of Offenders Act 1947.
- Sex Discrimination Act 1975.
- Race Relations Act 1976.
- Disability Discrimination Act 1995.
- Employment Rights Act 1996.
- Working Time Regulations 1998 (SI 1998 No 1833).
- National Minimum Wage Regulations 1999 (SI 1999 No 584).

Skilled and competent staff

13.36   Employers are under an obligation to service users and stakeholders that the people they employ to provide supported housing services are capable of performing their duties. Employers should use the recruitment process to ensure that the staff they employ have the requisite skills and are suitable for working with vulnerable adults. Where it is a statutory requirement when those working (either in a paid or volunteer capacity) with vulnerable adults, have to be checked by the Criminal Records Bureau (CRB).

Criminal Records Bureau Checks (CRB)

13.37   The CRB, an executive agency of the Home Office, runs a checking service on the confidential and criminal records of those applying to work with children and vulnerable adults. The Police Act 1997 made provision for these disclosures and there are additional definitions provided in later regulations, and in the Rehabilitation of Offenders Act 1974 and its accompanying regulations. This includes those who work with vulnerable adults, but any supported housing service which works with 16- to 17-year-olds is also subject to the provisions.

13.38   Employers should review the roles of all engaged in their service – this includes paid workers, volunteers, agency staff and others – to identify who is required to have a CRB check. Recruitment information should make clear where checks will be made on applicants prior to appointment and that offers will be subject to satisfactory CRB checks, as well as the usual references.

Box 13.11 Frequently asked questions

Once we have checked new and existing employees, do we have to run CRB checks again and if so how often?

For existing staff, employers should establish at what intervals re-checks will be made. In some cases, *Supporting People* or social services may prescribe how often re-checks should be made.

13.39   *Statutory requirements* – The Police Act 1997 describes working with vulnerable adults as 'being involved in regularly caring for, training, supervising or being in sole charge of them'. The Rehabilitation of Offenders Act 1974 (Exceptions) (Amendment) (England and Wales) Order 2002 (SI No 441) states that contact with the vulnerable person must be part of the normal duties of the worker or volunteer (reg 5). When deciding which member of staff should be subject to checks, the basic question to ask may be who can use their status as a staff member to gain access and potentially abuse a vulnerable service user?

13.40   *Definition of a vulnerable adult* – The regulations to the Police Act 1997 give the following three-part definition of a vulnerable adult.

13.41   A person must be aged 18 or over receiving services either:

(a) accommodation and nursing or personal care in a care home,
(b) personal care or support to live independently in their own home,
(c) any services provided by an independent hospital, clinic, medical agency or NHS body,
(d) social care services, or
(e) any services provided in an establishment catering for a person with learning difficulties.

because of having a condition of:

(a) a learning or physical disability,
(b) a physical or mental illness, chronic or otherwise, including an addiction to alcohol or drugs, or
(c) a reduction in physical or mental capacity.

and has a disability of:

(a) a dependency on others to assist with or perform basic physical functions,
(b) severe impairment in the ability to communicate with others,
(c) impairment in a person's ability to protect themselves from assault, abuse or neglect.

13.42   The Exceptions Order to the Rehabilitation of Offenders Act 1974 defines a vulnerable adult as:

A person aged 18 or over who has a condition of the following type –
(i)   a substantial learning or physical disability,
(ii) a physical or mental illness, chronic or otherwise, including an addiction to alcohol or drugs, or
(iii) a significant reduction in physical or mental capacity.

13.43   These definitions cover many of the client groups in the supported housing sector. Even those projects that provide services for clients who do not come within these definitions, such as hostels for homeless people, may still be required to have checks carried out on their staff on the basis that they may occasionally work with vulnerable clients. In most *Supporting People*-funded services, CRB checks will be required as part of the contract for funding the service.

Level of checks

13.44   The regulations referred to above require an enhanced disclosure to be obtained for people working with vulnerable adults, as defined above. This came into effect from March 2002. Enhanced disclosures include:

- details of convictions, including spent convictions, cautions, reprimands and warnings, recorded by the police at national level;
- information from local police records, including relevant non-conviction information; and
- checks on the Departments of Health and Education and Employment lists of people barred from working with the vulnerable.

13.45   Because of the sensitive nature of this information, enhanced checks can only be obtained by organisations registered with the CRB who have signed up to their code of practice on the handling and use of this information.

13.46   Standard checks are similar to the above, but exclude local police information and can also only be obtained by registered bodies. Basic checks can be obtained by any individual about themselves only, and show only unspent convictions held at national level.

13.47 There is a fee for checks, except for volunteers, for whom there is no charge.

13.48 *CRB Code of Practice* – An organisation wishing to get standard or enhanced disclosures from the CRB must either register with it or go through an umbrella body which is registered with it. The organisation must adopt policies and procedures which ensure compliance with the Code of Practice. This covers the use, handling, access to and storage of the information obtained. The Code of Practice can be viewed on the CRB's website on disclosure at www.crb.gov.uk; telephone: 0870 9090811.

13.49 Umbrella bodies have to ensure that all organisations using their services have policies which ensure compliance. Some provide model policies, but an organisation should ensure that these are integrated with their own personnel policies.

Support and supervision

13.50 Employers should ensure that staff who work with vulnerable people are supervised and supported to do the job effectively. There are no set rules as to how staff should be supervised and supported, and most organisations have both formal and informal systems. Employers should ensure that formal support and supervision sessions take place every four to six weeks and at least 60 minutes should be set aside for the session. An agenda should be drawn up that includes objectives of the post, workload and training and development needs. The employee should be given a record of the meeting and it should be confidential. Supervision provides an opportunity for:

- staff to raise concerns;
- development of good practice;
- support staff development;
- ensuring staff are capable and have the resources to carry out the duties of the post;
- identifying gaps in skills and competence and how these are to be met.

13.51 All employees have a legal requirement to allow employees access to minimum grievance and disciplinary procedure. We have signposted you to some procedural templates in Box 13.12.

Box 13.12 Signpost

Templates for standard grievance and disciplinary procedures, *Route to resolution, improving dispute resolution in Britain*, are available from the Department of Trade and Industry on www.dti.gov.uk.

Policies and procedures

13.52   Policies and procedures are two of the most important tools employed in delivering a service. It is the responsibility of employers to ensure that effective and up-to-date policies and procedures are in place. A policy is the statement of what an organisation aims to achieve and who is responsible for accomplishing those aims. The procedures are the practicalities of how to deliver those aims. Employers should ensure that all staff have:

- access to policies and procedures;
- an understanding of their obligations to adhere to the policies and procedures; and
- an understanding of the implications of non-compliance.

13.53   We have included an example to demonstrate the role of policies in Box 13.13.

Box 13.13 Example

An organisation provides accommodation and support in cluster flats to people with generic support needs. A support worker visits the property once a day and holds appointments in an office based on site. The office has an alarm system which can be activated either by a panic button in the office or by a portable device when the support worker has to enter a flat. Under the health and safety policy and procedure, it is the support worker's duty to ensure that the device is carried at all times when away from the office and that he or she is confident in using the equipment. The employer would have a duty to ensure that the system is regularly serviced and to supervise the employee's use of the system, providing training where necessary.

13.54   We have included guidelines on some key policies and procedures in our appendices. There is no definitive list of policies and procedures that are required in the provision of supported housing. The size and type of organisation will inform what policies and procedures are appropriate. Your organisation will have to give some thought to the range and detail of the policies and procedures it requires. For example, a large RSL may have a separate policy and procedure on 'dealing with death' as its occurrence will increase with the number of residents housed. A smaller organisation may include this in their accident and incident policy and procedure. In Box 13.14 we have given some examples of policies and procedures we believe a supported housing provider should consider putting in place.

Box 13.14 Examples of policies and procedures in the delivery of supported housing

- Equality of opportunity diversity and inclusion.
- Referral and selection (allocating and lettings).
- Support planning.
- Health and safety.
- Maintenance.
- Incident and accident.
- Protection of vulnerable adults.
- Confidentiality.
- Data protection.
- Harassment.
- Anti-social behaviour and nuisance.
- Challenging behaviour.
- Substance misuse.
- Rent setting, collection and arrears.
- Complaints.
- Tenure.
- Repossession (eviction).
- Move-on (resettlement).
- Code of conduct.

Employees' responsibilities

13.55 All employees have obligations arising out of employment law to do their best for their employer, and to the users of the service they provide. So, for instance, an employee is legally required to follow the instructions of their employer and to carry out their duties. Employees may feel this produces a conflict; for example, a manager may direct them to remove a service user's pet hamster from his or her bedroom.

The worker may feel that the hamster is not causing a problem and that service users should be entitled to keep pets. However, the employer may have a sound reason for the instruction. For instance, it may consider that if the hamster escaped it could cause a health and safety hazard by chewing through electrical wires. It is the employee's responsibility to carry out the instruction. The documents that set out what is expected from employees are:

- the contract of employment;
- the job description;
- the code of conduct; and
- the organisational policies and procedures.

13.56   Managers may also instruct employees to carry out tasks, either formally, perhaps in a supervision and support meeting, or informally, either verbally or by email. Employees are required by employment law to comply with the reasonable requests of their manager.

Box 13.15 Frequently asked questions

My manager has asked me to assist a service user to use the toilet. I am only expected to provide housing-related support – do I have to do what I am told?

If you believe a request is in contravention of your job description or contract of employment you should explain to the manager that you are not able to comply with the request. In the section on contracts of employment, we explain what employers are required to provide in relation to terms of your contract. If your explanation creates a problem, you should speak to a senior manager or to your union. If you feel that you are not qualified or sufficiently skilled to carry out the task, you can ultimately use the whistle-blowing policy and procedure. You may be able to use other avenues to avoid escalating the dispute, for example, negotiation or mediation.

Contract of employment

13.57   The Employment Rights Act 1996 requires employers to provide employees with a written statement of the main terms and conditions of employment within two months of starting work. Under the Employment Protection (Part-time Employees) Regulations 1995 (SI 1995 No 31), this applies to all employees whether or not they are full or part time, including those who work less than eight hours a week. The contract of employment will set out:

- hours of work;
- holiday entitlement;
- the job title and
- a brief description of the role.

13.58 The contract may also specify other responsibilities, for example, health and safety obligations, adherence to the code of conduct and confidentiality duties. When the contract is signed, both parties are agreeing to all the terms contained in it and have a legal duty to adhere to the terms of the contract. Breach of the contract of employment can trigger disciplinary procedures. The contract may give the employer the right to suspend an employee with or without pay whilst any breach is investigated or during the course of disciplinary or grievance procedures.

Job description

13.59 All staff should have a job description that enables them to understand what they are being employed to do. The job description should cover the following areas:

- the job title;
- to whom you are responsible, that is, which manager supervises your work and supports you in your role;
- the main purpose of the job;
- the duties you are expected to perform; and
- the role of the job what you are expected to achieve.

13.60 One of the dilemmas facing employers is ensuring that their employees are appropriately flexible. Job descriptions often include a term which says that the job description includes *any other duties as required*. The employer can only expect an employee to perform duties that are within the framework of the contract of employment.

Code of conduct

13.61 An organisation's code of conduct should leave staff, board members and volunteers in no doubt as to what constitutes acceptable and non-acceptable behaviour. The code of conduct can assist staff in areas where they may be confused as to the appropriate way forward or action to take. This may be particularly important in supported housing because of the relationships that exist between vulnerable people and those providing them with services

---

Box 13.16 Frequently asked questions

A service user has given me a gift for Christmas – should I refuse it and risk offending them?

Your organisation should identify when it is appropriate to accept gifts and when they should be refused. In some organisations you will be able to accept small gifts on behalf of the staff team. Generally, larger gifts should not be accepted. One good strategy is donating gifts accepted to a charity or raffling them amongst staff and the proceeds given to charity. In some organisations, staff are advised to ask service users who wish to make a gift to make a donation instead to a chosen charity. If you simply accept a gift from a service user you risk allegations of pecuniary abuse. If in doubt, check your code of conduct. The responsibility of becoming familiar with the code of conduct lies with you, the employee, and there will be consequences for not complying; in most organisations compliance with the code of conduct is a part of the contract of employment. If you choose not to follow the code of conduct, you could be disciplined. We discuss gifts again below in the section on professional boundaries.

13.62   In some areas the code of conduct will reflect legal or regulatory requirements; in others it will reflect the particular values of the organisation. Most codes of conduct cover use of organisational resources, behaviour, dress, confidentiality, relationships, finance and gifts. Some codes may cover specific areas, for example, consuming alcohol on duty or smoking. In the appendices we have included a checklist for the contents of a code of conduct.

Professional boundaries

13.63   Codes of conduct often require employees to work in a professional manner and/or adhere to professional boundaries. Professional boundaries separate the professional or work-related interventions of a supported housing worker from any behaviour, which, whether well-intentioned or not, could lessen the benefit of support to a service user because it steps beyond that professional limit. Boundaries give each party to a relationship a sense of control over the relationship and an understanding of what is legitimate behaviour. They set limits to the provider/service user relationship. This establishes a safe and supportive interaction between the person giving and the person receiving the support. Professional boundaries are therefore an essential part of supported housing work; some of your boundaries will be created by law, others will be set by your regulators. Organisations will establish their own limits. However, there may be areas where an employee's own ethics will inform their practice. We look at ethics in more detail in chapter 18. Most boundaries are made explicit by the job description, code of conduct and the policies and procedures expected to be adhered to. It is, however, crucial that employees recognise the difference between the relationship they have as a professional and other types of relationship. If employees do not observe professional boundaries, at best they will compromise their own and their organisation's integrity; at worst they could harm the service user, themselves and their organisation.

13.64 Providing services to vulnerable people places employees in a privileged but often difficult position. Service users often take staff into their 'hearts and their homes'. It is possible to be under-involved, which could result in neglect, as well as over-involved, where the relationship between the worker and service user takes priority over the customer's needs.

13.65 There are broadly speaking four 'categories' of relationships where the setting of appropriate boundaries may be complex.

Working relationships

13.66 Social housing and support services are limited resources and therefore there will always be a power imbalance between those who provide or deliver these services and the users of this service. The ways in which housing and support services are provided are usually set down by the policies and procedures of the organisation, which should incorporate legal and regulatory requirements. Both the Housing Corporation and *Supporting People* have requirements regarding how services are delivered. The priority of the staff should be in planning housing and support around the needs of the service user and being able to describe the reasons for their actions and decisions to the service user. Members of staff do not have the individual right to withdraw a service to 'punish' a service user or coerce their compliance. We have included an example of this in Box 13.17.

Box 13.17 Example

A worker should not advise a service user that he or she will withdraw support if the service user does not stop seeing a friend, who the worker believes is a 'bad influence'.

Dual relationships

13.67   Employees will have a number of roles within their private life, including partner, parent, family member and friend; they must not have any of these private relationships with service users. Some of these relationships appear clearer than others; most staff will probably know that it is *never* acceptable to have a sexual or intimate personal relationship with a service user. The distinction becomes more blurred if the relationship becomes more distant, for example, if a service user is a friend's son. A useful indicator is to identify all the problems that may occur and identify if these impede the provision of the service. In Box 13.18 we have included an example of this.

Box 13.18 Example

A support worker who finds that a service user's child is in the same school class as their own child will have to consider whether the support service will be compromised. The service user may be unwilling disclose the level of personal information required to provide the service and therefore should be assigned another support worker.

   The other problem with the dual relationship is caused by the very nature of supported housing provision. Workers want to establish a trusting relationship with service users and this may be the only relationship that service user has. However, staff need to be clear that they are not the service user's friend. They are employed or are volunteering to provide a professional service. The creation of a friendship with a customer compromises staff's integrity and increases the service user's vulnerability. Staff should not take service users to their home or to personal social occasions, for example, birthday parties, weddings.

Disclosure of information

13.68   A degree of self-disclosure may be appropriate for the development of trust and rapport in the relationship between a housing support worker and a service user. Staff need to be aware of their motives for disclosing information, that it is limited to what is supportive in value and always within an established working relationship. In Box 13.19 we have highlighted an example of this.

Box 13.19 Example

A worker in a women's refuge may disclose that she has experienced domestic violence in the past to develop some trust in the professional relationship. It would be inappropriate for the worker to suggest that the way she resolved the issue is the only solution open for the service user.

Gifts/financial relations

13.69   Staff should never make personal gains at the service user's expense, even if this is the service user's express wish. You may accept small tokens of thanks (perhaps chocolates) on behalf of your staff team. A worker should never personally accept a gift, as it will undermine their professional integrity and is dishonest – successful work with service users depends on team work. Box 13.20 provides an example of this.

Box 13.20 Example

In a mental health scheme a service user gives a supported housing worker a box of chocolates. The worker accepts them with thanks and sensitively advises the service user that all gifts are raffled amongst the staff and the proceeds used to buy gifts for a local children's home. In that way the gift will be enjoyed by a member of the team that is responsible for providing the service and also contribute to a good cause.

Whistleblowing

13.70   We hope that staff will never need to use the Public interest Disclosure Act 1998, which provides protections for employees who disclose malpractice, commonly described as 'whistleblowing'. If a staff member believes, however, that there is a possibility of serious malpractice, they have a professional duty to advise external agencies. The failure to whistleblow can have very serious consequences for the service user, staff and the organisation.

13.71   The Public Interest Disclosure Act 1998 gives protection to those acting in good faith and with reasonable suspicion that malpractice has, is or may be occurring who disclose this to a manager or employer. The Act came into force in 1999. It encourages people to raise concerns about malpractice in the workplace by protecting employees from victimisation and dismissal, and will help ensure that organisations respond by:

- addressing the message rather than the messenger; and
- resisting the temptation to cover up serious malpractice.

13.72   The Act applies to people at work raising genuine concerns about crime, civil offences (including negligence, breach of contract, breach of administrative law), miscarriage of justice, danger to health and safety or the environment and the cover-up of any of these. It applies whether or not the information is confidential and extends to malpractice occurring overseas.

13.73   Disclosures to others, for example, the police, media, MPs, non-prescribed regulatory bodies, are protected if they are not made for personal gain and, in addition to the above criteria, the whistleblower shows they:

- reasonably believed they would be victimised if they raised the matter internally or with a prescribed regulator;
- reasonably believed a cover-up was likely and there was no regulator; or
- had already raised the matter internally or with a prescribed regulator.

13.74   There are other considerations which an employment tribunal must take into account, including the seriousness of the matter, the degree of risk to those involved and the reasonableness of previous responses to expressions of concern. A whistleblower can bring a claim to an employment tribunal for compensation for victimisation or for an interim order to keep their job if they are dismissed. The Act also makes unenforceable any 'gagging' clauses in employment contracts or severance agreements when these conflict with the Act's provisions.

13.75   Should the employer refuse to take any action and the staff raising the concern wish to seek external advice, they should contact the charity, Public Concern At Work.

13.76   The *Supporting People* Quality Assessment Framework requires that a whistleblowing policy is in place in all organisations funded by *Supporting People*. The whistleblowing policy should set out how employees who raise concerns about malpractice within their organisation are protected, and must reflect the provisions of the Public Interest Disclosure Act 1998. In Box 13.21 we have included some good practice around whistleblowing and, in Box 13.22, signposted you to Public Concern at Work.

Box 13.21 Good practice in whistleblowing

Do:

- Keep calm.
- Think about the risks and outcomes before you act.
- Remember you are a witness, not a complainant.
- Get advice.
- Raise the matter; if it's a serious concern it should be addressed.
- Pass on your concerns to someone in authority.
- Remember details, record dates times, etc if necessary.

Don't:

- Turn a blind eye; you have a professional and personal responsibility to act if you have legitimate concerns.
- Forget there may be an innocent or good explanation.
- Become a private detective.
- Delay; you are raising concerns, not providing proof – that is some else's responsibility.
- Use a whistleblowing procedure to pursue a personal grievance.

Box 13.22 Signpost

If you need information and support regarding whistleblowing, you can contact Public Concern at Work, a charity that offers advice and practical help.

Website: www.pcaw.co.uk
Helpline: 020 7404 6609, 9 am to 6 pm, Monday to Friday.

Serious incidents

13.77   Employees who provide support to vulnerable people are quite rightly concerned that they may be personally liable if things go wrong. If there is a serious incident they will have to explain the decisions they have taken and failures to make decisions. Staff will be able to do this if they have:

- Taken reasonable care.
- Kept proper written records.
- Acted within a certain level of professional competence.

13.78   If there is a serious incident and a staff member is found to have made a mistake, there may be an official inquiry. If the staff member is at fault, they could be disciplined or even dismissed, or the organisation may be sued.

13.79   Staff are less likely to make a mistake if they:

- Know the policies and procedures of their organisation and work within them.
- Understand what duties their job description expects them to perform and are capable of performing them.
- Ensure that their manager is aware of any areas where they require training as they are not skilled or competent to carry out their duties.
- Undertake training to be and remain able to perform their duties.
- Receive regular supervision and support.

Summary

13.80   This chapter explains the structures of organisations and the role of officers and individuals within organisation including the role of the support worker. The purpose of this chapter is to help you understand what is meant by governance and how organisations are structured to ensure that services are provided for those who are most vulnerable in society.

13.81   We have looked at the role of the board and its officers and how they delegate their legal responsibility for the management of the organisation to the staff of the organisation. It is the responsibility of staff members to ensure they work within established policies and procedures to protect service users, the organisation and, just as importantly, themselves. This chapter should enable you to appreciate the responsibilities of employers and employees to the people who use your service. There may be times when staff feel that their organisation is expecting too much of them. Staff should use the support and supervision they are offered to ensure they are capable of carrying out their duties. They should not be expected to provide more than their contract of employment and job description. In the rare circumstances of organisational malpractice that cannot be resolved internally, staff may have to contact external organisations under the whistleblowing policy and procedure.

PART III

Managing the terms of occupancy agreements

Objectives

14.1   By the end of this chapter you will:

- Understand what kind of occupancy agreements are appropriate in different supported housing settings
- Know what terms are appropriate in different occupancy agreements
- Understand what landlord and resident rights and responsibilities should be set out in the agreement
- Appreciate the central importance of the agreement to the land-lord/tenant relationship

Case study

14.2   Nice View, a Housing Association registered with the Housing Corporation, is managing a temporary supported housing scheme for five people who have enduring mental health issues. Each resident has their own room, which has an en suite bathroom, and shares a communal kitchen. A supported housing officer provides the housing management and support services and visits the house to support residents, hold house meetings, supervise repairs and conduct monthly health and safety checks. Following a review, the purpose of the scheme was changed and residents are now expected to stay in the scheme for approximately two years and then move on to independent living. Prior to this, there were no time limits on length of stay. Current residents have assured tenancy agreements. The agreements need to be reviewed to ensure they are in line with legislation, regulation and good practice. The manager has suggested changing to licence agreements to give the housing association more management flexibility, enabling the organisation to take 16- to 17-year-olds, remove disruptive residents and ensure residents take up the support provided and move out and on when they no longer require support.

Overview

14.3   Like most residential occupiers who pay rent, all those living in supported housing have an agreement defining their occupation status and the terms relating to it. In previous chapters we have considered when a tenancy or a licence is appropriate in law, and the Housing Corporation requirements for RSLs and their managing agents. Occupancy agreements do not have to be in writing; however, it is both good practice and a Housing Corporation requirement that all occupants have a written copy of their agreement. It is also good sense: it would be virtually impossible to try to enforce a term of an agreement in court if you had nothing in writing to prove that the resident had agreed to the term.

14.4   In this chapter we will revisit the tenancy versus licence discussion, as it is a recurring problem for supported housing providers. Our focus here will be the practical issues and good practice considerations. In the case study, the housing association has quite properly recognised the need to review agreements from time to time. This avoids the agreement becoming a meaningless document which is only referred to when there is a problem. However, landlord organisations are not at liberty to decide what type of agreement would best suit their needs – it is the law which decides the status of the rental occupier drawing on the facts of provision.

14.5   This chapter looks at practical issues:

- What terms should appear in agreements?
- What responsibilities should be imposed upon residents?
- What is the relationship between support and the occupancy agreement?
- What can be done if a resident is not keeping to the terms of the agreement?
- Managing 'move on' when a resident requires a different type of accommodation, perhaps as a result of changing need for support.

Tenancy/licence debate

14.6   In chapter 4 we identified when the conditions for a tenancy existed in law and when it was appropriate to create a licence.

14.7   The case study is a useful reminder of the issues. The answer to whether the manager can issue licences hinges on whether the residents have exclusive possession of part of their accommodation.

14.8   The residents have their own room, they do not have to share a bedroom and the association does not need 'unfettered access' to the room. They have exclusive possession, so in law this would be a tenancy agreement. The fact that residents share the kitchen does not mean that a tenancy cannot exist. The resident need only have exclusive possession of part of their accommodation. Although the supported housing officer requires access to conduct health and safety checks, this is not inconsistent with residents' exclusive possession. Unfettered access means that the landlord would require access at all times to provide services that were required by the resident.

14.9   Some supported housing providers express a preference for licence agreements, as the lack of security for residents means the landlord has more flexibility to deal with those who are causing problems. Issuing a resident with an agreement labelled 'licence' *does not* mean a licence exists in law. If the manager did issue a licence and this was challenged in court (usually because a resident has been evicted), the court would look at the circumstances of the occupation and make a decision based on these. See chapter 4 for more information.

Assured and assured shorthold tenancies

14.10   Landlords can issue assured shorthold tenancies even if they intend to rent out the property for a long period of time – perhaps even permanently. However, Housing Corporation advice is that the most secure form of tenure must be granted to the occupier.

14.11   In the case study, Nice View grant the most secure form of tenure available to it – a full assured tenancy agreement. In this case study, the aims and purpose of the housing is now to provide only temporary accommodation and therefore a shorthold assured tenancy agreement is more appropriate. Indeed, in the case study the grant of a full assured tenancy may would create a false expectation that the provision was permanent potentially creating problems with 'move on'. In Box 14.1 we identify the decision-making process Nice View would have to go through as a registered social landlord operating post the 1988 and 1996 Housing Acts. In chapter 4, we identify the variety of occupancy agreements in both the private and public sector.

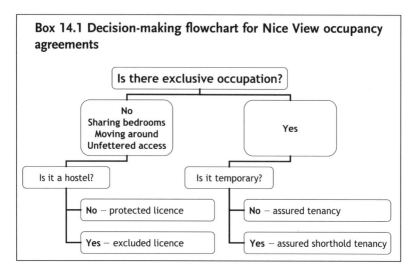

Box 14.1 Decision-making flowchart for Nice View occupancy agreements

Young people

14.12   Nice View wants to be able to accommodate young people aged 16–17 years. We discussed the legal position of young people and tenancies in chapter 4. In Box 14.2 we point you to good practice issuing tenancy agreements to young people.

Box 14.2 Good practice

Nice View need to get the young person to sign an equitable tenancy when he or she takes up residence. The young person will require a 'litigation friend' to represent them if the landlord applies to court for any reason during this time. When the young person reaches the age of majority, he or she should be given an opportunity (usually up to one month) to decide whether they want to take on a tenancy or repudiate (reject) their equitable tenancy. If they decide to take on a tenancy, they should sign a new tenancy. This may cause problems as any arrears from the first tenancy are no longer enforceable through possession proceedings but only through action for debt.

Changing agreements

14.13   In the case study, Nice View are currently issuing full assured tenancies, but assured shorthold tenancies are now more appropriate as the accommodation is short term. Nice View will now have to manage the change. It will have to be prepared to explain to tenants why the type of occupancy agreement has changed and ensure that stakeholders are aware of this. Nice View could then draw up an assured shorthold tenancy for the scheme and use the new agreement for future tenants.

14.14   Although it is legally acceptable to have different agreements in one scheme, this can often create problems as existing tenants will have a more secure agreement than new tenants. However, it is poor practice and legally very risky to replace assured tenancies with assured shorthold tenancies for existing tenants by asking them to sign the new agreements. Most residents, if properly informed, would not agree to sign a new agreement that substantially reduces their rights. If tenants did sign the new agreement, a court may conclude they only did so because they had not been properly informed or that they did not understand the implications of their action. Moreover, if the previous agreement has not been properly terminated, it is likely still to be in existence, and it would be difficult to argue that any surrender made by a tenant would be valid in these circumstances. Your stakeholders and the Housing Corporation would undoubtedly take a dim view of your practice. Some *Supporting People* teams have requested providers to change agreements of current residents from assured to assured shorthold tenancies. You may need to inform your *Supporting People* team why this is not appropriate for existing residents.

Terms of the agreement

14.15   Housing providers should review the terms of their agreements on a regular basis. In the case of new schemes or agreements, new terms will have to be drawn up. As seen in chapter 4, there are differences between the terms required by law for different occupancy agreements. A brief reminder:

- *Secure agreements* – come with a bundle of rights set out in the Housing Act 1985, for example right to take in lodgers, right to make improvements, etc.
- *Assured tenancy agreements* – the Housing Act 1988 sets out minimum statutory protections. These are usually supplemented by a written agreement or in some cases a verbal agreement.
- *Licence agreements* – licence holders have no specific statutory protection; their rights are limited to those available to all non-excluded occupiers under the Protection from Eviction Act 1977.

Accommodation in hostels (as defined in the Protection from Eviction Act) is excluded from those protections. The terms are set out in the agreement or contract.

- *Excluded tenancies* – tenancies which are excluded from the Housing Acts are common law tenancies. They have only the limited rights that all tenants have at common law. Common law tenants are entitled to the protections of the Protection from Eviction Act 1977 – as long as they are not also excluded from that Act. The terms are set out in the agreement or contract.

14.16   Differences in law should not stop organisations from ensuring that the terms of all the agreements used are as similar as possible. All occupancy agreement should contain the following general terms:

- landlord responsibilities;
- resident's responsibilities;
- resident's rights;
- ending the agreement; and
- signatures of both parties.

14.17   Occupancy agreements should be in plain English so the resident can understand their rights and responsibilities. It will be difficult to enforce a term in or out of court if the resident has no comprehension of what is expected by the term. The Unfair Terms in Consumer Contracts Regulations 1999 (SI 1999 No 2083) state that contracts should be in plain English. Something is probably not in plain English if:

- You do not understand what it means.
- You cannot explain to the user in simple language what it means.
- The terms contain 'legalese', for example, 'pursuant', 'aforementioned', 'apropos'.
- The sentences are long and you find that by the end both you and the service user have forgotten what the beginning was concerned with.

General terms

14.18   These terms set out:

- The parties to the agreement.
- Details of the property.
- The date the agreement commenced.
- If the property has a specific purpose, for example, to provide support as well as accommodation.

- The rent or charge, what that pays for and how and when it can be increased.
- The method for altering the agreement.
- The method for service of notices on the landlord.

Landlord

14.19 The landlord's name and address should appear on the document. If the landlord is a large RSL, for example, the address should be the registered address for company or charity purposes – usually the head office. If the property is managed by a managing agent, this should be detailed, but it should be clear that the legal relationship is between the landlord and the resident.

Resident

14.20 The resident's full name should be clearly spelt. This might cause problems if the resident is known by more than one name. We have set out a suggestion for how to deal with this problem in Box 14.3.

Box 14.3 Frequently asked questions

What happens if a resident has a 'street name' or changes their name through deed poll, marriage or divorce?

The occupancy agreement should identify any 'street name' if that is the name the resident is known by. Any documentation evidencing a change of name through marriage, divorce or deed poll should be attached to the agreement. It is important to ensure that the resident recognises any letter or notice is served on them, for example, a notice of seeking possession.

Address

14.21 This should be the address of the property, including flat or room number, letter or name. Where there are shared communal facilities, include all parts of the property the resident has exclusive or shared use of.

Furniture

14.22 Any furniture provided should be detailed on an inventory or schedule. You should also set out the condition of the furniture.

Date and duration of the agreement

14.23　*Secure and assured tenancies* – these are usually periodic, which means that the agreement runs from rental period to rental period until an event interferes with this. Examples of interfering events are when the court orders possession to be given to the landlord or the tenant terminates the agreement. In supported housing, the rental period is usually a week. This generally commences on a Monday to coincide with the housing benefit rent week. In the private sector, rent is often charged monthly, so the periods of a tenancy run from month to month.

14.24　　All instruments (including tenancy agreements) relating to property over a certain value have to be stamped in accordance with the Stamp Act 1491. In Box 14.4 we identify the implications of this and how you can avoid them.

Box 14.4 Stamp Act 1491

In reality most judges overlook the requirements of the Stamp Act. However, section 14 of the Stamp Act 1491 states that any instrument relating to property must be stamped in accordance with the law, otherwise it should not be given in evidence. In order to prevent this causing you any anxiety, we recommend you use the following wording which enables you to avoid the implications of the Stamp Act:

The Tenancy begins on .... and is an assured (*secure or shorthold*) tenancy for one week and weekly thereafter until determined, the terms of which are set out in this agreement.

The initial week's fixed term represents the value of the tenancy, which will always be below the Stamp Act 1491 limit, meaning it will not apply.

14.25　*Assured shorthold tenancies* – these can be fixed term or periodic. For fixed term, the tenancy should state the commencement date and the length of the fixed term in supported housing. This is usually six months. Do not forget, even if the agreement is periodic, the tenant is entitled to six months' security of tenure. In Box 14.4 we identify good practice from the Housing Corporation on length of stay for both fixed term and periodic assured shorthold tenancies.

Box 14.5 Housing Corporation Good Practice on Tenure

If periodic assured shorthold tenancies are used, the tenant should be advised of the intended length of stay either in the agreement or in the supporting documentation. If fixed term tenancies are used, the fixed term should reflect the intended length of stay. For example, if the aims and objectives are for a stay of 12 months, a fixed term tenancy of 12 months should be used. If this is the case, a section 21 notice requiring possession cannot expire until the end of the fixed term of 12 months – although it can be served before that date.

14.26   *Licence agreements* – licences do not create a legal interest in the property and are not instruments relating to property, so are not subject to the laws governing property. Licences can be for very short periods of time – even daily – and can start on any day of the week. We recommend setting out a start date, frequency of charge for the accommodation and services (weekly or daily) and the intended length of stay.

Support

14.27   In housing with care and/or support services, there has traditionally been a link between the accommodation and the support services provided. There is a question about whether support should be regarded as a condition of tenancy. In *Paddington Churches Housing Association v Boateng* (27 May 1998, Central London Civil Trial Centre), the landlord applied to the court for possession using ground 12 for breach of the term compliance with support. We provide details of the case in Box 14.6.

Box 14.6 *Paddington Churches Housing Association v Boateng*

RPS Rainer managed a scheme on behalf of Paddington Churches Housing Association. The aims of the scheme were to enable young women to acquire the skills to live independently and move out into independent living. Paddington Churches granted each tenant an assured tenancy, RPS Rainer managed the housing and support and the intended length of stay was two years. The assured tenancy agreement included a term stating that:

> ... the tenant agrees to participate in groups and individual programmes designed to assist with the tenants resettlement and to comply with the agents move on policies and

---

> procedures ... The project is not designed to provide permanent accommodation for the tenant and therefore the tenant also agrees to move into other accommodation if notified in writing by the agent that other accommodation is available.
>
> Ms Boateng was offered her move on accommodation and refused it. Paddington Churches applied for possession under the Housing Act 1988 Sch 2 ground 12 on the basis that the tenant had breached a term of the agreement. The judge in the case ruled that the term relied on was merely a personal obligation and not a term binding the tenant.

14.28   The rationale of the *Boateng* case becomes clear if you think of the tenancy as creating an interest in the land that is tangible and independent from the user. The terms of the tenancy must be obligations that can apply to anyone who can succeed to the tenancy, for example, the responsibility to pay rent or report repair can be carried out by anyone holding the tenancy. Support is based on personal need, and someone who succeeds to a tenancy will not have the same support requirements. You can succeed to a tenancy but not a support plan.

14.29   There is little point including an obligation to take part in support in a tenancy as it is highly unlikely that it is legally enforceable. This does not create a problem if the support can be delivered independently from the accommodation. This is the case in self-contained dispersed flats and houses for people with support needs.

14.30   However, many providers are still managing shared supported housing where the support is integral to the provision of the accommodation, for example, a shared housing scheme that enables young mothers to acquire the skills to live independently or a sheltered housing scheme with an on-site warden. In these circumstances we would advise the following.

14.31   1. *Secure and assured tenancy agreements* – the general terms of the agreement should include a term describing the purpose of the scheme. This term should make clear that it is not just for accommodation, but that there is a supportive or rehabilitative function. This should be followed by a term highlighting to the tenant how the provision of support interfaces with the tenancy:

> This tenancy is granted to facilitate the provision of support for you for which you are obliged to pay. The support services we provide and your

obligations are set out in the support contract in schedule [ ]. The support we provide is an essential part of your stay in your home. If you withdraw from support, do not require the support or break your support contract, we will review your support needs and we may take steps to end the tenancy by offering you suitable alternative accommodation.

14.32 In chapter 11 you will have seen that in long-term accommodation the user may have to pay for their support. Some providers include this charge in the service charge element as opposed to having a separate contract. We do not recommend this for two reasons:

- If this included as a resident responsibility the obligation to take part in support is not likely to be enforceable as an obligation of the tenancy.
- It is doubtful whether the court will include support charges as part of rent in a possession action.

14.33 We will examine how to regain possession in these circumstances in the next chapter.

14.34 *2. Assured shorthold agreements* – in short-term accommodation our advice depends on whether the provider is going rely on the mandatory avenue afforded by serving a section 21 notice requiring possession. If so, it is good practice to inform the tenant of this in the general terms of the agreement. After the term setting out the purpose of the scheme the following should be inserted:

> This Tenancy is granted to facilitate the provision of support to you. The support services we provide and your obligations are set out in the support agreement in schedule [ ]. The support we provide is an essential part of your stay here. If you withdraw from support, do not require the support agreed or require a different level of support we will review your stay and may take steps to end your tenancy by issuing a s21 notice. If we serve you with a notice we will use our best endeavours to assist you in finding alternative accommodation.

14.35 The circumstances when it is good practice to serve a section 21 notice are covered later in this chapter.

14.36 *3. Licences* – are not subject to the same legal constraints as tenancy agreements. Providers can include terms in residents' obligations, such as a requirement to take part in the key working session or attend house meetings. We think it is good practice to treat licence holders as if their legal rights are the same as tenants, when this is possible and when there is no legal reason preventing you from doing so. Just as we argued in connection with assured shorthold tenants, licence holders need to understand the circumstances in which their agreement could be terminated, including failure to comply with the support provision. After a term on the purpose of the scheme the following should be inserted:

> This licence has been granted so that you can receive support services. The support services we provide and your obligations are set out in the support agreement in schedule [ ]. The support we provide is an essential part of your stay here. If you withdraw from support or do not require support we will review your stay and may end your licence agreement by serving a notice to quit.

Support contracts

14.37 Support contracts are used when a person is obliged to make a payment for their support services; this ensures that they are under a contractual obligation to pay for the support. Service users in long-term services are expected to pay for support unless the administering authority subsidises the charge following a means test under fairer charging rules. Support contracts set out the support services provided and the responsibilities of the provider and service user. The Sitra website, www.sitra.org.uk, has examples of support contracts and agreements and guidance.

Rent, service charges and accommodation charges

14.38 All agreements should inform the resident of the level of rent or accommodation charge, what it pays for and how and when it is increased. Rents are discussed in more detail in chapter 17. In Box 14.7, we identify the Housing Corporation regulatory requirements regarding rents.

Box 14.7 Housing Corporation Regulatory Code and Guidance

3.1b All residents have information about their landlord's rent policy and rent levels across the associations' stock and in the relevant local authority area. All residents have information about their service charges including costs that their charges cover, how charges are budgeted and increases calculated.

In licence agreements the charge for accommodation should not be called rent as this refers to tenancies only. Lawyers can infer that a reference to rent indicates that a tenancy exists, not a licence. A charge for services is usually set out in addition to the rent or accommodation charge. If you are charging for additional services, they should be detailed on a schedule attached to the agreement.

Altering the agreement

14.39 As the case study demonstrates, all organisations need to review the terms of agreements from time to time. This means that it is necessary to include a clause which allows you to vary the terms of the agreement following agreement with the resident. It would be unfair for residents to end up with terms that were quite different from what they had originally agreed – and the law provides some limited protections. One source of protection is the Unfair Terms in Consumer Contract Regulations 1999 (SI 1999 No 2083) (UTCCR), which we discussed in chapter 3. Landlords cannot impose unfair terms on occupiers. We will look at the other unfair terms later in this chapter when we get to residents' responsibilities.

14.40 There is further protection for tenants. Generally, a tenancy can only be varied by the consent of both landlord and tenant. The Housing Act 1985 makes an exception to this rule for secure tenancies, which may be changed unilaterally by the landlord. The landlord must consult with the tenants by sending them a preliminary notice outlining the change and asking for their views. The landlord need only consider these before issuing a formal notice of variation which changes the terms of the secure agreement. However, local authority landlords are constrained in their actions by the requirements of public law which we discussed in chapter 2. The Housing Act 1988 did not make a similar exception for assured tenants, so any variation to the terms of the assured tenancy *must* be signed by the tenant and the landlord to take effect. For licences, there is no such protection; however, our recommendation is that licence holders should be treated the same as tenants as far as is legally possible and therefore we would advise that you seek the agreement of the licensee before you vary a term. In addition, the Office of Fair Trading has argued that a contract term which allowed the landlord of a registered care home to unilaterally change the terms of the contract is unfair. Box 14.8 points you to the Office of Fair Trading Guidance on tenancy terms.

Box 14.8 Office of Fair Trading Guidance

The Office of Fair Trading has issued guidance on unfair tenancy terms, most of which can be applied to licences. The guidance is available from www.oft.gov.uk/advice_and_resources/publications/guidance/unfair-terms-consumer/oft356; telephone: 08457 22 44 99.

Serving of notices

14.41 Lastly, in this section of the agreement, are provisions for notices to be served on the landlord. Most protections available to tenants require them to give notice to their landlord; it is therefore necessary and legally required for tenants to know where to serve such notices. As we explained in chapter 4, section 48 of the Landlord and Tenants Act 1987 applies to tenancy agreements. This first requires every landlord to serve a notice on the tenant giving the landlord's name and address and, secondly, an address where notices can be served. This does not have to be the same as the landlord's address. Including the name and address of the landlord at start of the general terms satisfies the first part of this requirement. To satisfy the second part you should include a term stating where notices should be served. For managing agents this could be the managing agents office; however, commonly the owning RSL's address is the appropriate one, as notices usually refer to the landlord's repairing obligations, which could result in the landlord being taken to court.

14.42 There should also be a term on how notices should be served on the resident. Most terms allow for notices to be validly served if hand-delivered to the premises or sent by first class or registered post. When the resident signs the agreement, he or she is agreeing to this method of service. The resident then cannot use a defence that he or she did not get the notice because he or she was away from the property. Although the term may refer to delivery by post, most providers hand-deliver notices for certainty of service.

Landlord responsibilities

14.43 It is common to outline the obligations of the landlord into sections of the agreement headed 'Landlord responsibilities' and 'Resident's rights'. Landlord responsibilities are usually obligations which include repairs and decorations. Resident's rights usually include complaints, access to information and participation. In an agreement, 'Resident's rights' normally comes after 'Resident's responsibilities'. In general, the landlord's responsibilities fall into three main areas, which are required by law:

- quiet enjoyment – a common law requirement of tenancies;
- repairs and upkeep – statutory obligations upon landlords; and
- provision of services.

14.44 Often, succession to partner or family members is included in this part of the agreement.

Quiet enjoyment

14.45   In legal terms this only applies to tenancy agreements as the concept is associated with that of excusive possession and is a crucial part of the common law understanding of a tenancy. The covenant of quiet enjoyment simply means that if the landlord has granted to the tenant the legal interest in the property, the landlord has given the tenant control over the property. Tenants should be able to enjoy their home without the landlord interfering, for example, by retaining a key and 'popping in'.

14.46   Quiet enjoyment is an obligation only upon the landlord. The concept is often misunderstood as meaning that the landlord should ensure that neighbours do not interfere with a tenant's right to enjoy their property by playing noisy music. Case-law has clarified that it does not cover actions by third parties. This is not to say that in shared or social housing the landlord would not take action if a tenant was experiencing anti-social behaviour from another tenant, but this would be as part of their policy and procedure and not as their landlord obligations. There is a balance to be struck, however, with the covenant of quiet enjoyment and the need to access a tenant's property to provide services. In Box 14.9 our frequently asked question outlines how we manage this balance.

Box 14.9 Frequently asked questions

How do we gain access without a tenant claiming we are interfering with their quiet enjoyment?

A problem arises in balancing the obligation of quiet enjoyment with the requirement to be able to access tenant's accommodation when necessary. Access is sometimes needed for health and safety inspections or to check on an individual's wellbeing. All landlords will require access to a tenant's property at some time, whether it is to repair something or to carry out the annual gas safety check. In the tenancy agreement the responsibility not to interrupt or interfere with a tenant's right to quiet enjoyment can be limited by terms being included in the agreement:

- To allow inspections to take place.
- To enable repairs to be carried out either to the tenants or adjoining property.
- To provide the services detailed in the agreement.

> • In an emergency where immediate repairs need to be
> carried out or there is concern for the health and safety of
> the tenant or others that may be in the property.
>
> We discuss this in more detail in the section on access.

Access

14.47   The landlord should specify how many days notice it will provide of its need for access. It should also make provision for immediate access in an emergency. An emergency can include the immediate need for repair, for example, where there is water pouring into flat or room below the tenants. In shared housing, where there may be a higher duty of care beyond the landlord and tenant relationship, providers walk a tightrope between keeping all tenants safe and respecting their right to enjoy their home in privacy. In such cases providers often insert a clause requiring immediate access if they have reasonable cause for concern about a tenant or another's health and safety. We believe that even with this clause a tenant could claim a breach of quiet enjoyment and would urge providers to exercise caution in this matter. When deciding whether immediate access is required, it is useful to consider why this action is defensible if the tenant claims breach of quiet enjoyment.

14.48   The nature of a licence is contractual – therefore there is no obligation of quiet enjoyment. This does not mean that the licence holder should not be afforded privacy, as the balancing exercise can be problematic – for example, it is inherent in the nature of a licence that the landlord requires 'unfettered access', or the bedroom is shared or there is a requirement for the licence holder to move bedrooms. Most providers adopt a sensible approach which allows the required access but respects privacy. This can be achieved simply by knocking on the resident's door and, if the licence holder objects to access at that moment, rearranging the visit for a more convenient time, if possible. The agreement will still allow for immediate access if required.

Repairs and maintenance

14.49   The responsibility of the landlord in ensuring the property is in good repair and complies with health and safety requirements is discussed in chapter 16. In brief, the occupancy agreement should detail the landlord's maintenance and repair obligations and the expectations of the resident, which will be set out in the resident's obligations.

14.50   The statutory responsibilities of the landlord are dependent on the type of agreement. The Landlord and Tenant Act 1985 imposes an obligation upon the landlord to repair the structure and exterior of a residential tenancy. This cannot be contracted out of. This includes keeping the supply for gas, electricity, water, heating and hot water in working order. This applies only to tenancies and not licences, but, in line with our advice elsewhere, licensees should be afforded the same standard of repairs to their accommodation.

14.51   The landlord responsibilities therefore usually include the structure and exterior of the property and any installations. The responsibility to repair or replace any fixtures, fittings, furniture and household items is dependent upon the nature of the accommodation. Most landlords accept responsibility for external decoration, but the responsibility for internal decoration tends to be dependent upon the nature of the housing. In a temporary shared house, for example, the landlord may agree to decorate communal areas every five years and resident's bedrooms every time they are re-let. We set out good practice for terms relating to repairs and maintenance in Box 14.10.

Box 14.10 Good practice suggestions for terms relating to repairs and maintenance

Repair of structure and exterior
We will keep in good repair the structure and exterior of your home including:

(i)   drains, gutters and external pipes;
(ii)   the roof;
(iii)   outside walls, outside doors, windowsills, window catches, sash cords and window frames including, where necessary, external painting and decorating;
(iv)   internal walls, floors and ceilings, door and door frames, door hinges and skirting boards but not in any case including painting and decoration;
(v)   pathways, steps or other means of access;
(vi)   plasterwork;
(vii)   integral garages and stores;
(viii) boundary walls and fences.

Repair of installations
We will keep in good repair and working order any installations we provide for space heating, water heating and sanitation and for the supply of water, gas and electricity.

> We will endeavour, so far as we are legally able, to maintain the supply of water and electricity and the proper functioning of any other services to the house. We are not liable for any loss or inconvenience caused by the failure or breakdown of any such supply.
>
> *Repairs of fixtures fittings and furniture*
> We will keep in a reasonable state of repair all internal and external fittings, furniture, cooking and washing appliances provided by us.
>
> *External decorations*
> We will keep the exterior of your home in a good state of decoration and normally will decorate these areas once every five years.
>
> *Internal decorations*
> We will keep the interior of your home in a good state of decoration and normally will decorate these areas once every five years.
>
> *Target times for repairs*
> Our priorities and target times for different kinds of repairs are available from staff.

Provision of services

14.52   Where the landlord charges for services such as water rates it has an obligation to pay for and provide those services.

14.53   Landlords usually insure the property and any fixtures, fittings, furniture and household items they provide. Any term on insurance should make clear if it does not cover the resident's personal possessions. In this case the resident should be advised to take out his or her own insurance. This can be a difficult area for residents living in shared housing, as most insurers are reluctant to provide insurance. Insurers who deal with students sometimes offer a service to residents of shared housing.

Succession

14.54   Succession is about the legal right of someone else to take over the tenancy when the person to whom it was granted dies. Succession rights are often confused with assignment, which is when a tenant transfers the agreement to someone else whilst they are still alive. A prerequisite for succession is the death of the tenant. Succession rights only apply to tenancy agreements.

14.55   Succession is a statutory right and landlords do not have to include a term relating to succession in the agreement for it to apply.

14.56   *Secure tenancy* – the Housing Act 1985 sets out the circumstances for succession. There can only be one succession to a secure tenancy. If the deceased tenant had already succeeded to the tenancy, it cannot be passed on to someone else. A secure tenancy can be passed on to the following people:

- Tenant's spouse – if they are living in the property as their only or principal home at the time of death. This includes married couples and civil partners.
- Family members – if they are living in the property as their only or principal home and have resided with the tenant for the 12 months preceding death. Family members include common law husband or wife, parent, grandparent, child, grandchild, brother, sister, uncle, aunt, nephew and niece (including half-blood relations).

14.57   If there is more than one qualifying successor, the spouse takes precedence, but otherwise it is up to the landlord to choose who succeeds if the family do not agree. As the succession is set out in statute this overrides any attempt the tenant may make to will the tenancy to someone else.

14.58   *Assured and assured shorthold tenancies* – succession under the Housing Act 1988 applies to assured periodic tenancies only, not to fixed-term contracts. Succession rights will apply to shorthold assured tenancies that have been periodic from the outset, or are allowed to lapse into periodic on the expiry of a fixed term. The Act provides that on the death of a tenant the periodic tenancy will pass to the tenant's resident spouse or common law partner. This applies only if they were living in the property as their only or principal home at the time of the tenant's death. Refer to Box 14.11 for some key information about succession.

Box 14.11 Key information about succession

- Death (and not assignment) triggers succession rights.
- It includes same sex couples (Civil Partnership Act 2004).
- There can only be one succession.
- Succession overrides any bequest made by the tenant.
- Succession rights are different for secure and assured tenancies.
- Landlords can give contractual rights above the statutory minimum.

14.59   Succession does not involve the creation of a new tenancy, so any rent arrears or notices served on the deceased tenant will apply to the successor.

14.60   Landlords sometimes adopt policies that allow other people to succeed where there is no one qualified to do so in statute. If a term to this effect is included in the tenancy, it becomes a contractual right that someone succeeding can rely on. If there is no such term, the landlord could allow a family member to remain in the property and create a new tenancy. This would mean that any rent arrears or legal action on the previous tenancy could not be enforced.

Survivorship

14.61   This is a common law right and not a statutory one. It applies when a tenant who holds a joint tenancy dies. The tenancy will pass to the surviving tenant(s) and takes precedence over succession. So if two sisters hold a tenancy and one dies, the survivor will become the sole tenant even if the deceased sister had a husband. Survivorship counts as a succession for statutory purposes – thus on the death of the survivor of an assured tenancy there can be no further statutory succession.

14.62   In the next chapter we discuss how to terminate the agreement:

1   in the event of a death when there is no one entitled to succeed; and
2   when the agreement is a licence.

Resident's responsibilities

14.63   This is usually the most expansive area of an occupancy agreement. When reviewing or developing occupancy agreements, you should bear in mind two things:

1   that the terms relating to resident responsibilities must not be unfair contract terms; and
2   the terms should be drafted so that they are enforceable in court.

14.64   Although there is continuing uncertainty about whether the Human Rights Act 1998 applies to RSLs, it is good practice for all providers to adhere to its principles as outlined below.

Human rights and resident responsibilities

14.65   A common term in supported housing occupancy agreements the prohibition of the use of alcohol on the premises. The most common reason given is to prevent the behaviours which are associated with alcohol consumption. This is probably not compatible with the spirit of article 8 of the Human Rights Act 1998. Such a term would interfere with a resident being able to enjoy a glass of wine or beer whilst watching the television, an activity that most of the population would expect to be able to do in their home.

14.66　　This does not mean that any interference with the right to drink alcohol is always in contravention of the Human Rights Act. In some cases it is necessary, legitimate and proportionate to interfere with the rights of one resident to protect other residents or to uphold the aims of the scheme. This is likely to include a term prohibiting alcohol in a 'dry' house for people with alcohol misuse issues. It may also be appropriate to prohibit alcohol in communal areas of a woman's refuge where small children use those areas regularly. See Box 14.12, where we examine compatibility with human rights. In chapter 7 we explain about human rights in more detail.

Box 14.12 Compatibility with human rights

A good test for human rights compatibility is to imagine how you would feel if you had the responsibilities that you are imposing upon the residents. What you think is reasonable may differ dependent upon whether the housing is long or short term. If a provision is restrictive, consider whether it can it be justified to protect other residents, or is it required to achieve the aims of the scheme?

Unfair contract terms

14.67　The Unfair Terms in Consumer Contract Regulations 1999 are based upon the need to protect residents from the inappropriate exercise of power by the landlord. This is because the ultimate sanction of a landlord is the ability to deprive a resident of their accommodation. Providers should ensure that terms do not cause a significant imbalance in the rights and responsibilities of the parties. Terms that have been found unfair in EU cases have included those prohibiting pets or flammable materials. An example of an unfair term on the OFT website is one that required residents to leave a property in a better condition that they found it in.

14.68　　*Pets* – there may be good reasons to require residents only to keep certain types of pet in different types of housing. In shared housing, for example, non-tropical fish or insects that would not cause infestations, for example, stick insects or great African snails. In other cases, providers may allow other pets to be kept but attach certain conditions. These can relate to the keeping of certain pets only where there is access to a garden and the resident has to sign a pet contract. We recognise that keeping pets poses dilemmas for supported housing providers and have signposted you to some guidance in Box 14.13.

Box 14.13 Signpost Guidance on pets in housing

The RSPCA has developed animal welfare guidance and advice for housing providers which takes account of vulnerable service users. The guidance includes formulating a pet's policy and other resources.

RSPCA
Wilberforce Way
Southwater
Horsham
West Sussex RH13 9RS
Tel: 0870 010 1141
Fax 0870 753 0284;
Website: www.rspca.org.uk.

14.69   *Flammable materials* – given the propensity for many items of clothing to be marked 'flammable keep away from fire', a term prohibiting all flammable materials is unreasonable. If providers do not want paraffin gas or electric heaters to be brought into a scheme, the term should specify just that.

14.70   *House rules* – many shared housing schemes have a list of rules that are attached to the occupancy agreement. Sometimes the occupancy agreement contains a term making the resident responsible for adhering to the house rules. The nature of house rules is such that they can change, depending on the demographics of the residents in the scheme at any one time. Staff or residents at a house meeting may change a house rule, possibly by a majority vote at a house meeting. Those residents not at the meeting or not agreeing to the change are, in strict legal terms, having their contract changed without their permission (see the earlier section on altering the agreement). Such a change is likely to be unenforceable.

Enforceability

14.71   There is no point having a term in an agreement if either:

- you do not intend to rely on it; or
- you do not seriously believe the court will give you possession if it is breached.

14.72   For example, a breach of a term that residents have to take part in the communal cleaning rota is unlikely to lead to possession. A term making the resident responsible for adhering to the house rules can also present a problem with enforceability in court. House rules are often a combination of rules relating to how the scheme operates and rules relating to behaviour. Rules relating to preventing serious problems – for example, illegal drug misuse – can be found alongside rules relating to leaving the communal toilet clean or checking the identification of contractors. A judge could query the importance the resident should place on the house rules, even if you are asking for possession for illegal drug misuse. In Box 14.14 we have identified some good practice on house rules. Lastly, some terms would not be enforceable as they rely solely on a subjective interpretation: one we have come across prevented the residents from hanging out unsightly washing. Are you prepared to give evidence in court that the washing was 'unsightly'?

Box 14.14 Good practice on house rules

All the serious and important terms should be contained in the occupancy agreement, for example, illegal drug misuse. The house rules could then become a house agreement that residents develop and agree among themselves. This enables the house agreement to be 'owned' by the people expected to adhere to it, and provides a mechanism through which the agreement can respond to changes in residents and/or their needs.

Possession

14.73   Statutorily protected tenants are expected to take up possession at the start of the tenancy and not to sublet their property. Secure tenants have a statutory right to sublet part of their property, but lose their security of tenure if they sublet the whole. Other types of agreement do not have this statutory right; the landlord can and usually does prohibit residents from subletting, and makes it a condition that residents use the property as their only and principal home.

14.74   Terms should include the length of absence that requires the resident to notify the landlord. This must be a fair term and will depend on the type of service and how often the resident is expected to meet with support staff. In chapter 3, we explain about the requirements of the Unfair Terms in Consumer Contracts Regulations 1999. For example, in a very short-term hostel for young vulnerable people with 24-hour staff cover, staff may want to know if a resident is going to be absent overnight. Alternatively, a permanent scheme, providing lower support in self-contained units for people with physical disabilities, for example, may only require absences of over two weeks to be notified.

14.75   Relating to this is a term that outlines what the landlord will do if a resident has not been seen for a period, and it is believed the resident has abandoned the project. The period of time the resident has not been seen for should be tied in to the period of time the resident can be absent without notifying the landlord.

14.76   *Assignment* – in common law a tenant may assign (hand over) their tenancy to someone else unless the tenancy prohibits it. Given the nature of supported housing, most agreements contain such a prohibition. Because licences are a personal as opposed to a property right, legally a licence cannot be assigned. A secure tenancy can be assigned to a potential successor, or to another tenant, if the tenant wants to exercise his or her right to exchange. All tenancies can be assigned as part of divorce proceedings under the Matrimonial Causes Act 1973.

14.77   The terms of an agreement usually provide for, or prohibit, sharing or lodgers. In secure tenancy agreements the tenant has a right to take in a lodger; in other types of agreements the landlord can decide if it is suitable. In shared housing, landlords usually have a term preventing the resident from having lodgers. This is reasonable for single-person accommodation when the lodger would have to share communal areas with the other residents in the house. In self-contained accommodation this would be more difficult to justify and would be indefensible in permanent housing. Such a term would not be compatible with the Human Rights Act 1998 article 8 *right to respect for private and family life*. If you do not want residents to have someone living with them, you need to carefully consider whether:

- you are justified in interfering with their basic human rights;
- this is a fair term; and
- if you went to court to prevent someone breaching this term, the court would give you possession.

Rent/charge payment

14.78 Residents are expected to pay the rent/charge for the accommodation and the term usually expects this payment be made weekly in advance. This is often confusing for residents when their housing benefit is paid directly to their landlord, four-weeks in arrears. Residents should be clear, however, that there are only two legal relationships in the landlord-resident-housing benefit triangle: see Box 14.15.

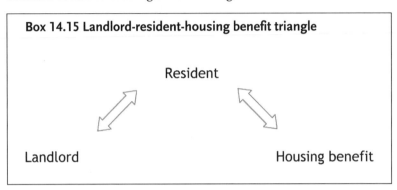

Box 14.15 Landlord-resident-housing benefit triangle

Resident

Landlord   Housing benefit

14.79 It is important to ensure residents are clear that there is not a legal relationship between housing benefit and the landlord. The resident is responsible for payment of the rent for which he or she may be entitled to housing benefit. For periodic agreements, the payment period of the rent, for example, weekly or monthly, denotes a period of the agreement. This is important when serving notices regarding possession or rent increases, which are covered below.

Behaviour

14.80 In most agreements, terms relating to behaviour make up the bulk of residents' responsibilities. The extent to which residents' behaviour impacts on others depends on the nature of the housing. A resident watching television at 4 am would be acceptable in a self-contained house, but not in a shared house. There is now an expectation on social landlords that they do not let their residents behave a way that is anti-social or causes a nuisance to others. You should include terms preventing the resident from causing anti-social behaviour nuisance, racial or other harassment or disruption to others. In Box 14.16 we demonstrate some good practice in relation to terms setting out the behaviour expected from residents.

> **Box 14.16 Good practice**
>
> A term relating to nuisance, anti-social behaviour, harassment or disruption should set out examples of what this can include. This will depend on the nature of the scheme and may include aggressive behaviour, noise nuisance, entering other resident's property without permission, etc. Harassment may include insulting words or gestures, damaging others property, etc. The term should also identify all those who may be affected by the behaviour, including other residents' neighbours, staff and contractors. The terms should be robust enough to manage seriously disruptive and violent behaviour, as well as swearing and telling offensive jokes.
>
> You may want to include a separate clause for noise nuisance, as this often represents the majority of the behaviour that impacts on others. This can include using all noise-making equipment that be heard outside the room, flat or house between certain hours, and can include loud voices.

Visitors

14.81   The issue of visitors presents difficulties for those working or managing housing with care and support. The behaviour of visitors often causes problems, particularly in shared housing. The most simple and effective way of making sure that residents are responsible for their visitors is to include visitors in any term relating to behaviour. An example of a term may be '*you or your visitors must not behave in a way that causes anti-social behaviour or nuisance*'. If the visitor causes a nuisance, the resident has breached their agreement. It is straightforward to explain to the resident that they are responsible for their visitors and their actions. You should make it clear that if a visitor causes a nuisance you will take action against the resident.

14.82   It is not uncommon to find terms in agreements restricting the resident from having overnight visitors, and in some cases, any visitors at all. Restricting a resident from having visitors should be carefully considered, as it is likely to be incompatible with human rights. It may be appropriate to limit the number of visitors and frequency of overnight stays in shared housing.

14.83   Some providers justify restricting visitors on health and safety grounds. In most cases this does not provide sufficient justification. You must always consider whether the restriction is necessary and proportionate. In some supported housing there may be compelling security reasons for restrictions on visitors, for example, in a scheme for women who have been trafficked for the sex trade or in women's refuges.

Health and safety

14.84 There is an expectation that residents should behave in a way that does not endanger their own or other's health and safety. This could include an obligation to leave the building when the fire alarm sounds or a probation on using fire extinguishers. A general term in the occupancy agreement would provide for most unacceptable behaviour. You should then elaborate upon the general term in your health and safety policy and procedure by providing details of what is meant by endangering health and safety. Some providers give detail in their agreement, and include terms, for instance, prohibiting the use of paraffin or portable gas or electric appliances for cooking and heating. Other terms could include allowing the landlord to check all electrical items brought onto the property to ensure they are safe. You may want to incorporate a term which requires that communal areas are kept free from obstacles that may cause an injury or obstruct a fire exit.

14.85 *Smoking* – the right to smoke and the right not to be exposed to passive smoking are contentious issues, and in supported housing these are exacerbated by concerns about fire, health and safety, particularly in shared environments. Box 14.17 summarises the legal position on smoking.

Box 14.17 Smoking ban

From 1 July 2007, under the Health Act 2006 almost all enclosed public places and workplaces in England became smoke free. The relevant regulations (the Smoke-free (Premises and Enforcement) Regulations 2006 (SI 2006 No 3368) and the Smoke-free (Signs) Regulations 2007 (SI 2007 No 923)) in England also came into effect on 1 July 2007.

The Health Act 2006 is public health legislation and the ban is designed to protect the public from the effects of secondhand smoking. There are very few exemptions, but these do include registered care homes. Providers may designate bedrooms or rooms as exempt if they wish – they are not required to do so. Designated rooms must be used only for smoking – and only by service users; they cannot be combined, for example, with a TV or games room. Between 1 July 2007 and 30 June 2008, services that provide residential accommodation for the treatment of those with a mental health condition are also able to designate rooms where smoking is permitted.

Hostels are also able to designate bedrooms for smoking, but no other rooms.

Self-contained supported housing is beyond the scope of the smoke free regulations, which is restricted to public areas. However shared hallways are considered public areas. Employers, however, have a duty of care to reduce workers' exposure to second hand smoking.

Shared supported housing communal areas are regarded as public places so will fall within the scope of the smoke free regulation. All offices would fall under the regulations as a place of work.

'No smoking' signs will need to be placed in a prominent position at every public entrance to 'smoke free' premises. The regulations make requirements as to the wording and size of signs. Local councils will be responsible for enforcing the new law. Employers will be responsible for ensuring that their premises are smoke free. They could be liable for a fine of up to £2,500 if someone is reported smoking. Failure to display a no smoking sign with the required wording in the appropriate place could result in a fine of up to £1,000 for the employer.

For more information about the regulations, visit www.smoke-freeengland.co.uk.

For more information on reducing the risk to staff of second-hand smoking, visit www.rcn.org.uk/publications/pdf/protecting_community_staff_smoke.pdf.

14.86   Most organisations have adopted a smoking policy that identifies areas that are available for smokers and identifies how to smoke responsibly and safely. This need not be detailed in the occupancy agreement. Behaviour such as consistently smoking in communal areas, or not putting out cigarettes properly or in the receptacles provided, should be covered by properly drafted nuisance and health and safety terms.

14.87   *Cleanliness* – for residents in self-contained accommodation, it is their choice as to how tidy and clean they want their home to be. If the lack of cleanliness poses a health and safety hazard or causes a nuisance, the terms in the agreement covering these should prove sufficient protection for the organisation.

14.88   Where residents have to share communal facilities, the issue of cleanliness becomes more relevant as different standards will impact on others. You may feel that a term in the agreement is necessary to enable residents to understand their responsibilities; but it still may be difficult to enforce. In Box 14.18 we identify some good practice on cleanliness.

Box 14.18 Good practice on cleanliness

- If a term is included in the occupancy agreement, it should state that residents clean up after their use of communal areas.
- Communal cleaning rotas should be in the house agreement and agreed to by residents; they are more likely to enforce the rotas than staff.
- Residents should be aware that ability to maintain a level of environmental hygiene is necessary for independent living.
- Explain to residents that if they do not clean, as landlord you have a responsibility to keep communal areas clean. You would have to employ a cleaner, the cost of which would be included in their service charge.

Repairs alterations and damage

14.89 The common law imposes a duty on all tenants to treat the property 'in a tenant like manner', and this includes taking reasonable care of the property. Although this is enshrined in law for tenants, both licence and tenancy agreements should contain a term making the resident responsible for reporting a repair. Terms should also include allowing access for inspections and repairs to be carried out (see earlier in the chapter). Repairs and replacements that result from fair wear and tear by tenants are the responsibility of the landlord, but a term should be included preventing residents or their visitors from causing deliberate or careless damage. The term should outline whether you are going to repair the damage, and expect the resident to reimburse you, or the resident is to make good the damage. If is the former you should give the resident an invoice so they can check the amount; if it is the latter you may want to inspect the 'making good' to ensure has been properly carried out.

Resident's rights

14.90 As explained earlier, landlords' obligations are usually divided into landlord responsibilities and resident's rights. The rights a resident can expect and which are usually contained in the agreement are outlined below:

- The right to be consulted before any changes are made in the housing management or maintenance.
- The right to be provided with information about the agreement and any related policy and procedure.
- The right to complain about the accommodation or services provided or about the landlord's adherence to the agreement.
- The right of access to personal information held under the data protection legislation (we explain about data protection in chapter 19).

Ending the tenancy

14.91 The terms of the agreement should include both the basis upon which the agreement can be terminated and terms setting out notice periods and the process of termination. There should also be a term explaining how the resident can terminate the agreement.

Termination by residents

14.92 The agreement should outline how residents can give notice and what notice period they are expected to give. You can include an additional term explaining what the resident should do when they move out. This term should include how the property is to be left and what will happen to any goods left behind. The Office of Fair Trading has identified that it is an unfair contract term to expect a property to be left in a better condition than when the resident took up residency. In some cases residents are required to agree that the condition of the property was acceptable when they moved in, but they are also obligated to leave the property in a good condition. This is likely to be unfair. We will be discussing termination of agreements and your responsibilities towards former residents' belongings in the next chapter. There should be a term identifying what will happen to any belongings left behind when residents leave, either voluntarily or are evicted. This term should be a reasonable term and not contravene the unfair contract terms regulations.

Box 14.19 Frequently asked questions

Is it reasonable to include a term disposing of residents belongings as soon as they leave?

Some providers state that goods will be disposed of at the end of tenancy through the local authority refuse and recycling services. The reasonableness of this term would take into consideration:

- Whether the tenant had been made aware of this term when they signed up and when they or the landlord terminate the agreement.
- The ability of the landlord to store the former resident's belongings safely and securely.
- Whether the accommodation is permanent or temporary.
- Efforts made in communicating to the resident, while a notice is expiring, what will happen to the goods.

14.93   The reasons that the landlord would terminate the agreement should be linked to the resident's responsibilities outlined in the agreement. In the case of secure and assured (including shorthold) tenancies, the grounds for possessions in the Housing Act should be referred to. In Box 14.20 we have outlined some good practice on terms relating to terminating the agreement. We will be outlining how to terminate agreements and the grounds for possession in the next chapter.

Box 14.20 Good practice

All tenancies
You should identify in all tenancy agreements which grounds for possession you are going to rely on when applying for possession. It is also helpful to give a summary of those grounds as an appendix to the agreement.

Assured shorthold tenancy
You should state in the agreement if you are going to rely on the mandatory ground for possession afforded by serving a section 21 notice requiring possession. You should also state in what circumstances it will be used, for example, if the resident refuses move on accommodation or does not engage with support.

Using the agreement

14.94 The occupancy agreement is often explained and signed when the resident takes up occupancy, then placed in their file. It is then frequently only taken out again if there is a problem or if the landlord is alleging a breach of agreement. The occupancy agreement is a valuable tool for both resident and support provider, and should be introduced at referral stage and referenced, regularly throughout the resident's stay, for example, during house/tenants meetings and key work/support sessions.

Referral stage

14.95 When a referral is made to a scheme, you should explain to the prospective resident:

- what type of agreement is being offered;
- whether it is a licence of a tenancy;
- what the rights and responsibilities of resident are;
- the amount of rent/charge; and
- that it is their responsibility to pay the charge unless there is an agreement that social services will meet the rent/charge (if so, when that agreement may come to an end, for example, for young people leaving care).

14.96 All this information should be repeated at the interview when the main points of the agreement should be discussed with the resident. In Box 14.21 we have outlined the Housing Corporation requirements and good practice.

Box 14.21 Housing Corporation requirements and good practice

- All applicants should be given a copy of the Housing Corporation charter.
- Referral agents should be given a copy of the occupancy agreement so the applicant has time to go through it prior to the interview.
- The main terms of the agreement should be summarised in plain English and translated, produced in Braille, spoken word on tape/CD as required.

Sign up

14.97 You will need two copies of the agreement both to be signed by the resident and you on behalf of or as the landlord. Most schemes have a standard agreement and you will be expected to fill in the details.

Tenancy start date

14.98 If you are granting a periodic tenancy, the start date must be the first day of your rent period – usually a Monday. You cannot allow someone to move in midweek as the tenancy would start from the date they moved in. This will then cause problems when you serve notices and rent increase letters, and they will probably be invalid. This has presented difficulties for providers who have a void room and a homeless person who needs accommodation. In these circumstances providers have:

- Backdated the tenancy to the previous Monday – this is probably fraudulent.
- Not charged rent – this does not negate the tenancy commencing when the resident took up residency, so the problem is not solved.
- Issued a bare licence until the tenancy start date on the Monday – if the resident has exclusive possession it would be deemed a tenancy from when the resident took up occupancy. Again, the problem is not solved.

14.99 The law is rigid in this matter – despite what you may consider to be unfortunate consequences. This problem does not occur with licence agreements, as the strict rules about notice periods and rent increases do not apply. What matters are the terms are set in the agreement.

14.100 You must ensure that the resident is aware that he or she is signing a legally binding agreement and understands the terms. If English is not the resident's first language you may need the agreement translated and an interpreter at the sign up. If someone has literacy needs the agreement can be recorded either onto cassette or CD, or for those with a sensory impairment you could provide a Braille or large print version or a video/DVD of a British Sign Language (BSL) signing of the terms of the agreement. In Box 14.22 we have identified a resource for tenancy agreements that are easy to read.

Box 14.22 Easy to read tenancy agreements

The National Housing Federation has produced some easy to read tenancy and support agreements for those with learning disabilities or who have difficulty reading. It is set out so that the key areas are clearly highlighted, using plain images, short sentences, simple punctuation and no jargon.

National Housing Federation
Lion Court
25 Procter Street
London WC1V 6NY
Tel: 020 7067 1010
Fax: 020 7067 1011
Website: www.housing.org.uk
E-mail: info@housing.org.uk.

14.101   You should go through the agreement verbally, explaining in more detail terms that involve subjective judgments, for example, nuisance and anti-social behaviour. You should make particular reference to the circumstances when the resident may lose their home. In RSL properties residents must be given a Corporation Charter so they know what to expect from their housing association landlord or the managing agent. In Box 14.23 we identify good practice on giving information to (prospective) residents.

Box 14.23 Good practice

You should also be prepared to give residents a summary of the rent arrears procedure, the anti-social behaviour procedure, the complaints procedure and any other related polices and procedures. If possible, you should interview a prospective resident before they take up residency. Ideally, go through the information over a couple of days, so they have time to take everything in. Prospective residents should be able to involve advocates and encouraged to ask questions about the agreement and their rights and responsibilities.

Reinforcing the agreement

14.102   *Supporting People* provides funding to pay for housing-related support. Support should be provided to enable service users to maintain their accommodation. Adhering to the terms of their occupancy agreement is an integral part of this, and you have many opportunities to reinforce the agreement. In shared housing the main terms of the agreement can be included in the agenda of house meetings. In support meetings one of the standard items on your agenda should be to consider how that person is managing the tenancy and the support they need to facilitate this. All this necessitates the occupancy agreement being visible to the residents and not remaining hidden in their files. The agreement should not only appear when it is perceived that a resident has breached a term and further action is required, or there is a complaint about the landlord not adhering to its responsibilities.

Summary

14.103 In this chapter we have introduced you to the occupancy agreement as an important tool in managing supported housing. The occupancy agreement establishes the relationship between the service user and the landlord. It identifies the rights and responsibilities of each party. The type of occupancy agreement which should be issued in your scheme is established by legal principles, regulatory requirements and good practice. Insecurity should not be used as a management tool; you should offer the most secure form of tenure available for the service user. You must not forget that you are dealing with vulnerable people, and their individual rights should be protected within a service as well as in society. The resident's rights and the landlord's obligations contained in the occupancy agreement provide the service users with a legal (contractual) remedy to reinforce their rights. The responsibilities of service users outlined in the occupancy agreement should be fair and allow supported housing schemes to operate without being oppressive. Lastly, the agreement should be referred to throughout the resident's stay. Part of the services provided in supporting housing is supporting residents in exercising their rights under their occupancy agreement and maintaining their responsibilities.

CHAPTER 15

Managing the occupancy agreement

Objectives

15.1   By the end of this chapter you will:

- Understand how to avoid the need for court proceedings
- Know how agreements can be terminated by the landlord
- Understand the different ways residents can terminate their agreement
- Know how to respond to abandonment of the premises
- Understand the legal consequences of the death of the tenant
- Understand your responsibilities for former resident belongings

Case study

15.2   Aurora Housing Project manages a block of studio flats for people with support needs on behalf of Mansion Housing Association, which is registered with the Housing Corporation. The project aims to house people who have previously been 'street homeless'. The service users are referred to Aurora by the local authority homeless person's unit. Residents are given an assured shorthold tenancy and are expected to stay in the project for approximately two years. They are then resettled into independent accommodation. Aurora is experiencing problems with breaches of tenancy as a result of rent arrears, noise nuisance and damage to property. In addition, one of the tenants appears to have abandoned the property. It is a term of the assured shorthold tenancy that tenants must advise Aurora in writing if they are going to be away from their home for a week. The agreement also states that if a tenant has not been seen for a week it will be assumed they have abandoned the tenancy and steps will be taken to recover possession of the property.

Overview

15.3   It is not uncommon for service users to breach their occupancy agreements. This should not be seen as automatically justifying eviction; providers are expected to work with service users to manage these breaches. One of the aims of supported housing is to provide an opportunity for service users to acquire those invaluable life skills which will enable them to achieve social inclusion, such as budgeting skills or identifying and managing unacceptable behaviour. However, in some circumstances breaches will be so significant that providers will have to take steps to terminate the agreement. The complexity of the legal system can mean providers are reticent about enforcing the agreement; the aim of this chapter is to enable you to avoid the legal pitfalls.

15.4   The case study contains a further complication. Aurora is managing the tenancy agreement on behalf of Mansion Housing Association, which is the landlord. Aurora is required to inform Mansion if it wants to take formal action in connection with any tenancy agreement. The legal relationship remains between Mansion (the landlord) and the particular tenant despite the fact that Aurora is performing the housing management services. It is Mansion which will need to be sure that Aurora is taking action within both the legal and the Housing Corporation regulatory frameworks.

15.5   This chapter starts by considering the mechanisms available to service providers to avoid legal action when a tenant breaches their occupancy agreement. We then go on to identify when it is appropriate to initiate legal action and on what grounds the landlord (or its managing agent) can serve a notice of intention to seek possession. There are, of course, two parties to any occupancy agreement, so the chapter also covers the range of actions that may indicate that a resident has terminated his or her agreement. In the latter part of the chapter we will look at how the landlord should terminate an agreement when a resident abandons the property, and what action the landlord needs to take following the death of a resident. The chapter ends with an explanation of what service providers' responsibilities are towards any belongings that have been left behind by a departing tenant.

Breaches of the agreement

15.6   There is both a legal and a regulatory expectation that Aurora should not serve a notice of termination on each and every occasion the occupancy agreement is breached. Aurora must make a judgment and only take immediate action when the behaviour that has led to the breach is serious, perhaps putting the health and safety of workers or other residents at risk. The Housing Corporation, which regulates Mansion, and the courts expect eviction to be the action of last resort. Both the courts and the Housing Corporation would expect Aurora not only to have policies and procedures managing residents' behaviour, but also to follow them. These policies should provide alternative ways to enable residents to resolve any behaviour that constitutes a breach, with support from the landlord or other agencies.

Warnings

15.7   Nearly all providers have a system of warnings that are either formal and codified or informal – in most cases there is a mixture of the two. The problems with an informal system are:

- warnings may be subjective and based on the decision of individual members of staff, who may have widely different views of when and what sanction is appropriate;
- new staff will only be inducted in this area via word of mouth, which will replicate the problems we set out above;
- there is a high risk that residents will not be treated fairly;
- if and when a notice is served on the tenant and the matter comes to court, it would be difficult to demonstrate to the court that eviction has been the last resort as there is no record of previous action.

15.8   Formal warning systems are often written into polices and procedures. In the case study we would expect Aurora to have thought about how it will respond to rent arrears and have set that out in its rent arrears policy – see chapter 17. In general, Aurora should respond to rent arrears while they are at a low level so that the problem can be easily managed and not escalate. Aurora should start with a system of verbal reminders about the obligation to pay rent, which would then lead to visits and formal letters pointing out what has been done to help the tenant deal with their problem and what the next steps will be. Only at this stage should a notice of intention to seek possession be served. Aurora should have similar processes for responding to noise nuisance, and in chapter 20 we discuss some of the formal mechanisms for managing anti-social behaviour. In general, Aurora should identify guidelines or set up a system of warnings that problems need to be dealt with or the tenancy is at risk. It will need to agree:

- what behaviour would attract what type of warning; and
- under what circumstances a final written warning will be given or when immediate service of a notice of intention to seek possession is appropriate.

15.9   There are no 'golden rules' regarding warnings; the rules need to be formulated by each individual organisation. Aurora will need to consider its aims and objectives, the type of occupancy agreement it provides, the terms of the agreement and the nature of the service it provides. We have given an example of types of warnings in the table in Box 15.1. Usually, a resident will first be given a verbal warning and then, if the behaviour does not improve, they will receive a written warning, and so on. There will also be circumstances when it may be appropriate for Aurora at any stage of the process to escalate the process and issue a final written warning or a notice of intention to seek possession.

15.10   Residents can be given warnings about different breaches of the tenancy agreement at different stages of the process. For example, if the resident has had a verbal warning for not paying the rent/charge and then damages the communal TV, you should issue a warning for the damage. Do not progress the warning for the rent arrears as it relates to a breach of a different term. It is good practice that warnings should be removed from the tenant's file after a set period, if the behaviour has not been repeated.

Box 15.1 Warnings guidelines

Warning	Reason	Period on file
Verbal warning	Minor breaches	3 months
1st written warning	If behaviour continues or more serious breaches	6 months
2nd written warning	If behaviour continues or serious breach	6 months
Final written warning	If behaviour continues or major breach	6 months
Notice	If behaviour continues or there is grossly disruptive or violent behaviour	Will differ dependent on agreement used

---

Ending the agreement

15.11   Tenancy agreements are contracts, and there are two parties (resident and landlord) to them. Termination is not only open to the landlord; agreements can be terminated by the resident. In this part of the chapter we deal first with termination by the landlord and then move on to discuss termination by the resident.

Terminating by landlord

15.12   If a resident breaches a term of their agreement, they breach the agreement, and the landlord can take action to repossess the property. In some cases the landlord can still take action to repossess the property even if the tenant has kept to the terms of their agreement. This happens most frequently in the private rented sector, but in the social sector it might happen when the property has been leased from the owner to provide short-life accommodation but the owner needs it back, perhaps for redevelopment purposes. The mechanisms available to the landlord to terminate the agreement depend on the type of agreement used. In the case study tenants have assured shorthold tenancy agreements, but you may work with a different agreement. Below we set out the different mechanisms available depending upon the type of agreement you use. Refer to chapter 4 to check which sort of agreement you use if you are in any doubt.

Secure

15.13   The Housing Act 1985 provides that a secure tenancy agreement can only be ended by court granting a court order. The landlord has to serve the tenant with a notice of seeking possession, which is commonly abbreviated to NOSP (also referred to as a notice of intention to seek possession, NISP or NSP). We have highlighted the characteristics of a NOSP in Box 15.4. The landlord has to prove to the court that there are grounds for possession, and these must be detailed on the NOSP, with an explanation of why these grounds are being relied on. There are therefore two critical stages, the notice stage and the court stage.

Notice

15.14   The notice served on the tenant must provide a date before which the landlord cannot apply to the court for an order of possession; this period between the service of the notice and the date of application to court is referred to as the notice period. The effect of common law and legislation means that for weekly tenancies the notice period must:

- be at least 28 days; and
- expire at the end of a period.

Box 15.2 Frequently asked questions

What is meant by a periods of the tenancy?

In chapter 4 we explain that tenancies can be periodic. A period of a tenancy is simply the length of time each payment of rent covers. In social housing, rent is usually paid weekly, the rent

> falls due on the Monday and applies to that week, which ends on the Sunday. The next Monday the rent falls due again, thus the period of a tenancy is one week. This is particularly important when either the landlord or tenant gives notice, as often the notice has to be a number of periods of the tenancy or expire in the last day of a period of the tenancy.

15.15　For weekly tenancies the landlord should serve the notice before the start of a rent period then allow four full rent periods starting from the following Monday. If the terms of the tenancy allow more than 28 days' notice, you are contractually obliged to follow this. For monthly tenancies, the notice must include a complete period of the tenancy. An example of this is where a monthly tenancy runs from the 5th of a month to the 4th of the next month. The landlord serves a notice on 15 August. The notice would not expire until the last day of a rent period and must be at least 28 days; the landlord would not able to apply to court until after 4 October.

15.16　Note there is an exception to the careful rules on notice periods. When the landlord uses the nuisance ground it can apply to the court for an order for possession immediately.

Grounds to be proved in court

15.17　All the grounds upon which possession of a secure tenancy can be granted are discretionary; this means that even if the landlord proves the ground the judge must consider whether it is reasonable to evict the tenant. You are therefore unlikely to get possession when the breach is minor. We have given you a summary of the grounds for possession in Box 15.3 and included the full text of the grounds in the appendices, together with a sample notice of seeking possession.

Box 15.3 Summary of grounds for possession of a secure tenancy

Requirement for reasonableness

Ground 1	Rent arrears or other breach of tenancy
Ground 2	Nuisance
Ground 2A	Domestic violence
Ground 3	Waste and neglect
Ground 4	Damage to furniture
Ground 5	Misrepresentation

Ground 6	Premium on assignment
Ground 7	Misconduct in tied accommodation
Ground 8	Temporary housing during repairs
Requirement for suitable accommodation and reasonableness	
Ground 9	Overcrowding
Ground 10	Demolition, reconstruction and major works
Ground 11	Charitable landlord
Ground 12	Tied accommodation
Ground 13	Accommodation for disabled persons
Ground 14	Accommodation for special groups
Ground 15	Accommodation for special needs
Ground 16	Under occupation by successor

15.18   The ground of possession commonly used in supported housing is the first ground, when the tenant has failed to pay the rent or has breached a term of the agreement. The court is, however, unlikely to give possession if the breach is minor or the term is unreasonable.

15.19   Ground 2 covers nuisance and domestic violence. We look at nuisance and anti-social behaviour more fully in chapter 20. It is useful to point out here that this ground was amended by the Housing Act 1996 in three ways:

1   It covers acts by visitors as well as tenants and others residing at the premises.
2   It can be used if the nuisance affects others in the locality, for example, staff or floating support workers, not just neighbours.
3   It includes behaviour likely to cause a nuisance – it is not necessary to show that nuisance had been caused when witnesses are too afraid to give evidence

15.20   This ground also allows for possession if the property is being used for immoral or illegal purposes or when an arrestable offence (carrying a sentence of five years or more) has been committed at the property or in the locality. Note that a criminal conviction is required here; it is not sufficient that the tenant has been arrested. Ground 2A, created by the Housing Act 1996, is available only to local authority RSLs or charitable housing trusts. It prevents a violent partner being in sole occupation of a family house following the departure of the victim of violence. This ground can be used even if the tenant is the sole tenant, and there is no need to offer alternative accommodation. This has been a problematic ground because it requires the departing spouse to give evidence that they are not intending to return to the premises, something that for understandable reasons victims of domestic violence are often reluctant to do.

15.21 Grounds 3 and 4 apply when the tenant or anyone living with them has allowed the property to deteriorate or has damaged the furniture provided. Ground 5 allows for possession if the tenant has misrepresented information that led to the landlord granting the tenancy. We will look at this in more detail in the section on assured tenancies as the same ground was inserted by the Housing Act 1996 for both types of tenancies. Ground 11 may be of interest to you if you work with secure tenancies, as it could be used if the successor to a secure tenancy did not meet the aims and objectives of the charity; however, grounds 13, 14 and 15 are more likely to be used.

Assured tenancy

15.22 The process of gaining possession of an assured tenancy is similar to the process for a secure tenancy: a notice of seeking possession must be served on the tenant by the landlord wanting to regain possession. We have set out the characteristics of a notice of seeking possession in Box 15.4. The notice must set out the grounds that the landlord relies on. The mechanisms are also available to landlords using assured shorthold tenancies – see below. The NOSP is often referred to as a 'section 8 notice'. Section 8 simply refers to the section in the Housing Act 1988 that sets out the requirement of the service of a notice. We have included a sample NOSP for an assured tenant in the appendices.

Box 15.4 Notice of seeking possession on secure and assured tenants

- Is in a special form that is laid down by statute.
- Does not end the tenancy – simply warns the tenant that you are going to apply to the court for possession.
- Must inform the tenant the grounds upon which the landlord is applying for possession. You can use as many grounds as you have evidence for.
- Must give enough information to enable the tenant to remedy the problem if they have breached the agreement. It must also provide the tenant with sufficient information to enable

---

> them to defend themselves from the allegations you make. For example, it cannot simply say 'caused a nuisance'; it needs to specify the relevant dates, times and events.
> - Must be validly served on the tenant.
> - It can be served on the property if the tenancy includes a clause enabling this – see chapter 14.
> - Must specify a date before which proceedings must not begin (the notice period).
> - Expires a year from the date it was served.
> - It is good practice to include an explanatory letter in plain English detailing why the NOSP has been served. If appropriate, include what you expect the tenant to do to remedy the situation, for example, 'come to an arrangement to pay off rent arrears in a reasonable amount of time'.
> - It is good practice to include a list of advice agencies, law centres, housing advice centres and/or solicitors.

15.23　The notice period required by law for an assured tenancy depends on the ground used. There are 17 grounds for possession for an assured tenancy agreement and these are set out in Schedule 2 to the Housing Act 1988. Unlike a secure tenancy agreement, where all the grounds are discretionary, there are a number of mandatory grounds for an assured tenancy agreement. This means that if the landlord proves the ground, the judge has to give an outright possession order. In Box 15.5 we have given you a summary of the grounds and the notice periods attached to each ground. It is good practice to exceed the statutory minimum notice and provide 28 days notice. If a term giving 28 days' notice is included in the agreement, it becomes a contractual right. As with secure tenancies where the nuisance ground (for assured tenants ground 14) is being used, the notice can expire as soon as it is served. In this case the landlord can apply to court any time after the service of the notice.

15.24　The notice period must encapsulate complete periods of the tenancy.

15.25　*Worked example* If an organisation with a term in the tenancy giving at least 28 days' notice serves a notice on ground 10 on Wednesday 15 August 2006, it must give four weeks' notice from the following Monday, 20 August, and proceedings cannot commence until after Sunday 15 September 2006.

Box 15.5 Summary of grounds for possession on an assured tenancy

		Notice period
Mandatory grounds		
1	Returning owner occupier	2 months
2	Mortgagee requiring possession	2 months
3	Tenancy proceeded by holiday let	2 weeks
4	Educational institutions	2 weeks
5	Returning minister of religion	2 months
6	Demolition or reconstruction	2 months
7	Death of a tenant (no succession)	2 months
8	Two months' (eight weeks') rent arrears	2 weeks
Discretionary grounds		
9	Suitable alternative accommodation available	2 months
10	Some arrears of rent due	2 weeks
11	Persistent arrears of rent	2 weeks
12	Breach of any other terms of tenancy (not rent)	2 weeks
13	Damage caused by waste, default or neglect of tenant	2 weeks
14	Nuisance; and 14a domestic violence	0 weeks
15	Deterioration of furniture	2 weeks
16	Tied accommodation	2 months
17	False information or misrepresentation	2 weeks

Mandatory grounds

15.26   A mandatory ground means that if the landlord proves the ground, the court has no choice but to grant possession. The court cannot use its discretion to refuse possession if, for instance, it considers that the breach is minor. The only mandatory ground commonly used in supported housing is ground 8. This is available if the tenant has eight weeks (for weekly tenancies) or two months' (for monthly tenancies) arrears at the time of service of the notice and at the date of the court hearing. The ground is about the total rent arrears, and you should not confuse this with (for those in shared housing) the element of the service charge that is not eligible for housing benefit, which usually amounts to £5 or £6. If the rent is £70 per week, of which £5 is ineligible for housing benefit, to use the ground the arrears must be

£560 not £40! Legally this ground can be used even if the arrears are not the fault of the tenant, perhaps because they arose as a result of housing benefit problems. Social landlords are obliged to follow the pre-action protocol for possession on rent arrears (we explain the protocol in chapter 17). The Housing Corporation regulates the use of ground 8 and possession action (we explain its requirements in chapter 10). In reality, most supported housing providers prefer to use the discretionary grounds and it is good practice to do so. It provides tenants with an opportunity to argue their case.

Discretionary grounds

15.27   You are most likely to use the discretionary grounds. Below we set out the circumstances that might be relevant.

15.28   *Suitable alternative accommodation* – this could be used where a tenant's support needs cannot be met by the scheme. As a result, you need the tenant to move from the designated supported housing to either more or less supported accommodation. The accommodation does not have to be available at the time the order is made; the court will accept a certificate from the local authority stating that accommodation will be available at a later given date. If possession is granted, the landlord must pay the tenant's reasonable removal costs.

15.29   *Rent arrears* – there are two discretionary grounds for rent arrears. Ground 10 does not specify an amount of arrears, but requires that arrears exist when the landlord applies to court and when the notice is served. Courts will not usually grant an order if the arrears are under £500. Ground 11 is available when a tenant consistently delays in the payment of rent. It could be used for instance to evict a tenant who only pays when a court date is imminent. We discuss eviction and rent arrears more fully in chapter 17.

15.30   *Deterioration and damage* – ground 13 applies when the tenant has allowed the property to deteriorate owing to neglect, and ground 15 when the tenant has damaged the furniture the landlord has provided.

15.31   *Nuisance* – the ground for nuisance is similar to the ground used for a secure tenancy (see above).

15.32   *Tied accommodation* – in older people's housing there is often residential accommodation available to wardens or support workers. If they hold an assured tenancy and that person ceases to be employed, the landlord has this ground to regain possession.

15.33   *Misrepresentation* – this ground was inserted by the Housing Act 1996 and was designed primarily to allow for possession if a tenant was granted a tenancy following misrepresentations about their status as homeless. The ground covers any false statement, but it has to be a statement and not simply an omission of a fact or information. It applies when the statement was made to a referral agency, which passed the information on to the local authority or the landlord in good faith. Some providers have used this ground to 'encourage' referral agencies to disclose all relevant information regarding their referral. Providers would have to include pertinent questions regarding the applicant's circumstances as omissions will not constitute a breach.

15.34   *Other breaches of tenancy* – ground 12 is the 'catch all' provision. However, as it relies on the judge's discretion, it is unlikely to result in possession on minor breaches or unreasonable terms. Although the requirement to pay rent is a term of the tenancy, this ground cannot be used for rent arrears.

Box 15.6 Frequently asked questions

What do judges take into consideration when exercising their discretion?

As the discretionary grounds rely on the judge's opinion as to whether it is reasonable for you to recover possession, you must be confident that:

- you have evidence to support the ground; and
- it is of a sufficient weight not to be regarded as trivial.

You should also be able to evidence that serving a NOSP is part of your policies and procedures, and that you have carried out other action prior to serving the NOSP to try to resolve the problem. In other words, you should demonstrate that possession is a last resort. The policies and procedure should outline in what circumstances you will use certain grounds. For example, the rent arrears policy and procedure should identify if and when you use ground 8 and ground 11, and at what stage you serve a notice using ground 10. The judge will not only check that your policy is appropriate, he or she will also check that you have followed it fully.

Assured shorthold tenancy

15.35   There are two ways for the landlord to gain possession of an assured shorthold tenancy:

- Assured shorthold tenancies are a type of assured tenancy, and you can serve a notice of seeking possession setting out the grounds following our advice set out above.

- Assured shorthold tenancies have an additional mandatory ground for possession. Landlords can serve a notice requiring possession without providing any reasons or grounds. This is called a section 21 notice because of the section of the Act which provides for this method of termination or is sometimes called a notice of determination. (Determination is another word for termination.) A section 21 notice gives two months' notice of the requirement for possession, and then the landlord gets automatic possession. This, of course, relies on the notice having been filled in correctly – the 'i's must be dotted and the 't's crossed, the notice period must have been calculated correctly and it must be correctly served on the tenant. If the form is correct there is no discretion available to the judge. It does not matter that the tenant has never have breached the agreement and has always paid the rent on time.

15.36　There is a great deal of confusion in the sector about whether to use the section 8 procedure or the section 21 procedure. Solicitors would probably advise you to use the mandatory route as it is simpler and cheaper, and if prepared and served properly will result in possession. The Housing Corporation (we explain about the role of the Housing Corporation in chapter 10) expects that for normal breaches of the tenancy you should serve an NOSP using the grounds for possession. In our case study, when eviction will be based upon non-payment of rent, causing noise nuisance or damaging property, Aurora, after exhausting the alternatives to court proceedings set out in their policies and procedures, should serve an NOSP. This gives the tenant the opportunity to defend their position in court and enables them to see and to test the evidence against them.

15.37　The mandatory ground for possession started by serving a section 21 notice should only be used if the resident's support needs can no longer be met by the scheme. Providers should have a policy and procedure identifying when it is appropriate to serve a section 21 notice and what internal appeal mechanism exists for the tenant. The policy and procedure should include how the process is monitored and controlled by managers and, in the case of managing agents, the owning RSL. In Box 15.7 we have identified good practice to follow before serving a section 21 notice.

Box 15.7 Good practice prior to serving a section 21 notice

- Have the tenant's support needs been reviewed?
- If the tenant has not been engaging with support, has an agreed action plan been in put in place?
- Does the tenant require another type of accommodation, or accommodation with less or more support?
- Has alternative accommodation been identified, or has the tenant refused alternative accommodation?
- Have other agencies involved in the support/care been informed as per the information sharing protocol?
- For managing agents – has the owning RSL been informed?

15.38 We have included a section 21 notice in the appendices. It does not require grounds, so you should include a letter explaining why the notice has been served and include a list of local advice agencies; law centres, citizens' advice bureaux and solicitors who practice legal aid. You will not be expected to demonstrate in court the reasons why a section 21 has been served unless you choose to include them in the court paperwork.

15.39 The most common reason possession actions fail using section 21 notices is because the landlord has miscalculated the length of notice which is required by law. If the notice expires a day too early or a day too late, it is invalid and possession will not be granted.

15.40 The notice period depends on whether it is fixed term (has an end date on the agreement) or periodic (running from week to week). Periodic includes fixed term agreements that have expired and not been renewed. If it is fixed term with over two calendar months to run the section 21 notice *cannot* expire until the end of the fixed term and it expires on the end date stated in the tenancy.

15.41 If it is periodic, it must expire on the last day of a period of the tenancy. The period is established by the frequency of rent payments and the time frame they cover. For example, in RSL accommodation, tenants usually are required to pay their rent every week, covering the period Monday to Sunday. Therefore, the last day of a period (rent week) is the Sunday. For a weekly (Monday to Sunday) periodic assured shorthold tenancy, if a notice was served on a Wednesday, we recommend that you start calculating the notice period from the next Monday's date. You should work out two calendar months from that date then go to the following Sunday for the notice expiry date.

15.42 *Worked example* An organisation uses a periodic tenancy where the period starts on a Monday and ends on a Sunday and the rent falls due on a Monday. If the landlord serves a notice on Wednesday 15 August 2007, it should calculate the notice period from the following Monday, 20 August 2007. The landlord would then calculate two calendar months, which would be 20 October 2007, which is a Saturday and the notice must expire on the last day of a period which is a Sunday. The notice would expire on Sunday 21 October 2007.

Box 15.8 Frequently asked questions

What happens if an assured shorthold tenancy agreements fixed term comes to an end while the section 21 notice period is expiring?

The fixed term assured shorthold tenancy will default into a statutory periodic assured shorthold tenancy when it expires. The notice period must be calculated on the basis that the tenancy is a periodic assured shorthold tenancy and must therefore expire on the last day of a period of that tenancy.

15.43   When the notice expires it does not end the tenancy agreement. The notice merely informs the tenant that you are going to apply to the court requiring the court to give you possession. A section 21 notice has no limits on its 'shelf life', unlike an NOSP; however, courts have indicated it should not be relied on if it was served several years earlier. It is poor practice to have section 21 notices hanging over tenant's heads; you should either proceed to court or withdraw the notice. It may be appropriate to have a notice on file for a period of time, for example, if you want to assess whether a tenant will continue to engage with support. Good practice requires that this time period should be defined; the decision to retain the section 21 notice should be regularly reviewed and should not exceed 12 months.

Protected licences and contractual tenancies

15.44   These agreements have the benefits of the Protection from Eviction Act 1977. To terminate a protected licence or a contractual tenancy, the landlord must serve a notice to quit.

15.45   *Notice to quit* – The notice to quit must comply with the Notice to Quit etc (Prescribed Information) Regulations 1988 (SI 1998 No 2201) in that it must include the following information:

- If the tenant or licensee does not vacate the dwelling, the landlord or licensor must get an order for possession from the court before the tenant or licensee can lawfully be evicted. The landlord or licensor cannot apply for such an order before the notice to quit or notice to determine has run out.

- A tenant or licensee who does not know if he or she has any rights to remain in possession after a notice to quit or a notice to determine runs out can obtain advice from a solicitor. Help with all or part of the cost of legal advice and assistance may be available under the legal aid scheme. He or she should also be able to obtain information from a citizens' advice bureau, a housing aid centre or a rent officer.

15.46 If you do not include the prescribed information, the notice will be invalid. The notice to quit must give a notice period of at least 28 days and it can expire on the last or first day of a period.

15.47 *Worked example* An organisation with a rent week Monday to Sunday which served a notice on Wednesday would have to give four weeks' notice from the following Monday. The notice can then expire on the Sunday or Monday. The notice should include the name and address of the landlord, and the address of the property, be served by the landlord or agent and received by the licence holder or tenant.

15.48 Legally, the notice to quit does not have to include the reasons it has been served. It is good practice to include reasons either on the notice or in the accompanying letter. These reasons should correspond with the terms of the licence agreement that identify the circumstances when the landlord would serve a notice. The accompanying letter should include a list of local advice agencies, law centres, citizens' advice bureaux and solicitors who practice legal aid. We have included a sample notice to quit in the appendices.

Excluded licences and tenancies

15.49 Those licence holders excluded from the Protection from Eviction Act 1977 have only the right to receive reasonable notice under common law. This can be verbal or in writing. There is no legal definition of reasonable notice. This can create a problem if a licence holder challenges the period of notice. The court will examine the period of notice in the light of the reasonable expectations of the licence holder, the nature of the breach and whether they have anywhere else to go. Excluded tenants are entitled in common law to a notice period of at least one period of their tenancy. So if the excluded tenant is given a monthly tenancy, you cannot evict him or her until the month has expired.

15.50 *Worked example* If the rent is paid weekly covering the period Monday to Sunday, a notice served on Wednesday 15 August 2006 would not expire until after Sunday 26 August 2006.

15.51   We have in Box 15.9 included some good practice in giving notice to licensees and tenants who are excluded from the Protection from Eviction Act 1977.

Box 15.9 Good practice for excluded licences and tenants

- It is good practice, although not a legal requirement, to give excluded licence holders and excluded tenants a 28-day notice to quit for normal breaches of the agreement. This would not apply if there is grossly disruptive and violent behaviour or the length of stay would prohibit this. For RSLs, the Housing Corporation expects a 28-day notice to quit in most circumstances.
- The circumstances that the agreement can be brought to an end and the notice a licence holder or excluded tenant can expect should be included in the agreement. These terms then represent contractual rights.
- If the licence holder or excluded tenant will not leave, you should obtain a court order. If you do not do so, you run the risk of committing an offence under the Criminal Law Act 1977. If the agreement is found to be a tenancy with protection, you could have unlawfully evicted the resident.

15.52   If circumstances require less than 28 days' notice, you should serve a notice terminating licence to occupy. We have included a sample in the appendices. While you do not have to include the reasons it has been served, it is good practice to provide reasons either on the notice itself or in the accompanying letter. These reasons should correspond with the terms of the agreement that identify the circumstances when the landlord would serve a notice. The accompanying letter should include a list of local advice agencies, law centres, citizens' advice bureaux and solicitors who practice legal aid. We have included a sample notice to quit in the appendices.

All notices

15.53   The following steps should be taken prior to serving any notice:

- Re-examine the occupancy agreement to establish which term has been breached.
- Establish that there are no problems regarding the occupancy agreement and the particulars set out in it. It is almost certainly too late to discover at any date after the notice has been served,

and especially at the court hearing, that the address on the tenancy agreement is incorrect.

• If any details are incorrect or if the original agreement has been mislaid, contact a solicitor.

• To prepare and serve a notice, it must be established that the person residing at the property:
  – has an occupancy agreement for the property, the possession of which is sought; and
  – the agreement is on the terms claimed by the landlord or its agent.

15.54　In Box 15.10 we provide you with guidelines to follow when serving any type of notice on a resident.

Box 15.10 Serving all notices

• It is not sufficient to serve a notice to a common hallway or post box. The notice should be served on the property. For example, if the tenant has their own bedroom and shares a kitchen and bathroom, it must be put under the door of the tenant's bedroom.

• The best way to serve a notice is to hand it to the resident. The best approach is arrange an interview or meeting with the resident. You can then explain the notice, what it means, what is going to happen next and, most importantly, what the resident can do to remedy the problem. Residents should be advised where they can obtain independent legal advice.

• Interpreters will need to be contacted or the notice translated where the resident may not have English as a first language or where there may be literacy problems.

• There should be one original of the notice that is served on the resident; all other copies should be photocopies of the original.

• Organisations should have polices and procedures that cover who is responsible for signing notices and who should serve them. Usually, managers sign notices and front line staff serve them.

• When serving a notice you will need to include a statement which details the date and time it was served, who served it and how it was served. This is to demonstrate to the court that the notice has been properly served. It is not sufficient to write 'by hand'; you need to state 'by hand under the door', 'in the post box', or 'in the tenants' hand'. We have included a sample statement of service in the appendices.

> • Ensure that your tenancy or licence agreement has a clause
>   stating the various ways in which a notice can be deemed to
>   be served. So, for example, it could state that a notice is
>   deemed to be served if hand-delivered to the premises, or if
>   posted to the tenant's last known address. The landlord or its
>   managing agent only has to prove that the notice has been
>   served, and not that the tenant or licensee has received it.

Termination by the resident

15.55   There are different methods of termination available to residents
depending upon whether they are a tenant or a licensee.

Tenants

15.56   A tenancy agreement represents a legal interest in the accommodation.
When a tenant wants to leave the property they have an obligation to
end or surrender that interest.

15.57   *Notice to quit* – the tenant can terminate the tenancy by serving a
notice to quit and the termination form often represents such a notice.
The notice to quit must:

- be in writing;
- provide at least 28 days' notice, not including the day it is served; and
- expire on the last or first day of a rent period unless there is a term
  in the tenancy, for example, allowing the tenant just to give 28 days'
  notice.

15.58   A notice to quit can be served unilaterally by a joint tenant and will bring
the tenancy of both parties to an end. The only recourse the other
tenant(s) has is to seek an injunction preventing the tenant from serving the notice or getting them to withdraw it within the notice period.

15.59   *Terminations of less than 28 days* – if the landlord accepts a termination that is less than the 28 days stipulated in the tenancy agreement, this is not a notice to quit. The tenant is deemed to have
surrendered the remaining period and assigned it back to the landlord by the agreement of all parties. This will present problems, however, if the tenant wants to move back within 28 days of the surrender.
Legal advice indicates that the tenant might still have a claim on the
accommodation. If you accept less than 28 days' notice, you need to be
aware that if you re-let the room the tenant can claim unlawful eviction.
You are working with vulnerable people who may act before they have

fully considered the consequences of their decisions, and a court is likely to take this into consideration in deciding how to treat your acceptance of the surrender.

15.60 There are two ways in which a tenancy can be surrendered.

15.61 *Strict legal surrender* – the tenant serves a deed on the landlord surrendering their interest. This is often known as a termination form or document. The document has to be received by the landlord or its agent, state the full address of the property, the tenant's intention to end the tenancy and be signed by the tenant or their 'guardian'. This is often used where the tenant gives less than 28 days' notice – however, see above for the problems that are associated with this.

15.62 *Surrender by operation of law* – case-law has developed over recent years to establish a type of 'implied surrender' of tenancy. Tenants can surrender a tenancy by performing an 'unequivocal act of surrender'. The tenancy is then deemed to have ended by operation of law.

15.63 The difficulty is that each determination of surrender is decided on the circumstances of the individual case. Examples include returning keys, or sending a letter that does not have the elements of a formal deed of surrender or removing all possessions from the property. Most organisations, however, treat this as abandonment, which we cover in the next part of this chapter.

15.64 There is an element of risk in repossessing a property without a strict legal surrender. Landlords have to balance the likelihood of a tenant claiming unlawful eviction with the need to fill voids and minimise rent arrears.

15.65 Organisations can protect themselves by having a clause in the tenancy which explains termination procedures and by adopting clear policies, procedures and practices that are applied consistently across the organisation.

Licences

15.66 Although licence holders do not have a legal interest in the property, they do have a contractual interest. Licence holders are obliged to bring that contractual interest to an end if they wish to leave the property. In the case of protected licences, the licence holder must give a 28-day notice to quit (see above). In the case of excluded licences, the agreement should specify how the notice is to be terminated and what notice period should be given.

> **Box 15.11 Frequently asked questions**
>
> **Can a tenant or licensee change their mind within the notice period and withdraw their notice?**
>
> Within the 28 days the tenant can withdraw the notice to quit and remain in the accommodation. This is particularly important if the tenant has moved out and wants to move back in again within the period. The tenant is able to move back into the property and withdraw the notice. If a licence holder wants to give less notice, in the case of a protected licence it could be interpreted that the licence holder has assigned the rest of their contractual interest to the landlord. For excluded licences the licence holder can, with consent, vary the term of the agreement to enable them to give less notice. If you accept less notice than 28 days or the period defined in the agreement, you are taking the risk that the tenant/licence holder could come back within the notice period. If you have re-let the room, the tenant/licence holder could claim unlawful eviction.

Abandonment

The legal concept of abandonment

15.67   An established principle of English law is that all goods and property are owned by someone. Ownership only ends when both the owner gives up the title to the goods and someone else receives lawful possession. In common law, abandonment is the voluntary giving up of those rights of ownership of goods or of occupation of land.

15.68   Tenants who abandon their homes will lose their security of tenure; a tenant relinquishing their occupation will result in their landlord automatically gaining possession. The safeguards of statutory protection do not apply because these rely on the tenant continuing to occupy the premises as his or her only or principal home. However, because the tenant has not formally renounced his or her interest in the property, he or she still has the benefit of a common law tenancy which the landlord must end by service of a notice to quit.

15.69   The common law understanding of abandonment is different from the ordinary meaning of the word. Abandonment in common law does not simply mean ceasing to be present in the property. Even after a prolonged absence a tenant can contest the presumption of abandonment if he or she can establish both:

- *an intention to return to the premises;* and
- *some physical evidence of that intention.* Physical evidence may be provided by the presence of a friend staying in the property to look after it or by the presence of furniture or personal items at the property.

15.70 The courts' approach to abandonment is demonstrated by the two contrasting cases in Box 15.12.

Box 15.12 Courts approach to abandonment

In *Brown v Brash* [1948] 2 KB 247, the plaintiff, a statutory tenant, had been sent to prison for two years. Although his family initially remained in the plaintiff's home with the intention of maintaining his tenancy, after a few months they left, taking with them all of the plaintiff's furniture except for three items. On release from prison the plaintiff sought to recover possession. The Court of Appeal decided that the plaintiff had ceased to possess the premises and therefore to enjoy the protection of the Rent Acts when his family left, and nothing which happened after that date could restore his possession or statutory status. There was no longer sufficient physical evidence of his intention to return to the property.

In *Crawley Borough Council v Sawyer* (1988) 20 HLR 98, the tenant went to live with his girlfriend in 1985. The electricity to the flat was cut off in June of that year and the gas the following year. In May 1986 the landlord was told that the premises were vacant. In July 1986 the tenant told the landlord that he was living with his girlfriend and that they intended to purchase her home. On August 29 1986 the authority gave the tenant notice to quit expiring on September 30. By that time the tenant and his girlfriend had broken up. He returned to the premises in October 1986. The judge found that during the period of the tenant's absence he had paid the rent and the rates, visited the premises once a month and at some time had spent a week at the premises. The tenant gave evidence that he had not abandoned the premises and had every intention of returning to them. The judge in the county court found that at all times the premises were the tenant's principal home. The Court of Appeal upheld his decision.

15.71 Abandonment can take many forms and often causes problems for all social housing providers. Some residents remove all their belongings, while others just appear to stay at the property less and less often. In the case study, Aurora may have the impression that the resident is never there. When the workers enter the flat they may note some belongings left in the room. The worker may notice that mail is piling up, but occasionally it is removed. Whenever there is some evidence that the resident is occasionally returning to the project, every attempt should be made to contact them and investigate the situation.

15.72 When new residents sign up to the occupancy agreement, Aurora should point out the clause obliging residents to inform it if they intend to be away from the project for over seven days. This would have to be a fair term, which would depend on how often the resident is expected to meet with the support worker. We explain about the terms of occupancy agreements in chapter 14. Residents also need to be reminded that they are responsible for paying rent/accommodation charges until they formally end their agreement. This is also an appropriate time to inform residents what will happen to any belongings they leave behind at the end of the tenancy.

15.73 When Aurora first suspects that a resident has abandoned their property, it is good practice to send a letter asking the resident to get in touch.

15.74 The letter should state that if the resident does not contact Aurora by a particular date, it will assume that the resident has abandoned the property and will take action to repossess the property. The period of time given to respond should be the same amount of time they are able to be away from the property without being required to inform the landlord. In our case study the period was seven days. If there is no clause in the agreement, the period should be at least seven days – or the rent period, whichever is longer.

15.75 There is no guaranteed risk-free way to deal with apparent abandonment. One of the risks is that the resident reappears. He or she may say they have been away on holiday, or helping someone out with an emergency. If Aurora has let the property to a new resident the resident can claim unlawful eviction. The action will be taken against the landlord – in our case study that would be Mansion Housing Association. Each case will be decided on its own circumstances and the courts have at times been very sympathetic to tenants. Whenever you deal with abandonment, we think it is helpful to imagine explaining in court why you thought it was reasonable to assume the property had been abandoned. How convincing do you believe your justification is? In Box 15.13 we identify what you would consider to provide evidence that the property has been abandoned. You will need to consider whether what you find supports your presumption of abandonment.

Box 15.13 Evidence of abandonment

- Are there any possessions in the rooms?
- Do they include personal possessions – toiletries, toothbrush, deodorant, razor, etc?
- Take photos of the property and the possessions in the property and put these on the resident's file, together with an inventory.
- Has the mail been collected? If not, when was the last time it was? Look at the date stamps on the letters and record them.
- Look in the dustbin – has it been used since the last time rubbish was collected?
- Do the other residents think that that property has been abandoned? Would they be prepared to sign a witness statement?
- Are benefits still being claimed from this address for the resident? The Benefits Agency will sometimes let you know, although it will not let you know where the person is now claiming from.
- Is the rent being paid? Note, however, that if housing benefit is being paid direct it may take some time to find out if the circumstances of the claim have changed. Remember also that under housing benefit regulations claimants are entitled to be away from their home for 13 weeks in any one year.

15.76 Assured or secure tenants who are not occupying their property as their *only or principal home* lose their assured/secure status and only have a common law tenancy. Therefore you should serve a 28-day notice to quit. For licence holders who have a protected licence, you should also serve a 28-day notice to quit. Excluded licences should have a term in the agreement detailing what notice will be given if the resident is believed to have abandoned. If there is no clause, serve a 28-day notice to quit.

15.77 In all cases serve a clear, covering letter explaining why the notice has been served. Aurora should ask the resident to get into touch with a named worker as soon as possible to confirm that they are living at the property. The letter should remind residents that they are in danger of losing their home if they do not respond within the notice period.

15.78   Do not pin notices or letters on the outside of the house, or flat or room door as this is a breach of confidentiality: the notice could be removed by other people in the project and it invites squatting. You can push notices under the door, but be careful they do not disappear under the carpet! If the agreement allows access to the property in the event of suspected abandonment, place the notice and the letter prominently in the room, or pin them on the inside of the room door. Have a witness with you when you serve the notice, and prepare a statement of service which you and the witness should sign. Keep a copy of the notice and statement on file. You should send a copy of the notice and the covering letter to anywhere you believe the resident may be or may visit, which can include any 'next of kin' address given on their referral form or their social worker. This should be addressed to them and marked 'private and confidential'. During the notice period you should make every attempt to find the resident by contacting their family or friends (if known), other agencies involved in their support or care, hospitals, prisons, probation, police custody and places of worship.

15.79   If the resident contacts Aurora, it will be able to investigate where the resident has been been, whether the resident has particular problems and/or whether they need a transfer. Most importantly, Aurora must ascertain whether or not the resident is occupying the property as their only or principal home. If the resident contacts either Aurora or the landlord to claim that they are still living there, Aurora *must not* proceed with the abandonment. In this case, Aurora would have the option of proceeding to court if the resident is not using the property as their only or principal home, or alternatively the resident could terminate their agreement. In Box 15.14 we identify what you should do if a resident comes back.

Box 15.14 What to do if a resident comes back

If a resident has not terminated their tenancy by serving the required notice or has abandoned the property, there is the possibility that they may come back and want to move aback in. If you have let the property or do not want them to come back, they may claim unlawful eviction. You should:

- Explain why you have taken the action and advise them of their entitlement to, and from whom they can get, legal advice.

- If the property is vacant you should consider allowing them to move back in; you will need to take into account the reasons they have given for their absence.
- If you have another vacancy you should consider offering them that tenancy. If they take an action for unlawful eviction any damages will include an amount to compensate the person for being homeless. If you can accommodate them, this will reduce your liability.
- If you do not have a vacancy ensure the person is accommodated elsewhere by contacting the local authority homeless persons unit or other agencies.
- If you can accommodate the person, this will not prevent you from formally terminating their occupancy agreement or defending a case of unlawful eviction.

Termination through death

Tenancy

15.80 In the previous chapter we dealt with the death of the tenant when there was a potential successor to the tenancy. The death of a tenant without a successor does not end the tenancy, which will form part of the tenant's estate. Secure tenancies will, however, lose their secure status and can be ended by serving a notice to quit. Assured tenancies are slightly different. If an assured tenancy has been willed to someone who has no succession rights, but occupies the property as their only or principal home, the tenancy remains assured. In this situation the landlord will have to rely on ground 7 of Schedule 2 to the Housing Act 1988. This ground allows for mandatory possession if a notice is served within 12 months of the tenant's death. If there is no inheriting person (or they are not living in the property as their only principal home), you must serve a notice to quit.

15.81 A notice to quit should be served on the beneficiary of the will, the tenant's executor or, if there is no executor or beneficiary, the Official Solicitor and Public Trustee at 81 Chancery Lane, London WC2A 1EE (telephone: 0207 911 7100). This will be the normal case for people living in supported housing. The notice to quit should also be sent to the late tenant's representatives at his or her last known address (usually the address of the property).

15.82　The tenancy can, however, contain an appropriately worded clause that allows for the tenancy to be terminated following the death of the tenant by serving a notice to quit on the property.

Licences

15.83　The situation is not the same for licences as these are merely personal permission for the individual to stay on the premises. Once the individual dies, the permission to reside dies with them.

Former resident belongings

15.84　If the tenancy or licence agreement has a clause giving you authority to dispose of any belongings left behind, once the tenancy is terminated you can arrange for their disposal or removal in line with the clause. Otherwise you need to proceed with caution.

15.85　Local authorities are subject to the Local Government (Miscellaneous Provisions) Act 1982 s41:

- The council is allowed to dispose immediately belongings that it would be unreasonably expensive or inconvenient to store or belongings that are perishable.
- The council has to serve a notice on the tenant to collect the goods. If belongings are not collected within one month, the council becomes the owner and can dispose of them.
- If the council has made inquiries before it took possession of the belongings and the resident or owner cannot be found, it can dispose of the belongings after a month.
- If the council only makes inquiries after it has taken possession of the belongings and the owner cannot be found, it must keep the belongings for six months before disposing of them.

15.86　All other landlords are obliged to follow the Tort (Interference with Goods) Act 1977:

- If reasonable efforts fail to trace resident, you are entitled to sell the goods.
- If the resident is traced, you must serve notice of collection details and storage costs. The notice must give a reasonable period for the tenant to collect the goods, after which time goods can be disposed of.

- Any monies obtained from sale can be used to offset the storage costs and credited to the resident's rent/charges account.
- Perishable goods can be disposed of immediately but should be recorded.

15.87 You should keep full and clear records of all action taken in relation to former resident's belongings. This will help you demonstrate that your organisation has acted reasonably. You should also be consistent in your practice. If you agree in the tenancy agreement to keep belongings for four weeks but in practice keep them for two weeks, a former resident would be justified in feeling aggrieved to find their belongings disposed of before the end of the two-week period. In Box 15.15 we have identified some guidelines on disposal of former residents' belongings. Remember, any passports or benefit books should not be disposed of, but returned to the issuing office, and any post received for the former tenant should be returned to the sender.

Box 15.15 Guidelines on disposal of a former resident's belongings

- Include a clause in the occupancy agreement regarding the disposal of ex-residents belongings.
- Ensure all termination forms have a forwarding address.
- Provide an incentive for residents to leave their property clear – for example, £20 of supermarket vouchers.
- Photograph all belongings and make an inventory that is signed by two members of staff.
- If you find any photos and personal papers, keep them in the resident's file/archive.
- Make it clear to the resident that they are responsible for removing all their belongings from the property. Make sure residents understand what will happen to any belongings left behind as soon as you know that they intend to leave.
- If a resident has apparently abandoned the property, any attempts to contact the resident should detail what will happen to any belongings when the notice to quit expires.
- Try to contact the resident using information on the referral application form, or the next of kin, and contact other agencies, for example, social services, probation services, prison service, etc.

Summary

15.88   In this chapter we have explained the myriad of ways a tenancy may be terminated. We reiterate throughout this book that terminating the occupancy agreement by the landlord should be a last resort. Landlords can use informal tools to manage inappropriate behaviour, and warnings provide a valuable opportunity to identify breaches of the agreement for service users. We do, however, recognise that in some instances serving a notice of seeking possession is appropriate. Supported housing landlords must follow due process of the law and conform to regulatory requirements and good practice. Serving a notice is the first formal step in the process which deprives service users of their home, so it is a step which requires careful consideration. The majority of service users will make their own decision to terminate their occupancy agreements, for instance, in leaving temporary housing to move to independent living in permanent accommodation. Service users also have responsibilities to terminate their agreement in accordance with the law. Great care is required to ensure that those with support needs do not inadvertently terminate their occupancy agreement. You should exercise caution in dealing with circumstances which look superficially like surrender or abandonment and ensure you do not deprive a service user of their home. Not only would that be inappropriate, but you would face the possibility of legal action as a result of unlawful eviction.

Managing the property

Objectives

16.1   By the end of the chapter you will:

- Understand in outline the statutory and common law responsibilities for disrepair
- Appreciate the public law responsibilities for health and safety, in particular, statutory nuisance, the Housing Health and Safety Rating System (HHSRS) and the significance of health and safety law
- Have an awareness of the role of the environmental health officer
- Understand how to assess the health and safety risks arising from the property

Case study

16.2   Starlight manages accommodation for young, pregnant women and mothers on behalf of Zest Housing Association, a registered social landlord. The women have exclusive occupation of studio flats which are equipped with kitchenettes; they also share facilities, including bathrooms and laundry. The accommodation has been acquired on a long leasehold from the freeholder, who lives next door. The newly appointed manager has noted that over the last three months the accident book and maintenance log has included the following:

1   A resident has fallen down the steep flight of stairs that leads to the laundry room in the basement. The resident, who was carrying a full laundry basket, experienced some bruising to her back.

2   A resident fell over a small, derelict wall separating the house from the freeholder's property whilst returning from a party late at night. The resident fractured her ankle, which was treated by the hospital the next morning. The resident had not sought first aid immediately as she said she had been drinking alcohol and did not realise the extent of her injury until the next morning.

3   The toilet in one of the bathrooms was blocked up with sanitary towels on three occasions as there are no disposal units in the shared bathrooms. There is some evidence that the toilet in another of the bathrooms has leaked on several occasions. The gas central heating is an old system and, in particular, the boiler takes a long time to heat up water for the bathrooms.

4   There have been several complaints about the standard of kitchen facilities provided in the studio flats – in particular, service users

have complained that the work surfaces are worn and need replacing.

5   There is an ongoing infestation of mice. The freeholder next door has complained that the infestation has spread to his property because Starlight is not addressing the problem.

Overview

16.3   This case study illustrates, perhaps in exaggerated form, the everyday realities of property management. In this chapter we consider the legal obligations for supported housing providers in connection with the physical condition of the property and the health and safety of the residents. We begin the chapter by outlining the private law obligations arising from the legal arrangement between the provider and the service user. There are extra obligations imposed upon landlords when the occupiers are tenants as opposed to licences. We then go on to discuss the public health obligations and outline the important changes to the law which have resulted from the implementation of the Housing Health and Safety Rating System (HHSRS) in the Housing Act 2004. Finally, we discuss the importance of health and safety legislation and your responsibilities to your employees and other people who use your premises.

The private law obligations to repair property

16.4   In private law, that is contract and tort, an occupier of a property, whether a licensee or a tenant, is entitled to a certain standard of repair from their landlord. If you are a managing agent, your responsibilities will depend on the nature of your agreement with the landlord. For the sake of simplicity in this chapter, when we refer to 'you' we mean your role as the landlord of the premises.

Contract

16.5   The contract is your first port of call in order to check the extent of your repairing obligations towards a service user. So the first step for the newly appointed manager in our case study is to check the terms of the contract with the residents.

16.6   If you manage the property on behalf of a registered social landlord (RSL) or a local authority, you will also need to look at the managing agreement, also a contract, between your organisation and the landlord. The managing agreement will set out those maintenance obligations which remain the responsibility of the owning landlord and those obligations that the managing agent has agreed to take on.

16.7   If the property is long leasehold, you also have a contractual relationship with the freeholder. It is very likely that the lease includes a covenant which states that you must not cause nuisance or annoyance to neighbouring properties. You must read the lease, which is the contract document. If you are in breach of the covenant you risk enforcement action by the freeholder which could, in extreme circumstances, result in him or her requiring you to forfeit the lease. If the freeholder threatens such action, you must take legal advice immediately. Starlight is likely to have breached any nuisance covenant by allowing the neighbouring properties to be infested with mice.

Statutorily implied terms

16.8   Contracts between landlords and occupiers have generally provided only for minimal standards of repair. Parliament has intervened in the relationship to impose certain terms in relation to disrepair. Sections 11 and 13 of the Landlord and Tenant Act 1985 set out the statutory obligations of the landlord to tenants. These obligations do not apply to licensees. A licensee can insist only on such repairs as are included in the agreed licence. As Starlight's service users are tenants, the Landlord and Tenant Act 1985 will apply. This means that Starlight must keep in repair the structure and exterior of the residential premises, which includes drains, gutters, and pipes. Starlight is also responsible for keeping in working order the supply of gas, electricity and water, and any appliances for heating and water heating. Additionally, it must ensure the sanitation facilities are in working order – lavatories, sinks, baths and showers. In the case study, the disrepair which is most likely to be caught by section 11 is the leaking toilet. It is a sanitary installation and as such must be kept in repair. The tenant is responsible for internal decoration. But if the need to redecorate is the result of the landlord's repairs, the landlord, not the tenant, must carry this out. In the case study, it is likely that the landlord has kept responsibility for internal decoration as this is the normal arrangement in short-term lettings.

Box 16.1 Frequently asked questions

Can a landlord avoid the statutory responsibilities to repair by excluding them from the agreement or by getting the tenant to agree not to enforce their rights?

A landlord cannot escape these obligations; they are statutory, and cannot be written out of a tenancy agreement for residential premises (unless it is for a fixed term of at least seven years).

16.9   The landlord must be allowed reasonable access to the property from time to time, both to inspect and to repair. The landlord should give the tenant notice of its intention to inspect, and should require access only during reasonable hours.

Limits on the obligations

16.10   The landlord is not obliged to repair damage caused by the tenant, unless the damage amounts to no more than normal wear and tear. More importantly, a landlord's duty to repair does not arise until it knows of the defects. This requirement is usually described as the landlord having to have 'notice' of the disrepair. However, as soon as complaints are recorded in an incident book – as in the case study – this means that the landlord is aware of them. There are other restrictions on the operation of the statutorily implied terms: courts will not order landlords to carry out repairs which are disproportionate to the value of the property or to a standard that is higher than the current standards of the locality. Since the obligations are implied in the contract, visitors injured as a result of disrepair are not able to sue, because they are not parties to the contract.

The definition of disrepair

16.11   Sections 11 and 13 of the Landlord and Tenant Act 1985 do not require the landlord to improve property, but to repair it. Frequently, a landlord can defend a repairs case by showing, for example, that serious damp is a design fault and not a disrepair matter. In the case study, the fact that the kitchen work surfaces are worn and need replacement probably does not count as a need for repair. The old boiler, despite being an appliance for water heating, may well not be in disrepair, but in need of modernisation. It is therefore not necessarily within the ambit of section 11.

Suing the landlord

16.12   These repairing obligations are implied in the contractual relationship between landlord and tenant. Therefore, a failure to carry out the repair is a breach of contract, for which the tenant can sue. Damages may include the cost of putting the premises right, if the tenant has had to do this, and may also include resulting losses, such as damage to clothing and furniture, additional heating costs and compensation for health effects and inconvenience.

Statutory tort

16.13   As well as contractual obligations towards your service users, you have, in certain circumstances, a duty of care towards them and their visitors. In particular, section 4 of the Defective Premises Act 1972 requires that you keep the property in a safe condition. In this Act, it does not matter whether the injury or damage to your service user was caused by disrepair or bad design. You must make the premises safe if you know or ought to have known of the defect. If you have a resident manager, or you have put a term into the contract granting yourself permission to inspect the property, then you will be presumed to have known about the defect, even if you have not been specifically informed. The accident book provides clear evidence of your knowledge. The type of defects which may give rise to breach of section 4 are the derelict wall and the steep staircase. In each case the service user has suffered injury and may sue for damages. It may be that the service user was drunk and contributed to her own injury, but this is unlikely to allow Starlight to escape liability completely.

Tort

16.14   The common law of tort of negligence may also provide a remedy to an occupier or a visitor who suffers injury or damage to goods as a result of disrepair. The tort of negligence applies only where the landlord owes a duty of care to the occupier. The common law does not impose a duty of care on a landlord normally, but where the landlord was the builder or designer of the property, then the duty of care will arise.

16.15   It is also likely that when the landlord provides support services to users then it will have a duty of care to those service users. This is quite different from the normal landlord and tenant relationship, when there is an assumption that the tenants operate autonomously from the landlord. Note that the duty of care is as likely to arise when the occupiers are licensees as when they are tenants. The occupier does have to show that there has been a breach of the duty of care and that the damage suffered was foreseeable. Once the occupier has shown there is a duty of care, it is relatively straightforward in most circumstances to overcome the other legal hurdles. It is likely that any injury caused by the derelict wall or the steep staircase will give rise to a claim for damages in tort by a service user against Starlight.

Public health

Statutory nuisance

16.16   There are other ways of making a landlord maintain property to an acceptable standard. A local authority can prosecute a landlord for statutory nuisance under the Environmental Protection Act 1990 s82. A statutory nuisance exists when residential premises are a danger to the health of the occupants. If a landlord is convicted, the court has a power and, unless there is a good reason to the contrary, an obligation to make a compensation order to the occupiers. Conditions in the property which cause a risk to health should be treated as a priority for action. Otherwise you run the risk of a criminal prosecution. In our case study, both the sanitary conditions and the mice infestation could be statutory nuisances.

Housing Health and Safety Rating System

16.17   The Housing Health and Safety Rating System (HHSRS), introduced by the Housing Act 2004, is a method for identifying faults in residential premises and of evaluating the potential effect of those faults on the health and safety of the occupiers or visitors. It is based upon the principle that residential premises should provide a safe and healthy environment for any potential occupier or visitor. It replaces the fitness for human habitation provisions of the Housing Act 1985. Local housing authorities are obliged to consider the housing conditions in their area on an annual basis, and obliged to inspect a premises if they receive a complaint from a Justice of the Peace (JP). It is probable that the statute also requires the local housing authority to inspect a premises if it receives a complaint from an advice centre or a lawyer.

16.18   The HHSRS is a risk assessment exercise which is carried out by local authorities to enable them to make informed decisions about enforcement action in relation to any risk to health disclosed by an inspection of property. It identifies potential housing hazards, such as the risk of structural collapse of the building, the risk of entry by intruders and the risk of contamination of water supply. The categories of hazards include a group that focuses on protection against infection. In our case study, there are potential hazards arising from pests, refuse, personal hygiene and sanitation. Another group of hazards focuses on protection against accidents. Again, our case study reveals a number of hazards, in particular, the steep staircase and the derelict wall, which suggest a risk of harm to occupiers.

16.19   Once an environmental health officer has inspected the property and identified the potential hazards, he or she will assess the risks posed by these hazards on the basis of the likelihood of an occurrence within the next 12 months that could cause harm and the probable severity of the outcome, if it did happen. The probable severity of harm is classified as either extreme (for example, death), severe (for example, asthma), serious (chronic severe stress, etc) or moderate (for example, severe bruising), and weighted accordingly. The hazard score is then calculated and categorised as either a category 1 hazard or a category 2 hazard. The local housing authority must take appropriate enforcement action if it considers that a category 1 hazard exists in any premises. When a category 2 hazard exists, there is no statutory duty on the housing authority, but only a power to take action.

16.20   We would argue that the hazards in Starlight's premises may well be found to be category 1 hazards. There is likely to be a high risk of serious or severe harm arising to a pregnant woman, for instance, from a fall down steep stairs, or a high risk of infection caught by a young child caused by inadequate sanitary disposal facilities.

Box 16.2 Frequently asked questions

We provide floating support to a service user in private accommodation. What enforcement action can the local authority take if it identifies a category 1 hazard? Can it board up his home as unfit to live in?

The type of enforcement action available to the local housing authority is very wide. It could indeed include prohibiting the occupation of the property, or, as in the case study, the demolition of the wall or the installation of proper sanitary facilities.

Statutory regulations

16.21   A number of regulations impose responsibilities upon landlords, which are enforced by the Health and Safety Executive.

16.22   The Gas Safety (Installation and Use) Regulations 1998 (SI 1998 No 2451) require landlords to maintain gas fittings and flues provided by the landlord in a safe condition. An annual gas safety check must be carried out on each gas appliance and flue by a CORGI-registered installer. All furniture and furnishings provided by a landlord must satisfy the Furniture and Furnishings (Fire) (Safety) Regulations 1988 (SI 1998 No 1324). The regulations cover upholstered furniture, mattresses, cushions and pillows, but exclude carpets, curtains and duvets.

Box 16.3 Heath and Safety Executive

The Health and Safety Executive has information available. Its address is:

Caerphilly Business Park
Caerphilly CF83 3GG
Tel: 0845 345 0055
Mincom: 0845 4089577
Fax: 0845408 9566
E-mail: hse.infoline@natbrit.com
Website: www.hse.gov.uk

16.23   The Regulatory Reform (Fire Safety) Order 2005 (SI 2005 No 1541) is an important order which replaced previous fire safety regulations and covers the workplace, shared areas of properties and hostels of shared housing for service users, as well as shops, nightclubs, etc.

16.24   Under the order the person in control of the premises must:

- Carry out a fire risk assessment.
- Consider who is especially at risk.
- Eliminate or reduce the risk and provide general fire precautions to deal with any residual risk.
- Ensure protection if storing flammable/explosive materials.
- Create a plan for dealing with emergencies.
- Provide a record of the findings from the fire risk assessment.
- Review the findings of the fire risk assessment.

16.25   For further information about compliance with the Fire Safety Order, see www.communities.gov.uk. We discuss risk assessments below.

16.26   In Box 16.4 we outline a summary of legal remedies connected with the case study. What is useful to note is that any particular instance of disrepair, for instance, a leaking toilet or a damaged gas fire, could give rise to several different remedies.

Box 16.4 Summary of legal remedies for disrepair

Problem	*Example*	*Remedy*	*Comment*
Failure to provide the standard of accommodation provided for in the contract	The contract says that the premises will be fit for human habitation and there is an infestation of mice.	Breach of contract – damages and repair.	Landlords rarely commit themselves to any standard of repair in the contract.
Defects in the structure, the exterior or the installations of the property	Leaking toilet.	Breach of implied term under section 11 of the Landlord and Tenant Act 1985 – damages and repair.	Note that the derelict outside wall is unlikely to be part of the structure or exterior. The need to improve the boiler is not the same as the need to repair it.
Dangerous state of the premises	Falling down steep stairs or over derelict wall.	Breach of section 4 of the Defective Premises Act 1972.	Applies where landlord knew or ought to have known of the defect.

Problem	Example	Remedy	Comment
Failure to take appropriate care of service users	Steep staircase. Derelict wall.	Negligence – damages.	Must establish duty of care, breach of that duty and injury.
Premises fails to provide a healthy and safe environment for occupiers	Risk of accident and risk of infection.	Enforcement action under the Housing Act 2004.	The risk of harm will be assessed under the HHSRS and, depending upon the category of the hazard, enforcement action may result.
Premises fails to provide a healthy and safe environment for employees and other users	Risk of accident and risk of infection.	Enforcement action by the Health and Safety Executive – breaches are criminal offences.	See below for a brief outline of the main statutes and regulations.

Health and safety obligations

16.27 The property you manage can also be the workplace of your staff. As such, there are legal requirements to look after the health and safety of your employees. The contract of employment should include a term requiring employees to observe health and safety requirements. There is also an obligation on employers to provide a safe place for employees to work. We have summarised the numerous statutory and regulatory obligations below. This is not a definitive list and you need to ensure that a manager has responsibility for keeping up to date with changes in health and safety legislation.

Health and Safety at Work etc Act 1974

16.28 The Act imposes a duty on all employers to ensure, as far as is reasonably practicable, the health, safety and welfare at work of their employees.

16.29 All employers must:

- provide and maintain systems of work which are safe and without risks to health;
- provide health and safety training to employees, including first aid and fire evacuation arrangements;
- ensure the health and safety of employees' working environment – heating, lighting, ventilation, noise;
- ensure that non-employees are not exposed to risks as a result of workplace activities;
- provide, free of charge, to employees anything necessary, or required by law, in the interests of health and safety at work;
- display a poster or distribute leaflets containing basic health and safety information.

16.30 Employees must:

- take reasonable care for the health and safety of themselves and others;
- co-operate with employers and any other persons to enable them to follow relevant statutory provisions;
- not intentionally or recklessly interfere with or misuse anything provided in the interests of health, safety and welfare.

16.31 An employer with five or more staff must prepare a written statement (health and safety policy) which contains the following information:

- a general statement of its intention to provide safe working conditions;
- the name of the director, secretary or manager responsible for ensuring the policy is implemented;
- the names of other key individuals responsible for health and safety, and what their responsibilities are;
- a description of any arrangements for joint consultation with a recognised trade union and the names of any safety representatives appointed by the union;
- a list of the main health hazards identified from the assessment of the working arrangements and workplace;
- the procedure for reporting accidents at work.

16.32   We have included guidance on developing a health and safety policy in the appendices.

Management of Health and Safety at Work Regulations 1999

16.33   The Management of Health and Safety at Work Regulations 1999 (SI No 3242) were introduced in their original form in December 1992 as SI No 2051. The single most significant requirement in the regulations was the introduction of the requirement to undertake risk assessments (see below).

16.34   The regulations deal with maintenance of the workplace and the equipment within it, ventilation and temperature, lighting, cleanliness and control of waste materials, room dimensions and space for employees, workstations and seating, condition of floors and traffic routes, windows, toilets and washing facilities, supply of drinking water, facilities for rest and eating food.

Manual Handling Operations Regulations 1992

16.35   The Manual Handling Operations Regulations 1992 (SI 1992 No 2793) cover any transporting or supporting of a load (including people and animals). Employers must assess the risk of injury from manual handling; establish measures to avoid hazardous manual handling; and provide information and training on handling loads.

Personal Protective Equipment at Work (PPE) Regulations 1992

16.36 The Personal Protective Equipment at Work Regulations 1992 (SI 1992 No 2966) set standards for employers on the provision of protective equipment for employees. PPE is defined as all equipment designed to be worn or held to protect against a risk to health and safety. This includes most types of protective clothing, and equipment such as eye, foot and head protection. There are some exceptions, for example, ordinary working clothes and uniforms (including clothing provided only for food hygiene).

Reporting of Injuries, Diseases and Dangerous Occurrences Regulations 1995 (RIDDOR)

16.37 Employers have a duty to report to the local authority environmental health department:

- fatal accidents;
- major injury;
- dangerous occurrences;
- accidents causing incapacity for more than three days;
- some work-related diseases (including tuberculosis, hepatitis).

16.38 RIDDOR 1995 (SI 1995 No 3163) introduced additional requirements, including:

- for the first time, injuries caused by acts of violence to people at work must be reported;
- the duty to report accidents to members of the public in any workplace.

16.39 Any accident, occurrence or case of disease, whether affecting residents, staff or visitors, should be recorded in an accident book. Accident books must be kept for three years. In Box 16.5 we signpost you to more information on the requirements of RIDDOR.

Box 16.5 Reporting accidents and dangerous occurrences

Visit www.riddor.gov.uk for more information about RIDDOR requirements and to report accidents and dangerous occurrences.

Control of Substances Hazardous to Health Regulations 1999 (COSHH)

16.40   The COSHH Regulations 1999 (SI 1999 No 437) require employers to make assessments of every hazardous substance used or generated in the workplace and to adopt appropriate control and monitoring procedures. Every workplace is covered, and substances include dust, fumes, chemicals and micro-organisms. Most hazardous substances carry a warning label and suppliers should be able to provide information on precautions to be taken.

Health and Safety (First Aid) Regulations 1981

16.41   Under the Health and Safety (First Aid) Regulations 1981 (SI 1981 No 917), employers are required to provide adequate and appropriate first aid arrangements. One first aid person for every 50 employees is recommended. The minimum requirement for all workplaces is that there should be an appointed person present at all times who will take charge in an emergency. All employers must be informed of first aid arrangements. Every workplace is required to have at least one first aid box, which is clearly identified (white cross on green background) and kept in a readily accessible place. No drugs should be kept in the box because most first aid people are not qualified to prescribe them.

Electricity at Work Regulations 1989

16.42   Under the Electricity at Work Regulations 1989 (SI 1989 No 635), employers are required to assess work activities which use electricity, or which may be affected by it, and to define all foreseeable risks associated with them. These include the suitability, design, construction and installation of electrical systems. Equipment must be regularly checked by a competent person.

Food Hygiene (England) Regulations 2006 (SI No 14)

16.43   All food businesses, whether run for profit or not, are covered by the Food Hygiene Regulations 2006 which implement EU legislation on food safety. A 'food business' includes canteens, clubs and care homes. Food prepared at home for consumption at home' is not covered. Helpful guidance on the implications of the regulations is available from the Food Standards Authority: www. food.gov.uk.

16.44   All food businesses must register with the competent authority, generally the local authority environmental health department. The legislation also requires food business operators to put in place, implement and maintain a permanent procedure, or procedures, based on Hazard Analysis and Critical Control Points (HACCP) principles. HACCP is an internationally recognised and recommended system of food safety management. It focuses on identifying the 'critical points' in a process where food safety problems (or 'hazards') could arise and putting steps in place to prevent things going wrong. This is sometimes referred to as 'controlling hazards'. Keeping records is also an important part of HACCP systems. The legislation is structured so that it can be applied flexibly and proportionately according to the size and nature of the food business.

16.45   One particular publication, 'Safer food, better business', has been developed by the Food Standards Agency in partnership with small catering businesses and more than 50 local authorities to help organisations manage food safety. If you would like to order a hard copy of 'Safer food, better business' call 0845 606 0667 or e-mail foodstandards@ecgroup.uk.com.

Regulation

16.46   Starlight manages the property on behalf of Zest Housing Association, an RSL. Starlight also has a *Supporting People* contract to fund its support services. Starlight will have to adhere to regulatory requirements.

16.47   The Housing Corporation Regulatory Code and Guidance requires that:

3.4.1   The homes their residents live in are well maintained and in a lettable condition.

16.48   Statutory housing management guidance includes requirements that:

3.4b   Housing stock is maintained in a lettable condition that exceeds statutory minimum requirements.

3.4d   There is a responsive repairs service that meets legal and contractual obligations and is efficient and effective.

16.49   In addition, the *Supporting People* contract will set out expectations about health and safety practices and compliance with the law. Under the Quality Assessment Framework, failure to achieve level C of the core service objective C1.3, Security, Health and Safety, represents a serious risk to service users and staff and action is likely to be taken against a provider.

Risk assessment

16.50   This brief outline of the law relating to the standard of repair and the health and safety of service users and employees demonstrates that it is a highly complex area. Failure to comply with legal requirements may have serious repercussions for your project. We have discussed at other points in this book the value of risk assessment. We consider that it is a particularly useful tool when it comes to managing the potential risks involved in repairing, managing and maintaining property.

16.51   Risk assessment involves five steps.

16.52   You must:

- Identify the hazards in the property
  - You can do this in a number of ways. Look back over your accident book and see what accidents have happened in the past. Walk around the premises and note the hazards. Think about what hazards may present themselves to your service users. If they are elderly, for instance, staircases may prove particularly hazardous. Ask your workers and your residents for their views.
- Decide who might be harmed and how
  - Think about your residents, their visitors, your workers, including cleaners and maintenance workers, and if members of the public have access, think about their needs too.
- Evaluate the risks and decide on precaution
  - Can you get rid of the hazard?
  - If not, can you reduce the risk? Starlight could, for instance, provide safety rails for the steep staircase and decent sanitary disposal facilities.
  - If you introduce new practices and procedures, check that they do not result in new hazards.
- Record your findings and implement them
  - The Health and Safety Executive provides a useful template for recording your findings. It is easily adaptable to the needs of a supported housing provider.
- Review your assessment and update if necessary
  - You should review your risk assessment annually. Think about

whether your present service users have different needs from those you have previously accommodated. Have you introduced new equipment into the premises, or new procedures?

Summary

16.53 This brief overview demonstrates the complexity and importance of the proper management of your premises. Providers have a number of relationships which impose a myriad of responsibilities in the management of property. First, they are landlords, and therefore are subject to contractual, tortuous and statutory obligations. Moreover, there is increasing regulation of standards in housing via public health legislation, in particular, the HHSRS. Secondly, they house vulnerable people and therefore are subject to regulation by the Housing Corporation and *Supporting People*. Finally, they are employers and must therefore provide their employees with safe places to work. What becomes clear is that one member of staff needs to take a lead responsibility in order to avoid potentially dangerous and expensive breaches of the law. That person needs to keep up to date with regulatory requirements and run regular risk assessments. However, the responsibility cannot be completely devolved to one person; all employees and managers need to understand their obligations and to act responsibly in connection with property management.

Managing rents

Objectives

17.1 By the end of the chapter you will:

- Have some familiarity with the framework for rent setting
- Understand the significance of the difference between rent and service charges
- Understand the different legal frameworks governing increases in rent
- Understand the importance of benefits in rent arrears prevention
- Appreciate how to manage rent arrears effectively
- Have an awareness of the grounds of possession available to landlords which are concerned with rent arrears
- Have an understanding of the procedural requirements of the county court in connection with obtaining possession of the property because of rent arrears

Case study

17.2 Goodmove is a small housing association, registered with the Housing Corporation, managing a number of properties for older people. Residents have a range of occupancy agreements: those in self-contained properties have either secure or assured tenancy agreements depending upon the date of commencement of the agreement; those in residential shared homes have assured shorthold tenancies; and those in registered care have licence agreements. The finance manager is concerned that the rents due to be increased in April are increased lawfully. Also, some of the residents have not been paying their charges and have built up considerable arrears. Staff have been reluctant to take any action as they feel serving warning letters is not supportive to residents. Managers do not feel confident in pursuing arrears: they are aware that the court has a protocol about this; however, they are unsure about what it is.

Overview

17.3 Many providers are nervous about the law in connection with rents. This is quite understandable. Not only is the law complex because of the different legal frameworks for different tenancy types, but providers are often acutely aware of the financial circumstances of their residents and the difficulties they face in dealing with housing benefit. Moreover, enforcement of rent arrears via the courts can seem particularly intimidating, and providers may have particular concerns about the disproportionate nature of the sanction of possession. At the same time, providers have a responsibility to safeguard the income of the project and to avoid problems caused by service users building up arrears.

17.4   Using the case study, we look at common problems connected with the payment, collection and increase of rents, and the action you should take to minimise arrears. In chapter 23 we give you further information on using the courts for possession proceedings. This chapter starts by considering the principles of rent setting and defining rents and service charges; the second part of the chapter explains the different legal mechanisms for increasing rents; the final part of the chapter concentrates on the problems of rent arrears, looking, first, at the range of available benefits, secondly, at how to manage rent arrears and, finally, at the vital steps you must take before issuing possession proceedings.

Important definitions

17.5   Before we begin explaining the law and procedures in connection with the payment of rent, it is necessary to clarify some key terms which we will use in this chapter.

17.6   There are two types of payment which service users may make in connection with their occupation of property. The first is *rent* and the second is a *service charge*. We have set out simple definitions of these in Box 17.1.

Box 17.1 Definitions of rent and service charge

Rent is a sum of money paid for the occupation and use of property. The amount and the regularity of payment is usually specified in a contract.

Technically, rent describes the payment made by tenants. The payment made by licensees is properly described as a fee. However, people generally do not make a distinction between the money paid by licensees and tenants, describing both as rent.

> A *service charge* is a sum of money paid for the services provided in connection with the provision of accommodation. So, for instance, the occupiers of a block of flats which has the benefit of a lift may well pay a service charge which covers the maintenance of the lift. In long-term supported housing, service charges are paid for the support services, such as care services, therapy and counselling, which are provided to the residents.

17.7 There is an important distinction between the remedies available for non-payment of rent and non-payment of service charges. Non-payment of rent can be pursued in the courts either as an ordinary debt or by possession proceedings, which can result in the eviction of the tenant. Non-payment of service charges can only be enforced as a debt. Note also that service charges are relevant in the calculation of fair rents for housing association tenants. However, service charges are not taken into account in calculating the market rent under the Housing Act 1988.

17.8 There is one further important distinction between tenancy types when considering rents: the distinction between fixed-term and periodic tenancies. If a tenancy agreement states that it lasts for a set period of time, such as six months or one year, then it is a *fixed* term tenancy. The landlord and the tenant are bound by the contractual agreement to let for that fixed period. If the tenant wishes to leave during that period, he or she can only do so with the agreement of the landlord. The rent payable is the rent agreed for the fixed period. Many assured shorthold tenancies are fixed-term tenancies. However, once the fixed term has expired, if the landlord does not grant a new fixed-term tenancy but allows the tenancy to continue, then the tenancy ceases to be fixed term and becomes periodic.

17.9 A tenancy agreement which does not specify that it is to last for a set time span is a *periodic* tenancy. The period of the tenancy is the *rent payment period*, so if the rent is paid monthly it is a monthly periodic tenancy and if it is weekly it is a weekly periodic tenancy. Rent can only be raised in periodic tenancies, which are governed by statutory regimes such as the Housing Act 1988 or the Rent Act 1977, by the statutory mechanisms set out in those Acts.

17.10 The first step for the landlord in our case study in making a decision to increase the rent is to determine whether any of the tenancies are fixed-term tenancies where the fixed term has not expired. If any of the tenancies are still in their fixed term, then the rents can only be raised in accordance with the agreement in the contract. Goodmove should also be clear about the terms of its periodic tenancies. Different rules about notices of rent increases apply dependent upon the period of the tenancy. We will explain this below.

17.11   There is one important legal requirement imposed upon landlords of weekly tenants. Tenants and licensees who pay rent weekly are entitled to a rent book, which provides a record of their payment: see section 4 of the Landlord and Tenant Act 1985.

17.12   The rent book must contain:

- the name and address of the landlord and the landlord's agent, if there is one;
- the amount of rent to be paid; and
- a description of the rental property.

17.13   Failure to provide a rent book when it is required or failure to provide the requisite information is an offence under the Act. The majority of landlords comply with this by ensuring that the written tenancy agreement includes these details.

17.14   Before we go on to describe how rents can be increased in accordance with the law, you should be familiar with the rent assessment committee, which is the forum to which you, as a landlord, or your tenants can complain if they consider that rent increases are not in accordance with the law.

17.15   Box 17.2 sets out the functions of the rent assessment committee.

Box 17.2 Rent assessment committee

When the Rent Act 1965 established the fair rent regime, it also created rent officers, to make decisions about fair rents, and rent assessment committees as independent appellate bodies where objections to rent officer decisions could be heard. The legislative basis for rent assessment committees is now contained in Part IV of the Rent Act 1977. Since the commencement of the Housing Act 1988, rent assessment committees have also dealt with disputes about market rents within the assured tenancy regime. Rent assessment committees have jurisdiction to hear disputes about rent levels for assured tenancies which arise at the end of a long lease at a low rent under the Local Government and Housing Act 1989. Rent assessment committees draw their members from five regional rent assessment panels. There is no appeal on decisions about the payable rent from the rent assessment committee, but appeals on points of law may be made to the High Court within 28 days of the decision.

> Rent assessment committees sit as tribunals, usually consisting of three members – a lawyer, a valuer and a lay person. They are generally chaired by either the lawyer or the valuer member. The tribunal has power to make decisions on the papers, following a hearing, and is able to make inspections of the property where appropriate. Rent assessment committees are part of the Residential Property Tribunal Service.

17.16   As our explanation of the functions of the rent assessment committee makes clear, the rent officer also plays an important role in the control of rents. Rent officers are employed by the Rent Service, which is an agency of the Department for Work and Pensions. Its work concerns the private rented housing sector. It has two main functions, which are carried out by rent officers:

- A rental valuation service for housing benefit purposes, determining local reference rents, single room rents and reasonable open market rents, as well as setting local housing allowances in support of the Path finder scheme.
- Fair rent determinations for landlords and tenants who fall within the regulated tenancy regime of the Rent Act 1977.

17.17   We provide more details on both housing benefit and fair rents below.

17.18   This chapter now concentrates on answering the important questions in connection with rent:

- How are rent levels set?
- How can rents be increased?
- What help is available to make rents affordable?
- What steps can be taken to manage arrears?
- What remedies are available to the landlord if a tenant persists on not paying rents and/or service charges?

Rent setting

17.19   Housing associations' rent levels, with a few exceptions, must be determined in accordance with Housing Corporation guidance on rent restructuring – *The rent influencing regime: implementing the rent restructuring framework*. In the past, each individual housing association calculated rents in slightly different ways, with the aim of covering their costs. Government was keen to establish a more coherent pattern of rents across the housing association and council sectors, and introduced a formula-based rent restructuring framework for setting rents over a ten-year period. The aim is to bring rents across the two sectors closer together; the Housing Corporation guidance offers detailed advice on how associations can apply the framework across their stock and is available on the Housing Corporation website.

17.20   Social landlords, such as Goodmove, are required to have a rent plan that helps them to move their rents towards a so-called target rent over a ten-year period, starting in April 2002 and ending in March 2012. In supported housing, housing associations were given the option of delaying applying the framework until 2003. Rents can go up or down, and to ensure tenants do not face large increases, the level of rent increases is regulated. For example, a housing association tenant's weekly rent cannot go up by more than the rate of inflation plus 0.5 per cent plus £2.

The statutory frameworks for increasing rent

17.21   In the case study three types of tenancy agreement are mentioned. These are:

- The secure tenancy.
- The assured tenancy.
- The assured shorthold tenancy.

17.22   When a housing association is the landlord of a secure tenant, although the terms of the tenancy are governed by the Housing Act 1985, the fair rent regime as set out in section 70 of the Rent Act 1977 applies to rent increases.

17.23   Periodic assured and assured shorthold tenancies under the Housing Act 1988 share the same legislative mechanism for raising rents. If the contract does not provide a rent review mechanism, then the rents can only be raised in accordance with the provisions of section 13 of the Housing Act 1988. The main difference with this piece of legislation is that it is based upon the notion of market rents, as distinct from the rent control mechanisms in the Rent Act 1977.

17.24   During the initial fixed term (or first six months if periodic) of an assured shorthold tenancy, tenants can challenge their rents through the rent assessment committee (section 22 of the Housing Act 1988). Further details of this procedure are available on the Residential Property Tribunal Service website at www.rpts.org.uk.

The fair rent regime

What is a fair rent?

17.25 In essence, a fair rent is a market rent less statutory disregards and a deduction for the scarcity (if any) of available rental accommodation. The statutory provision (see section 70 of the Rent Act 1977) requires a landlord which wishes to increase the rent to apply to a rent officer to register a new rent. Generally, a landlord must wait two years from the last registration before it can apply for a new rent.

Box 17.3 Frequently asked questions

We grant assured shorthold tenancies to our service users. In our mission statement we say we will charge a fair rent. Is that the same as the fair rent regime?

Supported housing providers often refer to their rents as fair or affordable. This is not the same as the statutory fair rent regime, which is only available for tenants who are protected by the Rent Act 1977 – the main legislative framework which applied before the Housing Act 1988 came into effect on 15 January 1989. Service users who have assured shorthold tenancies are covered by the Housing Act 1988 and not the Rent Act. We explain the provisions of the Rent Act 1977 in chapter 4

First registrations of fair rents

17.26 The rent officer will decide on the amount to be registered as the first fair rent by taking into account:

- all the circumstances of the letting (other than personal circumstances); and, in particular
- the age, character, locality and state of repair.

17.27 What is disregarded is:

- the impact on the rent of both disrepair which results from the failure of the tenant; and
- improvements carried out by the tenant (other than those required by the lease).

17.28 If you can provide evidence of market rent levels of comparable properties, this will assist the rent officer in making decisions about appropriate rent levels. You can quite easily tell the rent officer, for instance, what rents your tenants on assured or assured shorthold tenancies are paying. Scarcity, however, is a more difficult concept. Housing scarcity differs throughout the country, it differs according to property types and it can change quite quickly. For instance, it could be argued that there is a very limited supply of four-bedroom houses to rent in a particular town one year, but in another year there is sufficient availability for the demand. There is judicial authority suggesting that waiting lists for local authority or housing association properties can be used to demonstrate scarcity, but there would have to be evidence to demonstrate how many of those on the lists were actively seeking accommodation in the private rented sector.

17.29   Any fair rent (other than one arising on first registration) is subject to the Rent Acts (Maximum Fair Rent) Order 1999 (SI 1999 No 6). This limits increases by a formula based on the proportional increase in the retail price index since the previous registration. This mechanism was brought in because landlords had been arguing successfully before the courts that there was no longer any scarcity of rented accommodation, and that therefore fair rents were the equivalent of market rents. There are exceptions for first time registration and where the rental value of repairs or improvements has resulted in an increase in a fair rent of at least 15 per cent above the previous limit. What this means in practice is that the rent officer assesses the fair rent and then adjusts it in line with the formula set out in the order.

After registration

17.30   Once the rent officer has assessed the fair rent it is entered on the rent register, which is a public document available for inspection. If a landlord or a tenant objects to the registered rent then the matter is heard afresh by the rent assessment committee, which makes its own decision on the fair rent. Either party has 28 days within which to inform the rent assessment committee of its wish to object. If the landlord is a housing association, it must serve a notice of increase upon the tenant at least four weeks before the increase is charged, and the new rent can only commence at the start of a rental period. So if the tenant pays monthly, on the 15th of the month, the new rent can only commence from the 15th of the month after the four-week notice has expired.

17.31   A landlord cannot charge a tenant more rent than is provided for on the register, even if the tenant agrees to pay more. The tenant can recover any overpayment in the county court.

Service charges

17.32 Usually, the fair rent will reflect the value to the tenant of any services provided. However, if the tenancy agreement states that the landlord can from time to time vary the amount payable in respect of services and the rent officer accepts that the terms of variation contained in the tenancy agreement are reasonable, then the rent can be entered on the register as variable. This means that the amount in the fair rent that the rent officer considers to be attributable to services will be separately specified in the register. However, that element of the fair rent can still be altered from time to time in accordance with the terms of the tenancy agreement (for example, by notice from the landlord once a year).

17.33 In supported housing, in particular sheltered housing, there have been some problems when the cost of support is included in the rent payable by the tenant. Under section 71 of the Rent Act 1977, all payments paid by the tenant to the landlord, from whatever source, are treated as rent for fair rent purposes. This applies even if the charge is separate from the occupation of the dwelling or payable under separate agreements. Rent officers have been including any charge for support in the overall rent when assessing a fair rent, even if those charges are set out in a separate support contract. This can cause difficulties: if the charge for support is identified as covering substantial board or attendance, this can lead to the agreement being excluded from the provisions of the Rent Act and therefore the tenant is no longer entitled to a fair rent. This is a complex area and if you are experiencing problems, you should seek legal advice.

Summary

17.34 In Box 17.4 we set out a summary of the procedure for increasing fair rents. In our case study, if Goodmove want to raise the rents for its secure tenants in April, then it must time its application to the rent officer to give it sufficient time to get a decision and serve the necessary notice to increase rent.

Box 17.4

Step	Law	Comment
1 Check to see which tenants are covered by the fair rent regime.	Housing association tenants whose tenancy commenced before 15 January 1989.	Rent officers are a good source of advice on the jurisdiction of the Rent Act 1977.
2 Check to see when the registered rents were last increased.	Unless there are exceptional circumstances, then the registered rent can only be increased every two years.	Exceptional circumstances include extensive work on the property. A landlord can apply to the rent officer one year and nine months from the last registration.
3 Apply to the rent officer for a new fair rent.	The rent officer will calculate the market rent and then reduce it for scarcity, and finally apply the formula under the order.	You can provide evidence of market rents for similar properties and evidence of scarcity.
4 Once the new rent is registered, you must serve a notice of increase of rent.	This must provide at least four weeks' notice of the rent increase and the rent can only be increased from the start of a new rental period.	
5 If you are not happy with the registered rent, you can object to the rent officer.	Your objection must be in writing and within 28 days of receipt of the decision. The rent officer will then refer your objection to the rent assessment committee.	Ensure that you explain why you are objecting – if you have evidence to show that the market rent is higher than the rent officer decided or that there is less scarcity than the rent officer decided, then provide it in your letter of objection.

The assured and the assured shorthold rent regime

How the system works

17.35 The Housing Act 1988 introduced the assured tenancy. Assured tenants have limited rent protection. The Act was designed to provide for market rents. Therefore, tenants are bound by the rent provisions set out in their contract or by any subsequent agreement they make with their landlord. However, if the tenancy agreement does not provide a mechanism for the increase of rent, then section 13 allows the landlord to serve a notice proposing a new rent 52 weeks after the commencement of the tenancy or after the last increase in rent. If the tenant disagrees with the proposed rent, he or she may apply to the rent assessment committee, which will decide the market rent for the property.

Contractual terms which allow rent to be increased

17.36 As we have indicated above, landlords can include a term in the contract which enables them to increase the rents. So Goodmove should check its assured and assured shorthold agreements to see if there is a rent review clause. If there is such a clause, then Goodmove must follow the procedures set out in the clause. However, rent review clauses are not straightforward as tenancy agreements must conform to the requirements of the Unfair Terms in Consumer Contract Regulations 1999 (SI No 2083), ie they must be fair. This poses particular challenges for clauses which purport to raise rent. The Office of Fair Trading, which has published guidance on tenancy agreements, has provided its opinion on the requirements for fairness of rent review clauses in paragraphs 3.101–3.103 of that guidance. We have set out those paragraphs in Box 17.5. If the term in the contract is not fair, then it can be struck out.

Box 17.5 OFT guidance on fair rent variation clauses

Rent variation clauses are more likely to be fair as follows:

- where the amount and timing of any rent increases are specified (the precise amounts for each year or within narrow limits if not precisely stated), they effectively form part of the agreed price. As such, they may be regarded as 'core' terms setting the price, provided the details are

---

> clear, in plain intelligible language, and are adequately drawn to the tenant's attention;
> - terms that permit increases linked to a relevant published price index outside the landlord's control, such as the RPI, are likely to be acceptable;
> - rent review clauses that allow for an increase in the rent to be determined in the light of objective factors by a person who is wholly independent of the landlord. A fair alternative, where the parties cannot agree a new rent, is to agree that the matter should be referred to an independent expert.
>
> A fair rent term would also include provision for the landlord to give notice of the increase that was long enough to allow a tenant who did not wish to pay rent at the higher rate to leave before the increase took effect. However, such a provision would not necessarily render a rent variation term fair in itself.

17.37   What Box 17.5 suggests is that only rent review clauses which:

- genuinely inform the tenant about the future likely cost of renting the property;
- utilise objective criteria to determine the new rent level; and
- give the tenant sufficient time to find alternative accommodation if the rent becomes unaffordable,

are likely to be fair. This means that landlords must exercise caution if they are relying on rent review clauses to increase rents. If the rent was put up and the rent review clause was found to be unfair, then any possession proceedings to evict the tenant for unpaid rent would fail. Furthermore, all tenants would be entitled to reclaim payment of rent increases made in accordance with the unfair rent review clause – an administrative and financial nightmare!

Section 13 of the Housing Act 1988

17.38   If there is no rent review clause, then landlords have to follow the statutory procedure set out in section 13 of the Housing Act 1988. In our case study, it is most likely that Goodmove will use section 13 to raise the rents of both their assured periodic and assured shorthold tenants. Section 13 is an important piece of legislation. In its original form, it caused social landlords some specific difficulties because of the rules within the section that required rents to be raised no earlier than the anniversary of the commencement of the tenancy. This made it impossible to have an annual date for rent increases, which imposed a heavy administrative burden on landlords with a large number of properties. However, the Regulatory Reform (Assured Periodic Tenancies) (Rent Increases) Order 2003 (SI No 259) amended the section so that now the landlord of an assured periodic tenancy of less than one month is able to set a fixed day (such as the first Monday in April) on which a rent increase is to take effect. The rules now are that the first increase under section 13 subsequent to its amendment must take place not less than 52 weeks after the commencement of the tenancy or, if the rent had been increased prior to the date on which the order came into force 11 February 2003), not less than 52 weeks after the date of the last increase. Second and subsequent increases may take effect not less than 52 weeks after the last increase, unless that would result in the increase taking effect on a date falling a week or more before the anniversary of the first increase after the date on which the order comes into force. In such a case, the increase may not take effect until 53 weeks after the date of the last increase. We have provided a copy of the amended section 13 in the appendices to this book.

17.39   In order to raise the rents of the assured and assured shorthold tenants, Goodmove, like every landlord, will have to complete the appropriate form – Form 4B – for the purposes of the section.

17.40   The most important points to note when completing this form are:

- When the proposed new rent can start
  - The date in section 3 of the notice must comply with the following three rules:
    - First, a minimum period of notice must be given before the proposed new rent can take effect. That period is:
      - one month for a tenancy which is monthly or for a lesser period, for instance, weekly or fortnightly;
      - six months for a yearly tenancy
      - in all other cases, a period equal to the length of the period of the tenancy – for example, three months in the case of a quarterly tenancy.
        (So Goodmove must check the period of its tenancies. It is highly probable that it will have to give one month's notice of the proposed new rent.)
    - The starting date for the proposed new rent must not be earlier than 52 weeks after the date on which the rent was last

increased using the statutory notice procedure or, if the tenancy is new, the date on which it started, unless that would result in an increase date falling one week or more before the anniversary of the date in paragraph 3 of the notice, in which case the starting date must not be earlier than 53 weeks from the date on which the rent was last increased.

17.41   This allows rent increases to take effect on a fixed day each year where the period of a tenancy is less than one month. For example, the rent for a weekly tenancy could be increased on, say, the first Monday in April. Where the period of a tenancy is monthly, quarterly, six monthly or yearly, rent increases can take effect on a fixed date, for example, 1 April.

17.42   *So Goodmove, in our case study, must check when it last raised the rent on these tenancies – the statute only allows for rent increases after 52/53 weeks.*

17.43   There are two exceptions to the 52/53-week rule. Where the tenancy was originally for a fixed term (for instance, six months) but continues on a periodic (for instance, a monthly) basis after the term ends; and where the tenancy came into existence on the death of the previous tenant who had a regulated tenancy under the Rent Act 1977. In these cases the landlord can propose a new rent immediately.

- Thirdly, the proposed new rent must start at the beginning of a period of the tenancy. For instance, if the tenancy is monthly and started on the 20th of the month, rent will be payable on that day of the month, and a new rent must begin then, not on any other day of the month. If the tenancy is weekly and started, for instance, on a Monday, the new rent must begin on a Monday.

17.44   *So Goodmove must check the date of its tenancies if the period is monthly, or the day of the week that the tenancy began if the tenancy is weekly.*

17.45   Note the situation of new tenants. Their rents cannot be raised for 52/53 weeks from the commencement of their tenancy. This means if you want to raise all rents from April you will have to allow more than one year to pass before raising the rents for new tenants. The only way round this would be to have a robust contractual review clause – but we have already highlighted the difficulties posed by the Unfair Terms in Consumer Contract Regulations.

Challenging the proposed increase

17.46 Tenants who are not happy with the proposed new rent set out in the notice of increase can refer the notice to the rent assessment committee. The notice of proposed increase gives the tenant details on how to do this. The tenant must refer the notice to the rent assessment committee before the starting date of the proposed new rent, and case-law has made it clear that it is not sufficient for the tenant to send the notice to the rent assessment committee – the committee must receive the notice before the starting date of the new rent. Unless it does so, the committee has no jurisdiction to hear the referral.

17.47 The rent assessment committee will consider the tenant's application and decide what the maximum rent for the property should be. In setting a rent, the committee must decide what rent the landlord could reasonably expect for the property if it were let on the open market under a new tenancy on the same terms. The committee may therefore set a rent that is higher, lower or the same as the proposed new rent.

Raising rents in assured shorthold tenancies

17.48 Assured shorthold tenancies are simply a subcategory of assured tenancies, so Goodmove should follow the procedures set out above. However, if the shorthold agreements were originally fixed term agreements, and the tenants are now periodic tenants, the anniversary rule in section 13 of the Housing Act 1988 does not apply in the same way. The anniversary which is relevant is the anniversary of the creation of the periodic tenancy. However, all the other formalities are relevant.

Raising rents in licences

17.49 Licences are contractual agreements. Therefore, any increase in rent should be done in accordance with the terms of the contract. If there is no rent review term, then a landlord can terminate the licence and issue a new one at the new rent. Do not forget that if you terminate the licence, the provisions of the Protection from Eviction Act 1977 may apply (see chapter 4).

Housing benefit

17.50   The principal way that unemployed tenants or tenants on low or irregular wages afford rent is through claiming housing benefit.

17.51   Housing benefit is a notoriously complex benefit. What we intend to do is to provide you with a basic outline of the workings of the benefit. If a service user requires further advice you should refer him or her to an agency such as Citizens' Advice. Chris Smith has also written a helpful guide, *Housing benefit for Housing Managers in the Social Sector*, which is published every year – visit www.HBhelp.co.uk. It is vital that you do your best to ensure that service users claim the maximum benefit that they are entitled to. Not only does this allow them to keep their home, it also prevents the accumulation of unnecessary arrears and allows providers to carry out effective financial management of their project.

What is housing benefit?

17.52   Housing benefit is an income-related benefit designed to assist people on income support and low income to pay their rent.

Who is entitled to claim housing benefit?

17.53   Someone may be entitled to housing benefit if:

- they are liable to pay rent;
- their capital (ie savings and investments) is less than £16,000;
- they receive income support or income-based jobseekers allowance or are on a low income as prescribed by the Housing Benefit (General) Regulations 1987 (SI 1987 No 1971).

17.54   Certain people are generally excluded from receiving housing benefit. These include:

- people who live in residential care homes;
- people subject to immigration control or defined as persons from abroad;
- full-time students (there are exceptions here, and further advice will be necessary);
- people who live with their landlord or are a close relative;
- people whose landlord is a former partner of the claimant;
- people whose landlord is a parent of the claimant's child;
- people whose tenancy is not made on a commercial basis.

17.55 Anyone excluded from housing benefit should seek further advice.

How much rent is payable by housing benefit?

17.56 Not all of the money payable to the landlord will be covered by housing benefit. Payments for charges such as water charges, personal light and heat fuel costs, meals and other services, such as support, are excluded. This exclusion is particularly relevant for supported housing service users.

17.57 There are other restrictions that may affect the amount of housing benefit which will be paid. Under housing benefit regulations, rent officers use local reference rents to determine the level of rent payable. These are worked out by the rent officer examining the rents of properties of a similar size in the locality. There are special rent restrictions for young people, where the rent is limited to a single room in a shared house. Some types of tenancy are 'excluded', which means that they do not automatically have to be referred to the rent officer. This includes RSL tenancies. In these cases, the housing benefit officer can decide that the rent is reasonable without making a referral to the rent officer. These rents, however, can be referred if housing benefit officers believe they are unreasonably high or the accommodation unreasonably large.

17.58 Some accommodation is also designated exempt (Housing Benefit (General) Regulations 1987 regs 95 and 10(1), (6)) from referencing and often referred to as 'old regulation 11'. Exempt accommodation is defined as including accommodation 'provided by non metropolitan council ... a housing association, charity or voluntary organisation where that body or a person acting on its behalf also provides the claimant with care, support or supervision'. A social security commissioner's decision in August 2006 (CH/423/2006) clarified that this did not apply where support was provided by a managing agent, separately from the landlord under contract with another body, and reference rents are applicable in these circumstances.

Box 17.6 Frequently asked questions

We are a voluntary agency who have just opened a refuge for women fleeing violence. The housing benefit officer is asking us to provide invoices to prove the amount of rent and service charge we are charging.

Your accommodation is exempt accommodation which does not have to be referred to the rent officer as you are a voluntary

> organisation that provides care, support or supervision, unless the council believes the rent is unreasonably high or too large. You should ask the housing benefit officer if he or she believes the rent is unreasonably high and what accommodation they are comparing you with. The council can reduce the rent if it can show it is unreasonably high compared with suitable accommodation. The council should compare you with other provision for women fleeing violence and accommodation would not be considered suitable if the tenant is likely to be subject to violence from a former partner.

Landlords and housing benefit

17.59 Problems with housing benefit are often the cause of rent arrears. The Communities and Local Government guide, *Improving the Effectiveness of Rent Arrears Management,* published in June 2005, which we discuss more fully below, argues that landlords can assist tenants with housing benefit claims by implementing good practice. It suggests:

- informing tenants, in general terms, about how housing benefit operates;
- advising potential new tenants of what information they will need to bring with them to support a full housing benefit claim;
- advising tenants about which elements of rent and service charges will be paid by housing benefit and calculating their likely entitlement;
- assisting tenants in completing forms accurately and make direct referrals to housing benefit departments;
- making it clear where tenants can receive ongoing support and advice about their benefit entitlement (at the same time make it explicit that rent payment remains the tenant's responsibility);
- reminding tenants to inform the landlord and housing benefit office about changes in their household circumstances as soon as possible;
- where individuals are identified as being vulnerable or have previous arrears, undertake regular reviews of their circumstances.

Managing rent arrears

17.60 The starting point for managing rent arrears is that your role as a supported housing provider is to maintain tenancies, and that eviction should be used as a last resort. This view is supported by the regulatory provisions of the Housing Corporation. The Department for Communities and Local Government has produced two helpful publications which provide guidance on effective rent arrears management: the *Guide on Effective Rent Arrears Management*, published in August 2006, and *Improving the Effectiveness of Rent Arrears Management*, published in June 2005. These are available free of charge from Communities and Local Government Publications, PO Box 236, Wetherby LS23 7NB; Telephone: 0870 1226 236; Fax: 0870 1226 237; Textphone: 0870 1207 405; E-mail: communities@twoten.com. We suggest that you read these publications and devise your own policies on dealing with rent arrears.

17.61 We can apply some of the advice provided in these publications to the case study. Goodmove staff are concerned about sending letters to tenants who are in arrears because they do not think this is supportive. The problem is that they have not taken any other action in connection with the arrears. This has allowed arrears to build up, which of course exacerbates the financial difficulties the tenants face. Research suggests that tenants themselves welcome early contact about rent arrears problems.

17.62 *Improving the effectiveness of Rent Arrears Management* suggests that the key points in dealing with rent arrears are:

- In communicating with tenants about rent arrears, landlords should place emphasis on direct personal contact rather than correspondence – particularly where this involves written correspondence through standard, system-generated, letters. However, for audit trail purposes, written correspondence should not be discounted.
- Personal contact is generally preferable to impersonal communication because letters can be more easily ignored or misunderstood, because personal contact helps staff understand reasons for arrears and because this provides an opportunity for negotiation.
- Landlords should make use of a variety of methods to facilitate personal contact with tenants in arrears – for example, office interviews, home visits, telephone contact. E-mail or text messaging

can be useful in alerting tenants to problems and/or setting up interviews.

- Attempts to negotiate arrears repayment agreements should continue alongside any legal action and should not cease until the bailiff's visit.

- In negotiating repayment agreements, landlords should offer tenants the option of lump sums, instalments or a combination of the two. Direct deductions from benefits or earnings should also be considered.

17.63   Letters can be useful, and are often the main tool that landlords use to communicate with tenants. However, care should be taken in using such letters. The aim should be to promote early settlement of the problem, and to make it clear to tenants what the next steps are if the problem is not resolved.

17.64   *Improving the effectiveness of Rent Arrears Management* suggests that arrears letters should:

- be written as plainly and clearly as possible;
- be provided in different languages, large print, Braille or other formats as required;
- state clearly the amount due;
- indicate that support is available to tenants to resolve the problem, including payment by instalments, whilst at the same time stating clearly the potential seriousness of continuing inaction on the part of the tenant;
- set out the next stage in the process, so that tenants are clear about further action;
- encourage tenants to get in touch – a threatening tone is likely to discourage contact;
- provide a range of means for tenants to make contact, including telephone, office interviews, after-hours surgeries, where these are provided, and the offer of a home visit;
- provide contact details of local advice centres and encourage tenants to contact these centres; and
- provide a clear timescale and deadline for making contact.

Evictions for rent arrears

Secure tenants

17.65 It is extremely unlikely that you will be considering evicting secure tenants for rent arrears. These tenants have been tenants for a very long time – at least since 1988 – so their history of rent payment must have been good and any difficulties they may face should be only temporary. However, where it is necessary, there is a discretionary ground for evicting secure tenants under the Housing Act 1985. We have outlined the ground in Box 17.7.

Box 17.7 Ground 1 text from Schedule 2 to the Housing Act 1985

Ground 1: Rent arrears or other breach of tenancy

Rent lawfully due from the tenant has not been paid, or an obligation of the tenancy has been broken or not performed.

Assured tenants

17.66 One aim of the Housing Act 1988 was to introduce a market system for private rented housing. Part of this involves providing the landlord with much more certain methods of repossessing the property, particularly when its income stream is at risk. There is a mandatory ground for eviction for rent arrears, ground 8, which is available to the landlords of assured tenants where there are two months' arrears of rent outstanding at the date of the notice of seeking possession and at the date of the eviction. This means that if the facts are made out, the court has no option but to grant the possession order. The rent could be in arrears because of housing benefit delays or because of problems within the family, but the reasons for non-payment of rent are irrelevant. The court must order possession. Many housing association landlords choose not to use ground 8. We have set out the text of ground 8 in Box 17.8. The Housing Corporation set out its criteria for the use of ground 8 in circular 02/07 (we explain about this circular in chapter 10).

Box 17.8 Ground 8 text from Schedule 2 to the Housing Act 1988

Ground 8: Substantial rent arrears

Both at the date of the service of the notice under section 8 of this Act relating to the proceedings for possession and at the date of the hearing –

(a) if rent is payable weekly or fortnightly, at least eight weeks' rent is unpaid;
(b) if rent is payable monthly, at least two months' rent is unpaid;
(c) if rent is payable quarterly, at least one quarter's rent is more than three months in arrears; and
(d) if rent is payable yearly, at least three months' rent is more than three months in arrears; and for the purpose of this ground 'rent' means lawfully due from the tenant.

17.67   The protocol on evictions for rent arrears, which we discuss below, makes it difficult for housing associations to use the ground even if they choose to do so. The Housing Corporation provides regulatory guidance on the use of ground 8 in its circular 07/04, which states that that ground 8 should only be used as a last resort, after all other reasonable alternatives have been pursued. It also refers to Department for Work and Pensions good practice guidance – for example, obtaining a certificate to confirm that there are no outstanding benefit inquiries to ensure that rent arrears are not linked to housing benefit administration.

17.68   There are two discretionary grounds in the Act which relate to rent arrears: ground 10 and ground 11. We have set these out for you in Box 17.9.

Box 17.9 Grounds 10 and 11 of Schedule 2 to the Housing Act 1988

Ground 10:
Some rent lawfully due from the tenant –

(a) is unpaid on the date on which the proceedings for possession are begun;
(b) except where subsection (1)(b) of section 8 of this Act applies, was in arrears at the date of the service of the notice under that section relating to those proceedings.

Ground 11:
Whether or not any rent is in arrears on the date on which proceedings for possession are begun, the tenant has persistently delayed paying rent which has become lawfully due.

17.69   Housing associations generally prefer to use these grounds. It means that the tenant has an opportunity to argue their case, and the housing association can have the reassurance of knowing that the court agrees that it is reasonable to evict in the circumstances of the case.

Preparing for court

17.70 There has been concern that housing associations and other social landlords sometimes issue possession proceedings inappropriately, for instance, where arrears are at a very low level, or to provoke a response from housing benefit. As a result, there has been a great deal of emphasis on reducing the use of the courts to collect rent arrears. One particular initiative by the courts is the publication of a pre-action protocol which should be adhered to prior to court proceedings. It recognises that it is in the interests of both landlords and tenants to ensure that rent is paid promptly and to ensure that difficulties are resolved wherever possible without court proceedings. The aim of the protocol is to encourage more pre-action contact between landlords and tenants and to enable court time to be used more effectively. Courts should take into account whether the protocol has been followed when considering what orders to make. RSLs are also required to comply with guidance issued from time to time by the Housing Corporation. We have set out the protocol in full below because it is essential that you follow its steps and are aware of its contents prior to the issue of possession proceedings.

Pre-action protocol for possession claims based on rent arrears

Initial contact

1. The landlord should contact the tenant as soon as reasonably possible if the tenant falls into arrears to discuss the cause of the arrears, the tenant's financial circumstances, the tenant's entitlement to benefits and repayment of the arrears. Where contact is by letter, the landlord should write separately to each named tenant.

2. The landlord and tenant should try to agree affordable sums for the tenant to pay towards arrears, based upon the tenant's income and expenditure (where such information has been supplied in response to the landlord's enquiries). The landlord should clearly set out in pre-action correspondence any time limits with which the tenant should comply.

3. The landlord should provide, on a quarterly basis, rent statements in a comprehensible format showing rent due and sums received for the past 13 weeks. The landlord should, upon request, provide the tenant with copies of rent statements in a comprehensible format from the date when arrears first arose showing all amounts of rent due, the dates and amounts of all payments made, whether through housing benefit or by the tenant, and a running total of the arrears.

4. (a) If the landlord is aware that the tenant has difficulty in reading or understanding information given, the landlord should take reasonable steps to ensure that the tenant understands any information given. The landlord should be able to demonstrate that reasonable steps have been taken to ensure that the information has been appropriately communicated in ways that the tenant can understand.

    (b) If the landlord is aware that the tenant is under 18 or is particularly vulnerable, the landlord should consider at an early stage –
    (i)   whether or not the tenant has the mental capacity to defend possession proceedings and, if not, make an application for the appointment of a litigation friend in accordance with CPR 21;
    (ii) whether or not any issues arise under Disability Discrimination Act 1995; and
    (iii) in the case of a local authority landlord, whether or not there is a need for a community care assessment in accordance with National Health Service and Community Care Act 1990.

5. If the tenant meets the appropriate criteria, the landlord should arrange for arrears to be paid by the Department for Work and Pensions from the tenant's benefit.

6. The landlord should offer to assist the tenant in any claim the tenant may have for housing benefit.

7. Possession proceedings for rent arrears should not be started against a tenant who can demonstrate that he has –
    (a) provided the local authority with all the evidence required to process a housing benefit claim;
    (b) a reasonable expectation of eligibility for housing benefit; and
    (c) paid other sums due not covered by housing benefit.

    The landlord should make every effort to establish effective ongoing liaison with housing benefit departments and, with the tenant's consent, make direct contact with the relevant housing benefit department before taking enforcement action.

    The landlord and tenant should work together to resolve any housing benefit problems.

8. Bearing in mind that rent arrears may be part of a general debt problem, the landlord should advise the tenant to seek assistance from CAB, debt advice agencies or other appropriate agencies as soon as possible.

After service of statutory notices

9. After service of a statutory notice but before the issue of proceedings, the landlord should make reasonable attempts to contact the tenant, to discuss the amount of the arrears, the cause of the arrears, repayment of the arrears and the housing benefit position.

10. If the tenant complies with an agreement to pay the current rent and a reasonable amount towards arrears, the landlord should agree to postpone court proceedings so long as the tenant keeps to such agreement. If the tenant ceases to comply with such agreement, the landlord should warn the tenant of the intention to bring proceedings and give the tenant clear time limits within which to comply.

Alternative dispute resolution

11. The parties should consider whether it is possible to resolve the issues between them by discussion and negotiation without recourse to litigation. The parties may be required by the court to provide evidence that alternative means of resolving the dispute were considered. Courts take the view that litigation should be a last resort, and that claims should not be issued prematurely when a settlement is still actively being explored.

   The Legal Services Commission has published a booklet on 'Alternatives to Court', CLS Direct Information Leaflet 23 (www.cls-direct.org.uk/legalhelp/leaflet23.jsp), which lists a number of organisations that provide alternative dispute resolution services.

Court proceedings

12. Not later than ten days before the date set for the hearing, the landlord should –
   (a) provide the tenant with up to date rent statements;
   (b) disclose what knowledge he possesses of the tenant's housing benefit position to the tenant.

13. (a) The landlord should inform the tenant of the date and time of any court hearing and the order applied for. The landlord should advise

the tenant to attend the hearing as the tenant's home is at risk. Records of such advice should be kept.

(b) If the tenant complies with an agreement made after the issue of proceedings to pay the current rent and a reasonable amount towards arrears, the landlord should agree to postpone court proceedings so long as the tenant keeps to such agreement.

(c) If the tenant ceases to comply with such agreement, the landlord should warn the tenant of the intention to restore the proceedings and give the tenant clear time limits within which to comply.

14. If the landlord unreasonably fails to comply with the terms of the protocol, the court may impose one or more of the following sanctions –

(a) an order for costs;

(b) in cases other than those brought solely on mandatory grounds, adjourn, strike out or dismiss claims.

If the tenant unreasonably fails to comply with the terms of the protocol, the court may take such failure into account when considering whether it is reasonable to make possession orders.

Summary

17.71 Good financial management of projects is essential to ensure survival. It is obviously important to ensure that rent rises are implemented in accordance with the law, that service users receive the benefits they are entitled to so that the rents are affordable and that the payment of rent and service charges is prompt. It may in certain circumstances be necessary to evict service users for non-payment of rent. However, you should ensure that you have followed the appropriate guidance and the requirements of the pre-action protocol before taking such drastic action.

Managing vulnerability

Objectives

18.1 By the end of the chapter you will:

- Understand the legal requirements in connection with the capacity of individuals to make decisions
- Appreciate your responsibilities to protect service users from abuse
- Have an awareness of the role of other professionals in protecting service users from abuse
- Understand that services for vulnerable people should be delivered within a professional and ethical framework that promotes dignity

Case study

18.2 Amethyst project manages housing for people with learning disabilities on behalf of Stoneway Housing Association. Amethyst has shared house for five men who require 24-hour support, which is provided by support staff, some of whom provide the sleep-over cover. The staff at the scheme received a complaint from the parents of Martyn, a service user. The parents demanded that staff take Martyn's benefit away from him, as he has been spending it on prostitutes. Staff have agreed and have included in Martyn's support plan that he will be given £5 per day. Staff are also conducting daily searches of his room to ensure that he is not hoarding his money or using it to buy pornography. These checks take place at random times of the day, without prior warning, and Martyn is disturbed by staff when he is not fully dressed.

Overview

18.3 In this chapter we will consider how the law protects those who may have capacity issues and who may be vulnerable to abuse. As in many of our chapters, the dilemma facing the project is how to protect vulnerable people while at the same time protecting their rights and enhancing their dignity. We have already considered capacity in contracts in chapter 3. First, we will examine how the law ascertains that individuals are capable of making decisions. We will consider the implications of the Mental Incapacity Act 2005 and the accompanying guidance produced in April 2007 by the Ministry of Justice, Department of Health and the Public Guardianship Office. We then consider how the law protects service users from abuse and what you can do if you suspect or discover abuse. We also look at the roles of other professionals who may be involved in providing or managing services to those who are vulnerable. Finally, in the absence of a professional code of ethics within supported housing, you will need be aware of the ethical values that should underpin providing services to vulnerable people.

Capacity

18.4   In this case study the staff have taken a decision that Martyn does not have the capacity to make decisions as how to spend his money. Whilst there has been considerable pressure from his parents, the staff must consider the issue of Martyn's capacity within the framework of the law. It is important to recognise that just because you or others consider a service user's decision to be ill-considered, irrational, immoral or potentially dangerous, this does not mean that they do not have capacity to make the decision. This is often difficult for service providers because they are balancing an individual's autonomy with responsibility for their welfare.

18.5   The law in general has taken a functional approach to capacity which was endorsed by the Law Commission in their 1995 report on *Mental Incapacity.*

> ... whether an individual is able at the time when a particular decision has to be made, to understand its nature and effects. Importantly, both partial and fluctuating capacity can be recognised. Most people, unless in a coma, are able to make at least some decisions for themselves, and many have levels of capacity which vary from week to week or even from hour to hour.

18.6   Common law indicates that the individual does not have to have total understanding of any decision, but must understand the nature and effect of the decision. This is the basis of the Mental Capacity Act 2005.

Mental Capacity Act 2005

18.7   This Act received Royal Assent in 2005, but the provisions did not come fully into force until October 2007. It provides a statutory framework to protect and empower adults (16 years and above) who may lack capacity to make decisions. It also makes clear who can make decisions for an individual, in what circumstances and how to go about it.

18.8   Section 1 of the Act sets out five principles. The summary of the Act produced by the Ministry of Justice explains these clearly:

- A presumption of capacity – every adult has the right to make his or her own decisions and must be assumed to have capacity to do so unless it is proved otherwise.
- Individuals being supported to make their own decisions – a person must be given all practicable help before anyone treats them as not being able to make their own decisions.
- Unwise decisions – just because an individual makes what might be seen as an unwise decision, they should not be treated as lacking capacity to make that decision;
- Best interests – an act done or decision made under the Act for or on behalf of a person who lacks capacity must be done in their best interests.
- Least restrictive option – anything done for or on behalf of a person who lacks capacity should be the least restrictive of their basic rights and freedoms.

Test for capacity

18.9   The Act sets out a test for assessing lack of capacity that is 'decision specific' and 'time specific'.

18.10   According to the Act, a person 'lacks capacity in relation to a matter if at the material time he is unable to make a decision for himself in relation to the matter because of an impairment of, or a disturbance in the functioning of, the mind or brain'. This can be a temporary or permanent problem – what is important is that it is present at the time the decision needs to be made.

18.11   Under section 3(1) a person is unable to make a decision for him- or herself if he or she is unable:

(a) to understand the information relevant to the decision;
(b) to retain that information;
(c) to use or weigh that information as part of the process of making a decision; or
(d) unable to communicate his or her decision.

18.12   The explanation of the information relevant to the decision needs to be communicated appropriately, for example, using makaton or sign language. It also does not matter if the information is only retained for a short period, as long as that period covers when the decision was made.

Best interests

18.13   Once someone has been assessed as lacking capacity actions taken on their behalf must be in the best interests of the service user. This should not be based on someone's age or appearance or any condition that may lead to unjustified assumptions about the service user's best interests. This should prevent blanket assumptions being made about the best interests of groups of service users, for example, those living with dementia are not able to manage their own finances. The Act also provides a checklist of factors you will need to consider when assessing best interests:

- Whether the person will at some time have capacity in relation to the matter in question.
- If so when this is likely to be.
- If lacking capacity the service user must participate as much as possible in any act or decision taken on his or her behalf.
- Action must be taken to improve the service user's ability to participate as much as possible in any act or decision taken on his or her behalf.
- Any act should take into account the service user's past and present wishes, feelings, beliefs and values likely to influence their decision if they had capacity.
- Consultation must take place with anyone named by the service user to be consulted, anyone engaged with caring for the service user or interested in their welfare and anything done under a lasting power of attorney granted by the service user.

18.14   In our case study, the action taken by staff should be the result of an assessment of Martyn's capacity to make decisions as to how he spent his money, and the related issues in relation to pornography and the use of prostitutes. If he is able, at the time of engaging the services of a prostitute, to understand the information relevant to the decision, retain the information, use and weigh that information and communicate his decision, then he is capable of making the decision. Given this arrangement has taken place on more than one occasion, and money has exchanged hands, it would be difficult to rebut the presumption of capacity. The balance that staff need to address is between Martyn's individual rights and their duty of care in respect of supporting him to manage risks around relationships, health and personal safety. Although staff and his parents may feel unhappy about his decision, it is his decision and he has the capacity to make it. The wider issues relating to duty of care should be addressed through the assessment and support planning process.

> **Box 18.1 Frequently asked questions**
>
> We are working with people with mental health problems who may lack capacity when they become unwell. Often they state what they would like to happen when they become unwell, for example, allow someone else to look after their pet. However, when this happens they are reluctant to part with their pet.
>
> It would be good practice in these circumstances to ask service users to formulate a plan that encapsulates their wishes if they become unwell. When they become unwell, however, and express a different wish, you should apply the principles of the Mental Capacity Act. If the person does lack capacity following the plan will be a strong indication of acting in their best interests.

Code of practice

18.15   Under the section 42 of the Mental Capacity Act 2005, the Lord Chancellor was required to produce a code of guidance. The statutory code of practice was approved by parliament in April 2007. A number of people have a formal duty to have regard to the code, including those being paid for acts on behalf of, or in relation to, a person who lacks capacity. This includes care assistants, care workers and others who have been contracted to provide a service to people to lack capacity to consent to that service, and applies to supported housing providers who provide services to those who may lack capacity. In Box 18.2 we direct you to the code of practice and some useful guidance about the Act.

> **Box 18.2 Mental Capacity Act 2005**
>
> *The Code of Practice* can be downloaded from the Ministry of Justice website, www.justice.gov.uk. The British Medical Association has produced useful guidance, which can be found at www.bma.org.uk/ap.nsf/content/mencapact05.

18.16   The code has statutory force, which means that, although it is not a primary legislation, providers will have to justify disregarding it, and failure to comply can be used in legal proceedings.

Court of Protection

18.17   The jurisdiction relating to the Act is managed by a Court of Protection. The court will make decisions or appoint deputies to make decisions for those who lack capacity. It will also be important in resolving issues of disputed capacity or, in the case of lack of capacity, what is in the service user's best interests. In our case study, if Amethyst continues to manage Martyn's money, he could apply to the court either to dispute Amethyst's finding of incapacity or to argue that Amethyst is not acting in his best interests, or both.

Protection of vulnerable adults

18.18   The vulnerability of some service users in supported housing, as demonstrated in the case study, identifies the need for providers to ensure that abuse does not occur. Abuse was defined by the Department of Health in their 2000 guidance document, *No Secrets*, as 'the violation of an individual's human and civil rights by another person'.

18.19   Previously, Action on Elder abuse had defined it as a 'single or repeated act or lack of appropriate action occurring in a relationship in which there is an expectation of trust, which causes harm or distress to an older person'. Both these definitions are useful for you to start thinking about the relationship between staff and service users and when abuse may occur.

18.20   There are several types of abuse.

Physical abuse

18.21   Physical abuse is the deliberate infliction of pain, physical harm or injury, including: hitting, slapping, punching, pushing, kicking, hair-pulling, restraint, withholding or misuse of medication.

Psychological and emotional abuse

18.22   Psychological and emotional abuse is any pattern of behaviour by another that results in the psychological harm to a vulnerable adult. This may include: verbal abuse, humiliation, insults, ridicule, bullying, threats, enforced isolation, coercion, lack of privacy or choice, denial of dignity.

Sexual abuse

18.23   Sexual abuse is any sexual act carried out without the informed consent of a vulnerable adult. Examples may include: fondling, sexual intercourse, offensive or suggestive language, inappropriate touching.

Financial abuse

18.24   Financial abuse is the misappropriation of the funds of a vulnerable adult. Examples include: misuse of finances, exploitation, theft or fraudulent use of money, embezzlement, misuse of property.

Neglect

18.25   Neglect may be deliberate or by default, when the abuser is not able to provide the care needed and may not recognise the need for that care to be given.

Abusive regimes

18.26   There has been debate amongst academics that there is a further type of abuse: institutional abuse. Similar to institutionalised racism this is does not fall into the definitions identified earlier as it is abuse by regime rather than by individuals. On occasion, institutions develop practices which are abusive of the residents. In Box 18.3 we identify where environment and practices may lead to abuse regimes.

Box 18.3 Abusive regimes

In residential and nursing homes this may include:

- lack of flexibility and choice for residents in waking/bed times;
- lack of opportunity to obtain drinks and snacks;
- lack of choice over meals;
- lack of appropriate bedding;
- lack of appropriate heating;
- lack of personal possessions;
- lack of procedures in financial management, medical requirements and other matters pertaining to the person's care;
- lack of privacy in personal care, such as bathing, dressing, editing mail, restricting visits;
- derogatory remarks;
- public discussion of matters private to residents;
- restraint of residents that cannot be justified;
- lack of action to deal with abuse.

In supported and sheltered housing indicators this may include:

> - staff using master keys without due cause;
> - staff entering flats/rooms without permission or not waiting for reply after knocking;
> - breaches of residents' confidentiality;
> - restrictive practices in the use of communal facilities.

18.27   In the case study, it could be argued that Martyn is experiencing a range of abuse, which includes psychological or emotional abuse due to the lack of privacy or choice. It could also be claimed that Martyn is experiencing an abusive regime in that staff are entering his room without permission and not allowing him control of his money. It could be argued that Martyn is also experiencing financial abuse; however, as the object is not the misappropriation of funds but to 'protect' Martyn, this would be more difficult to prove.

Legal framework

18.28   The *No Secrets* guidance discussed above was published in March 2000. We have outlined the key measures of *No Secrets* and where it can be found in Box 18.4. This provides guidance on developing and implementing multi-agency policies and procedures to protect vulnerable adults from abuse.

18.29   The guidance has been issued under section 7 of the Local Authority Social Services Act 1970. This means that the guidance must be implemented unless local circumstances justify a variation.

Box 18.4 *No Secrets* guidance from the Department of Health

This is guidance for local agencies that have a responsibility to investigate and take action when a vulnerable adult is believed to be experiencing abuse. Its key measures are:

- Social services departments have a co-ordinating role in developing local policies and procedures for protecting vulnerable adults.
- There is a requirement for all relevant agencies to work collaboratively to protect vulnerable adults and develop inter-agency policies, procedures and protocols within to do so

No Secrets is available from www.dh.gov.uk/publications.

Legislation

18.30 There are two strands of the relevant law: protection and prevention. There is no specific legislation for protecting vulnerable adults, as there is for children, since the law generally assumes that adults are responsible for their own actions.

18.31 Vulnerable adults at risk may sometimes remain in dangerous situations because:

- staff have no power to gain access to remove them from such a situation or investigate the conduct of their affairs; or
- the vulnerable adult refuses all help.

18.32 Protection is available through criminal and civil courts, both to prevent a person being abused and to take action against the abuser. One of the problems you may encounter is the 'patchwork' of law relating to abuse, which can make it difficult to understand and/or enforce. There is a scarcity of case-law in this area, which may be due to the unwillingness of agencies and service users to undertake legal proceedings. There can also be difficulties in obtaining sufficiently reliable evidence from witnesses with some kind of disability or illness. This means that evidence in often uncorroborated, which deters people from going to court. These potential legal difficulties should not prevent you from reporting suspected abuse, or from becoming involved in inter-agency work to assess and attempt to resolve it.

18.33 Relevant areas of legislation include the following

Criminal law

18.34 Vulnerable adults are protected in the same way as other person against criminal acts. In Box 18.5 we have identified where abuse is criminal. If a person commits theft, rape, or assault against a vulnerable adult, they should be dealt with through the criminal justice system. Legislation in this category includes the Offences against the Person Act 1861, the Theft Act 1968, the Criminal Justice Act 1988, the Domestic Violence and Matrimonial Proceedings Act and the Sexual Offences Acts 1956, 1967, 1985 and 2003.

Box 18.5 When abuse is criminal

Physical	Assault.
Sexual	Rape, sexual assault, harassment.
Financial/material	Theft, extortion, embezzlement, fraud.
Psychological/emotional	Threats to kill, physical/sexual harassment. Often hard to evidence.
Discriminatory	(Not criminal: employment law covers race, gender, disability, sexual orientation and faith.)
Institutional	Corporate manslaughter.
Neglect	Actions that lead to endangerment of life.

Specific statutory offences

18.35   Section 127 of the Mental Health Act 1983 recognises that ill-treatment or neglect of patients with a mental disorder by professional staff is an offence. This Act also gives power of guardianship if the vulnerable adult is mentally ill and believed to be ill-treated or neglected.

18.36   The Sexual Offences Act 2003 protects vulnerable people by making it an offence to engage in or induce sexual activity with a person who has a mental disorder impeding their choice. The Act includes a separate offence concerning sexual activity between care workers and those who have mental disorder impeding their choice. You will need to consider the implications of this Act, particularly if you work in a care home or with service users aged 16 or 17. For more information. visit www.homeoffice.gov.uk

Civil law

18.37   This includes family law, property law, contract law and tort, including the 'duty of care' and 'negligence'. Thus, for example, the Court of Protection Rules Act 1984, the Enduring Powers of Attorney Act 1985 and Part IV of the Mental Health Act 1983 all provide for financial protection of vulnerable adults. Family law allows an individual to take an injunction against a member of their own household who is threatening their safety. Employment law is also relevant.

Law regulating provision

18.38 The Care Standards Act 2000, for example, enables the Commission of Social Care Inspection (CSCI) to take action where abuse is alleged or discovered. We look at the work of CSCI in chapter 10.

Statutes empowering agencies or professionals to act

18.39 These include:
- The NHS and Community Care Act 1990, which requires local authorities to assess need, which includes the need for protection due to vulnerability or the risk of being abused, and, in conjunction with other agencies, develop a care plan to meet the assessed need. This duty makes it appropriate for social services to have the lead responsibility, although this may not always apply.
- The Chronically Sick and Disabled Person Act 1970, which requires local authorities to provide services to disabled people.
- The Housing Act 1996, which allows local authorities and registered social landlords (RSLs) to apply for injunctions against anti-social or abusive tenants.
- The National Assistance Act 1948 s47, which is occasionally used to remove vulnerable but mentally competent older people from their home against their will.
- The Police and Criminal Evidence Act 1984, which gives the police powers to enter premises to save life.

Compensation

18.40 The law of tort enables a private action to be taken against an individual in the civil courts for compensation, and the Criminal Injuries Compensation Scheme provides compensation for criminal injury or damage.

Anti-discrimination legislation

18.41 This includes the law relating to disability rights, race relations, gender issues and human rights. We look at this area of law in chapter 6. Examples of statutes relating to discrimination are the Sex Discrimination Act 1975, the Race Relations Act 1976 and the Disability Discriminations Act 1995.

Regulatory framework

18.42   The Housing Corporation, in its Regulatory Code and guidance, expects that:

2.3 Housing association must maintain the highest standards of probity in all their dealings.
2.3.1   Acting to maintain the good reputation of the sector and not bringing it into disrepute.

18.43   In its guidance, the Housing Corporation advises there is a code of conduct for the governing body and staff, adherence to which should prevent abuse.

18.44   The Housing Corporation Code goes on to state that:

3.5 Housing Associations must provide good quality housing services for residents and prospective residents.
3.5.6   by providing high standards of customer care.

18.45   The guidance requires that:

3.5.7   Vulnerable and marginalised residents are provided with appropriate responsive housing services. Support and care arrangements (including liaison with other agencies) are in place, where appropriate.

18.46   Protection from abuse is one of the core service objectives of the quality assessment framework under the *Supporting People* framework. Providers are expected to have up-to-date policies and procedures to ensure protection from abuse. A failure to do so is seen to represent a serious potential risk to service users and/or staff. *Supporting People* teams expect that staff working with vulnerable adults are checked by the Criminal Records Bureau. We look at this in more detail in chapter 13. From July 2004, individuals who have abused, neglected or otherwise harmed vulnerable adults or placed them at risk of harm have to be included on a protection of vulnerable adults (POVA) register. Providers must make POVA checks if employing staff for care homes adult placements or domiciliary care.

Policies and procedures

18.47 Each organisation should have a policy and procedure on abuse or suspected abuse of vulnerable adults. Protection cannot rely on one policy and procedure; there are a number of related polices and procedures:

- Whistleblowing.
- Child protection.
- Recruitment.
- Equal opportunities.
- Health and safety.
- Confidentiality and information sharing.
- Financial management and accounting.
- Cash handling.
- Staff training and supervision.
- Code of conduct.
- Conflict of interest.
- Gifts.
- Incident and accidents.
- Dealing with violence and aggression.
- Harassment.

18.48 This is not an exhaustive list, but will give you an indication of the depth of work that is needed to ensure vulnerable people are protected.

Reporting abuse

18.49 If a staff member suspects that Martyn is being abused, they must report it in line with Amethyst's policies and procedures. This may be difficult if Martyn does not want anything to happen; the staff member should reassure him that his wishes will be taken into consideration. In Box 18.6 we outline when it may be necessary to take action against service users' wishes.

Box 18.6 Capacity and consent in referring abuse

The issue of capacity discussed earlier in this chapter is important in reporting abuse. If the service user has the capacity to make a decision and does not consent to a referral of abuse, their wishes should be honoured unless:

- they or others are in physical danger; and/or
- they are not the only person affected and risk to others is significant.

18.50 The staff member should report alleged or suspected abuse immediately to social services or the police if they believe that Martyn is at risk of serious harm or a serious criminal act has taken place.

Social services

18.51 Social services has a duty in collaboration with all other involved agencies to assess the needs and provide care to vulnerable adults. In the government *No Secrets* guidance, social services departments have been appointed as the lead agency for protecting vulnerable adults. It is usually social workers (also referred to as care managers) who fulfil this function for individual victims of abuse.

Social workers

18.52 The Local Authority (Social Services) Act 1970 imposes social service functions on local authorities. We summarise these duties in Box 18.7. Social workers were created to carry out the statutory duties required of social services departments. The legislation lists the duties imposed on social services in connection with children and adults. As this list has been added to or amended several times since the 1970s, it is less than coherent. In our case study, Martyn is likely to have a social worker under the provisions of the National Assistance Act 1948 or the National Health Service and Community Care Act 1990.

Box 18.7 Social services duties

- National Assistance Act 1948
  Providing care services in the community or residential care for those who cannot cope without such services.
- National Health Service and Community Care Act 1990
  Requirement to plan community care services, assess individual needs and make appropriate provision.

18.53 Anyone who suspects Martyn is being abused should inform social services. They can do this via Martyn's social worker (if he has one), the duty social worker, the social services intake team or, if Martyn was in hospital, a hospital social worker.

18.54 The social worker's response should include all or any of the following:

- Act as a key worker co-ordinating the involvement of appropriate parties and, if necessary, organising multi-agency case conferences.
- Arrange a package of care which, might include home care, day care, meals provision, etc.
- Assess the needs of the victim's carer relief to support the situation.
- Monitor the situation and provide emotional support to the victim and family.
- Instigate Court of Protection or other methods of handling victim's finances.
- Work with other agencies to resolve any accommodation issues.

Police

18.55 Sexual abuse, physical abuse, some forms of psychological abuse, financial exploitation, theft or fraud all constitute criminal offences. In such cases, you should contact the police, either directly or through social services. The police must always be informed immediately if current sexual abuse is suspected or if allegations involve staff.

18.56 The police have a duty to the service user to assist, support and obtain evidence of alleged offences, and a responsibility to investigate a reported crime, as well as interview any identified suspects. The best interests of the service user as well as their wishes should be taken into consideration. This process may not always result in criminal proceedings, and criminal proceedings will not always result in a conviction.

Box 18.8 Frequently asked questions

How can we ensure that someone we want to employ as a support worker hasn't been abusive to service users in a previous job?

You would need to take up professional references for anyone who has been previously employed, particularly the current or most recent employer. For those working with vulnerable people, you would be expected to carry out a Criminal Records Bureau check. This would identify any abuse that was criminal. We cover CRB checks in chapter 13. The Safeguarding Vulnerable Groups Act 2006 establishes a vetting and barring scheme for people working with children and vulnerable adults. Individuals are to be placed on the barred list if there is evidence that they have harmed or attempted to harm a vulnerable adult, caused or incited them to be harmed or put them at risk of harm. This will be administered by the CRB and is expected to be in operation in Autumn 2008. Employees should be able to get an online snapshot of those unable to undertake certain activities relating to those who are vulnerable. It does not cover all client groups, so you may still have to rely on the CRB checks and following up references.

For further information see www.everychildmatters.gov.uk or www.dh.gov.uk.

Health

18.57   Health service provision is broadly divided between purchasers and providers. The purchasers (health authorities and primary care groups) influence policy and determine how money is spent. Providers deliver health services to the public in hospitals or in a variety of community settings.

18.58   There is a range of healthcare providers, employed by trusts or part of the primary healthcare team (your GP surgery), who may be involved in assessing and meeting the needs of an abused vulnerable adult and determining capacity. These include:

18.59   In the community:

- *Ambulance Service* – accessed through 112 (the new number for 999) or 999 when it is an emergency. If a crime is suspected, the police should be contacted first and they will arrange for an ambulance.
- *General practitioners (GPs)* should be contacted in non-emergency abuse situations where the victim's mental or physical health has been affected. They can also spot signs and symptoms of abuse in their patients. The GP can refer the service user to other health services, including district nurses or specialist health professionals.
- *District nurses and health visitors* are part of the primary care team and are accessed either via the GPs or through direct referral. Some service users may feel more comfortable with health practioners as apposed to social workers.
- *Community psychiatric nurses (CPNs)* – these are usually part of an NHS trust. They may be involved when a mental illness (including

dementia) of the victim or the abuser is a contributory factor. Access routes to CPNs vary across the country but social services care staff should know how to involve them, if appropriate.

- *Specialists* such as *geriatricians, psycho-geriatricians, nutritionists, occupational therapists, physiotherapists* can be called in depending on the needs of the situation. Psycho-geriatricians have a particular contribution to make establishing the capacity of older vulnerable adults.

18.60   In hospital:

- *Hospital personnel* including *doctors, nurses, occupational therapists, physiotherapists* and *other health specialists* play an important part in responding to an emergency and setting the wheels in motion to ensure the future safety and wellbeing of the victim. They also have a key role in spotting the signs and symptoms of abuse which may have been overlooked in the community.

18.61   Healthcare providers, like other agencies, are required under government guidance to work in a collaborative, multi-disciplinary way.

Human rights

18.62   In the last part of this chapter we examine the importance of delivering services that promote service users' rights and afford them dignity. In chapter 7 we introduced you to the Human Rights Act 1998, which provides a mechanism to those whose rights have been infringed. As we highlighted, the question of whether 'third sector' providers can be proceeded against as public bodies is not clear. Despite this, we are confident you want to provide services that respect service users' human rights. To facilitate this, we discuss delivering services within an ethical framework and identify the values that should underpin your work.

Values and ethical framework

18.63   Ethics can be defined as the fundamental principles that inform a person's values and determine their moral duties and obligations; crudely, they describe a motivation based on what is considered to be right or wrong. In your private lives, your ethics will influence the way you behave. For example, you may decide not to eat meat, based on your belief that killing animals is wrong or you may buy only free-range eggs, based on your belief that factory farming is wrong. Individuals all have their own beliefs about what is right or wrong. However, the law is based on a framework of what society as a whole believes is right and wrong. For example, you may feel that you are capable of driving quite safely at 75 miles per hour on the motorway; but the law has set the speed limit at 70.

18.64   At work, ethical practice often refers to a code of professional standards, containing aspects of fairness and duty to that profession. In supported housing, there is no statutory or even agreed ethical code, compared with social care provision by social workers or health care provision by nurses. This is probably because there is no statutory duty to provide supported housing services. Ethical practice is largely determined by a number of requirements. Legal requirements may provide ethical standards, for example, the Data Protection Act 1998 protects information held about service users. Housing Corporation regulatory requirements expect RSLs to compensate service users under certain circumstances. Lastly, organisations have their own policies, procedures, codes of conduct, job descriptions, etc which set particular ethical standards. For example, a worker's job description usually obliges them to adhere to the organisation's equal opportunities policy and procedure.

18.65   What follows is our interpretation of the basic values and ethics that inform supported housing service provision. This is often referred to as the 'value base' of supported housing, or the philosophy upon which the sector provides services. For those directly involved in provision, this requires reflective practice. This means that you will have to examine your own beliefs and attitudes to ensure that they are not negatively impacting on those people to whom you are providing a service.

Respecting and promoting service users' rights

18.66   Rights more generally can be described as service users' entitlements. They are often linked to the needs that service users have, for example, the basic needs for accommodation and food, and those more complex needs of health and social care. As we have outlined throughout the book, the rights that service users expect from supported housing are driven by legislation, regulation and policies and procedures. Workers in supported housing have a huge impact upon whether service users enjoy, or are deprived of, their rights. In Box 18.9 we identify how service users' rights may be limited by attitudes or practices.

Box 18.9 Reasons that rights may be limited for service users

- The stereotyping that accompanies attitudes towards minorities or disability. For example, a service user with enduring mental health problems may be given a less secure form of occupancy agreement because he or she is seen as unreliable.
- Paternalistic attitudes of workers that lead to a risk adverse service delivery. For example, not allowing a service user with a learning disability to go swimming on their own without assessing risk.
- Lack of information in an accessible form regarding rights. For example, relying on written information where service users may have a low level of literacy or English may not be a first language.
- Lack of resources, for example, there may not be funding to ensure that all accommodation-based service schemes are wheelchair accessible.

18.67 Workers should ensure that they know what rights service users have within the service, and where information about them can be found. In Box 18.11 we identify what regulators expect in relation to service user rights. These may be found in the occupancy agreement, in a service user handbook or in policies and procedures. Service users should be advised of their rights, not just when they move in but throughout the period support is provided to them. Workers may also be expected to advocate for service users to ensure that their rights are respected in the wider community. For example, if a service user with a substance misuse issue is not receiving adequate health care, a supported housing worker may negotiate better provision with their GP or healthcare services. Sometimes workers may find upholding a service user's right presents them with a conflict of interest, when it is their organisation that is alleged to be responsible for infringing that right. A service user can be supported by staff in making a complaint, but it may be appropriate to refer them to an external advocate or advice agency.

Box 18.10 Regulatory requirements on service users' rights

The Housing Corporation expects that all applicants and residents are given the Housing RSL, available at www.housingcorp.gov.uk.

For services funded by *Supporting People*, the administering authorities usually require that service users are given particular rights, for example, the right to complain. Contact your local Supporting People team at www.[*name of local authority*].gov.uk.

The National Minimum Standards for Care Homes for Adults (16–65), published by the Department for Health, identifies a number of ways in which service users' rights are protected. For example, Standard 16: 'Service users rights are respected and responsibilities recognised in their daily lives': see www.csci.org.uk/PDF/care_homes_for_adults_18_65.pdf.

Acting in the best interests of the service user

18.68   There is a tension in the provision of housing and support as workers are employed to provide a service to the service user, but also are often expected to advocate on behalf of, and advise, the service user. The primary responsibility is to provide services that are in the best interests of the service user. As we have highlighted, at times this may be in conflict with what the service user wants, for example, if their wishes endanger their health and safety. Service users have a right to self-determination and are entitled to autonomy, and should therefore be supported in reaching informed decisions, as long as these do not conflict with their safety or the safety of others. As we have identified earlier, the interpretation of safety may need to be carefully negotiated when service users have family members, friends or other agencies involved in their support or care.

Acting in a non-discriminatory and inclusive way

18.69   Chapter 6 looks at the legal protection service users can expect in shielding them from discrimination. The protection of the law is sometimes not enough because of the difficulties that service users face in enforcing legal rights. Good practice and the requirements of external regulators that services are delivered within a non discriminatory and inclusive framework are necessary to supplement the law. All organisations should have an equal opportunity policy and procedures that staff are expected to follow. Supported housing services should be provided in a non-judgmental way, with an awareness of the effects of poverty and deprivation on the service users. Regulators expect staff to know and understand organisational equal opportunities and anti-discriminatory policies and procedures. This is an area where attitudes and experiences have a direct influence on behaviour. As prejudices develop from a very early stage, our own learned behaviour will affect how services are delivered. This requires that we reflect upon our own practices and change them where necessary. Organisations should ensure that all staff receive anti-discriminatory training to enable them to identify discrimination, understand why it exists, consider its effects and actively work to reduce it. In the appendices we have included information on the practical approaches for the supported housing sector. In Box 18.11 we explain methods of working in a non-discriminatory way.

Box 18.11 Working in a non discriminatory way

- Be prepared to challenge offensive remarks and behaviour, for example, service users telling racist jokes.
- Avoid harmful generalisations, for example, 'all travelling people cause anti-social behaviour'.
- Identify when discrimination occurs and be prepared to challenge it. This may be either on an individual basis, for example, a worker speculating about the HIV status of a gay man, or on an organisational basis, for instance, a policy and procedure for a scheme for people with learning disabilities preventing service users from having overnight guests.
- Ensure that you understand how to implement your organisation's anti-discriminatory guidelines and procedures, and support service users in making a complaint when this is appropriate.

Involving service users in service provision

18.70 Ethically informed supported housing provision should involve those who receive services. Regulators and/or funders, such as the Housing Corporation, *Supporting People,* the Audit Commission and the Care Standard Commission for Inspection, expect that organisations ensure that service users' needs and aspirations are central to the service provided. This should include involvement in decision making, for example, involving service users in planning services and delivery. This involvement should not be limited to the organisation of services.

It should also work at an individual level – a service user should be involved in deciding how his or her personal support services are delivered – for example, when support meetings take place and who has control over the process. The issue of service user involvement can be challenging for staff, as it implies the transfer of power from the support provider to the recipient of support, which can cause insecurity for staff – they have lost status as part of the process. Service user involvement is critical in maximising choice for service users. Although resources and external constraints may place restrictions upon provision, providers should enable service users to choose between different actions and possibilities. In order to exercise choice, service users need to be informed about the services available, the implications of making the choice and how it will affect themselves and others. In Box 18.12 we direct you to further resources on service user involvement.

Box 18.12 Signpost Further information on service user involvement

ODPM, *A guide to service user involvement for organisations providing housing related support,* November 2003, www.communities.gov.uk.

Audit Commission and Housing Corporation, *Housing: Improving services through resident involvement,* June 2004, www.auditcommission.gov.uk.

Summary

18.71   The supported housing sector along with other welfare provision is moving from paternalism to empowering users, and the law on capacity enhances this move. There is a presumption that service users are capable of making decisions about life choices, and the law supports this. You may feel that service users make unwise or irrational decisions – the law gives service users the right to do this; all of us have the right to make mistakes. The legislation protecting service users from abuse is more disparate – this is not surprising, given the range of abuse that may occur and the slowness of society to recognise this. It is expected that you will have robust policies and procedures to give staff and service users the confidence to report and respond to abuse. Lastly, we have touched on the value base that should be the foundation of support service delivery. You should understand how your experiences shape your beliefs and how this in turn will influence the way you deliver a service. Individuals are assumed to work in the supported housing sector because they want to make a difference to the quality of life for service users. It is therefore your responsibility to enable service users to have the same rights and choices as you would expect for yourself. Developing the habits of reflective practice is a crucial tool to help you deliver effective provision.

CHAPTER 19

Managing information

Objectives

19.1   By the end of the chapter you will:

- Appreciate the need to protect the confidentiality of information
- Understand when it is appropriate and necessary to share information
- Appreciate what your duties are in relation to data protection
- Understand how information should be stored and service users' rights to access information held about them

Case study

19.2   New Start, a charitable agency, manages an accommodation-based scheme for care leavers on behalf of Partner, a registered housing association. Young people are referred by social services and the aim of the scheme is to provide temporary accommodation and support to enable service users to acquire the skills to live independently. Mike, a service user, has just disclosed to his support worker that he has been tested for HIV and has had a positive result. Mike has said that he does not want anyone else to know. The worker also supports Kim in the project, who has confided that she is having a sexual relationship with Mike and believes she may be pregnant.

Overview

19.3   This case study provides an opportunity for us to explore the dilemmas in the supported housing sector in deciding what confidential information to disclose and under what circumstances. The common law and the Human Rights Act 1998 are designed to safeguard the privacy of vulnerable people, but there are times when information sharing is essential for the protection of vulnerable people. What are the legal and good practice issues that this case raises? How can we balance individual rights and professional responsibilities? We will explore these questions as we go through the chapter.

19.4   There has been a tendency for both statutory and voluntary agencies to be cautious about sharing information. The Laming Inquiry (January 2003), into the death of Victoria Climbie, and the Bichard inquiry (June 2004), into the conviction of Ian Huntley for the murder of Holly Wells and Jessica Chapman, examined the reluctance of agencies to share information and the potential legal barriers to information sharing. The Laming Inquiry was concerned that information was not shared between agencies because staff thought they ran the risk that their actions would be considered unlawful. This was seen as not compatible with serving the needs of children and families. The Bichard Inquiry identified the lack of confidence that police and other officers had in their ability to share information because of their perceptions of the Data Protection Act 1998. Michael Bichard identified that:

> ... the legislation was not the problem [but that] better guidance is needed on the collection, retention, deletion, use and sharing of information, so that police officers, social workers and other professionals can feel more confident in using information properly.

The Ministry of Justice has issued very helpful guidance on information sharing, which can be found at www.justice.gov.uk

19.5   In this chapter we set out the legal framework which draws upon both common law and human rights to help you to understand the principles that should inform your day-to-day practice. We then go on to look at disclosure and the difficult balance between maintaining confidentiality and disclosure of information in the private or public interest. Lastly, we look at the Data Protection Act 1998, which ensures that information is handled appropriately and requires that individuals should have access to the information held about them.

The law relating to confidentiality

The Human Rights Act 1998

19.6   We have already looked at the Human Rights Act 1998 in chapter 7 and we think it is useful for organisations to measure themselves against the conventions of the Act in terms of good practice, whether or not they are public bodies.

19.7   The article that is of particular relevance to confidentiality is:

Article 8 – Rights to respect for private and family life

Everyone has the right to respect for his private and family life, his home and his correspondence.

There shall be no interference by a public authority with the exercise of this right except such as is in accordance with the law and is necessary in a democratic society in the interests of national security, public safety or the economic well-being of the country, for the prevention of disorder or crime, for the protection of health or morals, or for the protection of the rights and freedoms of others

19.8 In the case study set out at the beginning of the chapter, New Start would have to determine whether it would be lawful, proportionate and necessary to interfere with Mark's right to respect for his privacy. We will look at disclosure later.

The common law duty of confidentiality

19.9 In chapter 2 we looked at the sources of law. It is the common law which imposes a duty of confidentiality and provides individuals with a cause of action for damages if there has been a breach of that duty. Breach of confidence is a tort that protects the collection, use and disclosure of personal information. There are three basic legal requirements before the duty arises:

- The information must be confidential; it must not be in the public domain or readily available from another source. For example, if an actress disclosed in the news that she had attended a rehabilitation clinic for substance misuse she could not claim breach of confidence if a substance misuse worker disclosed that they had supported her in managing her substance misuse. The courts, however, can act to limit further disclosure even if the information is already in the public domain, so the worker may be prevented from giving interviews to the press on the matter.
- The information must be disclosed as a result of circumstances giving rise to an obligation of confidence. The obligation of confidence is likely to arise because of your professional relationship, so this means that the service user can assume that information they disclosed will be kept in confidence. This extends to information you receive indirectly but in your professional capacity. For example, if a referring agency disclosed that a service user had an eating disorder.
- There must have been an unauthorised use of the information. If a service user gives you permission to divulge information, you have not breached your duty. However, you need to be careful about how you deal with permission: a service user may give you permission to disclose financial information on their behalf to a debt collection agency, not that the reason they experienced problems in payment is a result of mental health problems.

19.10 Some providers require service users to sign blanket consent to share all information with any party. We do not recommend this approach, and in any case this probably would not constitute a defence in court. Implicit in the relationship between service provider and service user is the relationship of confidentiality. Such a blanket would negate the duty.

19.11 Confidentiality is not an absolute right, and defences for disclosure of information include:

- acting in the public interest; and
- just cause or excuse, for example, to prevent a serious crime.

19.12 In some cases legislation or regulation requires you to disclose information. For example, if a service user's rent is paid directly to you as their landlord, you are under an obligation to disclose a change in circumstance to the housing benefit department.

19.13 In many ways, the common law expects that you balance the justification for disclosure of information with the proportionality of the need for that information to be shared – a very similar balance to that required by the European Convention on Human Rights. We will look at the instances when it might be appropriate to share information later in the chapter.

Importance of confidentiality

19.14 We have identified the legal framework that works to protect confidentiality, but there are other reasons why confidentiality is important in the housing, care and support sector. On a practical level, confidentiality:

1 prevents exploitation;
2 preserves dignity and self-esteem;
3 establishes trust;
4 upholds the client's right to know what happens to information disclosed;
5 promotes respect;
6 promotes choice.

19.15 Organisations should have a clear written confidentiality policy and procedure, and we have included guidelines on developing a policy in the appendices. Many regulators or commissioners will expect organisations funded by them to have a policy and procedure on confidentiality. The starting point is the presumption of confidentiality: the legal principle is that it is the duty of the person seeking the disclosure to make a positive case to justify breaching the code of confidentiality. For example, in *S v S (Chief Constable of West Yorkshire Police Intervening)* [1999] 1 All ER 281, a woman had fled to a refuge with her child and the father asked the court to order the police to divulge the address to the court. The police successfully resisted the request as they were able to satisfy the court of the child's safety without disclosing the address.

19.16   The duty of confidentiality is usually set out in an employee's contract of employment and the organisation's code of conduct. Volunteers are also bound by the duty of confidentiality. Service users cannot be bound in law to keep each other's confidences as they have no professional relationship with each other. The only instance where a service user could be accountable for disclosing information is through the terms of their occupancy agreement, and then only if that term were reasonable. For example, a requirement not to not disclose the address or the identity of a service user in a women's refuge is likely to be a reasonable term of a refuge's occupancy agreement.

19.17   In the case study outlined at the beginning of the chapter, the presumption is that the information disclosed by both Mike and Kim would be confidential and that there is a duty of confidentiality imposed upon the worker. The next section outlines the instances where information can and should be shared.

Sharing information

19.18   It is difficult to provide services to vulnerable people if information is not available to the full range of professionals concerned with their welfare. Assessments (especially risk assessments) and decisions need to be based not on half-truths, but on full and accurate information.

Information is confidential to the individual not the organisation

19.19   Where information is shared, it should be made clear that the information is confidential to the organisation and not the individual member of staff. There should be procedures in place that outline how information will be shared. Information should be handled in a way that promotes respect and trust. This does not mean that every detail of a service user's life should be divulged to every member of staff in an organisation; information should be shared on a 'need to know' basis.

19.20   In the case study, information about both Mike and Kim should be shared with the line manager in the first instance. Then a decision should be made about what information should be shared with other support workers. Only workers who 'need to know' the information should be provided with it. The information that Mike is HIV positive does not need to be shared with the cleaner or maintenance staff, for example.

Multi-agency work

19.21 Supporting vulnerable people increasingly relies on multi-agency work, which can only be effective if information is shared between the professionals involved in the service user's support/care. The 'third sector' is increasingly being expected to deliver public services, which involves a close relationship between statutory agencies and other voluntary or private organisations. However, information must be shared in a responsible way. Disclosure is only defensible/lawful if it is in the public or individual's interest and, if disclosure is by a public body, it must be proportionate and necessary under the Human Rights Act 1998. Good practice is to negotiate an information sharing protocol both for the scheme and each service user at the beginning of their stay. We have outlined considerations for an information sharing protocol in Box 19.1.

Box 19.1 Information sharing protocol

1   Who are the nominated staff?
2   What information is to be shared – justification?
3   Audit trail and documentation.
4   What consent has been asked for and given by the service user?
5   Accuracy of information shared.
6   Record keeping.

Disclosure to the police and other bodies

19.22 Legislation provides some very specific circumstances when information must be disclosed to the police. For example, the Prevention of Terrorism Act 1989, the Police and Criminal Evidence Act

1984 and the Misuse of Drugs Act 1971 require some information you may come across in the course of your duties to be disclosed to the police. Generally, you can disclose information to the police for the prevention and detection of crime or for the apprehension or prosecution of offenders.

Box 19.2 Frequently asked questions

We manage a hostel for those who have offended or are at risk of offending. The police have asked us it they can have a list of those housed.

It would be a defence to a breach of confidentiality if the information was for the prevention and detection of a crime or the apprehension or prosecution of an offender. There is an also an exemption in the Data Protection Act 1998 that allows organisations to provide information to the police. This exemption does not cover all information. You are only able to disclose information which, if not disclosed, would prejudice the police being able to catch a suspect or prevent crime. In this case, the police appear to be on a 'fishing exercise', and you could refuse to disclose the information until the police can explain why having this information prevents crime or allows them to catch a suspect.

19.23   For housing benefit purposes, the Fraud Act 1997 obliges the staff of landlords to disclose prescribed information about service users to the housing benefit office, where the housing benefit is paid directly to the landlord. In Box 19.3 we summarise the key points when information should be shared.

Box 19.3 Key points when information should be shared

1   When the service user consents to enable effective delivery of support, social care, health and other services.
2   If the service user or third party may be in danger.
3   Child protection.
4   Court instructs or the police acting on behalf of the court.
5   Under care management, probation, etc systems.
6   Where there is a lawful basis under legislation, common law or Crown prerogative.

19.24   In the case study set out at the beginning of the chapter, the worker must carefully consider what information, if any, should be shared with whom.

19.25   *Other members of staff* – the information is confidential to the organisation not to the individual worker but the worker should consider who 'needs to know' this information.

19.26   *Social worker* – the worker should have to establish whether there is an ongoing relationship with social services for both Mike and Kim. In an ideal world, the ongoing arrangement would be covered by an information sharing protocol. In the absence of such an agreement, the worker would have to make a decision within the framework outlined above. In both cases, the information is confidential so a decision to share it must be defensible. Is it in the interests of Mike and Kim to have the information shared with their social worker?

19.27   *Police* – the worker is not under a duty to disclose information to the police. The prevention or detection of a crime can be a defence to a breach of confidentiality. The worker should speak to Mike about implications of continuing to have unprotected sex with Kim without divulging his HIV status.

19.28   *Kim and other service users* – the information should not be disclosed to Kim, though the worker does have a role in encouraging Mike to discuss his status with his partner. Confidential information about Mike or Kim should not be disclosed to other service users under any circumstances.

19.29   The ideal solution in the case study would be for Mike's key worker to support Mike in disclosing his health status to his sexual partner(s), including Kim. Kim could then be supported by her key worker in making decisions regarding ascertaining her own status and make informed decisions regarding her own health especially if she is pregnant. Another solution would be to seek Mike's consent to the worker disclosing the information to Kim. This could only happen if Kim agreed to her key worker disclosing to Mike that she had informed the key worker of their sexual relationship.

Data protection

19.30   The increasing professionalisation of the sector and the requirement for accountability for the services has increased the amount of information held about service users. Information held is subject to the statutory framework that controls information handling, and you should be aware of your obligations.

Data Protection Act 1998

19.31   The Data Protection Act 1998 came into force on 1 March 2000 and governs information held by providers. *The Act requires organisations or individuals who process personal data to register with the Information Commissioner.* Personal data means information about an identified or identifiable living individual which is processed automatically, for example, by computer, or recorded manually, for example, in a filing system. Processing includes collecting, holding and destroying information and also disclosing it. We have included details about the Information Commissioner in Box 19.4.

Box 19.4 Signpost

The Information Commissioner Office provides information, at home and oversees, and enforces the Data Protection Act 1998, the Freedom of Information Act 2000, the Environmental Information Regulations 2004 (SI 2004 No 3391) and the Privacy and Electronic Communications (EC Directive) Regulations 2003 (SI 2003 No 2426). There is a range of user-friendly and useful explanations of information legislation on the Information Commissioner Office website, www.ico.gov.uk.

19.32   The Data Protection Act 1998 requires people or organisations who decide how or why personal data is processed (data controllers) to comply with eight principles.

19.33   Personal data shall be:

1   *Fairly and lawfully processed* – processing the information must not breach the common law duty of confidentiality or infringe individuals' human rights. Also, the organisation must not be operating outside of its authority, for example, a hostel for young people should not be keeping the credit card details of the young people.

2   *Processed for limited purposes* – the information should be held for a particular purpose and only used for that purpose, for example, information on ethnicity to ensure that equality targets are met.

3   *Adequate, relevant and not excessive* – information should only be held if it is necessary, for example, someone's credit card details are unlikely to be relevant even when support is being offered to help them manage rent arrears.

4   *Accurate* – the information processed should be accurate, and information held on service users should be checked with the

service user, for example, service users should be asked to sign records made or their support plan.

5 *Not kept longer than necessary* – if there is no reason for holding on to information, it must be destroyed, for example, if a written warning only lasts six months it should be destroyed after six months.

6 *Processed in accordance with the data subject's rights* – there is no breach of the obligations set out in Schedules 2 and 3 to the Act.

7 *Secure* – non-authorised people should not be able to gain access to the information, and each organisation should be clear who has access, for example, service users' referral information should be password protected or kept in a locked filing cabinet.

8 *Not transferred to countries without adequate protection* – information should not be automatically sent to new countries, for example, if a service user moves abroad.

19.34 We have included some guidelines you may find helpful when keeping records in Box 19.5.

Box 19.5 Record keeping

1 Ensure it is readable – word processed or clearly handwritten.

2 Ensure it is understandable – use plain language, short sentences, accurate grammar and punctuation. Avoid jargon – if you need to use specialised terminology or abbreviation, you should explain these terms when you first use them.

3 Follow your scheme guidelines; use standard formats where appropriate.

4 Record date and time of any incident or meeting and of the report being written.

5 Write your report as soon as possible after the meeting or incident, while you can still remember clearly. At the very least, make notes that you can refer to.

6 Record what *you* have observed or make it clear if you are recording hearsay.

7 As a rule, state facts rather than expressing opinions, for example, 'his speech was slurred, I could smell alcohol on his breath and he was unsteady on his feet', rather than 'he was drunk'.

8 If it is relevant to state an opinion, make it clear that this is what you are doing and whose opinion it is: 'she said she was depressed' or 'I thought she was depressed because she

> was unusually quiet and tearful at times during our meeting
> ...' rather than 'she was depressed'.
> 9 Be specific – about what occurred, when it occurred, who
>   was present, what was agreed, any deadlines, for example,
>   'We agreed that I would accompany Tony to the review session
>   with his social worker on 29 March', or 'At 10.00 am I was in
>   the project office with support worker, Samantha Jones. I
>   heard shouting from the kitchen and the fire alarm sounded'.
> 10 Written records are *legal documents*, and you should always
>   remember this. Imagine that anything you write could be
>   read out in court – are you being objective, professional and
>   non-discriminatory in what you write?

Fair processing

19.35   The Act expressly provides that personal data is not to be treated as processed fairly unless certain criteria are met (as far as practicable).

19.36   Criteria to be met include:

1 You must inform the service user of the identity of the data controller.
2 You must inform the service user of the purpose for which the data is to be processed.
3 The service user should not have been mislead or deceived as to the purpose of the processing of the data.

Conditions for processing

19.37   Processing may only be carried out when one of the following conditions has been satisfied:

1 The individual has given his or her consent to the processing.
2 The processing is necessary for the performance of a contract with the individual.
3 The processing is required under a legal obligation.
4 The processing is necessary to protect the vital interests of the individual.
5 The processing is necessary to carry out public functions.
6 The processing is necessary in order to pursue the legitimate interest of the data controller or certain third parties.

Sensitive information

19.38 Data should not be processed unless one of the conditions set out in Schedule 2 to the Act is met; in the case of sensitive personal data, one of the conditions in Schedule 3 to the Act must also be complied with.

19.39 Sensitive personal data includes information relating to racial or ethnic origin, political opinions, religious or other beliefs, trade union membership, physical or mental health, sex life and criminal convictions. In relation to your work, the conditions for disclosure set out in both Schedules 2 and 3 include the service user giving consent to the disclosure. If no consent is given the, schedules include circumstances where disclosure is needed to protect the vital interests of the service user.

Rights of the service user as a data subject

Access to personal information

19.40 The Data protection Act 1998 provides a right of access to personal information held by both public and private bodies. This includes:

1 Computer records.
2 Manual records.
3 Where files or papers are organised in a way that makes it easy to find information about a particular individual, for example, a scheme log book.

19.41 Organisations should have a policy and procedure that allows service users to access the records held on them. In most cases, you would be expected to respond to a request to see records within two working days, which will give you time to remove exempt information. Exempt information under the Data Protection Act 1998 includes:

1 Personal information about someone other than the service user. In the case study, if there was a record of the information disclosed by Kim on Mike's file.
2 Information that would identify someone who has supplied information, for example, a complaint about a service user where the complainant had wanted to remain anonymous.
3 References cannot be accessed from the individual or organisation who supplied it and also cannot be accessed by the holding organisation if they identify the individual who gave it.
4 Information held for the purpose of preventing and detecting crime

or apprehending or prosecuting offenders, for example, some court records.

5   Information about the course of legal negotiations between the data controller and the individual if access to the information would prejudice those negotiations.

19.42   There is also an important safeguard preventing access to records. Information can be withheld if disclosure would be likely to cause serious harm to the service user or to any other person's (including staff) physical or mental health. You should not use this safeguard lightly and require evidence to support its use. In Box 19.6 we outline some good practice to enable you to share information appropriately when requested.

Box 19.6 Good practice

Staff should satisfy themselves of the identity of any individual requesting information, including the service user. Some organisations give service users a password for use on the phone or email so that they can be easily identified when requesting information such as rent account balances. Information sharing protocols should include named individuals, who should be expected to provide identification.

Enforcement and remedies

19.43   The Information Commission has powers of entry and inspection and may investigate processing of information and serve an enforcement notice where a principle has been contravened. It is a criminal offence under the Data Protection Act 1998 knowingly or recklessly to obtain, disclose and procure to sell personal data without the consent of the data subject.

Box 19.7 Frequently asked questions

We manage a scheme for people with substance misuse issues. One of the service user's GPs has advised her parents that she has become sexually active. Can she claim compensation?

The service users can seek compensation under section 13(1) of the Data Protection Act 1998 and damages for distress under section 14. A service user can also sue through the civil courts for damages and distress caused because a data controller has contravened the Act.

19.44 Contravention of the Act can result in a £5,000 fine in a magistrates' court or unlimited fine in a Crown Court. Directors and other officers can separately be held personally liable. In Box 19.8 we have identified some action points to support you in complying with data protection requirements.

Box 19.8 Action points

1 Ensure a member of staff is a data protection compliance lead/officer.
2 Check your data protection security.
3 Carry out a data protection audit – a manual is available from www.ico.gov.uk/tools_and_resources/document_library/data_protection.aspx.
4 Ensure you are able to distinguish between personal and sensitive data.
5 Are storage methods secure?
6 Are staff and volunteers aware of the obligations?
7 Are service users aware of their rights?

Retention of records

19.45 Principle 5 of the Data Protection Act 1998 sets out that records should be held for the minimum amount of time. This principle dictates that records should be destroyed and not kept. Your organisation should have a retention policy that outlines how long information should be kept. This should include information on existing and former service users, depending on the need to access those records. In some cases this is clear, for example, if a service user is given a warning for a breach of their occupancy agreement and that warning lasts for six months. The warning must be destroyed after six months unless further action is to be taken. For other information, for example, information on former service users, the organisation will need to assess how often it has to refer back to the records once the service user has left and over what time period. For example, if you only refer to the records of former service users within six months of their leaving, you should destroy information after six months.

> **Box 19.9 Frequently asked questions**
>
> **We have residents records dating back for eight years. Is there any information we have to keep for any specified length of time?**
>
> Some information may need to be kept for a certain period of time, for example, anything relating to a contract, including the occupancy agreement and rent account, should be kept for six years. The Limitation Act 1980 imposes this limit for breach of contract and arrears of rent claims. A claim for negligence is also limited to six years under the Limitation Act 1980. We would advise you to develop a retention policy and procedure that distinguishes between different types of information.

Freedom of Information Act 2000

19.46   This Act enables you to support your service user in accessing information about them, both personal and non personal held by public authorities. The exemption from this requirement cover a category of information relating trade secrets, court proceedings or investigation or proceedings conducted by public bodies. There is another exemption where disclosure would prejudice the interests of the UK abroad or the prevention or detection of crime.

CCTV

19.47   There has been an increase in the use of CCTV, both by public bodies in public areas and by providers in communal areas. Under the Data Protection Act 1998, CCTV systems that process data must be notified to the Information Commissioner. In Box 19.10 we have included a checklist for smaller use of CCTV.

> **Box 19.10 CCTV small user checklist**
>
> The Information Commissioner has published a checklist to ensure that small users of CCTV are able to comply with data protection, see www.iso.gov.uk.

19.48   Providers should ensure that they are not in breach of the Human Rights Act 1998, by infringing a service user's right for privacy, by positioning cameras to ensure that they do not capture images that are intrusive. For example, cameras that only capture images of one particular flat room or house.

Summary

19.49   Confidentiality is important as it enables providers to support service users by establishing a trusting relationship. Work with service users does involve the disclosure of personal information and providers have duty under law to respect confidentiality. You also have a duty to ensure that the information that is kept on service users in record files, even on CCTV complies with data protection.

19.50   Services users often require services from a number of different agencies, and the Bichard and Laming Inquiries highlighted the importance of lawful information sharing. Both for you and your organisation, a balance needs to be struck between protecting those who are vulnerable and the right to privacy. The law, however, is moving towards greater sharing of information, provided it is proportionate and necessary. A carefully considered information sharing protocol that clarifies parties' legal responsibilities will support you in making decisions about the people who you work with.

CHAPTER 20

Managing behaviour

Objectives

20.1 By the end of the chapter you will:

- Understand your responsibilities both to service users and the community to manage anti-social behaviour and nuisance
- Be aware of a number of early intervention strategies to prevent anti-social behaviour escalating
- Understand how to apply the law to help you reduce anti-social behaviour
- Understand the particular legal consequences of racial harassment and racial violence
- Have a basic appreciation of the legal responsibilities of the managers of rented accommodation in connection with drugs

Case study

20.2 Lotus Housing Association manage a scheme for young men at risk of offending. The residents have their own flats and there is a communal lounge for residents use, with a television. The support worker arrives at the block of flats on Monday morning to find the communal area has been badly damaged and the TV has been thrown through the window into the garden. There is a message on the answer phone from a neighbour complaining about being disturbed on Saturday night because of a fight in the block of flats. There is evidence of substance misuse, with cannabis roaches in saucers that have been used for ashtrays, despite the lounge being a no smoking area and the letting agreements including a term preventing the consumption of drugs on the premises. One of the residents, Taj, discloses to the support worker that another resident, Rollo, and his visitors had 'trashed' the place on Saturday night. Rollo overhears Taj's complaint and storms into the office to threaten Taj with a 'beating', calling him a 'Paki grass'. Taj has made previous complaints about Rollo's behaviour, including include noise nuisance, constant visitors and racist behaviour.

Introduction

20.3 Anti-social behaviour has been a major concern for government, which has introduced a range of measures to deal with the issue. This chapter considers the management of anti-social behaviour and draws on the case study to suggest practical ways to tackle problems. We begin by considering the definition of anti-social behaviour and the importance of managing behaviour, including the statutory duty in connection with anti-social behaviour policies and procedures. We then consider the government's Respect agenda and the Respect standard for Housing Management. We look at possible remedies and suggest a variety of both supportive and enforcement initiatives which may help to prevent future recurrence of the behaviour. In the light of the serious consequences of racist behaviour, we provide an outline of the law relating to racial harassment and racially motivated crime. Finally, we outline the responsibilities of those who manage accommodation to prevent the consumption of drugs on their premises.

What is anti-social behaviour?

20.4   Anti-social behaviour is broadly defined to cover behaviour which impacts negatively upon other people. It can be thought about as disorder or nuisance and it may include behaviour which is criminal. Hate crime, such as racist abuse and threats of racial violence, is clearly anti-social behaviour. Other types of behaviour, such as young people congregating at bus stops, are more difficult to categorise as anti-social. A lot depends upon the context of the behaviour.

20.5   We set out in Box 20.1 two statutory definitions which are useful to demonstrate the scope of anti-social behaviour.

Box 20.1 Statutory definitions of anti-social behaviour – the Housing Act 1996 and the Crime and Disorder Act 1998

Section 153 of the Housing Act 1996 defines anti-social behaviour as:

> '... conduct which is capable of causing nuisance or annoyance to any person and directly or indirectly relates to or affects the housing management functions of a relevant landlord'; or 'conduct which consists of or involves using or threatening to use housing accommodation owned or managed by a relevant landlord for an unlawful purpose'.

Section 1(1) of the Crime and Disorder Act 1998 defines acting in an 'anti-social manner' as acting in 'a manner which causes or is likely to cause harassment, alarm or distress to one or more persons not of the same household' as the perpetrator.

20.6   The flexibility of the definition provides the basis for a wide range of interventions. However, there are two other important points:

- Providers must consider carefully the type and level of the anti-social behaviour in order to target their response appropriately.
- The definitions are very 'victim' orientated. In a desire to manage the perpetrator, you must not forget the needs of the victim.

20.7   The first step which Lotus Housing Association must take in connection with the incident of anti-social behaviour is to investigate the allegations. The housing association's statement of policy and procedures in relation to anti-social behaviour (see below) should make the process of investigation explicit. It should include who will investigate it, assurances of confidentiality, where appropriate, and any appeals procedures. It is particularly important that the investigation should be open-minded about the incident and not assume that Rollo was responsible for all, or indeed any, of the problematic behaviour.

20.8   On the other hand, it is important to demonstrate to Taj that the landlord is taking his complaints and his needs as a victim seriously. This is particularly necessary when there are racially motivated threats of violence. It is also important to talk to the neighbour who complained.

20.9   Once Lotus Housing Association has established what has happened, it must then decide what action to take. We discuss the possibilities later in the chapter.

Managing anti-social behaviour

20.10   There are a number of reasons why providers must take the management of anti-social behaviour seriously. These include:

- *Safety of service users and workers*
  Safety has to be your priority. If you consider that Taj is at risk of assault, you must do everything you can to protect him. One hostel worker has told us that she realised that her project had to take bullying more seriously when, following a serious incident of racial abuse, a resident left, saying they felt safer on the street than in the hostel.
- *Accountability to service users and the local community*
  Social landlords use public money and are accountable to users and the local community for the ways in which they spend it. One particularly important responsibility for social landlords is to manage behaviour appropriately.

- *Continued existence of the project*
  Many projects only exist because of the tacit support and agreement given to them by the local community. It is very easy to forfeit that support if the community has to suffer anti-social behaviour from your service users. Funders will also be concerned if there are unmanaged behaviour problems, for these will prevent the project achieving its aims.

20.11   The government takes the management of anti-social behaviour extremely seriously. One strategy it has tried to ensure that social landlords manage effectively is to impose, from 30 December 2004, a statutory duty on social landlords to publish anti-social behaviour policies and procedures. It is to this statutory duty that we now turn.

The statutory duty on social landlords to publish an anti-social behaviour policy and procedures

20.12   Section 218A of the Housing Act 1996 imposes a statutory duty upon social landlords, defined as local housing authorities, housing action trusts and registered social landlords, to prepare:

- a policy in relation to anti-social behaviour; and
- procedures for dealing with occurrences of anti-social behaviour.

20.13   The Housing Corporation provides statutory guidance on the contents of the policy and the procedures – this means it must be taken into account in the drafting of policies and procedures. This guidance is essential reading for you and can be found on the web at www.housingcorp.gov.uk/upload/pdf/ASBpolicyproc.pdf.

20.14   The guidance points out that the statutory duty involves the preparation and publication of the following documents:

- 'Statement of policy on ASB' (the policy statement);
- 'Statement of procedure on ASB' (the statement of procedures) and
- 'Summary of current policy and procedures on ASB' (the summary).

20.15   We have set out the paragraphs which elaborate upon the differences between these documents in Box 20.2.

Box 20.2 The prescribed documents

The policy statement should outline your general approach to ASB and also include specific policies. For example, these could relate to your commitment to eradicating ASB, the obligations of tenants, support for witnesses of ASB, racial harassment, domestic violence, multi-agency partnerships and the use of available legal remedies.

The statement of procedures should outline your procedures when dealing with ASB. For example, it could include information on how and to whom people should complain about ASB, how you will maintain contact with the complainant, and how you will monitor the progress of the case. It should contain enough information to enable a tenant to understand how you will deal with a complaint of ASB and what you expect of them.

The summary should be briefly restate the main points in the above two documents.

20.16　The guidance suggests you begin your policy with a general statement of your policy intentions. This should set out your attitude and general approach to anti-social behaviour, for example, to communicate clearly what standards of behaviour are acceptable. It could also identify what specific commitments you are making to your tenants or the wider community in terms of dealing with ASB, and what service standards they can expect. You should describe the range of services you offer on ASB, and how these will deliver a proportionate and flexible response to challenges that ASB presents. You should also explain how these services fit within your organisational structure.

20.17　It is important to be specific about the obligations upon tenants. You should set out the standards of behaviour that you expect of your tenants, those who live with them and their visitors. Make clear that the tenant is responsible for the behaviour of people who live with or visit them. Refer specifically to any tenancy clauses relating to anti-social behaviour or nuisance. The guidance also emphasises the importance of supporting complainants. You should commit yourself to dealing with their complaint promptly, keeping them informed of any developments relating to their complaint, and referring them to appropriate support services where necessary. Your policies to support complainants should be included in your policy statement.

20.18　The guidance is very specific about the importance of racially motivated anti-social behaviour. We have set out the relevant paragraphs of the guidance in Box 20.3. Note how policies on anti-social behaviour should reflect your policies on equal opportunities and diversity.

Box 20.3 Racial and other harassment policies

Incidents of harassment could fall within the description of ASB and should be addressed in your policy statement.

Our Regulatory Code states that associations must demonstrate their commitment to equal opportunity and that their governing body has adopted an equalities and diversity policy. Policies on ASB should take these policies into account.

We would expect you to reflect in your policy statement your policies for dealing with reported incidents of racial harassment, and to have policy and procedural commitments to:

- eliminate unlawful discrimination and harassment;
- promote good relations between people of different racial groups;
- encourage people to report racially motivated incidents;
- support complainants and their families; and
- take action against perpetrators.

20.19   The guidance is clear about what is required in the procedural statement. It should set out the operational procedures that you have introduced to implement your policies on anti-social behaviour. Whilst the statement of procedures will vary according to the policies you have adopted, the statement is expected to address the making of a complaint, the processing of a complaint, support to complainants, the use of enforcement action, support for the perpetrator, and the monitoring of complaints about ASB. You should also include any relevant procedures relating to multi-agency partnerships and professional witness schemes.

20.20   Support for complainants is seen as particularly important. We have set out further details in Box 20.4.

Box 20.4 Supporting complainants

You should consider the support needs of complainants, including:

- How best to assess and meet their needs
- How to refer complainants to external sources of support, and when.
- A list of the available support services.

> The support mechanisms you provide to the complainant may include:
>
> - risk assessment for their home and installation of appropriate witness protection measures, such as alarms, new locks and panic buttons;
> - access to counselling services;
> - allocations and lettings policies that are sympathetic to complainants and effective – where appropriate they may include temporary and/or permanent re-housing;
> - witness support;
> - access to telephone and/or face-to-face interpreters; and
> - regular visits or patrols by housing officers, community support workers or neighbourhood wardens.

20.21 Finally, the guidance makes it clear that the range of options which a landlord may consider should be set out in the procedural statement, together with an explanation of the circumstances in which each might be appropriate. These could include:

- mediation.
- acceptable behaviour contracts;
- anti-social behaviour orders;
- injunctions and exclusions orders under sections 153A, 153B, 153C or 153D of the 1996 Act;
- in connection with any of the injunctions above, applications for powers of arrest;
- possession proceedings;
- demoted tenancies; and
- any other legal action which could be taken with the support of the police or local authority, for example, action under the Environmental Protection Act 1990 or criminal prosecution.

20.22 We elaborate upon some of these options later in this chapter.

Review

20.23 Policies and procedures must be kept under review. Lotus Housing Association could use the incident set out in the case study as a trigger to review their policy and procedures. It may be relevant to ask:

- Is there a need for additional security measures when no support workers are available?

- Would CCTV be a useful device in preventing anti-social behaviour?
- Should procedures be introduced so that Taj is able to complain about Rollo's behaviour without being overheard?
- Is there an adequate system of recording incidents, including incidents where a decision has been made to take no further action?
- Does the tenancy agreement need amending to ensure that there are specific clauses relating to anti-social behaviour, drug taking, racism and responsibility for visitors?
- Are the procedures introducing new tenants sufficiently explicit about drug taking and racist behaviour?
- Is there a need for a risk assessment in connection with the behaviour and safety of the service users?

20.24   Social landlords must comply with the statutory duty and the Housing Corporation guidance. We consider that thoughtful compliance which responds to the particular challenges of individual projects will go a long way to ensuring that providers are well equipped to manage anti-social behaviour.

20.25   Another voluntary mechanism, which is part of the government's Respect agenda, is the development of a voluntary standard for social landlord's management of anti-social behaviour. This aims to elaborate upon the statutory duty and to improve practice and disseminate best practice. We now consider some of the details of that voluntary standard.

The respect standard for social landlords

20.26   The government launched the Respect agenda in January 2006 as part of its campaign to maintain momentum in combating anti-social behaviour. To download a copy of the Respect Action Plan visit www.respect.gov.uk. We think you will find it useful as it sets out government future plans in managing anti-social behaviour. A crucial part of this agenda is its work to improve the management of anti-social behaviour by social landlords. In August 2006, the Department for Communities and Local Government published the Respect standard for social landlords, which outlines the essential components to deliver an effective response to anti-social behaviour and build stronger communities.

Box 20.5 Frequently asked questions

Do landlords have to sign up to the standard?

Signing up to the Respect standard is entirely voluntary. For registered social landlords, however, inspection by the Audit Commission includes assessing performance on the principles of the standard.

20.27   Social landlords can sign up to the standard which commits them to six core principles which are set out below. Note that you do not need to take the lead on each of these standards. You may work in partnership with other agencies on the commitments. However, there are some areas, such as involving service users, where you will have direct responsibility.

1   *Accountability, leadership, and commitment*
Landlords need to make a visible commitment to the community so that everyone is clear they take issues of anti-social behaviour and respect seriously and will deliver what they say they will.

2   *Empowering and reassuring residents*
Landlords and the community need to work as one by involving residents and giving them input into decision making. Engagement and effective communications act to reassure and empower communities.

3   *Prevention and early intervention*
Landlords can play a key role in preventing anti-social behaviour from occurring. Where it does, addressing problems quickly often gets the best results.

4   *Tailored services for residents and provision of support for victims and witnesses*
Success rests on people being prepared to report and then give support to agencies in taking action. Every case and every person deserves a robust, tailored and sensitive response.

5   *Protecting communities through swift enforcement*
Government has provided landlords with the tools they need to tackle a wide range of anti-social behaviour. Landlords need to understand how these tools work and be prepared to use them quickly to protect communities.

6   *Support to tackle the causes of anti-social behaviour*
Provision of support can put an end to unacceptable behaviour by tackling underlying causes. This leads to sustainable outcomes and gets people's lives back on track.

20.28   The government considers that accountability to residents will be critical to the success of the standard. If you sign up to the standard, you should consider how you can let your residents know about the action you have taken. However, the standard is concerned with overarching strategic priorities. What is equally important is that you are familiar with the range of possible responses to particular incidents, and that you have decided when it is, and when it is not, appropriate to employ them. We turn to the more specific detail now, and we begin by considering a range of interventions which concentrate on achieving necessary behavioural changes.

Supportive interventions

20.29   There are a number of strategies which you could employ to persuade a service user that his or her behaviour is anti-social and that it is necessary for him or her to change that behaviour. If these are successful, then it will avoid eviction or other enforcement action. Whatever you choose to do, you must communicate your decisions to the victims of any anti-social behaviour.

Advice and counselling

20.30   If your project does not offer targeted advice and support for its service users then you should ensure that you know how these can be accessed in your local area. In the case study, it may be that the priority for Lotus Housing is to ensure that Rollo gets some help with his behavioural issues. Of course, Taj, as the victim of anti-social behaviour, should also be offered counselling and support. Rollo may be someone who could be helped through youth inclusion programmes (YIPs).

Mediation

20.31   It can be very difficult for groups of people to live together successfully. Sometimes it helps for the group to meet together to work out why disputes happen and how to avoid them in future. A trained mediator may be able to help facilitate this. Mediation may help everyone to understand how to live together more successfully. It may also help to deal with complaints made by the neighbours, particularly if this can be organised before feelings get entrenched. You can contact Mediation UK to find out if there are local mediation services available to you. The web address is www.mediationuk.org.uk.

Warnings

20.32   It is important to warn a service user that his or her behaviour is anti-social, and early intervention warnings can be an effective way to help change behaviour. In the context of the case study, this would mean meeting with Rollo to explain why his behaviour is unacceptable, to make him aware of the impact of his behaviour on Taj, on other service users and workers and on neighbours. In particular, you should explain why his racism was unacceptable. You should explain what further action you will take if his behaviour does not improve, and confirm the warning of further action in writing. You may choose to involve the police, social services or the youth offending team in the interview.

Acceptable behaviour contracts (ABCs)

20.33   An acceptable behaviour contract is a flexible tool designed to engage with an individual to acknowledge his or her anti-social behaviour and its effect on others, with the aim of stopping that behaviour. It is a written agreement made between a person who has been involved in anti-social behaviour and their local authority, youth inclusion support panel (YISP), landlord or the police An ABC or agreement is completely flexible and can be adapted for the particular local need. It can include conditions that the parties agree to keep. It may also contain the agreed consequences of a breach of the agreement.

20.34   The individual may agree to:

- stop specific behaviour that has been causing disruption to the community;
- positive requirements such as engaging in a community group, attending school regularly or attending a local youth diversion scheme.

20.35   The agency may also agree to provide support that will help the individual to keep to the terms of the ABC. It may also refer the person to agencies that are able to provide further intervention or support. Involving the individual in drawing up the ABC may help them to recognise the impact of their behaviour and take responsibility for their actions. ABCs and agreements usually last for about six months, but can be renewed by agreement between both parties.

20.36   Lotus Housing Association may consider that an ABC would be a useful tool to help manage Rollo's behaviour. It would enable it to be explicit about the consequences of continuing anti-social activity and racism, and to provide some positive actions for Rollo to take to demonstrate his commitment to improving his behaviour. It would also avoid the potentially negative consequences of eviction for Rollo. An ABC is frequently a prelude to an anti-social behaviour order (ASBO) (see below) and Lotus Housing Association should be prepared to face the consequences of possible escalation of the action against Rollo.

Box 20.6 Frequently asked questions

We work with vulnerable young people and think that acceptable behaviour contracts would support our service users in managing behaviour. Are they legally binding?

ABCs are not legally binding, although they are formal written agreements. Often representatives from the local authority or police will attend a meeting to sign an ABC, and it may prevent more serious action being taken at that juncture. ABCs can be used in legal proceedings for possession ASBOs and injunctions if behaviour continues and they are breached. They can represent evidence that the young person was responsible for anti-social behaviour, support has been offered or a warning given.

20.37   Lotus Housing Association, once it has considered the implications of the incident, may decide that it has no choice other than to take more punitive action against Rollo. This may be the consequence of reviewing the history of past behaviour by Rollo, or because of the serious implications for the project of the cannabis consumption or the impact of Rollo's racism on Taj. We now consider the range of responses which are more focused on enforcing good behaviour. Whilst these are often not punitive in themselves, if these orders are breached there is a significant risk of criminal sanctions being applied.

Enforcement

20.38   Anti-social behaviour can be prevented through the use of a number of enforcement mechanisms. Social landlords should consider the possibilities of injunctions, exclusion orders and anti-social behaviour orders before thinking about evicting perpetrators, because the consequences of eviction can be extremely damaging. However, in appropriate circumstances the last resort of eviction may be the only response available to a social landlord. We set out the details of these enforcement mechanisms below.

Injunctions and exclusion orders

20.39 Section 153 of the Housing Act 1996 provides social landlords, including registered social landlords, with extensive injunctive powers. There are three different types of injunction available:

- the anti-social behaviour injunction;
- the injunction against unlawful use of premises; and
- the injunction against breach of tenancy agreement.

20.40 The anti-social behaviour injunction will be granted by the court once two pre-conditions have been met. The first condition is that the person against whom the injunction is sought is engaging, has engaged or threatens to engage in anti-social conduct which has a connection with the housing management functions of the landlord. The second condition is that the anti-social conduct is capable of causing nuisance or annoyance to:

- a person with a right to reside in or occupy housing accommodation owned or managed by the relevant landlord;
- a person with a right to reside in or occupy other housing accommodation in the locality of the housing accommodation owned or managed by the relevant landlord;
- a person engaged in lawful activity in or in the locality of the housing accommodation; or
- a person employed by the relevant landlord wholly or partly in connection with his or her housing management functions.

20.41 This covers neighbours, whether tenants of the same landlord, tenants of another landlord or owner-occupiers; it covers all other tenants of the same landlord; it covers those who visit, carry out businesses or other activities in the locality; and it covers the landlord's employees.

20.42 The other two injunctions are largely self-explanatory. Where there has been an unlawful use of the premises, for instance, as a result of illegal consumption of drugs or using the premises to fence stolen goods, then the social landlord can obtain an injunction to restrain such activity. Finally, where the anti-social behaviour specifically breaches the tenancy terms, an injunction can be obtained to restrain such behaviour. We explain how to apply for an injunction for anti-social behaviour in chapter 24.

20.43 A court will be able to attach an exclusion order and/or a power of arrest to the anti-social behaviour injunction where the anti-social conduct involves violence, threats of violence or a significant risk of harm.

20.44 In the case study it is likely that Lotus Housing Association will be able to obtain an injunction against Rollo, particularly if it can be proved that he used drugs on the premises. If the threat of violence is a serious one, then Rollo can be excluded from the premises pending possession proceedings and Lotus Housing Association can ask for a power of arrest, which will mean that the police can respond to any breach of the injunction by arresting Rollo.

Anti-social behaviour orders (ASBOs)

20.45   The Home Office published guidance on ASBOs in August 2006, which is available at www.crimereduction.gov.uk/antisocialbehaviour/antisocialbehaviour55.pdf.

20.46   Much of the following material has been taken from that guidance.

20.47   ASBOs, which originated in the Crime and Disorder Act 1998, are civil orders designed to protect the public from behaviour that causes or is likely to cause harassment, alarm or distress. An order contains conditions prohibiting the offender from carrying out specific anti-social acts or from entering defined areas and is effective for a minimum of two years.

20.49   Applications for ASBOs can be made by a number of 'relevant authorities', including local authorities, the police, registered social landlords and housing action trusts. Applications are generally made to magistrates' courts, but can be made to county courts when there are relevant connected proceedings, such as possession proceedings, and can be requested in the course of criminal proceedings. Regardless of which court issues the order, it is a civil order, which has important consequences in connection with evidence since hearsay evidence and professional witness evidence is admissible in civil proceedings. Where necessary, courts can make interim orders, so immediate protection against anti-social behaviour is available. Breach of an order is a criminal offence and criminal procedures and penalties apply. For further details on ASBOs see chapter 25.

20.50   Once a provider has decided to apply for an ASBO, the Home Office guidance at appendix E provides a useful summary of the next stages, which we have reproduced in Box 20.7.

Box 20.7 Extract from Home Office Guidance (August 2006)

Appendix E

Step-by-step process for anti-social behaviour orders and orders on conviction

Process for anti-social behaviour orders

Collect evidence
Agencies applying for orders should strike a balance and focus on what is most relevant and necessary to provide sufficient evidence for the court to arrive at a clear understanding of the matter.

Undertake statutory consultation
Documentary evidence of consultation, not agreement, is required although it is not a statutory requirement for orders on conviction (see below).   The stages for orders in county court proceedings will be available on publication of the practice direction in the updated Civil Procedure Rules.

Partnership working
Lead agencies should liaise with other agencies which can add value to the application. Involve the youth offending team and social services at the start of the process if the subject of the application is a child or young person, in order to ensure that any assessment required is carried out in parallel with the application process. If the perpetrator is aged 10 to 17, the court is obliged to consider making an individual support order (ISO). Consideration needs to be given at an early stage to the positive interventions which could be included in such an order to address the individual's anti-social behaviour.

Identification of the need to protect the community
An order is necessary to protect person(s) from further anti-social acts by the perpetrator.

Identification of anti-social behaviour
There is behaviour that is causing, or likely to cause, harassment, alarm or distress to one or more person(s) not of the same household as the perpetrator.

The hearing
The lead officer in charge of the case should ensure that all the evidence and witnesses are available at the hearing, including any evidence in support of the need for the court to make an immediate order. The defendant(s) should attend but an order can be made in their absence.

contd

Step-by-step process for anti-social behaviour orders and orders on conviction

Applying for an interim order

Where there is an urgent need to protect the community, an application for an interim order may be made with the application for the main order. The appropriate form in the Magistrates' Courts (Anti-Social Behaviour Orders) Rules 2002 should be used. An application for an order without notice to the defendant may be made subject to agreement of the justices' clerk or other court clerk with delegated authority. The clerk shall grant leave for an application for an interim order to be made where they are satisfied that it is necessary.

The hearing for a without notice interim order will take place without the presence of the defendant. Where the hearing is made on notice, the defendant should be summoned to attend the hearing.

If an interim order is granted, the application for the main order (together with a summons giving a date for the defendant to attend court) should be served on the defendant in person as soon as practicable after the making of the interim order. The interim order will not take effect until it has been served on the defendant. If the interim order is not served on the defendant within seven days of being made, then it shall be set aside. The interim order shall cease to have effect if the application for an anti-social behaviour order is withdrawn or refused.

Make an application to the magistrates' court

An application for an ASBO is by complaint to the magistrates' court using the appropriate form in the Magistrates' Courts (Anti-Social Behaviour Orders) Rules 2002. The complaint must be made within six months from the time when the matter of the complaint (the behaviour) arose. A complaint may be made on the basis of one incident if sufficiently serious. Earlier incidents may be used as background information to support the case and show a pattern of behaviour. The application may be made to any magistrates' court. A summons together with the application, as set out in the Rules, should be either given to the defendant in person or sent by post to the last known address.

Draw up prohibitions

The order should be drafted in full, including its duration, and a court file prepared.

Process for an order made on conviction in criminal proceedings (in the magistrates' court or the Crown Court)

Since the case of *R v Wadmore and Foreman* [2006] EWCA Crim 686 Court of Appeal Criminal Division, the court should record on the face of the order its findings of fact in relation to the alleged anti-social behaviour.

Verdict

If found guilty of breaching the order, the offender is convicted or given a conditional discharge.

Criminal hearing

This is to establish guilt of criminal charge only.

Signal intention to seek an order

Prior to, or at the start of, the criminal stage or hearing, the police, Crown Prosecution Service or local authority involved in the case may advise the subject and court that an order will be sought on conviction. This is not a requirement; the issue can be raised for the first time post-conviction.

Draw up prohibitions

The police or other agency involved in the case may draw up the prohibitions necessary to protect the community from the subject's anti-social behaviour for consideration by the court post-conviction. This is not a requirement.

contd

Collect evidence

Evidence may be collected for presentation to the court post-conviction. This is not a requirement as the court may make an order on conviction on its own initiative.

Other matters

Application for variation or discharge by either the applicant or the defendant is to the same magistrates' court that made the order. Appeal is to the Crown Court. Breach of the order will go to the magistrates' court, which may refer it to the Crown Court in the more serious cases. Mode of trial decision determines whether breach of ASBO is dealt with in the magistrates' court or the Crown Court.

Immediate post-order procedure

Where an ASBO is granted, it is preferable for a copy of the order to be served on the defendant in person prior to their departure from court. If this is not possible, personal service should be arranged as soon as possible thereafter. In the case of a child or young person, the order should also be served on the parent, guardian or an appropriate adult. In all cases, service should be recorded.

The lead agency, if not the police, should ensure that a copy of the order is forwarded immediately to the police. Copies should also be given to the anti-social behaviour co-ordinator of the local crime and disorder reduction partnership, the other partner agencies, and to the main targets and witnesses of the anti-social behaviour.

An order comes into effect on the day it is made. But the two-year period during which no order shall be discharged starts from the date of service.

Other matters

Where the order is made on conviction in the magistrates' court, application for variation or discharge by either the applicant or the defendant may be made to any magistrates' court within the same local justice area as the court that made the order. Appeal is to the Crown Court. Breach of the order will go to the magistrates' court, which may refer it to the Crown Court in the more serious cases.

Where the order is made on conviction in the Crown Court, application for variation or discharge by either the applicant or the defendant is made to the same Crown Court which made the order. Appeal is to the Court of Appeal. Breach of the order will go to the magistrates' court, which may refer it to the Crown Court in the more serious cases.

Immediate post-order procedure

If the offender is given a custodial sentence, the court may make provision for the requirements of the order to come into effect when the offender is released from custody. See above for details for immediate post-order procedure for ASBOs.

Post verdict – hearing for order on conviction

The hearing for the order post-conviction is civil.

The issue of an order may be raised by the magistrates or judge without any request from the prosecution or the police or local authority; the Crown Prosecution Service may make an application for an order on conviction. Additional evidence relating to the request for the order and the need for the prohibitions may be produced.

20.51 Lotus Housing Association could consider the possibility of obtaining an ASBO against Rollo. Relevant prohibitions could relate to Rollo's drug use, his racist behaviour, the noise nuisance and to the people he associates with. The housing association will have to take into account the possibility of management problems arising from obtaining an ASBO against Rollo. It is likely that his continued presence in the project will depend upon him accepting the ASBO as a useful strategy to improve his behaviour.

Comparing ASBOs and injunctions

20.52 The Respect website has set out a useful table which compares the ASBO and the injunction. We set this out in Box 20.8.

Box 20.8 A comparison of anti-social behaviour orders and injunctions

Anti-social	Injunctions behaviour orders	
Which court	Magistrates' court (stand alone or on conviction). Youth court (on conviction). County court (related proceedings). Crown Court (on conviction).	County court High Court
Immediate protection	Interim ASBO Made without notice.	Interim injunction. Made without notice.
Age of defendant	10+	Age of defendant is not relevant; rather, the mental capacity of the defendant to understand what they are doing and how to modify their behaviour is the test.
Duration	Minimum two years.	Can last forever.

Geographical extent	Can extend to whole of England and Wales but location must be specified.	Specific location.
Standard of proof	Criminal standard equivalent.	Civil standard.
Hearsay and professional witnesses admissible	Yes	Yes
Who can apply	Police Local Authorities Registered social landlords (RSLs) British Transport Police (BTP) Housing association trust (HAT) County councils Environment agency Transport for London	Local authority Social landlord – behaviour must be housing related.
Penalty for breach	Criminal offence. Criminal penalties apply.	Contempt of court penalty. Imprisonment and or fine.
Reporting	No automatic restrictions.	No restrictions. Restrictions in place for juveniles.

Possession proceedings

20.53   Possession proceedings should be used as a last resort. If Rollo is evicted, he is likely to be found intentionally homeless by the local authority and will end up living on the street or drifting in the private rented sector with no support for his problems. Nonetheless, Lotus Housing Association may consider that it has insufficient resources to protect other residents from Rollo's behaviour and has no alternative but to evict him.

20.54   The nature of possession proceedings will depend upon the security of tenure that Rollo enjoys. As an assured shorthold tenant, Rollo can be evicted without specifying a ground for eviction following two months' notice, or Lotus Housing Association will have to issue possession proceedings based upon the anti-social behaviour ground (ground 14) of the Housing Act 1988. Housing Corporation guidance suggests that using ground 14 is good practice: it requires that the landlord proves its case in court and gives the resident an opportunity to state his or her case. Whichever route is chosen, there is likely to be a delay before obtaining a possession order. The housing association should consider applying for an injunction together with an exclusion order for that period.

20.55   There is no requirement for a notice period before issuing possession proceedings on ground 14. The notice and the proceedings can be issued on the same day. Note also that ground 14 is a discretionary ground. The court will have to be convinced that it is reasonable to evict Rollo before it will make an order. However, the courts have taken a robust line on anti-social behaviour and legislation has structured the exercise of their discretion (section 9A of the Housing Act 1988). When the courts exercise their discretion, they are required to consider the past impact of the anti-social conduct on other people, the likely continuing effect of the nuisance and the likely future effect of any repetition of the conduct when considering whether it is reasonable to make an order for possession.

Summary of possible responses to the case study

20.56   In Box 20.9 we have set out those matters which should be considered by Lotus Housing Association in response to the incident.

20.57   In the remainder of this chapter we outline the potential serious consequences of two elements of the case study, racist behaviour and drug use on the premises.

Box 20.9 Responses to incidents of anti-social behaviour

Incident	*Strategic response*	*Contractual response*	*Supportive response*	*Enforcement response*
Damage to property	Check the selection process and your admission procedures.	Check that the terms of the contract are explicit about damage.	Consider a warning or an ABC.	Injunction or possession proceedings depending on context.
Complaints from neighbours	Inform the local community how you will respond to anti-social behaviour.		Mediation.	
Cannabis use	Do you have a drugs policy? Have you anticipated how to respond to breaches of it?	Ensure that the contract makes your policy on drugs and your response explicit.		This may justify possession proceedings because of your legal responsibilities (see below).
Misbehaviour by visitors	Do you need security when there is no support worker present at the project?	The contract should make residents responsibility for the behaviour of visitors explicit.		Possession proceedings are possible for the behaviour of visitors.

Incident	Strategic response	Contractual response	Supportive response	Enforcement response
Racist abuse	Do you have a code of conduct for residents which makes your attitude to racism explicit?	Should be covered by the contract.	Mediation may make the consequences of low-level racism clear to residents.	An ASBO or an injunction may be appropriate.
Threats of racially aggravated assault	What sort of relationship with the police have you got? What support are you able to offer victims?		In less serious cases, warnings or an ABC may deal adequately with this.	This may be a serious criminal offence and possession proceedings may be your only alternative. If, following investigation, you consider that the threats were less serious, then an injunction may suffice.

Racial harassment and violence

20.58 Service users who are suffering racial harassment and racial violence will require extensive support. In this part of the chapter we briefly outline the criminal consequences of racist behaviour.

Race crimes

20.59 The Association of Chief Police Officers (ACPO) defines a racial incident as:

> ... any incident in which it appears to the reporting or investigating officer that the compliant involves an element of racial motivation; or any incident which includes an allegation of racial motivation made by any person.

20.60 Someone who harasses or is violent towards someone because of their race is committing a criminal offence. A broad range of criminal offences, from murder to criminal damage, may be relevant. There is a particular offence of incitement to racial hatred, which may be committed if a person uses threatening, abusive, or insulting words or behaviour; publishes or distributes threatening, abusive, or insulting written material, or possesses such written material with a view to its publication or distribution.

20.61 The Crime and Disorder Act 1998 ss29–32 created a number of racially aggravated offences. These are racially aggravated assaults, racially aggravated criminal damage, racially aggravated public order offences and racially aggravated harassment. The offences are all pre-existing offences which become more serious as a result of the racial motivation for the offence.

The role of the police and the Crown Prosecution Service

20.62 Racial incidents have been separately recorded by the police since 1988, and figures have risen in almost every year since that date. Most police forces run community safety units, with dedicated staff who receive special training in community relations, including local cultural issues, to enable them to respond appropriately to racial incidents.

An outline of the law of drugs as it relates to the management of supported housing

20.63   In the final part of this chapter we briefly consider the consequences of residents' possession of or dealing in illegal substances in supported housing.

Penalties for possession and dealing

20.64   Class A, B and C drugs are described as controlled substances under the Misuse of Drugs Act 1971, with class A being considered most harmful. It is important that providers are aware of the range of offences under the Misuse of Drugs Act 1971. There are four possible offences under the Act, the consequences of which depend upon the class of drugs involved. It is an offence under the Act to:

- Possess a controlled substance unlawfully.
- Possess a controlled substance with intent to supply it.
- Supply or offering to supply a controlled drug (even where no charge is made for the drug).
- Allow premises you occupy or manage to be used for the purpose of drug taking – see below for further details.

20.65   In Box 20.10 we outline the penalties for possession and dealing with drugs.

Box 20.10 Penalties for possession and dealing

Class of drugs	Possession	Dealing
Class A		
Ecstasy, LSD, heroin, cocaine, crack, magic mushrooms, amphetamines (if prepared for injection).	Up to seven years in prison or an unlimited fine or both.	Up to life in prison or an unlimited fine or both.
Class B		
Amphetamines, methylphenidate	Up to five years in prison or an	Up to 14 years in prison or an

(Ritalin), pholcodine	unlimited fine or both.	unlimited fine or both.
Class C		
Cannabis, tranquilisers, some painkillers, gamma hydroxybutyrate GHB), ketamine	Up to two years in prison or an unlimited fine or both.	Up to 14 years in prison or an unlimited fine or both.

The responsibilities of managers in connection with drug use

20.66 There has been considerable confusion about the legal responsibilities of managers for the use of drugs on their premises. These are covered in section 8 of the Misuse of Drugs Act 1971. We have set this out in Box 20.11.

Box 20.11 Section 8 of the Misuse of Drugs Act 1971

A person commits an offence if, being the occupier or concerned in the management of any premises, he knowingly permits or suffers any of the following activities to take place on those premises, that is to say—

(a) producing or attempting to produce a controlled drug in contravention of section 4(1) of this Act;

(b) supplying or attempting to supply a controlled drug to another in contravention of section 4(1) of this Act, or offering to supply a controlled drug to another in contravention of section 4(1);

(c) preparing opium for smoking;

(d) smoking cannabis, cannabis resin or prepared opium.

20.67 The government proposed amending section 8 through the Misuse of Drugs Act 1971 (Modification) Order 2001 (SI 2001 No 3932). The amendment would have changed section 8(d) of the 1971 Act in such a way that hostel providers, or any landlord, could be held criminally liable if they failed to prohibit and prevent any and all illicit drug use on their premises.

20.68 Sections of both the homelessness and drugs sectors protested that the amendment would criminalise their staff, create cultures of secrecy around drug use which increase risk and undermine opportunities for intervention, or require projects to exclude many of their most vulnerable clients. The amendment was repealed in 2005, having never come into force, and section 8 of the Misuse of Drugs Act 1971 remains unchanged. What it means is, with regards to drug use on premises, landlords may not 'knowingly permit or suffer' the smoking of cannabis or opium, but that landlords have no legal responsibility to prohibit the use of other illicit drugs. In the case study, Lotus Housing Association did not 'knowingly permit or suffer' the smoking of cannabis as there was no one from the housing association present on the premises at the time. If you do see cannabis use on the premises, you must insist that it is stopped immediately, otherwise you will be committing a criminal offence.

20.69   The issue of drug dealing is distinct from that of drug use. It imposes serious legal responsibilities on landlords and service providers, as was demonstrated in 1999 when two managers from the Wintercomfort day centre in Cambridge were convicted and imprisoned under section 8(b) of the Act.

Summary

20.70   This chapter has provided an overview of the range of remedies available to landlords to deal with anti-social behaviour and has provided further information in connection with racially motivated behaviour and the specialist area of drugs. There is an increasing emphasis on the responsibility of landlords to manage the behaviour of residents. The government, in particular, has extended the range of legal avenues for landlords and expects that they will be used. As social welfare professionals, it is easy to prioritise the needs of the perpetrator of anti-social behaviour. It is important not to forget the needs of victims, and your responsibilities for the health and safety of all your residents. On the other hand, perpetrators are often victims too – so deciding on the right course of action in particular instances can be demanding. Moreover, the government's agenda on anti-social behaviour is constantly evolving. We suggest that you regularly check the Respect website to keep up to date. Sitra also publishes regular updates in its monthly bulletin for members. Most importantly, you need to keep your policies and practices up to date and ensure that all staff understand what action should be taken and when.

Managing and preventing emergencies

Objectives

21.1 By the end of this chapter you will:

- Understand what you can do in an emergency and what legal steps are available to you
- Understand what different agencies can contribute to managing an emergency
- Appreciate what can be done to minimise an emergency
- Appreciate what post-incident action should be taken

Case study

21.2 Fountain Housing Project manages a scheme for women with enduring mental health problems on behalf of Casa Housing Association. The scheme houses five people in a shared house. The manager is called out to the house during one weekend. One of the service users has reported a fire in the property. The service user tells the manager that another service user deliberately set fire to the communal bin. This appears to have been in the course of an argument between the service users, which took place in the kitchen. The kitchen is damaged and the emergency fire-fighting response team have disconnected the electricity and gas supply.

Overview

21.3 In most circumstances, sharing housing is difficult. Within supported housing, service users are often very vulnerable and are given limited choice as to with whom they share. Problems are therefore exacerbated. Providers are responsible for the health and safety of occupiers and for workers and neighbours. In the case study above, the manager would be expected to make decisions and take action that will put the property into a safe condition. Emergencies are, of course, not limited to shared accommodation. In self-contained accommodation, problems are more likely to be directly about the behaviour of individual service users or their neighbours.

21.4 This chapter will look at what action to take during and immediately after an emergency. We first set out a checklist for action by a manager and then look at the roles of the police, mental health professionals and other statutory and non-statutory bodies. We examine your legal responsibilities and what actions you can take to protect those you are responsible for. We then consider what needs to be in place before a crisis occurs so that you can manage an emergency as effectively as possible. In this case study, or in any emergency, good policies and procedures on referral and selection, risk and needs assessment and management, possession and disaster planning will not avert the emergency, but they can minimise its effects. Staff will have the confidence to deal with emergencies if they have been properly trained and are conversant with the policies and procedures. Lastly, we briefly examine the action you can take after an incident, to enable your response to inform improvements in future performance.

During an emergency

21.5   The most important priority is to deal with the incident that has caused the emergency and ensure the safety of the service users. When the wellbeing of the residents and staff is assured, you will be able to investigate what caused the crisis. It is important not to apportion blame or make decisions about who is responsible until you have investigated. Emergencies may be triggered by a variety of causes; in our case study it is the fire, but in other cases it may be a violent or aggressive incident. You should:

- Establish whether anyone has been hurt or injured. All staff should have some basic training in first aid. If you are uncertain how to administer first aid or the injury is serious, an ambulance must be called.
- If there is a violent or dangerous incident in progress, you should minimise the number of people exposed to risk. You should aim to put a barrier between the danger and the residents. This may include locking a door on a violent person or evacuating the property. If there is a violent person on the premises, you should not tackle this problem yourself, but call the police.
- Contact other members of staff and/or members of management who have the authority to provide finance for repairs, alternative accommodation, etc.
- Once other staff have been contacted, appoint a project manager for the incident, who will be responsible for co-ordinating what is required. The project manager does not always need to be physically present, but needs to be constantly contactable.
- Contact maintenance services if immediate repairs are required.

- In most cases you will have to involve other agencies; in the case of agency managed schemes the owning registered social landlord (RSL) must be informed. Below we outline what you can expect from other organisations.

The police

21.6   In the case study, the manager may suspect a criminal offence of arson has been committed and needs to contact the police. If you need to contact the police because an incident has not been resolved or you are worried about a repetition, you should call 999 and ask for the police. In less pressing circumstances, you should contact your local police station. Calling 999 will enable you to contact the other emergency services – fire and ambulance – if they are required. The police are obliged to respond to 999 calls and must attend and investigate the matter. When they get to the property, the police will want to interview any service users involved in an incident. The police then have the following options:

1   They may decide to take no further action if they believe there is no evidence that a crime has been committed.
2   They may decide to investigate the crime, but not take action at this stage.
3   The perpetrator can be arrested and taken to the police station.
4   The perpetrator can be given a caution, either at the property or taken to the police station.
5   The perpetrator can be taken to the police station for further questioning.

21.7   *Police investigation* – when a crime is reported the police will send officers to the scene to investigate. This involves taking witness statements and may involve taking photos. In some cases, the police may seal off an area if they believe it has important forensic evidence that should be examined or collected by specialist officers. In Box 21.1 we outline how you can support service users in their contact with the police.

Box 21.1 Supporting service users

The service users involved in an incident will be asked to make a statement. You should ask the police to explain what will happen to the statements given and what will be expected of the service users in the future. Service users may be expected to attend

---

> identification parades and/or court. If a crime involves serious violence, service users need to be aware that the police have powers to search them even if they are not suspected of direct involvement.

21.8   The police have the power to take the following actions.

21.9   *Caution* – a caution is a first official warning given for first time or minor offences such as damage to property. The police will issue a caution if there is evidence of the service user's guilt and he or she admits to the offence. The service user must consent to the caution; if they do not do so, they may be charged with an offence instead. There are two types of caution: (i) simple cautions, where no further action will be taken by the police; and (ii) a conditional caution, which has specific conditions attached to it, for example, to pay for damage caused. If the service user fails to comply with the conditions, they face the possibility of criminal proceedings for the original offence. Cautions are only given to adults; those aged 17 and under are given reprimands and/or final warnings.

21.10   *Arrest* – If a service user is arrested they are taken to a police station. Once arrested, a service user can be:

- Released without being charged with a criminal offence.
- Cautioned (see above).
- Charged with a criminal offence.

21.11   *Custody* – the police may keep the service user under arrest in custody. The police can take a service user into custody if they have 'reasonable grounds' to suspect they he or she has committed an offence. For those under 17 and those who are 'mentally vulnerable', an 'appropriate adult' must be present during any questioning to ensure the service user understands what is happening. The service user can be kept at the police station for 21 hours without being charged. This can be extended to 36 hours with the authority of a superintendent and to 96 hours by a magistrate. If the police decide there is not enough evidence to charge the service user, he or she will be released on police bail.

Charged with an offence

21.12   The Crown Prosecution service decides whether to press charges. Once the service user has been charged with an offence, he or she will be taken to the magistrates' court as soon as possible. At the magistrates' court a decision is made whether the service user should be released on bail or held on remand. In Box 21.2 we explain how you can influence bail.

Box 21.2 Influencing bail

The service user will not be granted bail if the court considers he or she will fail to return to court, will commit an offence whilst on bail, will interfere with witnesses or will obstruct the course of justice. You may believe there is a danger that a service user who is bailed back to your property will present a risk to other service users or staff. If this is the case, you should contact the police immediately and be prepared to make representation in court to this effect.

Mental health

21.13   In our case study, it may be that the incident is linked to deterioration in a service user's mental health. Fountain may wish to refer the service user to mental health services. In the event of an emergency, the service user may have to be admitted to hospital, ideally by agreement. It is not inconceivable, however, that the service user requires compulsory admission if they present a serious risk to themselves or others. Compulsory admission under the Mental Health Act 1983 would normally require the intervention of a doctor and approved social worker (ASW) and, in some cases, the police. In Box 21.3 we briefly outline what local mental health services may be available and how to find them.

Box 21.3 Local mental health services

Mental health trusts manage a number of community- and hospital-based services. Under the National Service Framework for Mental Health, crisis and assessment teams and home treatment teams have become more widespread. The support and treatment these teams can offer in the community can be a welcome alternative to hospital for service users experiencing mental ill-health.

To find out what is in your area, contact your local mental health trust or GP, or visit www.nhs.uk.

Mental Health Act 1983

21.14   Here we provide a brief outline of the admissions procedure under the Mental Health Act 1983.

Admission in an emergency

21.15   Section 4 of the Mental Health Act 1983 allows for an admission and detention for 72 hours. An application for admission can be made by the nearest relative (see Box 21.4) or an approved social worker on two doctor's recommendations (one in an emergency). If possible, the doctor should have some knowledge of the service user. An emergency must be demonstrated by evidence of:

- an immediate and significant risk of mental or physical harm to the patent or others; and/or
- the danger of serious harm to property; and/or
- the need for physical restraint of the patient.

Box 21.4 Nearest relatives in order of priority

- Spouse (excluding those who are separated but including same-sex couples registered under the Civil Partnership Act 2004).
- Cohabitee of six months' standing.
- Son or daughter.
- Parent.
- Brother or sister.
- Grandparent.
- Grandchild.
- Uncle or aunt.
- Niece or nephew.
- Anyone who has lived with the person for five years if there is no spouse.

Admission for assessment

21.16   During those 72 hours, the detention can be converted into a 28-day admission for assessment under section 2 of the Act, if a second doctor's recommendation in support is received. For admission for assessment under section 2, the service user:

- must be 'suffering' from a mental disorder of the nature and degree that warrants the detention of the patient in a hospital for assessment for a t least a limited period; and

- ought to be so detained in the interests of 'his' own health and safety or with a view to the protection of others person.

Admission for treatment

21.17   In some circumstances, a service user can be detained under section 3 of the Mental Health Act 1983. This is known as admission for treatment. Section 3 is usually used when a service user has gone into hospital voluntarily or under one of the shorter sections, section 2 or section 4. It allows a person to be detained in a mental institution for a period of up to six months. The purpose of the detention is to allow for treatment in hospital that could not otherwise be given.

21.18   The criteria for admission under section 3 are as follows:

(i)   he or she is suffering from mental illness, psychopathic disorder or mental impairment and his or her mental disorder is of a nature or degree which makes it appropriate for him or her to receive medical treatment in a hospital; and

(ii) in the case of psychopathic disorder or mental impairment, such treatment is likely to alleviate or prevent a deterioration of his or her condition; and

(iii) it is necessary for the health or safety of the patient or for the protection of other persons that he or she should receive such treatment and it cannot be provided unless he or she is detained under this section.

21.19   Recommendation for admission under section 3 must be made in writing by two medical practitioners who state that the above criteria have been met.

Box 21.5 Frequently asked questions

We suspect one of our service users has become mentally unwell. They have barricaded themselves in their bedsit and are refusing to come out. This has been going on for 48 hours – what can we do?

Section 135 allows the police to enter a premises, by force if necessary, with a warrant issued by a magistrate and remove a 'mentally disordered' person to a place of safety for up to 72 hours. The person does not have to be named. There has to be evidence that the person is living alone and unable to look after him- or herself or is being neglected, ill-treated or otherwise not under 'proper care and control'. The police can also detain in a place of safety a person who appears to be mentally disordered under section 136. This power can only be exercised if the person is in a public place. In these circumstances, we assume this would not cover the communal areas of the property, for example, the kitchen or lounge of a shared house. A public place, however, would cover a landing on a block of flats.

21.20   In Box 21.6 we identify some of the key mental health personnel you or service users may come into contact with.

Box 21.6 Key Mental Health personnel

Approved Social Worker (ASW) – this is a social worker who has been specifically trained in mental health care and legislation. The ASW is responsible for the social and not the medical care of service users and is responsible for decisions to compulsorily admit someone to hospital under mental health legislation.

Psychiatric nurses – responsible for the care of patients in hospital, including key working and dispensing of mediation.

Community psychiatric nurse – responsible for the care of patients in the community, and may do home visits or see service users at the community mental health team base.

Senior house officer – a junior doctor and the person most likely to have day-to-day responsibility for a service user who is receiving treatment.

Specialist registrar – the next most senior doctor who oversees the work of the senior house officer.

Consultant psychiatrist – the most senior doctor, who has ultimate responsibility for the clinical care of the patient.

Psychotherapists – offer therapy to those who are referred to them, mostly patients who have been referred by psychiatrists, GPs, social workers and psychologists.

Counsellors – counselling aims to identify the problems a person is facing in any sphere of life and to help them discover effective ways of dealing with these. Counsellors work in various settings, such as the independent or voluntary sector, GPs' surgeries and hospitals.

Local authority

21.21   Fountain may contact the local authority during an emergency. There will be different departments of the local authority that will be involved dependent on the nature of the service and the type of emergency. In Box 21.7 we identify how you can find out what the local authority can do in an emergency.

21.22   *Social Services* – if the service user has a social worker or care manger, you must inform the specific social worker what has happened. The information sharing protocol should set out contact points for emergencies. If you are unable to contact the specified social worker, or it is out of hours, contact the duty social worker.

21.23   *Housing department* – if you have no accommodation to temporarily house service users, they will have to present to the homeless persons unit. See below.

21.24   *Buildings control* – most areas operate a 21-hour emergency service that will assess dangerous or unstable buildings. A surveyor will assess the danger and decide on a best course of action. The local authority has powers under the Building Act 1984 ss77 and 78 to get landlords to take direct action to make buildings safe.

Box 21.7 Local authority services

To find out what the local authority can offer in an emergency, contact your local authority visit their website, www.*[local authority name]*.gov.uk

---

Fire services

21.25   The fire service will attend all fires and ensure that the property is made safe. This may involve shutting off the gas and electricity supplies. If they do this it will be the landlord who has the responsibility to arrange for reconnection. The fire service may contact the local authority surveyor directly if they believe a building is unsafe. The fire service will compile a report regarding the details of the fire. Your insurance company may request the report. If you have any questions regarding a fire, you should contact the attending crew or the incident commander.

Other agencies

21.26   Depending on the type of emergency, you may contact other agencies, for example, victim support, advice agencies and counselling services. Most local authorities have information on the services that are offered locally.

Re-housing service users

21.27   If any property has become uninhabitable or service users do not feel safe, alternative arrangements must be made to accommodate them. The lead member of staff should ensure that suitable accommodation is found. Ideally, you will have a policy and procedure on disaster planning which identifies what accommodation is available to be used. The best course of action would be to house service users in your own managed properties. In some cases, it may be appropriate to ask service users if they have relatives or friends they can stay with in the short term. If you are not able to do this and are a managing agent, contact the owning RSL, which may have some provision. In some cases, you may need to get management authority to use hotel accommodation.

Box 21.8 Frequently asked questions

We are a small voluntary organisation that has a property that became unsafe following the tornado in north-west London. We have no other housing provision. Does the local authority have a duty to house the residents?

You will need to contact the homeless persons unit. The local authority has a clear duty to house service users in the immediate aftermath of a disaster under homelessness legislation (see chapter 5).

21.28   A member of staff should accompany the service users to the alternative accommodation to ensure that it is appropriate for their needs and that they have the wherewithal to eat, sleep and wash. A brief risk assessment should be made on the suitability of the accommodation along with the other agencies involved in the support and care of service users. Service users should be reassured that you will continue to provide a service and advised:

- when they will next be visited; and
- how long the temporary arrangements will last (if known).

21.29   If service users are moved from the property, you will need to contact the next of kin, or encourage service users themselves to inform them of the alternative arrangements.

Civil proceedings in an emergency

21.30 In chapter 21 we explain how to commence possession proceedings. Possession proceedings have to follow the legal formalities so that people threatened with eviction are able to defend themselves. Fountain would have to contact the owning landlord, Casa Housing Association, to get approval if it wanted to commence possession proceedings. In an emergency which involves allegations of nuisance, the processes can be expedited (speeded up) because the notice period is curtailed – see chapter 8. These are cases where you will need the advice of a solicitor – see chapter 9. You can, however, serve a notice as most licences and tenancies allow for immediate notice to be given for violence and disruptive behaviour. In chapter 21 and chapter 25 we outline other ways of managing behaviour, for instance, by using injunctions and anti-social behaviour orders (ASBOs). Both injunctions and ASBOs can be used to exclude someone from their home. Injunctions and ASBOs do not end a tenancy or licence agreement; they do provide for immediate relief and allow you to pursue a permanent solution.

Preventing emergencies

21.31 Ideally, Fountain will have policies, procedures and practices in place that prevent emergencies or minimise their effects when they happen.

Referral and selection

21.32 In chapter 19 we outline the importance of sharing information about service users within the parameters of the law. This chapter concentrates on the process of referral to your project and your decision to accommodate and support them. Obtaining accurate information about service users is critical to assessing their needs and managing risk.

21.33 An important part of the referral process is to ensure that referral agencies have accurate information about the services a scheme provides, staffing levels and the level of support provided. You should invest time and resources in ensuring that this information is accurate and up to date, as this is key to the prevention of inappropriate referrals. Building good relationships with referral agencies, including social services, homeless persons units, day centres or other voluntary agencies, is also vital. You need a clear statement of eligibility for the service and information on accessing the service. This information should all be in the referral and selection policies, which are key tools in ensuring the service is provided fairly and equally to those in need.

21.34   The aim of the referral selection and assessment process is to:

1   gain information from the applicant and referring agency on predetermined areas (from the selection criteria) and to assess the applicants suitability for the project;
2   give information to applicants so they are able to assess whether the project is suitable for their needs;
3   make decisions about the priority between applicants.

21.35   The usual process is to use an application form, which is completed by both the applicant and referring agency. If the application form indicates that the applicant's support needs can be met by the scheme, then the application should be followed by an interview. The interview is usually based on standard questions and should allow the applicant and providers to see if the scheme can meet their needs. The best way to avoid an emergency is through good assessment of needs and risks. You will need to have a process that is robust enough to identify service users' needs and any risks that they may present. This will enable you to draw up a support plan which incorporates management of the risks identified in the assessment. In many local authorities, *Supporting People* commissioners are introducing a single assessment process prior to referral. You will still need to ensure that you have accurate and up-to-date information about referrals in order to ensure that you can provide the appropriate support.

Box 21.9 Frequently asked questions

We are a specialist RSL with a scheme for people with mental health problems. We take all of our referrals from the community mental health team. Can we refuse applicants when we clearly can't meet their needs?

The Housing Corporation expects RSLs to maintain their independence as organisations. In practical terms, this will support your policy, as even if all of your referrals come from one source, you still have the right to refuse referrals if they do not meet your selection criteria.

Risk assessment and management

21.36　Assessing and managing risk is fundamental to reducing the potential for emergencies. Risks that could contribute to an emergency can be broadly identified as:

1　Service user risks, for example, risk associated with a service user's behaviour, as in the case study, or risks to the service user from others.
2　Service delivery risks, for example, suspension of staff due to allegations of abuse.
3　External factors, for example, fire, flood, flu pandemic or extremes of weather.

21.37　Risks may be presented by an emergency to:

1　Service users, who may experience physical or psychological harm.
2　Staff, who may experience physical or psychological harm.
3　The property, that may experience damage.
4　External agencies, for example, police, fire brigade, etc.
5　Neighbours and the local community.
6　The organisation and stakeholders

Policies and procedures

21.38　The management of risk in relation to emergencies will be greatly facilitated by having clearly written policies and procedures which provide staff with direction about what to do and how to do it. Policies and procedures should include:

1　Anti-social behaviour.
2　Challenging behaviour.
3　Support.
4　Confidentiality and information sharing.
5　Anti-harassment.
6　Anti-discrimination.
7　Substance misuse.
8　Possession.
9　Disaster recovery planning.

21.39　We have included guidelines developing a number of policies in the appendices. Here, we examine disaster recovery planning in more detail.

Disaster recovery planning

21.40   Disaster recovery plans should reflect the nature of your organisation, its services and the risks to which it is exposed. An effective plan should cover certain key business risks normally associated with disasters, such as:

- death or injury to staff and clients;
- alternative accommodation;
- loss of business assets including computerised records;
- interruption or disruption of services;
- breakdown of communication with key stakeholders;
- human and financial resources to maintain services or rebuild the organisation.

21.41   Effective recovery planning is an organisation-wide activity requiring active involvement of the board, management, staff, funders and service users. The following teams will play a leading role in successful recovery:

1   The board will take overall responsibility and staff should have emergency contacts for the named members who are responsible for providing a role in direction and delegating authority.
2   The planning team will establish the contingency plan, including:
   (a) identifying the risks;
   (b) the human and financial implications of those risks;
   (c) producing a timetabled sequence of critical disaster recovery activities.
3   The disaster recovery team, which will implement the plan, including allocation of resources and tasks.
4   Any number of ad hoc teams to carry out allocated tasks.

21.42   Realistically, the primary aim of disaster recovery is to:

- keep the human and financial costs to a minimum;
- resume an acceptable level of service quickly;
- return the organisation to pre-disaster capacity within a fixed period of time.

21.43   We recommend that you buy an insurance policy that is tailored to your organisation's size and activities.

21.44   There are also a number of tasks that will enable you to manage a disaster or emergency more effectively:

1   Details of emergency services, for example, ambulance and hospitals, mental health, social services, local authority homeless unit,

police and fire brigade, should be on communal notice boards, on any communal phone and contained in the residents' handbook.

2 Invest some time in establishing good relationships with individuals or organisations that can support you in an emergency, for example, local solicitors, community support officers, community psychiatric services and local authority emergency provision, including social services and environmental health.

3 Work with other supported housing providers on plans to collaborate in the event of an emergency and pool resources.

4 Work with partners, for example, *Supporting People* teams and partner RSLs, on roles and responsibilities in an emergency.

5 Activate the recovery plan and a disaster recovery team as soon as an emergency occurs.

6 Plan how to inform staff, committee, clients, funders, insurers and stakeholders of the disaster or emergency and the recovery plan.

7 Check the availability of finances, and procedures for claiming under insurance policies.

8 Ensure there are adequate arrangements to support service users and maintain the functions of your organisation.

9 Plan to restore critical utilities and services, such as accommodation for service users, access to paper or computerised records including those of the service users, and do not forget office furniture and equipment.

Induction and training

21.45 When service users move into a scheme, they should receive a comprehensive induction. Service users should be made aware of their obligations under their occupancy agreement and be given a summary of the policies and procedures outlined earlier. They should also be made aware of what emergency arrangements are in place, and details of arrangements and contacts should be given to them and prominently displayed in the property. You should consider how residents are given information to ensure that appropriate methods are used for service users with communication or literacy needs.

21.46 Induction for new staff should cover policies and procedures, in particular, what will be expected of them in an emergency. Appropriate training should be provided to staff in:

1 Managing difficult or challenging behaviour (including self defence).

2 Legal remedies in an emergency, including possession, injunctions and the criminal law.

3 Anti-social behaviour.
4 Emergency first aid.
5 Fire safety.
6 Personal safety.

21.47 This is list is not exhaustive and the training will depend on the nature of services you provide and on your environment

Other preventative work

21.48 All fire-fighting equipment should be checked and serviced regularly. The fire alarm systems in the office and shared houses should be checked regularly and serviced quarterly. The fire brigade is now involved in preventative work, visiting homes and giving advice – use this service. We discuss your fire safety and other property obligations in chapter16.

21.49 Computer records should be backed up weekly and the discs kept off site by the finance and administration manager. The housing support worker should keep information on each tenant, which includes next of kin, GP and any other useful information.

Post-emergency action

21.50 Management post an emergency is almost as important as during the emergency. Members of staff and board members will need to be clear about their continuing responsibilities and what support they can expect in fulfilling these. Service delivery to service users should be maintained. Moreover, this is an important learning opportunity – following a review of the incident, the results should be used to assess and review practices polices and procedures.

Service users

21.51 Immediately after an incident, you may have to investigate the events that led up to the incident. In order to get a picture of what happened, you will need to interview service users and witnesses. As a result of the investigations, you may need to take further action, for example, issuing warning to other service users involved. In some cases, you may have to take formal action, for example, commencing possession proceedings or advising the police that a criminal offence has occurred, if you have not already done this.

21.52   If there has been a violent incident, you may need to consider transferring service users to alternative accommodation if you have concerns about their safety and security. This may be particular appropriate if service users have agreed to be witnesses in formal or legal proceedings.

21.53   The organisation will still have a duty of care in law for the service users. You will still have to provide services to service users even if they have been temporarily placed elsewhere. This will continue until that support is transferred to another organisation. If they have been located in other supported housing within the same organisation, their support may be transferred to the staff of the new scheme, although where possible continued contact with existing support staff is desirable. If service users have been placed with other providers, staff should ensure they still receive the services they require. Other agencies involved in their support and/or care should be informed.

21.54   Service users should have a formal review of their support plan, and this should include a reassessment of needs and risk assessment. A new risk management plan should be drawn up, which will include any interim plans formulated during the emergency. You may need to refer service users to specialist counselling or support to enable them to manage the after-effects of the emergency. There are specialist organisations that provide support services, for example, dealing with sexual assault or racial harassment.

Support for members of the organisation

21.55   The support needs of the staff and any board members should be considered as part of the action required following the emergency. Some organisations have arrangements with specialist counsellors who are trained to support staff and board members in these circumstances. Staff can also be referred to specialist agencies. In law, employers have a duty of care and a duty in contract to ensure that the employee is kept safe from psychiatric as well as physical harm.

Policies and procedures

21.56   The afternoon of an emergency is a good time to re-evaluate and review your response and to consider how robust the policies and procedures proved to be. The policies and procedures need to contain information that allows staff and board members to be aware of their legal and management obligations and the obligations of external agencies, for example, the police and mental health services.

Other agencies

21.57   Within the confines of your information sharing protocol you may need to contact the other agencies that are involved with the support/care. Relevant agencies should be advised of what has happened and that ongoing plans are in place. In some cases, they may need to be involved in reviewing the support needs and risk of the service user.

21.58   In some cases, funders and commissioners such as *Supporting People*, will have to be contacted. For instance, if the property is out of commission or there has been a serious incident.

21.59   In some cases, the local authority must be contacted under Reporting of Injuries, Diseases and Dangerous Occurrences Regulations 1995 (SI 1995 No 3163) (RIDDOR) – we discuss the requirements of RIDDOR in chapter 16.

21.60   You may need to keep regular contact with the police, health services and fire brigade to ensure that you are informed about any further action to be taken and your responsibility in connection with this. It is useful to ask for a named point of contact. If you are a managing agent of an RSL, you may have to inform the RSL, depending on the severity of the emergency. This is almost certain to be necessary if there is a need for formal proceedings or if the property has been damaged. The RSL should have provided you with the details of when it should be informed.

Property

21.61   The landlord (or managing agent) will still be responsible for the property even if you have to move all the residents out. You should ensure that it is secure, and you will have a duty of care for keeping any possessions of the service users safe and secure under these circumstances. You may find that your insurance does not cover service users' possessions, so you may have to arrange for their removal to a safe location or even into storage.

Summary

21.62   In supported housing, services are being provided for those most vulnerable in our society. The nature of supported housing means that emergencies are almost inevitable and staff will be expected to deal with them. It is useful if you are aware of your legal and management responsibilities and the responsibilities of the other agencies you should be able to rely on, such as the police. In this chapter we have outlined the action to take in an emergency and how you can minimise its effects. Appropriate training and induction of staff, good policies and procedures, robust risk and assessment practices can minimise the likelihood of an emergency. A disaster plan can support you in dealing with an emergency effectively. An organisational approach to managing emergencies should seek to support staff and post-emergency reviews should avoid blaming staff. Similarly, any investigation that involves service users should be impartial, recognising how easy it is to jump to conclusions about who is responsible in the turmoil surrounding an emergency.

PART IV

Introduction to the court system

Objectives

22.1   By the end of this chapter you will:

- Be familiar with the functions of the different courts
- Understand the constitution and jurisdiction of the civil and criminal courts
- Appreciate the role of key personnel involved in the administration of the law

Overview

22.2   In chapter 2 we examine the sources of English law. This chapter builds on that information and provides a basic introduction to the court system in England and Wales. The aim is not to provide a full description of the court system, but to facilitate your understanding of the final section of this book. We first look at the role and structure of the civil court system, as most housing disputes are civil in nature. We will then look at the role of the criminal courts, as you may come into contact with the criminal justice system, for example, if a service user commits an offence. Lastly, we will briefly examine the coroner's court, as you may be required to attend this court in the event of a service user's death. Throughout the chapter we identify key judicial personnel. For more information on the court system we recommend that you visit www.judiciary.gov.uk.

22.3   When an individual is alleged to have committed an offence against the state, or a dispute or problem relating to contracts, property or professional relationships cannot be resolved between the individuals or organisations involved, our legal system provides for a decision to be made by a court or tribunal. Even when a dispute has been resolved, it is sometimes necessary to attend court to formalise the agreement, for example, to vary the terms of a possession order. The criminal and civil court systems are separate. In chapter 2 we have provided a diagram of the court system. Because we operate a common law system of law in England and Wales, our courts are arranged in a hierarchical structure. This means that a lower court must follow decisions of a court higher than itself. This also allows a system of appeals against the decision of one court from one level to another.

Civil courts

22.4 Civil law concerns disputes or problems that give rise to actions between individual citizens. Civil courts were set up to provide a formal means for individuals or organisations to obtain a remedy for an injustice they had experienced. Judges makes decisions in civil cases based on the balance of probabilities; that is, after hearing all the evidence, they decide what a reasonable person would conclude is most likely to be the facts of the case.

The county court

22.5 If you want to regain possession of a property or start a debt action for arrears of rent, you will apply to the county court. The county courts were established in 1846 and there are now 270 county courts, each covering a different locality. The county court deals with actions such as:

- Possession of land.
- Claims in contract or tort up to a certain value (for example, small claims for rent arrears).
- Equity trusts and mortgages.
- Winding up companies and bankruptcy.
- Probate.
- Some family matters, including undefended divorces, adoption and guardianship.
- Extortionate credit agreements under section 139 of the Consumer Credit Act 1974.

22.6 The case is heard by one judge, and can be heard in a traditional court setting or in the judge's chambers. Chambers are less formal and the judge does not appear robed and wigged. Some cases have to be heard in private; this includes possession cases. Cases heard in chambers are always private. The county court system allows the judge to read written statements of evidence from both parties and consider the dispute before the court hearing. In the next chapter we look at the submissions that are expected in possession proceedings. In Box 22.1 we identify the key personnel of a county court.

Box 22.1 Key personnel

District judges, who are solicitors or barristers of at least seven years' standing, hear cases. These are normally debt cases and

---

> possession cases. Assistant district judges perform a similar role.
>
> *Circuit judges* are more senior – they have to be barristers of ten years' standing or have worked as a recorder for at least five years. They can hear more complex or higher value cases. Circuit judges travel around defined geographical areas (circuits), and hear cases in the county courts that fall within their locality.
>
> *Recorders* are part-time circuit judges who work as barristers or solicitors for the remainder of the time.
>
> *Court managers* manage the day-to-day administration of the court.
>
> *Ushers and clerks* are administrative staff who are responsible for managing the list of cases and assisting the judge.

High Court

22.7   The High Court hears appeals from inferior courts or tribunals and can hear cases for the first time.

22.8   Normally, your action would only be referred to the High Court if it involved:

- A complicated dispute of fact.
- A point of law of general importance.
- The amount of value of the claim was over the jurisdiction of the county court.
- You are claiming against trespassers and there is a substantial risk of public disturbance or of serious harm to people or property which requires immediate resolution.
- If you or the person you are in dispute with appeals a decision made in the county court. An appeal does not usually mean hearing the case again; it simply involves the higher court considering the process by which an inferior court reached its decision.

22.9   The Administrative Court is part of the High Court and hears applications for judicial review, the process by which the court reviews the lawfulness of a decision by a public body. We explain judicial review in chapter 2.

22.10   In Box 22.2 we identify the key personnel of the High Court.

> **Box 22.2 Key personnel**
>
> A *High Court judge* or *puisne* (pronounced puny) judge usually hears cases.
>
> Court of Appeal judges (or former Court of Appeal judges), circuit judges, recorders or former High Court judges can also hear cases.

Court of Appeal

22.11   In its civil capacity, the Court of Appeal hears appeals from the county court and High Court. It can also hear questions of law from administrative tribunals, for example, the lands tribunal. It can order that appeals are allowed, dismissed or order a new trial.

House of Lords

22.12   This is the highest appellate court. It hears appeals from the Court of Appeal, but in some cases decisions made in the High Court can circumvent the Court of Appeal and appeal directly to the House of Lords if all parties agree and the case concerns an important interpretation of a statute or point of law.

22.13   In theory, an appeal is made to the whole House of Lords; however, only the law lords hear the appeal.

Criminal courts

22.14   The criminal law involves the prosecution by the state of criminal offences. It is designed to protect the public from attacks on persons or property. Its object is to punish those who offend against the state and to protect the community. You are only likely to be involved in criminal law proceedings when a crime is committed or you work in a scheme that involves the criminal justice system; for example, substance misuse services or schemes for people at risk of offending. In Box 22.3 we signpost you to a useful information resource about the criminal courts, criminal justice on line.

> **Box 22.3 Signpost**
>
> Information about the criminal courts is available from www.cjsonline.gov.uk. This enables you to 'walk through' court procedures as a witness, victim, defendant or offender.

Magistrates' court

22.15   The vast majority (95 per cent) of criminal cases are first heard in the magistrates' court. Criminal offences are classified as follows:

22.16   *Summary offences* – these are the least serious offences and are tried in the magistrates' court. For example, public order offences such as being drunk and disorderly, common assault and criminal damage which has caused less than £5,000 worth of damage.

22.17   *Triable either way offences* – these can be described as intermediate offences and include a wide range of crimes, for example, theft and more serious assault causing actual bodily harm. These can be tried in either the magistrates' court or Crown Court, but may heard in the magistrates' court and committed to the Crown Court for sentencing. Magistrates are only able to impose sentences that do not exceed six months imprisonment (12 months if consecutive sentences) or fines exceeding £5,000.

22.17   *Indictable offences* – these are serious crimes and include murder, manslaughter and rape. All indictable offences must be tried at the Crown Court, but the first hearing is dealt with at the magistrates' court. The magistrate will decide if the defendant should be given bail.

22.19   Cases are usually heard by a panel of three magistrates, collectively known as a bench. In Box 22.4 we have identified key personnel of the magistrates' court.

Box 22.4 Key personnel

Justices of the Peace – also referred to as lay magistrates, are members of the community appointed by the Lord Chancellor and are supported in matters of law and procedure by a legally qualified court clerk.

District judges – formerly known as stipendiary magistrates, district judges sit alone and deal with more complex or sensitive cases, for example, serious fraud.

22.20   The magistrates' court also houses the youth court, which deals with young people aged between 10 and 17. The magistrates and district judge are specially trained in youth matters, and this court is not open to the public and reporting restrictions apply.

22.21   The magistrates' court can also act in a civil capacity, for example, in some family matters.

Crown Court

22.22   The Crown Court is where serious criminal cases are heard before a judge and jury. The jury, made up of a random selection of lay people, decides a case on the facts based on the evidence it hears in court. The judge is the authority on the law.

22.23   The Crown Court deals with:

- Cases on indictment, wherever committed.
- Appeals from the magistrates' court against conviction or sentence.
- Sentencing referred by the magistrates' court.

22.24   The sentence imposed by the Crown Court is limited by the statute governing the crime or the common law.

Box 22.5 Key personnel

Judges of the Crown Court include:

- *Judges of the High Court*, if requested by the Lord Chancellor.
- *Circuit judges* with ten years' experience in the Crown Court or county court, who move around the circuits (areas).
- *Recorders* (part-time circuit judges).
- *Justice of the Peace*, who must sit with the judge when hearing appeals.

Court of Appeal (Criminal Division)

22.25   The Court of Appeal hears appeals against decisions of the Crown Court or from those convicted in a magistrates' court but sentenced by the Crown Court. Appeals can be made as of right on points of law, but appeals on other matters, such as sentencing, require the leave of the court.

22.26   The Court of Appeal can:

- Quash (dismiss) the inferior court decision.
- Vary the sentence, which can be made longer or shorter.
- Order a new trial.

House of Lords

22.27   As with civil cases, this is the highest court of appeal in the UK.

Coroner's court

22.28   The coroner's court manages inquests into the death of people who died from an unknown cause, in prison or from a violent or unnatural death. Coroners are usually lawyers, but in some cases they can be doctors. Coroners must apply the law in determining the cause of death. If a service user dies in a scheme, the matter may be referred to the coroner's court if the cause of death cannot be determined by the attending doctor or if it was sudden or unexpected.

22.29   The coroner will hold an inquest, which is an inquiry to find out:

- who has died, and how;
- when and where they died;
- the information needed by the registrar of deaths, so that the death can be registered

22.30   The purpose of the inquest is not to find out if anyone is to blame for the death. However, if the verdict of the inquest is murder, the coroner may commit the person for trial. In most cases the coroner conducts the inquest alone. However, a jury may be called if the death occurred in prison or in police custody or if the death resulted from an incident at work. In this case the jury, not the coroner, makes the final decision about the cause of death. The coroner's court is not governed by requirements relating to burden of proof, such as beyond reasonable doubt or on a balance of probabilities; it is merely an inquiry, although it is influential.

Summary

22.31   This chapter has briefly described the court system. You will most probably use the county court in commencing civil actions on behalf of your organisation. In some circumstances, you may be required to attend the magistrates' court as a witness or to support a service user. If a service user dies, there may be an inquest if the death is sudden or the cause cannot be determined. Attending court may cause anxiety for you and the service user. It will be helpful if you understand the role of the court and what is expected of you. We advise you to seek legal advice where you are uncertain and we explain how to do this in chapter 9. You will also find it informative to visit the Judiciary and Community Legal Service website we signposted earlier in the chapter, or visit www.direct.gov.uk/en/Gtgl1/GuideToGovernment/Judiciary/ DG_4003097.

CHAPTER 23

Possession proceedings

23.52   Appeals

23.53   Court costs

23.54   Summary

Objectives

23.1   By the end of this chapter you will:

- Understand when it is appropriate to go to court to recover possession
- Know what documentation is required to obtain possession from the court
- Understand the court process and the landlord's responsibility in possession proceedings
- Appreciate the powers of the court and what the possible outcomes may be

Overview

23.2   In part three of this book we looked at managing supported housing. We pointed out that the occupancy agreement is critical to effective management as it sets out the expectations of both parties. We have looked at the responsibilities of the parties in relation to rent, behaviour and vulnerability and repair, and explored ways of working with service users in ways that maintain their accommodation.

23.3   There are circumstances, however, when action for possession of a service user's home is necessary. We have deliberately placed this discussion in the last part of the book because possession should always be the last resort for a landlord when all other tools have failed. In this chapter, we will first look at the process of applying to court and the necessary paperwork; we will explain what happens at a court hearing for landlord and service users. Lastly, we will look at what the court is able to order and the range of outcomes you can expect from court proceedings.

Deciding to go to court

23.4   In part four of this book we identify the range of tools available to resolve disputes between service users and landlords that do not necessitate the service user losing their home. The decision to go to court is one that should be taken in a way that reflects the gravity and importance of depriving someone of their home.

Legislative requirements

23.5   One of the most important legislative checks on repossession is the need for 'due process' to be followed. For the majority of occupancy agreements, the landlord has to serve a notice that complies with appropriate legal requirements. The notice serves as a warning to the resident that the landlord intends to apply to court and facilitates them in seeking legal advice. The exceptions to this requirement are those agreements excluded from the Protection from Eviction Act 1977 identified in chapter 4.

23.6   The serving of a notice does not compel the landlord to go to court; notices can be withdrawn if the reason for their service ceases, or they can just remain on file. In the case of licences, however, the notice must be withdrawn if not relied upon, as the expiry of the notice brings the licence agreement to an end. If it is not withdrawn and the licence holder remains in residence and pays accommodation charges, a new licence may have been created. In Box 23.1 we have reminded you about good practice about serving notices. There is more information about serving notices in chapter 15.

Box 23.1 Good practice

Only serve a notice if you intend to rely on it. If the reason for serving the notice is remedied, the notice should be withdrawn formally. The resident should be informed in writing that the notice has been withdrawn.

23.7   The court performs two important roles:

- It checks to ensure that the notice is legally correct and that the appropriate legal process has been followed.
- Where the court has discretion, it will consider the reasonableness of the action in line with the statutory requirements. The court will consider the proportionality of the action and whether there is an alternative remedy available. For example, most courts will not entertain an application for possession on discretionary ground 10 of the Housing Act 1988 if the arrears are less than £500.

23.8   In 2000/01 there was a major reform of civil procedure following a review by Lord Woolf, the then Lord Chief Justice. One important effect of the reforms is to ensure that all possible steps have been taken to resolve a problem prior to it going to court. This is reflected in the paperwork required by the court and in the areas where the judge has discretion. In Box 23.2 we have outlined the procedural rules that apply to civil actions.

Box 23.2 Civil Procedure Rules

All cases that go to the county court or High Court are now governed by the Civil Procedure Rules (CPR). These are sets of rules to enable the courts to deal with cases fairly and equitably. The rules are expanded by practice directions, which set out procedures to enable the rules to be applied.

23.9 This new culture has been extended by the requirements of pre-action protocols in areas such as disrepair litigation and rent arrears. The requirements of the latter are discussed in chapter 20. The pre-action protocol for rent arrears is particularly important for supported housing providers.

Litigation friend

23.10 In law, someone who is deemed by the court to be incapable of understanding legal proceedings must have a litigation friend. A litigation friend acts on behalf of an individual and represents their best interests. Residents who may require this type of representation include:

- people with mental health problems;
- people with a learning disability; or
- people with alcohol or substance misuse issues that cause 'mental impairment'.

23.11 All those under the age of 18 are also required to have litigation friends; this can be formal legal representation, but can also include social workers. If the resident does not have a litigation friend and the court feel one is required, the Official Solicitor will be appointed and the landlord will have to meet the costs while the resident applies for legal aid.

Regulatory requirements

23.12 The Housing Corporation, in its Regulatory Code and guidance (paragraph 3.5.c), expects that legal possession of a property is sought only as a last resort. This is statutory housing management guidance.

23.13 The Audit Commission, in its Key Line of Enquiry (KLOE) 6 on Tenancy and Estate Management, expects that where action is being taken to reduce anti-social behaviour, possession proceedings are the last resort, to minimise eviction (6.4.3.1).

Policies and procedures

23.14   Throughout this book we have emphasised the need for effective policies and procedures to ensure consistency of treatment and to enable staff to be confident about the decisions and action taken. All organisations need clear guidelines for staff, which include:

- the circumstances in which cases are taken to court;
- who takes that decision;
- how this is overseen and monitored;
- in which cases workers can represent the landlord and in which cases should professional legal representation be obtained.

23.15   For managing agents, the owning registered social landlord (RSL) will need to sanction any court action, and in some cases it will be the managing agents who will take the case to court.

23.16   You can either choose to have a separate eviction policy and procedure that considers all potential actions that might proceed to court or, alternatively, there could be a section on proceedings to court within each of your policies and procedures on harassment, anti-social behaviour and rent arrears.

Box 23.3 Signpost

Sitra have published a *DIY Possession* workbook that guides staff through the county court process on recovering possession from assured and assured shorthold tenants on rent arrears grounds. For more information see www.sitra.org.uk; Telephone: 0207 793 4713; Fax: 0207 793 4715.

23.17   In most cases, simple undefended cases do not require lawyers and are usually dealt with by staff – for example, rent arrears. In Box 23.3 we have signposted you to more information about representing your organisation in court. Solicitors are normally instructed for more complex and defended cases, for example, nuisance. If you choose to instruct a solicitor, you should consider preparing the court paperwork and getting the solicitor to check this as a means to cut costs. In Box 23.4 we outline some good practice on the management of possession proceedings that could be incorporated into your policies and procedures.

> **Box 23.4 Recommended practice**
>
> - Senior manager reviews each case prior to issuing court papers.
> - The service user is informed of the intention to proceed to court and supported in seeking independent legal advice.
> - The service user is made to understand that this step could result in them losing their home and they could incur costs.

Court paperwork

23.18 The process of going to court begins when proceedings are issued; that is, when the landlord sends details of the claim against the service user to court. This can only happen when the notice has expired. If the resident has voluntarily moved out, there is no requirement to go to court.

23.19 The court paperwork is sent to the county court which covers the geographical area the property is located in. These areas do not correspond with local authority boundaries, so if in doubt telephone the court and speak to the issue clerk. In Box 23.5 we have identified the court website from which the forms can be obtained. We recommend you visit the website, as it has helpful guidance.

> **Box 23.5 Court forms**
>
> The court forms, and guidance on completing the forms, are available at www.hmcourts-service.gov.uk.

23.20 To issue a claim, a landlord must complete:

- form N5, which is the claim form for the possession of land; and
- particulars of claim (the details of why the claim is being made).

23.21 For tenancy agreements, the particulars of claim have to be on form N119. Licence agreements have no set form, but in order to comply with the CPR you should use the template of the form N119 to prepare the particulars that support your claim.

23.22 The particulars of claim require you to provide evidence to support your claim. In the case of rent arrears this may just consist of a rent statement, but in nuisance cases this may involve statements, diary logs, incident reports, etc. In Box 23.6 we outline the common form used for possession for an assured shorthold tenancy.

> **Box 23.6 Accelerated possession proceedings for assured short-hold tenancies**
>
> In chapter 6 of the book we refer to the availability of accelerated possession proceedings for assured shorthold tenancies. For this possession action the landlord simply has to fill in an N5b form, which combines the claim for the possession of land and the particulars of claim.

23.23　The court forms (and prepared particular of claim) should include a statement of truth, which verifies that the information contained in the claim is true and accurate. The statement of truth must be signed by the landlord or its legal representative (if the landlord is an organisation, it must be signed by a senior member of staff). This means that managing agents cannot sign the statement of truth.

> **Box 23.7 Frequently asked questions**
>
> **What happens if the person who has served the notice is not able to attend the court hearing?**
>
> When a notice is served, it is good practice for the person who has served the notice to fill in a statement of service. We have included a sample statement of service in the appendices. When a senior officer signs the court forms they agree that it is a true and accurate record the information contained, including that a notice was served by that person. There is no longer a requirement for the person serving the notice to go to court unless there is a dispute as to whether the notice was served. In some cases, the judge will ask the person attending court if they recognise the signature of their colleague who served the notice.

23.24　When the court receives the paperwork, the issue clerk logs it onto the computer system. This generates a claim number and defence papers with guidance for the resident. The resident should also receive a copy of the claim form and the particulars. The resident has at least 14 days from receiving the paperwork to make a defence and a counterclaim. We look at counterclaims later in the chapter. If the landlord believes it will be difficult for the court to serve the papers on the resident, it can elect to serve the court paper itself.

23.25　　The court will fix a date for the hearing and this should be between four and eight weeks from the date the claim was issued. In practice, the case-load of some of the inner city courts means that landlords can wait between 10 and 13 weeks for a hearing. The court has the power to reduce the time taken for a hearing in cases of emergency (we referred to expedited court proceedings in chapter 24. In Box 23.8 we have given you some good practice guidelines to follow once you have issued proceedings.

Box 23.8 Good practice

If a possession action is due to a breach of the occupancy agreement that can be remedied by the resident, you should continue to support the resident in resolving the problem. In cases where the court has discretion, the judge may ask you what steps have been taken since issuing the proceedings to enable the resident to address the breach. The contact you have with the resident should inform your decision as to whether to proceed to court. It should also inform your choice about which order or action you will be requesting the court to consider.

Court hearing

23.26   Possession cases are usually heard in private, and can be heard in court or in the judge's chambers. The former are in a formal court setting, with the judge sitting at the head of the court (the bench) and those attending being asked to stand in the witness box to give evidence. In Box 23.9 we have identified the key personnel you may come into contact with at court.

23.27   The object of the court hearing is for the court to hear evidence to decide:

- if the landlord has a claim for possession; and
- if that claim can be disputed because the resident has a defence or the notice is inaccurate.

Box 23.9 Key personnel

Issue clerk – processes the papers received by the court and checks the papers received to ensure all information has been included. The issue clerk will not usually pick up mistakes in the address or name unless contradictory information is given. The issue clerk will refer the papers to a judge if they involve a legal issue, for example, a managing agent acting on behalf of an RSL.

Court manager – supervises the work of the court administrative staff who issue claims, list appointment and draw up orders. All correspondence to the court should be addressed to the court manager

Court usher – ensures all claimants are represented and ushers people into the court. They can also give advice on which court to go to and the facilities of the court. In some courts the function of the court usher and clerk are performed by the same person.

Court clerk – is the administrative officer of the court and sits in front of the judge in the court. The court clerk calls the court into session announces the cases, swears in the witnesses and ensures information is passed to the judge. The court clerk also notes the judgment.

Judges – the judges responsible for the county court are detailed in chapter 22.

23.28   All parties will be called into the court; both parties, if present, will give evidence supporting their claim or defence. Both parties may have someone representing them or supporting them (in the case of service users). In Box 23.10 we have outlined the role of the advice teams which are often located in county courts. Usually, parties are asked to give evidence under oath. This means that the court clerk or usher will ask the party giving evidence to affirm (when the party does not follow a religion) or swear on a holy book of choice that the evidence is true. Knowingly to give false evidence under oath is a criminal offence. At the hearing (or any adjourned hearings), the judge will make a decision about the claim or give case management directions, ie instructions which on how the court is going to deal with the case.

Box 23.10 Advice teams

Some courts have teams who advise residents and make representation on their behalf to try to prevent them losing their home. These teams are made up of solicitors/barristers and housing advice workers. You should be prepared to negotiate with the resident or their representative regarding the case.

Evidence

23.29 The particulars of claim should include the evidence up to the date that the proceedings were issued. You must also provide evidence of any other action or incidents that occur between issuing proceedings and going to court that you want to rely on. If you have witness statements, they need to be sent to the court, to allow them to be served on the resident at least two days before the hearing. This allows the resident to prepare a defence.

23.30 Possession is a civil action, and therefore evidence can include: rent statements, hearsay, video and CCTV evidence, professional witnesses, complaints (including those anonymously given) and witness diaries, as well as direct witness statements. Although a witness statement can be relied on in court, this does not have as much weight as a witness attending court to give evidence. This is because the party making a defence should have the opportunity to cross-examine the witness and challenge the evidence. When the judge makes a decision in a civil case, it is on the balance of probabilities – what the reasonable person would believe having considered all the evidence. We look at evidence in more detail in the next chapter, which is concerned with injunctions.

Court outcomes

23.31 There is a range of possible outcomes of court proceedings.

Application dismissed

23.32 The case may be dismissed if the judge feels that a ground for possession has not been established. This may occur, for example, if a landlord is pursuing a possession action against an assured tenant relying on ground 8 and the tenant has brought their account to less than eight weeks in arrears. An application may also be dismissed where the court has discretion and feels that it would be unreasonable to make an order. We will look at reasonableness later in this chapter.

Adjournment

23.33 The judge has the power to adjourn an application for possession. This means that the case remains 'live' in the court system until a time that it can be heard by the court. The judge may adjourn the case with 'liberty to restore', which means that the landlord can 'reactivate' the hearing at a later date. The judge usually puts a time limit on the 'liberty to restore'. If not, you need to be careful as some courts close the claim if they have not had contact with the claimant for 12 months. The judge adjourns a case with 'liberty to restore' under the following circumstances:

- In rent arrears cases where the arrears are small. In these cases the judge may set terms of repayment that the resident has to adhere to, allowing the landlord to return to court if there is a breach of those terms.
- When the landlord requests the judge to consider this if the resident has made an agreement regarding a breach.
- If the judge will not allow staff to represent the landlord but allows time to instruct a barrister or a solicitor (as only they have the right of audience).

23.34   The judge may adjourn the hearing with directions in the following circumstances:

- The judge feels that the landlord is not properly prepared. In busy inner city courts, around 30 cases can be expected to be heard in any one session. If the landlord's representative appears unprepared, for example, not having the correct information to hand, this would cause the court difficulties. Judges have been known to adjourn cases to the next available date after giving a week to enable the landlord to 'prepare adequately for the hearing'.
- If the resident has made a defence and more time needs to be allocated for the hearing.
- If the resident has a defence and/or counterclaim, but has not had the opportunity to properly instruct legal representatives.

23.35   When the judge adjourns the hearing, the directions will include how the court is going to manage the case and when it will be heard. For example, in a rent arrears case, if the resident counterclaims for damages for disrepair then the judge may direct the case to be listed for a one-day hearing, on the first available date after two weeks have elapsed to allow the landlord to inspect the property.

Outright possession order

23.36   The judge will grant this order when the landlord has proved a mandatory ground for possession. This includes:

- For assured and assured shorthold tenancies where a notice of seeking possession has been served and proceedings issued on a mandatory ground for possession.
- For assured shorthold tenancies where the section 21 notice has been used to require the court to give possession.
- For introductory tenants where the tenancy was still in its introductory form and had not defaulted to a secure tenant.

23.37 An outright order will also be given:

- For protected licences and excluded and contractual tenancies where a notice to quit has been served.
- For excluded licences where a notice terminating licence to occupy has been served.
- If the judge finds that the notice is valid and where discretion can be exercised so that it is reasonable for the defendant to give outright possession, as the notice has the effect of ending the licence or tenancy.

23.38 The order usually takes effect forthwith (immediately) or after a period of time, usually 14 or 28 days. This can be extended to up to six weeks if the resident can prove they will experience exceptional hardship if the order were to take effect earlier. In reality, if the landlord then has to apply for a warrant of execution (we discuss this in chapter 29), the resident will have some additional time.

Postponed (suspended) possession order

23.39 The judge has the power to 'postpone' an order for possession where a discretionary ground for possession has been used. This was previously referred to as suspending a possession order. However, in March 2006 the Court Service issued a new wording for the order. This followed the Court of Appeal decision in *Harlow DC v Hall* [2006] EWCA Civ 156, 28 February 2006, which highlighted that the unintended effect of the wording of a suspended order was to end a secure tenancy and create a tolerated trespasser (we discuss the concept of tolerated trespasser in chapter 26). The situation for assured tenancies was previously unclear. However in May 2007 the Court of Appeal held in *White v Knowsley Housing Trust* [2007] EWCA Civ 404 that a possession order suspended for a period of time also terminates an assured tenancy agreement on the date for giving possession. The Court of Appeal did recommend that the direction to the courts to use postponed orders instead of suspended should apply to assured as well as secure tenancy agreements. Current legal advice is that you should request the judge to use the N28A form of the order which identifies that the order is postponed for both secure and assured tenancies.

23.40   The postponed order does not require the judge to set a date for possession; it allows the order to be postponed until the landlord applies to the court if the tenant breaches the conditions set by the court.

23.41   Previously, the order was known as a suspended order. This order was suspended for 28 days or until the tenant breached the conditions set by the court. You may come across both orders and we refer to postponed (suspended) orders to cover both orders.

23.42   The postponed (suspended) order is usually used in rent arrears matters where the order is postponed (suspended) on condition that the tenant pays the current rent plus an amount of the arrears, known as 'rent plus'. In Box 23.11 we point you to some good practice as to when to use postponed (suspended) orders. The amount the judge sets should be in line with the tenant's circumstances, but for those on benefit the amount is £2.95 as at April 2006 and usually rises by 5p a year. The postponed (suspended) order is also becoming more common in nuisance cases, wherein the conditions set by the court relate to the tenant's behaviour. The breach of the conditions relating to the postponed order does not end the tenancy agreement and we will look at post-hearing action in chapter 29. We outlined above the position relating to secure tenancy agreements with suspended orders and advise providers to seek further legal advice. In the case of assured tenancy agreements with suspended order, the suspended order does not take effect if the conditions set by the court are met. If the conditions are breached it is not clear whether this brings the assured tenancy to an end, and again providers should seek further legal advice.

Box 23.11 Good practice

It is good practice for providers to seek a postponed (suspended) possession order in the first instance unless taking action for violence or extremely disruptive behaviour. This enables the tenant to maintain their home if they keep to the terms of the conditions set by the court, effectively giving them a further opportunity to remedy the problem.

Reasonableness

23.43   There is a range of circumstances when judges can exercise their discretion in possession proceedings, for example, when they are making decisions about either outright or postponed orders on the discretionary grounds for possession. The judge has to be satisfied that it is reasonable to grant an order. If the judge fails to consider reasonableness, it means that the order can be nullified even if the tenant has agreed to it. Examples of what a judge may take into consideration in exercising his or her discretion include the age and health of the tenant, the reason the landlord requires possession, the public interest and previous conduct. The judge may also look at whether the landlord has followed its policies and procedures, if the tenant is entitled to welfare benefits and whether they have been claimed. Since the Human Rights Act 1998, judges are expected to look at proportionality, for example, whether a possession order is necessary to enable the landlord to recover the rent owed. In the case of small arrears the judge might decide that it is not proportionate for a tenant to lose their home when the landlord could use the small claims process to recover the debt.

23.44   In Box 23.12 we have identified some good practice guidelines to follow in the case of different court outcomes.

Box 23.12 Good practice

If you are granted a possession order or the case is adjourned you should contact the resident explaining the court outcome and what will happen next. If the order is postponed you should detail the terms set by the court, what is expected of them and what support you will be offering to enable them to keep to the conditions. If the order is an outright order, you should support the resident in securing alternative accommodation by contacting the local authority housing unit and other agencies to prevent the them from becoming homeless. If they are vulnerable or have dependants, you should contact the local authority social services department.

Defences

23.45   The resident has 14 days to file a defence and any written evidence they are going to rely on in court. If the resident fails to acknowledge the papers, they can attend the hearing but it is up to the judge whether they can make representations. In practice, most judges would agree to hear what the resident has to say if they attended hearing.

23.46   There are two main defences to possession proceedings:

- The first is procedural. For example, the notice is inaccurate in terms of dates or details, if the resident has not received the notice or if the claim is defective.

- The second is substantive. This means the landlord cannot rely on the ground used with the evidence provided on the balance of probabilities. An example would be if a ground for rent arrears was being relied upon and the resident could demonstrate their rent had been wrongly allocated to another resident's rent account. Or if the ground has been proved, but there is a condition to be met (the most common in tenancy agreements is reasonableness) that the landlord has not proven on the evidence and balance of probabilities. An example of this would be if the resident had breached a term of their occupancy agreement relating to health and safety as they were hoarding newspapers. They could demonstrate to the court it would not be reasonable for them to lose their home, when what they needed was support for their compulsive behaviour.

Counterclaim

23.47   The resident may also make a counterclaim; they should apply for the court's permission to do this. The most common example is for disrepair. For example, the resident has a problem with damp in the property and as they are dissatisfied with the landlord's response, they stop paying rent. The landlord then takes them to court on the grounds of rent arrears. The tenant counterclaims for damages for disrepair which will be set off against the rent arrears. In Box 23.13 we have signposted you to a useful publication if you are supporting service users through the possession process.

23.48   In court the resident may be represented by a solicitor or barrister. Residents could also be represented, with permission of the judge, by one of the lay representatives attached to the advice team. Service users can also be accompanied by a 'McKenzie friend', a term given to someone who is able to support them in court by making suggestions as to what they should say. McKenzie friends cannot speak on a service user's behalf.

Box 23.13 Signpost

Legal Action Group publishes *Defending Possession Proceedings* (6th edn, 2006) by Nic Madge, John Gallagher, Derek McConnell and Jan Luba QC, which is a mine of information, not only for defendants, but for claimants as well: www.lag.org.uk; tel: 0207 833 2931; fax: 0207 837 6094.

Changing the terms of possession orders

23.49   Once a possession order has been granted by the judge, there are a number of ways in which it can be altered by the courts.

Setting aside possession orders

23.50   If the defendant can prove certain circumstances, the possession order can be set aside. The court can either order a new hearing and give directions for this hearing or hear the case there and then. The most common reason for setting aside a possession order is that the resident did not attend the hearing. This can be used even after the warrant of possession has been executed. The resident would have to prove they acted as soon as they found out the order had been made, they had a good reason for not attending and they had a reasonable chance of success at the hearing. The effect is as if the order had never been made.

Changing an outright to a postponed order

23.51   If an outright order is made on a discretionary ground for possession, the tenant can apply to change it to a postponed order if there has been a significant change in their circumstances.

Box 23.14 Frequently asked questions

We obtained a suspended possession order some time ago against an assured tenant when she was unemployed. The conditions set by the court are that she pays £2.85 per week off her arrears. Can we ask the court to increase this amount?

The landlord can apply to the court to vary the terms of a postponed (suspended) order if the tenant's circumstances change. There is a charge for this (at July 2007, £35) and you may wish to weigh up how much it will cost you against how much extra per week you will recover. The tenant can also apply to the court if the situation were reversed. For example, if they are no longer working and on reduced income they can apply to have the repayments reduced.

Appeals

23.52   Either party can bring an appeal against the decision made by the judge. We discuss the hierarchy of courts in chapter 22. The appeal can be made on the basis that the judge has not applied the law properly, including the reasonableness of making an order. However, superior courts are reluctant to interfere with the decision of inferior courts because they consider that the judge at first instance has had the benefit of hearing the evidence first hand. They are particularly reluctant to interfere in the exercise of judicial discretion.

Court costs

23.53   The costs of going to court include the court fees and the cost of legal representation. Residents on low income may be entitled to public-funded legal representation and, under the Legal Help scheme, free initial advice and assistance. The judge has discretion over whether costs incurred by one party should be paid by the other party, the amount of those costs and when they should be paid. If you take a possession action, you may want the resident to pay the costs of the court case if you get an order. It is common for all residents to pay the costs of the court fees if the landlord is successful in a possession action. If the landlord has incurred the costs of legal representation, it is unlikely that publicly funded residents would be expected to pay the cost of the landlord's legal representation.

Box 23.15 Court fees

The Court Service website,www.hmcourts-service.gov.uk, has details of the cost of making an application to the court.

Summary

23.54   This chapter has looked at the practicalities involved in taking a case for possession to court. Although the motivation for those working in supported housing is to help residents maintain their accommodation, not to deprive them of their home, the court process is a necessary element of your work. The legislative requirements of the court provide a check on the process of a landlord regaining possession of a resident's home. The procedures ensure that the service users are given every opportunity to prepare a defence. The landlord has to demonstrate and provide evidence to support the ground for possession, and in most cases that possession is reasonable. The formality and seriousness of court action, as embodied in the CPR, accompanied by the requirements of your regulators, mean that you will not pursue this action lightly.

CHAPTER 24

Injunctions

Objectives

24.1   By the end of this chapter you will:

- Know about the different types of injunctions available to manage behaviour in supported housing
- Understand how an injunction can be used as a tool in managing behaviour
- Know how to apply for an injunction and what evidence is required to support that application

Overview

24.2   In chapter 8 we looked at injunctions in the context of managing anti-social behaviour. In this chapter we will examine how injunctions can be used to help you carry out your work with residents, and we consider the process of applying for an injunction. We will start by setting out the basic legal principles underpinning injunctions, we look at how regulators expect injunctions to be used and consider how they should feature in your policies and procedures. We will then go on to identify how injunctions could be used to enable residents to remain in their home. Lastly, we will look at the legal process of applying for an injunction and how this can be managed.

The legal nature of injunctions

24.3   Injunctions are part of the remedies available in civil law. These remedies are designed to compensate or protect parties and not to punish individuals, which is the role of the criminal law. However, common law remedies, such as damages and eviction, were not sufficiently flexible to provide a full range of responses to a legal dispute. The courts therefore developed the injunction as an equitable remedy which would improve the limitations of common law remedies. One example to illustrate this is where a resident is harassed by his or her landlord. The common law remedy for this would be damages. Damages, however, do not really provide a remedy for the harm the tenant is suffering. What he or she wants is for the harassment to stop. Injunctions provide a way to stop the unwanted behaviour. However, the resident is not entitled to the injunction as of right. He or she must issue proceedings for breach of the covenant of quiet enjoyment and then apply for an injunction in the course of those proceedings.

24.4   Because injunctions are civil remedies, the judge will make a decision about the evidence of the behaviour you are trying to restrain based on the balance of probabilities, having examined all the evidence. Note that breach of an injunction is contempt of court which carries sanctions, including imprisonment.

24.5   Injunctions are equitable remedies. What this means is that even if the facts of the case are made out, the applicant has no right to an injunction. The judge has the discretion to decide whether an injunction is fair, appropriate and necessary in order to resolve the problem. This means, for instance, that injunctions are unlikely to be granted if you delay your application, as this would suggest it is not necessary.

24.6   There are two different types of injunctions:

- A mandatory injunction has the effect of making a resident do something, for example, removing a dog that has been brought into a shared house. Judges can be reluctant to grant mandatory injunctions.
- A prohibitory injunction prevents a resident from acting in a certain way, for example, tampering with the fire extinguishers.

24.7   The vast majority of injunctions are ancillary to other court proceedings. What this means is that you can apply for an injunction for instance at the same time as commencing possession proceedings. The injunction would be granted to stop a resident from continuing to breach their occupancy agreement while the landlord waited for a court date for possession.

24.8   There are some exceptions to this, known as free-standing injunctions. These are created by statute to deal with specific problems. In the housing world, the most relevant free-standing injunctions are available to restrain domestic violence and to restrain anti-social behaviour. We look at the details of anti-social behaviour injunctions in chapter 8 and discuss their use in chapter 20.

Box 24.1 Frequently asked questions

Can you obtain an injunction against a service user under 18 years or who has a mental health problem?

Injunctions can, in theory, be obtained against any age of person. However, courts are very reluctant to grant them against people aged under 18 years because there is no sanction available to the court for non-compliance; moreover, the person who is

> subject to the injunction must have the mental capacity to under-
> stand what they are doing and how to modify their behaviour.
> Because the law presumes that adults have mental capacity, it
> would be for the defendant to argue that they lack capacity. How-
> ever, it would be sensible for you to provide evidence that the
> defendant had the capacity to understand the significance of the
> injunction.

24.9   Breach of an injunction can result in two years' imprisonment and/or
an unlimited fine for breach of court.

24.10   In some circumstances, such as domestic violence and anti-social
behaviour, statutes have given courts the ability to attach a power of
arrest to the injunction. This is a serious reduction of someone's civil
liberties, so there are quite restrictive circumstances when the power
of arrest can be applied. You can read details of the circumstances
when a power of arrest is available in cases of anti-social behaviour
in chapter 8.

Regulatory requirements

24.11   The Housing Corporation's Regulatory Code and guidance emphasises the value of injunctions as an alternative to taking possession
proceedings.

24.12   These principles have been expanded by Circular 07/04, 'Tenancy
management: eligibility and evictions'. This circular states that registered social landlords (RSLs) should use the full range of tools now
available for tackling anti-social behaviour and should only consider
evictions when other interventions have failed to protect the wider
community. There is an expectation that RSLs use injunctions both to
prevent breaches of tenancy and to ensure residents adhere to the
terms of the tenancy. This enables both the RSL to deal with the problem and the resident to keep their home. The circular describes another
practical example when an injunction may be useful: a mandatory
injunction could be used when a resident refuses to allow access to
the property, for instance, to enable the statutorily required annual
gas safety checks to take place. The main cause of action in this example would be breach of the tenancy agreement.

Policies and procedures

24.13   Guidelines for staff on the use of injunctions will usually be found in
the policies and procedures that govern behaviour, for example:

- Anti-social behaviour.
- Anti-harassment.
- Racial harassment.
- Challenging behaviour.
- Breach of tenancy.

24.14   In Box 24.2 we have identified some good practice concerning the
user of injunctions.

Box 24.2 Good practice

If there is no specific policy and procedure on injunctions, staff
should be given guidelines on their use. This will enable staff to
be aware of how injunctions are applied for, what they can expect
if an injunction is granted and what to do if the injunction is
breached.

Housing injunctions

24.15   Providers can apply for injunctions for a number of different purposes, such as enforcing the access conditions of the tenancy. You
would need to issue proceedings for breach of contract and apply for
a mandatory injunction as part of the proceedings. Residents can also
apply for an injunction, for example, to prevent a provider from disclosing information about them to another party. This would be as
part of proceedings against the landlord for breach of the common
law obligation of confidentiality or for breach of data protection legislation.

24.16   The majority of injunctions in supported housing are used to
manage the behaviour of residents, members of their household or
visitors. The government has introduced a wealth of legislation on
anti-social behaviour and section 13 of the Anti-social Behaviour Act
2003 introduced provisions that allow RSLs to apply for injunctions to
prevent anti-social behaviour that affects their management of their
housing stock. We set out details of these injunctions in chapter 8 and
discuss their use in chapter 20.

Box 24.3 Frequently asked questions

One of our tenants collects items from skips in the neighbourhood. She lives in a block of flats and is storing her belongings in the communal hallway and on the communal stairs. She has refused to move them and we are concerned that other tenants may injure themselves stepping over the items. Can we apply for an injunction?

In these circumstances you could apply for a 'stand alone' housing injunction under the Housing Act 1996 for anti-social behaviour or breach of tenancy agreement. For both of these injunctions you would have to demonstrate that in storing the items the tenant was causing a nuisance or annoyance to the other tenants or staff. If you think it would be difficult to prove this but want to ensure the health and safety of other residents, you could follow another course of action. You could commence possession proceedings on ground 12 – breach of tenancy agreement. You could then apply for an injunction as part of the proceedings. When you receive the injunction, you could either let the possession proceedings lapse or withdraw the possession proceedings. Alternatively, you could simply request at the possession hearing that the tenant to makes an undertaking to the court that she will remove the items. On that basis, you could withdraw the proceedings.

Application to the court

24.17   An application for an injunction must be made as part of legal proceedings, for example, for breach of the tenancy agreement. The procedures for applying for an injunction are governed by the Civil Procedures Rules (CPR). There are specific rules for anti-social behaviour injunctions: see CPR Part 65, Proceedings relating to Anti-social Behaviour and Harassment, which modified the existing Part 8 alternative procedure for claims. In Box 24.4 we signpost you to where you can find the CPR.

Box 24.4 Civil Procedure Rules

CPR Parts 8 and 65 can be found on the Ministry of Justice website, www.justice.gov.uk.

Applications for anti-social behaviour injunctions

24.18   Any application for an anti-social behaviour injunction must be made on a claim form N16A and be addressed to the court manager. The form sets out details of the case, including:

- the name of the individual or organisation applying for the injunction (the claimant) and service user (the defendant); and
- the behaviour the claimant want to prohibit.

24.19   The form must be accompanied by written evidence supporting the grounds.

Application on notice

24.20   If the application for the injunction allows for a hearing (with notice), the landlord must serve the application and copy of witness statement on the resident personally. The service user has 14 days to acknowledge the notice if they want to make representations. If the resident does not acknowledge service, it is up to the judge on the day whether he or she will allow representations. In urgent circumstances, the date for the hearing may be less than 14 days. In these cases the service user must be given the application and evidence at least two days prior to the hearing. The service user can make representations in even if no acknowledgement of service is received.

Application without notice

24.21   If the situation is an emergency, you can apply without giving notice to the service user. There must be written evidence supporting the reasons why notice has not been given. The court may order that notice must be given or allow the application. If the injunction is granted, the service user must be given the chance to make representations as soon as possible.

Application for an injunction with a power of arrest attached

24.22   The judge may decide to attach a power of arrest if it is within his or her powers to do so. If you believe that the behaviour is serious, you should include a request for a power of arrest within the application for the notice or in the evidence accompanying the application. If you are granted an injunction with a power of arrest, you must deliver a copy of its provisions to the police station that covers the area where the conduct took place.

Evidence

24.23　The success of obtaining an injunction is dependent on the evidence that is presented at the application hearing. There are different types of evidence that can be used:

- Witnesses who appear in court, for example, those the injunction is intended to protect. This could be neighbours, staff from the organisation requesting the injunction, an environmental health officer from the local authority, housing officers, etc. This type of evidence carries the greatest weight as the judge will be able to hear the facts and asses its truthfulness.
- Written statements from those affected. For example, neighbours, staff, police, etc. The statements from those employed to manage the housing or statutory services are often called witness statements. This can include diary sheets, log books, warnings and occupancy agreements terms. This evidence should demonstrate why the injunction is needed, and should include any support that has been given to the service user and any agreements they have made and broken. If those affected are too intimidated to appear, they can provide written statements (if necessary, anonymously). This becomes hearsay evidence, which is admissible in a civil court. This can be strengthened if the professional who has taken the statement appears in court and evidences that the individuals making the statement were upset, distressed and intimidated.
- Photos, CCTV, sound and video recordings can also be used as evidence as the proceedings are civil.

24.24　All the evidence you are relying on must be disclosed to the court and the service user so that they can prepare a defence. If you do not want to disclose hearsay evidence to protect witnesses who may fear reprisals, you can refuse to do so. The judge, however, has the discretion to order you to disclose the information. If you do not want to do this you can withdraw that piece of evidence.

Terms of the injunction

24.25   If the judge grants the injunction, the order will be made using form
N16 and issued to the service user. The order will set out the prohibited
conduct, and make clear that if the service user breaches the injunction
they will be guilty of contempt of court and may be sent to prison. If
the injunction is an interim one, the form will detail the date, time
and place of the hearing where it will be reconsidered. The court
can vary or discharge an injunction if you or the service user
applies using form N244. In Box 24.5 we identify some good practice
concerning the use of injunctions.

Box 24.5 Good practice

If you are granted an injunction you should contact the service
user explaining what happened at the court hearing and what is
expected of the service user. You should review the service user's
support plan and risk assessment and consider what support
is needed to ensure they comply with the terms of the injunction. The service user should be made aware of the consequences
of breaching the injunction and whether this will be used as evidence for possession proceedings.

Breach of the injunction

24.26   A breach of injunction is dealt with by proceedings for contempt of
court. As soon as you are aware of the breach, you should make an
application to the court using form N244 for a hearing. You will need
to provide evidence of the alleged breach. Where a power of arrest is
attached, the defendant can be arrested if a police constable has reasonable cause for suspecting the defendant has breached the order.
The defendant will be then brought before the county court.

24.27   If the judge is satisfied that the terms of the injunction have been
broken, he or she may decide to impose a fine or a prison sentence of
up to two years. If a service user receives a prison sentence they can
write to the court apologising for the behaviour, acknowledging that the
contempt needed to be punished and undertake to keep the terms of
the injunction in the future. If the judge is satisfied by this, they can be
released before the end of their sentence.

Summary

24.28   An injunction is an equitable remedy which has proved to be a useful tool in supported housing. It is not intended to punish the service user or deprive them of their home. Instead, it can be used to demonstrate that certain behaviour is unacceptable and indicate what is required for someone to keep their home. The injunction has value as a formal legal tool, and the process of going to court and receiving the order can make the seriousness of the situation clear to the service user.

24.29   In this chapter we have outlined how to use injunctions with a specific reference to their use in managing antisocial behaviour. In the next chapter we will look at anti-social behaviour orders, a different civil order designed exclusively to tackle anti-social behaviour.

CHAPTER 25

Anti-social behaviour orders (ASBOs)

Objectives

25.1   By the end of this chapter you will:

- Appreciate the different types of anti-social behaviour orders (ASBOs) available
- Understand the application process for an ASBO, including the evidential requirements
- Know what happens when an ASBO is issued and what happens if it is breached
- Understand how an ASBO can be appealed against, varied or discharged

Overview

25.2   In chapter 8 of this book we consider the general legal remedies for managing anti-social behaviour. In this chapter we concentrate on one of those remedies, the ASBO. ASBOs have attracted a great deal of attention from a variety of sources. The government has heavily promoted their use in tackling 'loutish and unacceptable behaviour'. The media has alternatively celebrated their use, in particular against young people who are seen as out of control, or highlighted their absurdity when they have been given to prevent sarcasm or singing in the bath. Supported housing providers may come across ASBOs in two quite distinct ways. Service users can be perpetrators of or experience anti-social behaviour. You could be supporting a service user who has an ASBO who may wish to appeal against its imposition or wish to vary the order. Alternatively, you could be applying for an ASBO to protect a service user or to manage the behaviour of visitors or to manage a service user's behaviour 'in situ'. This chapter will first outline the different type of ASBOs that are available and then explain how regulators expect the orders to be used. We will then describe the court process for obtaining an ASBO and the evidence required. Lastly, we will look at what happens when an order is made and what happens if an order is breached. We will specifically address the issue of young people, as to date nearly 50 per cent of ASBOs relate to young adults under 18 years of age.

Legislation

25.3   The Crime and Disorder Act 1998 introduced the ASBO. It is a civil order which prohibits the defendant from specific anti-social acts and from entering defined areas (exclusion zones). The order is itself is not a criminal order, and its purpose is not to punish the defendant but to restrain his or her behaviour. The order prevents the defendant from continuing to act in an anti-social manner or enter a defined location in order to protect a person(s) or the public.

25.4   There are three types of ASBO:

25.5   *Stand alone* – this order is unrelated to any other legal proceedings and made in the magistrates' court acting in its civil capacity.

25.6   *County court order* – this can be obtained where other proceedings are being taken against the defendant, most commonly possession proceedings. Changes made in the Anti-social Behaviour Act 2003 enable people who have behaved in an anti-social manner who are not party to the proceedings in the county court to be joined to proceedings and made the subject of an ASBO. This means, for instance, that where the defendant to the possession proceedings is not the perpetrator of the behaviour, but he or she is the parent of the perpetrator, the child can be joined to the possession proceedings. The purpose is to avoid the waste of court resources and the need to present the same evidence twice in two different courts.

25.7   *Order made on conviction of a criminal offence* – the magistrates' court, Crown Court or youth court can make an order against an individual convicted of a criminal offence.

Box 25.1 Frequently asked questions

Can we get an order in an emergency situation even if the person causing the problem isn't at court?

In these circumstances you could apply for an *interim order*. This order can be used for all three types of ASBO. It can be made by the magistrates' court or county court at an initial court hearing in advance of a full hearing of an application for an ASBO. It can be made without notice to the defendant and enables the court to put an immediate stop to the behaviour.

Regulatory requirements

25.8   The Housing Corporation expectations are set out in their Regulatory Code and guidance, which provides in paragraph 3.5c that '*legal possession of a property is sought as a last resort* and paragraph 3.5d *strategies are in place to tackle antisocial behaviour*'. This part of the Regulatory Code and guidance has been expanded by Circular 02/07, 'Tenancy management: eligibility and evictions'. This circular states that registered social landlords (RSLs) should use the full range of tools now available for tackling anti-social behaviour, only considering eviction when other interventions have failed to protect the wider community. In supported housing, providers might use ASBOs as a tool to manage behaviour, rather than eviction or withdrawing support.

25.9　*Supporting People* services are often provided to those who have or are at risk of legal sanctions for their behaviour. Examples of these services are the intensive family intervention projects that support challenging families. For more information about these schemes visit www.respect.gov.uk/members/news/article.aspx?id=10316. The services may include support in enabling service users to adhere to the conditions of an ASBO.

Policies and procedures

25.10　Providers who are RSLs or local authorities are required under the Anti-social Behaviour Act 2003 to have policies and procedures on anti-social behaviour. The use of ASBOs should form part of the policy and procedures, which should outline, for instance, when an ASBO should be applied for. In chapter 20 we specifically address policies and procedures in the management of anti-social behaviour.

The application for an ASBO

25.11　The agencies able to apply for ASBOs are referred to as 'relevant authorities'. These include the police, local authorities, RSLs and housing action trusts. RSLs have to consult with the local authority and the local police force before issuing an application. The local authority and the police do not have to give consent. A signed document of consultation is required by court. However, for an interim order this could simply be a record of a phone conversation between the various parties. RSLs would require legal representation to obtain an ASBO. The average cost of applying for an ASBO is estimated at £2,500.

25.12　Applications can be made to the following

Magistrates' court

25.13　Magistrates acting in their civil capacity applications can make stand alone orders on application from a relevant authority. The relevant authority should arrange for an application form and three copies of the summons form to be completed and serviced on the court. The defendant should then be served with the summons, the application form, evidence of consultation, guidance about legal advice and representation, notice of hearsay evidence and any other evidence to be relied on, and a warning regarding witness intimidation. If the person is under 18, the person with parental responsibility must also receive a copy of this information. In the magistrates' court, the complaint must have occurred within the six months prior to the application. However, previous incidents can be included as background to support the application.

24.14   In their criminal capacity, magistrates can make ASBOs following convictions in criminal proceedings. The court may make an order of its own volition or on application by the prosecutor or the police or local authority.

Crown Court and youth courts

25.15   An ASBO can be made on convictions in criminal proceedings that take place in the Crown Court or in youth courts.

County court

25.16   The judge can make an order on a person against whom possession proceedings are being taken or on a non-party who is joined to the proceedings. For example, an order is required to prevent a resident's visitors from harassing neighbours. There must be principal proceedings, ie the landlord must be evicting the tenant. The relevant authority making the application for the ASBO must be a party to the principal proceedings. Other relevant authorities may become parties in order to apply for an order if they apply to the court to be 'joined'. As stated earlier, a visitor who has caused anti-social behaviour may be 'joined' to the proceedings. An application for an ASBO is made on court form N113.

Procedure

25.17   The agency applying for an ASBO needs to satisfy what is commonly referred to as the two-stage test. Under section 1 of the Crime and Disorder Act 1998, the agency must demonstrate:

- the defendant behaved in an anti-social manner; and

- an order is necessary for the protection of people from further anti-social behaviour by the defendant.

25.18   In chapter 8 we looked at the legal definition of anti-social behaviour. What may be useful now is to look at the type of behaviour identified by the Home Office that can be tackled by ASBOs:

- Harassment of residents or passers-by.
- Verbal abuse.
- Criminal damage.
- Vandalism.
- Noise nuisance.
- Writing graffiti.
- Engaging in threatening behaviour in large groups.
- Racial abuse.
- Smoking or drinking alcohol while under age.
- Substance misuse.
- Joyriding.
- Begging.
- Prostitution.
- Kerb-crawling.
- Throwing missiles.
- Assault.
- Vehicle vandalism.

Burden of proof and evidence

25.19   An ASBO is a civil order. However, the standard of proof required is criminal. This means that the agency must prove that the defendant acted in an anti-social manner so that it is beyond reasonable doubt that the behaviour occurred.

25.20   The evidence that is required to demonstrate the defendant acted in an anti-social manner should explain to the court the context of the anti-social behaviour and its effect on other people, as well as demonstrating the actual acts of anti-social behaviour. Because of the civil nature of the order, evidence can include hearsay, video and CCTV evidence, professional witnesses, complaints (including those anonymously given), witness diaries, as well as direct witness statements (including the attending police officers), details of previous arrests, convictions or proceedings and evidence of breaches of acceptable behaviour contracts and warnings. In Box 25.2 we have included the range of evidence that can be used in an application for an ASBO.

Box 25.2 Evidence for ASBO

The Home Office guide to ASBOs identifies evidence to be used in ASBO applications to include:

- Professional witness statements.
- Hearsay evidence.
- CCTV footage.
- Letters of complaint (including those made anonymously) to the police, the council or the landlord.
- Articles in the local press.
- Number and nature of the charges against the defendant.
- Defendant's character and conduct as revealed by the evidence.
- Victim's personal statement.
- Other offences that have been taken into consideration.
- Warnings or previous convictions.
- Risk assessment in any pre-sentencing reports.
- Record of other intervention acceptable behaviour contracts.
- Community assessment statement.

The guide is available from www.homeoffice.gov.uk

25.21 A community impact statement is often used in ASBO proceedings. This can be prepared by a police officer or a housing officer. The purpose of this statement is to outline the effect of the behaviour on the wider community. It is designed to give the magistrate or judge a picture of what it is like living and working in the community and how the behaviour complained about has impacted on the community. It can enable the housing officer to present evidence when witnesses are too intimidated to appear. The statutory definition of anti-social behaviour includes 'likely to cause harassment alarm or distress', which enables someone other than the victim to give evidence. You, as a member of staff, can give evidence if witnesses are worried about intimidation or reprisals. In the supported housing sector, you may also be working with people who are likely to be accused of perpetrating anti-social behaviour. In Box 25.3 we signpost you to a publication to support your work.

Box 25.3 Defending ASBOs

The wide-ranging effect of the order may concern those of you who work with people vulnerable to allegations of anti-social behaviour. Legal Action Group publishes *ASBOs: a practitioner's guide to defending anti-social behaviour orders* by Maya Sikand: Website: www.lag.org.uk; tel: 0207 833 2931; fax: 0207 837 6094.

The order

25.22   The applicant should draw up its proposals for appropriate conditions and the duration of the order. However, it is up to the court to decide the terms of the order. It should be clear to the defendant what behaviour is expected of him or her, so the order must be specific and easy to understand. If the ASBO prohibits a defendant from a particular area, it must include street names and a map. What is not helpful is a prohibition from going within 50 metres of a particular point. The effect of the order should be explained to the defendant and the terms stated in open court. The duration of the order is for a minimum of two years, but can last for any period up to a lifetime. This is not so worrying for the 87-year-old man who has an ASBO preventing him from being sarcastic; it is more so for the 14-year-old prohibited from entering Leeds city centre.

Breaches of the order

25.23   A breach of an ASBO is a criminal offence that is arrestable and recordable. Usually, prosecutions for breaches are brought by the Crown Prosecution Service, although the local authority can also pursue prosecutions. The maximum penalty on conviction in the magistrates' court is a six-month prison sentence and a fine of up to £5,000. Community penalties are available, but a conditional discharge is not.

Appeals, variations and discharge

25.24   When an ASBO has been made, there are various rights of appeal depending on its origin.

25.25   For stand alone and post convictions from the magistrates' court, appeals can be made to the Crown Court. If the ASBO has been made by the Crown Court, an appeal must be made to the Court of Appeal

(Criminal Division). In some cases of procedural irregularity there can be an appeal from the magistrates' court or Crown Court to the High Court. Lastly, a judicial review can be used to challenge the lawfulness of the court's decision, for example, to argue that the court has acted in excess of its jurisdiction or failed to follow the rules of natural justice. ASBOs made in the county court can be appealed to the High Court or the Court of Appeal. An appeal can also be made by the applicant against a decision to refuse to grant an order.

25.26   The order, once made, can be varied or discharged by applying to the court that made it. The order cannot be discharged within two years of being made. The conditions of the order can be varied, removed or added to at any time. Providers may find it necessary to support an application for variation of an ASBO if the perpetrator is unable to use the support services because, for instance, he or she is restricted from entering a particular area.

Young people

25.27   Young people and children from 10 years of age can be subject to a stand alone, and on conviction or interim ASBOs. Agencies are able to apply for ASBOs against young people in much the same way as they do against adults. The youth offending team (YOT) has a role to play in explaining the order and offering support to young people to aid compliance. In Box 25.4 we signpost you to a report explaining its role. In cases of a breach of order, a pre-sentence report should be provided by the YOT. The pre-sentencing report can address the issue of parenting that may lead to a parenting order being made. If the young person is under 16 and a parenting order is desirable to avoid repetition of the anti-social behaviour, the court must make such an order. The other order that may be available when an ASBO is imposed on a minor is an individual support order (ISO). This order requires the young person to comply with specified activities for a period of six months. Failure to comply with an ISO is punishable by a fine, and when the child is under 16, the parent would be expected to pay the fine.

Box 25.4 The role of the youth offending team

Anti-social behaviour: A guide to the role of Youth offending Teams in dealing with Anti-social behaviour, available at www.youth-justice-board.gov.uk.

25.28　As the youth court has no civil jurisdiction, applications for stand alone orders are heard in the magistrates' court unless the order is made on conviction. In the county court there is no general power to make an order on a minor. There has been a pilot scheme in operation in 11 county courts to enable this to happen.

Box 25.5 Frequently asked questions

Why do papers publish photographs of people who have been given ASBOs? Aren't there reporting restrictions when young people are involved in criminal activities?

There are no reporting restrictions in relation to ASBO applications, whatever the age of the defendant. The justification for publishing photos is that the ASBO would be an ineffective prohibitive tool if the public does not know of its existence. In the case of young people, the court does, however, have the power to impose a restriction on media reporting. Judges have to balance the detrimental effects of 'naming and shaming' on the young person with the need for the identity of the individual to enable the order to be effective.

25.29　One positive change brought in by the government is that ASBOs for young people must be reviewed every year.

Summary

25.30　The ASBO is a powerful tool. Its critics, and there are a number (visit www.asboconcern.org.uk), are concerned that it criminalises what was considered to be unattractive but not criminal behaviour. ASBOs, however, appear to be 'here to stay' and, as social housing providers, we are increasingly expected to use them as a tool to manage behaviour. As supported housing providers, we are also expected to work with service users who are in the process of having an ASBO imposed. This chapter has aimed to provide you with an understanding of the mechanics of the ASBO to enable you to be a party in making an application or to support a service user through the process.

CHAPTER 26

Evictions

Objectives

26.1   By the end of this chapter you will:

- Understand what action is required following obtaining possession in the county court
- Understand the roles of the court bailiff and police in an eviction
- Appreciate what organisational action is required in an eviction

Overview

26.2   In chapter 23 of this book we looked at possession proceedings in the county court. We identified the possible outcome of a court hearing, and when it was appropriate to seek a suspended or outright/immediate possession order. The end of the possession process results in a service user being physically evicted from their home. In this chapter we will look at the legal process that is necessary for eviction, which is dependent on the order for possession obtained from the court. We will then look at the practical steps you will need to take to safeguard the security of the property and other residents. Lastly, we identify what steps should be taken to ensure the former resident does not become homeless.

Immediate order

26.3   An immediate or outright order ends a tenancy or licence on the date it takes effect. This is the date identified by the judge in the court hearing. For example, if you go to court on 2 June and the judge grants an outright order 'forthwith', the agreement ends on that date. If the judge grants an outright order to be effective in 14 days, it will end on 16 June. However, you cannot simply change the locks on that date; you must apply to the court for a warrant for possession of land (see below). Legal advice indicates that if you obtain an immediate order, you should apply for a warrant and take possession of the property as soon as possible. If you choose to do nothing, the resident becomes a 'tolerated trespasser' – we will explain more about this later.

Postponed order

26.4 Judges have the power to postpone possession orders only when the occupancy agreement is a tenancy. A postponed order (previously known as suspended order) is one which does not take effect immediately. Instead, the tenancy continues as long as the resident keeps to the conditions or terms of the order imposed by the judge. What this means is that the postponed possession order does not end the tenancy. However, if the terms are breached, you can apply to the court to fix a date for possession. The date identified by the court is the date the order becomes effective, and the tenancy comes to an end.

Suspended orders

26.5 The previous position, when orders were described as suspended, was problematic. Suspended orders came into effect if and when the resident breached the terms set by the court – at this point the tenancy came to an end. This meant that if you allowed the resident to continue living at the property after he or she had breached the order (thereby terminating the tenancy), he or she became a tolerated trespasser. For secure tenancies, this was further complicated in February 2006 in the case of *Harlow DC v Hall* [2006] EWCA Civ 156. The Court of Appeal decided that the usual type of possession order suspended for 28 days ended the tenancy after the 28 days even if the tenant kept to the terms set by the court. This means that the tenant became a tolerated trespasser despite complying with terms. The position for assured tenancies and old-style suspended possession orders is unclear as the court cases have been contradictory. In May 2007 however the Court of Appeal held in *White v Knowsley Housing Trust* [2007] EWCA Civ 404 that a possession order suspended for a period of time also terminates an assured tenancy agreement on the date for giving possession. What is suspended is the execution of the order by the landlord not the possession order. If the occupant keeps to the terms set by the court although they are no longer a tenant they can stay in the property as a tolerated trespasser.

26.6 If the resident breaches the terms set by the court you have a choice. If you want the tenant to leave then you should apply for a warrant of possession of land. If you want the tenant to stay you can write to them stating you are expressly waiving the breach and allowing them to continue to stay as a tolerated trespasser.

Tolerated trespasser

26.7   The term 'tolerated trespasser' was established in the case *Burrows v Brent LBC* [1996] 4 All ER 577, HL. It was used to describe an occupier who had lost his or her legal right to remain on the property but the landlord has continued to allow them to remain without granting them a fresh tenancy. It has only been used in tenancy arrangements as it has been linked to losing the legal interest in the property. Subsequent court cases have allowed 'tolerated trespassers' some of the rights of tenants. The postponed possession orders should reduce the numbers of 'tolerated trespassers', as they will only occur when an outright order has not been acted upon by the landlord.

Applying for a warrant of possession of land

26.8   You must apply for a warrant of possession of land (a warrant) unless the former resident voluntarily leaves. The warrant is commonly known as the eviction order; it enforces the judgment made. In most cases (which tend to be straightforward rent arrears cases), the warrant is granted by the court without the need for a hearing. For some, more complex cases, the judge will order that a warrant can only be granted with the leave of the court. The judge will indicate at the possession hearing whether the case requires a hearing before a warrant is granted. If so, you must apply to the court for a hearing. In Box 26.1 we indicate good practice to follow before a warrant is applied for.

Box 26.1 Good practice

The possession or eviction procedure of your organisation should ensure that tenants are treated fairly and homelessness is prevented. Before a warrant is applied for you should ensure:

- The relevant authorisation procedures have been followed. All applications should be agreed by a senior manager; in some organisations this may mean the chair of the management board. In the case of managing agents, the owning registered social landlord (RSL) usually sanctions the application.
- The resident has been advised of the action and their right to appeal to the board of management in the case of a breach of a postponed order.

> - The resident is advised to seek legal advice.
> - Other agencies involved in the support or care of the resident are informed in line with the information sharing protocol.
> - You still continue to support the tenant and make efforts to secure alternative accommodation.

26.9 When the decision to apply for a warrant is authorised by your organisation, you can request a warrant from the county court where the judgment was made. The Request for Warrant for Possession of Land is court form N325 and attracts a fee. You can download all court forms and details of the fees charged from www.hmcourts-service.gov.uk.

26.10 In the case of a postponed order, the court will want to see evidence that the conditions attached to the order have been breached. In simple rent arrears matters there is usually no hearing and the warrant is issued by court personnel, who will simply expect a rent statement. In more complex nuisance cases you may be expected to have another hearing and present evidence. The county court will process the papers and contact you with a warrant number. It will also send a date for the eviction, either at the same time or shortly afterwards. On this date the court bailiff will attend the property to give you possession.

Eviction date

26.11 The court will send a copy of the date for the eviction to the resident. Once you have the date for the eviction, you will need to contact the resident. You should explain what will happen to the resident and their belongings. We discuss your responsibility for former resident's belongings in chapter 15. The Housing Corporation expects, and it is certainly good practice, that those evicted from social housing do not become homeless. This may present difficulties as the inevitable result of the eviction process is that a resident is deprived of their home. Providers should do all in their power to support the resident in finding alternative accommodation. In Box 26.2 we provide some advice in preventing service users from becoming homeless.

Box 26.2 Preventing homelessness

- Contact the local authority housing unit, which should be able to advise you what options the resident has (see chapter 5 on homelessness).
- Refer the individual to other agencies who provide supported housing.
- Contact other agencies involved, for example, the probation service.
- If the person is vulnerable, contact social services.
- Investigate any opportunities for rent deposit/guarantee schemes for private rented accommodation.
- Identify whether the resident can access floating support to support them in maintaining their new accommodation if it is unsupported.

Changing locks

26.12   You will need to arrange for the locks to be changed, so contact a locksmith and ensure you have a spare key. If the accommodation is shared, remember you will have to change locks on the communal door. Remember to give other resident's a copy of the new keys beforehand so they can gain access.

Contacting other residents

26.13   At some stage you will need to meet or contact the other residents in shared housing to explain what is happening. Other residents should be given an opportunity to discuss any concerns or fears they may have. You should also instruct the other residents not to let the evicted resident back into the building after the eviction.

Contacting the police

26.14   If you or other residents have concerns that the eviction may lead to aggressive behaviour you should contact the police. You can advise the police that you believe that a breach of the peace may occur.

> **Box 26.3 Frequently asked questions**
>
> **What happens if the resident refuses to leave when the bailiff attends?**
>
> It is a criminal offence to interfere with an officer of the court in the performance of his or her duties. If the resident refuses to leave when the court bailiff attends to deliver up possession, the bailiff will contact the police. The bailiff has to ensure the property is vacant when he or she delivers up possession to the landlord.

Suspending or withdrawing the warrant

26.15 Once the warrant has been issued you can apply to suspend it (with the resident's consent) or withdraw it. If the order is suspended, it remains 'live' on the court system for one year and can be revived by using court form N445, Request for Reissue of Warrant. If a year has lapsed, you usually have to apply for leave of the court before it can be revived. If you suspend a warrant you do not have to pay another fee to revive it.

Stay of execution

26.16 The resident can apply to the court for a stay of execution of the warrant. The court has discretion to postpone the date of possession or stay the execution of the warrant for such period or periods as it thinks fit. The application is heard by a judge, and can be heard following two days' notice to the landlord. For imminent possession it can be heard *without notice* – that is, without the landlord knowing of the application. This hearing can be as late as the day of the eviction. Court bailiffs therefore carry mobile phones to enable the court to contact them if a stay of execution has been granted. The normal practice of judges is to grant a stay in the first instance. If the hearing is without notice the judge will stay the execution of the warrant until a hearing date can be set for the application by the resident. At the stay hearing the court may set new conditions attached to a postponed order. For example, in the case of rent arrears, it may alter the amount at which the arrears are to be repaid. The stay, once granted, remains in force unless or until the resident breaches the terms set by the court, either at the original hearing or the stay hearing.

Box 26.4 Frequently asked questions

We are supporting a tenant who has an outright order – can he apply to the court to stay the order?

If the court has granted an outright order, it has very little power to stay (stop) the possession. The court may be able to give the resident more time to allow them to find alternative accommodation, in the case of 'exceptional hardship'. The court could stay the order if the tenant applies to have the possession order set aside or changed to a postponed order. The order would be stayed until the result of the application hearing. We look at legal mechanisms to change possession orders in chapter 23.

Summary

26.17 The chapter has detailed both the practical and the legal action required for the legal eviction of a resident. It is important that providers do not miss out this important stage in the repossession of a property. A concern highlighted by the Law Commission in its work on the reform of the law relating to renting homes is the lack of judicial scrutiny. Most commonly, at this stage the decision to grant a request for a warrant is made by court personnel not by the judge. It is your responsibility to ensure that residents are supported through this process and are treated fairly. Residents should be made aware of their opportunity to appeal breaches of postponed orders and of their ability to suspend or stay possession dates.

CHAPTER 27

Tribunals, ombudsman services, alternative dispute resolution and proportionate dispute resolution

Objectives

27.1   By the end of this chapter you will:

- Understand the distinction between tribunals and courts
- Be aware of the growing importance of tribunals and government actions to increase their 'fitness for purpose'
- Have an outline knowledge of the jurisdictions and practices of the Residential Property Tribunal Service
- Understand the role of ombudsman services in general and the Housing Ombudsman in particular
- Appreciate the forms of dispute resolution that provide an alternative to the courts and tribunals
- Understand the government objective in seeking to develop principles of proportionate dispute resolution

Introduction

27.2   Providers of supported housing run complex services and have to reconcile a number of competing priorities. Moreover, as we have demonstrated throughout this book, the service they provide is highly regulated. It is inevitable that some of the conflicts that arise in the course of operating will not be solved by internal processes, but will require the intervention of an outside agency. We have already discussed the role of the courts, which is relevant to possession proceedings, injunctions and anti-social behaviour. This chapter concentrates on tribunal justice and forms of dispute resolution that are an alternative to the courts and tribunals. We discuss the emergence of tribunals at the beginning of the welfare state and the differences between courts and tribunals. We go on to explain why tribunals are increasing in importance and the development of the Tribunal Service. We then provide you with an outline description of the Residential Property Tribunal Service, since it is the tribunals within its remit which are those you are most likely to encounter. The latter part of this chapter provides an outline of the available alternative dispute resolution mechanisms. It also points out that courts are increasingly likely to police the use of these mechanisms, requiring people to have at least attempted to resolve their differences prior to initiating court proceedings. Finally, we describe an important government initiative which is likely to have an impact on the future shape of dispute resolution services, the government white paper on proportionate dispute resolution.

The history of tribunals

27.3   Whilst tribunals have been in existence in some form or other for more than 200 years, our current system is a consequence of the growth of the post-war welfare state. The provision of services by the state to individuals in the areas of housing, social security and education gave rise to particular rights, but also to new forms of dispute. For instance, is a particular child entitled to a place in a specific school, or is someone entitled to a particular welfare benefit? For a number of reasons, in particular the potentially huge number of disputes and the specialist nature of the legislation involved, the state considered that the court system would be an inappropriate forum for the resolution of these disputes.

27.4   Tribunals have always been controversial. Their advocates argue that they represent an improvement on the courts because they are both more informal and more expert. Their opponents worry that they provide second class justice and that they are too close to the workings of the administration of the state to be effective in challenging its decisions.

27.5   In 1957 the Franks Committee investigated the workings of tribunals. It considered that tribunals were likely to become an increasingly important part of the machinery of justice and recommended that their proceedings be governed by three crucial principles:

- *Openness* – hearings should be in public and the reasoning behind decisions should be explained.
- *Fairness* – there should be clear procedures which allow parties to know their rights and present their case fully and to be aware of the case against them.
- *Impartiality* – tribunals should be free from undue influence or the appearance of undue influence of the government departments with whose work they are concerned.

27.6   The development of tribunals from that date can be seen as a working out of the practical application of these principles. What should be noted, however, is that tribunals are required to comply with the same principles of natural justice as the courts, and their proceedings are overseen by the courts through the process of judicial review.

27.7   Recently the government, as part of its programme of constitutional reform, has considered the role of tribunals again. One strand of this was the commissioning of the Legatt Review, which was concerned with putting in place the necessary reforms to create a tribunal system which is independent, coherent, professional, cost-effective and user-friendly. Its recommendations were published in 2001 (*Tribunals for Users One System, One Service*). We will consider the response of government to those proposals below. At this point we will summarise the distinctions between the courts and tribunals.

The distinct features of tribunal justice

27.8   With over 80 tribunals handling around a million disputes every year, any summary of the features of tribunal justice can only deal in generalities. It is best to think of a dispute resolution spectrum, with courts generally being more formal and tribunals tending to the informal. However, certain court procedures, such as the small claims procedure, appear to operate in a more informal and user-friendly way than some tribunals. In Boxes 27.1–27.3 below we summarise the features of tribunals and their advantages and disadvantages. You will note how the advantages and disadvantages of the tribunal system are interlinked. For instance, there are advantages in a largely lawyer-free environment: proceedings can be more straightforward and speedier. At the same time, a party to a dispute who has difficulty in understanding the complexities of the legislation may well be disadvantaged by the lack of a lawyer.

Box 27.1 What is distinct about tribunal justice?

- Inquisitorial – the tribunal can and does intervene to work out the facts of the case.
- Less formality – the tribunal can set its own procedure.
- Legal representation not necessary – although evidence shows that unrepresented parties can be disadvantaged.
- Specialist jurisdictions – emphasis on state/citizen disputes.
- Do not charge fees – although this is not true in all cases.
- No cost orders – although certain tribunals do have powers to make cost orders where the parties are behaving frivolously or vexatiously.
- No enforcement powers – decisions have to be enforced through the courts.

Box 27.2 The advantages of tribunal justice

- Speed – it is considerably quicker to reach a hearing date.
- Cost.
- Informality.
- Flexibility.
- Specialisation – tribunals usually specialise and have members, such as surveyors, who bring a specialist knowledge to bear on decision making.
- Relief of congestion in the ordinary courts.
- Awareness of policy – tribunals are very close to the development of their specialist area and tend to understand the aims of legislation.
- Privacy – in general, the press has little interest in tribunal proceedings, although employment tribunals are an exception.

Box 27.3 The disadvantages of tribunal justice

- Lack of openness – procedural rules may be complex or incomplete and the ability of tribunals to decide on their own procedures may make parties feel disadvantaged.
- Unavailability of state funding – if you cannot afford to bear your own costs, you are excluded from the system.
- Reasons for decisions not always given.
- Lack of accessibility.
- Lack of coherence – understanding one tribunal does not necessarily help you to understand another.
- Not user-friendly – some tribunals have been criticised for their services.
- Not independent of government, or do not appear to be independent.

Recent developments in tribunal justice

27.9 The government did not immediately embrace the principles of the Legatt Review. However, after further consultation it announced the establishment of a new Tribunals Service in 2003, with the aim of increasing the administrative coherence and independence of the tribunal system. It explained that:

The new Service will be established as a distinct part of the justice system, accountable to the Lord Chancellor. The Service will bring together the 10 largest tribunals from across central Government, with smaller tribunals joining as appropriate.

27.10   In July 2004, the government published a white paper, *Transforming Public Services: Complaints, redress and tribunals*. This white paper forms the basis of Part 1 of the current Tribunals Bill, which is expected to receive Royal Assent during 2007. We have summarised in Box 27.4 the main features of the bill.

Box 27.4 The main features of Part 1 of the Tribunals, Courts and Enforcement Bill

- New simplified statutory structure for tribunals, with two tiers of tribunals, the First Tier Tribunal and the Upper Tribunal.
- The Lord Chancellor will have the power to transfer existing tribunals to the new structure.
- New judicial office – the Senior President of Tribunals – is to oversee tribunal judiciary.
- New provisions for tribunal membership, rights of appeal from tribunals and new tribunal rules.
- The Upper Tribunal will have certain powers of judicial review.
- The Administrative Justice and Tribunals Council will replace the current Council on Tribunals and have a broader remit over the whole of the administrative justice system.

27.11   Tribunals are likely to increase in importance and number over the coming years. This is as a result of a multiplicity of factors, including the Human Rights Act 1998, devolution and other constitutional reform and the increasing complexity of state regulation of everyday life. In addition, the government is seeking to ensure that our dispute resolution system is proportionate, by which it means that simple disputes should be solved by simple means, which suggests that a number of disputes will be taken out of the court system and resituated within tribunals. It will be interesting to see if the new structure proves sufficiently robust and responsive to these changes and ensures an acceptable framework for the administration of such an important part of our legal system. In the next part of this chapter we concentrate on one tribunal service which is likely to feature in your work, the Residential Property Tribunal Service.

The work of the Residential Property Tribunal Service (RPTS)

27.12 Like all tribunals, the work of the RPTS has developed in an ad hoc way over a number of years and in response to particular disputes. Its origins lie in fair rent legislation, but its remit has expanded considerably. The RPTS is in fact an umbrella organisation for five regional offices called rent assessment panels. The members of the rent assessment panels, which includes lawyers, surveyors, other professions with expertise in housing and lay members, sit in a variety of tribunals which are concerned with residential property disputes in the private rented and leasehold sector. The aim is to provide a quicker and more accessible means of solving these disputes than courts would provide. The tribunals are set out in Box 27.5.

Box 27.5 The tribunals of the RPTS

- *Rent assessment committees* – which determine disputes about fair and market rents. You are most likely to use these tribunals when challenging the decision of a rent officer about the level of fair rents or market rents. There is no fee for these hearings.
- *Leasehold valuation tribunals* – which determine disputes involving leasehold property. You are most likely to use these tribunals when involved in a service charge dispute with leaseholders or when you are planning major work to property which you intend to reclaim via service charges charged to leaseholders.
- *Residential property tribunals* – which determine certain appeals against denial of the Right to Buy scheme and decisions in connection with the Housing Act 2004. You are most likely to use these tribunals if you are involved in a dispute with your local authority about the Housing Health and Safety Rating System.

27.13 The tribunal, which sets its own procedures and is inquisitorial, usually consists of a legally qualified chair, a surveyor or valuer member and a lay person with experience of property matters. However, there are a number of chairs who are surveyors rather than legally qualified. Each of the regional panels operates in a distinct way, responding to the quantity and type of property disputes within its area. In London, for instance, which has the greatest volume of work, there are procedures for pre-hearing reviews, which enable the issues to be clarified and the area of dispute to be narrowed, making hearings operate more efficiently. It also offers a mediation service where it considers that may provide a more appropriate form of dispute resolution. The RPTS website, at www.rpts.gov.uk, is a mine of useful information, with outlines of the relevant law, procedures and application forms. It also has a database of decisions. If you have to attend a hearing at the RPTS, we would advise that you prepare by visiting the tribunal and watching a similar case. The panel does its best to put people at ease and to help them present their case. If your facts are prepared and you have an understanding of the legal framework of the decision you are challenging, you should not find it too difficult an experience.

Box 27.6 Frequently asked questions

If you are not happy with the decision of a tribunal, can you still apply to a formal court?

The jurisdictions of tribunals and courts are quite distinct. You do not have a choice whether to use one or the other. However, if you are dissatisfied with the decision of a tribunal, you may be able to appeal against the decision to a supervisory court. You should seek legal advice if you want to do this.

27.14　Tribunals and courts provide a critical and valuable service, not only in dispute resolution, but also in checking the exercise of power by the state and certain individuals. For instance, it is appropriate that the eviction of a tenant is controlled by the court because the potential loss of one's home is a major infringement of rights. However, there are a number of disputes where it may be inappropriate or even destructive to resort to legal mechanisms of dispute resolution. One example is noise nuisance, where explaining problems and reaching solutions together may be far more constructive than taking legal proceedings. In such cases you should consider alternatives to the courts. In the next part of the chapter we consider the different ways of resolving disputes outside of the formal court arena. One way in which service users can complain without going to court is to use the services of an ombudsman.

Ombudsman services

27.15　Ombudsman services are designed to provide a source of redress when private individuals have suffered through the poor administration of a public body, such as a local authority or a body which provides public services. 'Poor administration', which is also termed 'maladministration', is the key to the basis of ombudsman service complaints because the ombudsman is concerned only with this area. What the ombudsman looks at is not the failure of the organisation to obey the law, but its failure to implement the law in a competent way. Ombudsmen are not able to investigate complaints where legal proceedings are possible.

The Parliamentary Ombudsman

27.16 The first ombudsman created was the Parliamentary Commissioner for Administration, who deals with the administrative failings of government departments. The public does not have direct access to this ombudsman. Complaints must go first of all to members of parliament. MPs are not obliged to refer the complaints they receive to the Parliamentary Ombudsman if they consider that they can deal with the matter themselves. This filter was introduced to preserve the primary responsibility of parliament to call the administration to account.

The local government ombudsman

27.17 The local government ombudsman (technically called the Parliamentary Commissioner for Local Government) deals with complaints about local government services, including social services and local authority housing and community care services. Typically, in any year there are 15,000 complaints to the local authority ombudsman, 37 per cent of which relate to housing departments – mainly the administration of housing benefit. The objective of the local government ombudsman is to provide, where appropriate, satisfactory redress for complainants and assist in the improvement of administration by local government. The local government ombudsman has the power to issue general advice on good local administration. The local government ombudsman is not able to investigate personnel complaints or complaints about the internal running of schools.

27.18   More information is available on the local government ombudsman's website, www.lgo.org.uk. The site also contains reports of the local government ombudsman's decisions and details on how to make a complaint.

Other ombudsman services

27.19   There are several other examples of ombudsman services which may provide useful redress for your service users. The Health Service Ombudsman investigates complaints about the failures of NHS hospitals or community health services and other NHS provision. Any member of the public may refer a complaint direct, though normally only if a full investigation within the NHS complaints system has been carried out first. More recently, a range of specialist ombudsman has been created. For instance, the Legal Services Ombudsman handles complaints about services provided by lawyers. More information about these services can be found on their respective websites, www.ombudsman.org.uk/hse and www.olso.org.

The Housing Ombudsman Service

27.20   Social landlords, including all registered social landlords and landlords who have taken over the responsibility for council housing from local authorities, are required to be members of the Housing Ombudsman Service. This does not include council tenants, who have to complain to the local government ombudsman. The Housing Ombudsman Service investigates complaints about shortcomings in the way homes are managed. Complaints must be made by the resident affected or an authorised representative. Internal complaints procedures must have been completed before a resident can complain to the Housing Ombudsman Service. The Housing Ombudsman Service is free to use. In Box 27.7 we have set out the conditions which must be met prior to a complaint being investigated.

Box 27.7 Before making a complaint to the Housing Ombudsman Service

- You must first make your complaint through the internal procedure of the landlord, agent or park home, within the time limits they stipulate, and not later than 12 months from the time you become aware of the problem.
- That internal procedure must be completed before submitting the complaint to the ombudsman. The Service cannot deal with it unless the landlord or agent is given a full opportunity to resolve the problem directly. If you are having difficulties using the internal procedure, please let us know.
- You have to submit the complaint to the ombudsman as

soon as possible after completing the internal procedure, and not later than 12 months afterwards.

- Your complaint must be about something which the landlord or agent has not yet resolved. The ombudsman primarily deals with maladministration – that is, with wrongdoing which affected you and which has not already been addressed locally. The ombudsman cannot punish landlords or agents, nor can he or she ask them to do things if they have done nothing contrary to required standards, or if they have already remedied any mistake for which they were responsible.
- The ombudsman encourages a conciliatory approach to resolving housing disputes. He or she will only investigate complaints when there is early evidence of serious maladministration. Otherwise, he or she may recommend instead the use of mediation or other alternative forms of dispute resolution, which he or she makes available at no extra cost.

27.21   If the conditions are met, then the service user can make a complaint. This can be done via the website or by downloading a form. The website address is www.ihos.org.uk. Box 27.8 sets out the procedure once a complaint has been received.

Box 27.8 Processing complaints to the Housing Ombudsman Service

If we agree there is an unresolved problem, we may first try to deal with it informally, for instance by letters or phone calls suggesting possible solutions.

We may recommend that you and the member organisation use mediation or other ways to resolve the complaint with help from us, and we will send you more information about that. Mediation can only go ahead if you and the member organisation agree.

If we decide to adjudicate or to investigate in order to make a formal decision, we will usually send a copy of the complaint to the member organisation for comments. We may ask for more information from you or the member organisation, and perhaps from other bodies who know about the complaint. If you want to send us supporting information, please leave out anything you want us to treat in confidence because we will probably not be able to use it as evidence.

> We will establish what has happened, then we will make a decision. At this point we will write to you and the member organisation. Our letter will explain our findings and say what, if anything, should be done to put matters right. This may include some compensation for you, but the Ombudsman is mostly concerned that any shortcomings by the member organisation are tackled effectively. This might be by carrying out specific work, by changing its policies or procedures, or by training its staff better.
>
> We do not punish member organisations. That is to say, we can only ask them to do what is necessary to put a person back in the position he or she was in before something went wrong, and to ensure that the problems we identify do not happen again. Sometimes, of course, that is not possible, so we can ask that other things be done to achieve a fair solution.

27.22   The Housing Ombudsman Service publishes an annual report, which makes general points about deficiencies in the provision of housing by registered social landlords. This is particularly useful as it allows for complaints to drive strategic change in the quality of provision, rather than allowing solely for individualised responses.

27.23   You will have noticed that the Housing Ombudsman refers to the possibility of using mediation between the parties to resolve disputes. Mediation is a form of alternative dispute resolution. We now describe what is meant by this.

Alternative dispute resolution (ADR)

27.24   ADR is an umbrella term for a number of different approaches to the resolution of disputes. These vary in the extent to which they are distinct from court procedures, but share the objective of resolving disputes without the necessity of judicial intervention. The Ministry of Justice defines ADR as:

> The collective term for the ways that parties can settle civil disputes with the help of an independent third party and without the need for a formal court hearing.

27.25   Box 27.9 outlines the main forms of ADR.

Box 27.9 The main forms of ADR

Arbitration

In arbitration an independent third party hears both sides in a dispute and makes a decision to resolve it. The arbitrator is impartial; this means he or she does not take sides. In most cases the arbitrator's decision is legally binding on both sides, so it is not possible to go to court if you are unhappy with the decision.

Most types of arbitration have the following in common:

- Parties both agree to use the process.
- It is private.
- The decision is made by a third party, not the people involved.
- The process is final and legally binding.
- There are limited grounds for challenging the decision.
- Hearings are often less formal than court hearings. (Note, however, that some forms of arbitration do not involve hearings, but are decided on the basis of documents only.)

Conciliation

Conciliation involves a third party helping the people in dispute to resolve their problem. The conciliator should be impartial and should not take one party's side.

All conciliation has the following elements in common:

- It is voluntary – the parties choose to conciliate or not.
- It is private and confidential.
- The parties are free to agree to the resolution or not.
- Conciliated agreements are usually non-binding, although they can be made into binding contracts. In employment disputes, however, a signed conciliated agreement is binding.

Mediation

Mediation involves an independent third party helping disputing parties to resolve their dispute. The disputants, not the mediator, decide the terms of the agreement. The mediator has an important role, however, in 'reality testing' any agreement – that is, in checking carefully that the parties are able to do what they agree to do.

All types of mediation have the following in common:

- It is voluntary – the parties choose to mediate or not.

- It is private and confidential.
- The parties make the final decision on how to resolve the dispute.
- The mediator is impartial – he or she does not take sides or say who is right and who is wrong.
- The mediator is independent.

27.26   You can find further information about ADR on the Ministry of Justice website, www.justice.gov.uk/whatwedo/alternativedispute resolution.htm, and about local mediation services from Mediation UK on www.mediationuk.org.uk.

Growth of ADR

27.27   There are a number of reasons why ADR is growing. Civil litigation does not necessarily benefit the client:

- It is a 'winner takes all' game.
- It is stressful for the parties.
- It is expensive.
- Many people and many disputes are excluded from litigation.

27.28   Civil litigation may be particularly difficult for vulnerable service users.

27.29   However, we should also note that litigation is a very expensive social service and government will benefit from reduced expenditure if it successfully reduces the use of courts. Lawyers in particular are sceptical of the growth of ADR. In their opinion:

- Cases often involve a serious imbalance of power.
- A fear that prescribing mediation for state-funded clients will lead to a two-tier justice system.
- Mediated cases can disguise fundamental causes of certain problems.
- Some problems are not amenable to litigation – domestic violence, racial harassment.

27.30   Nonetheless, the pressures to use ADR are growing. The Civil Procedure Rules, which govern the procedures of litigation, require consideration of the use of ADR and pre-action protocols, which are requirements placed upon parties prior to litigation being initiated, before proceedings are begun. Moreover, legal funding for representation may be refused if ADR is available and not used. Increasingly, parties can expect there to be costs penalties if they fail to use ADR before going to court.

> **Box 27.10 Frequently asked questions**
>
> **We are an RSL which often uses mediation to resolve neighbour disputes. This is proving costly. Would it be better to get the tenants to sue each other so they could use the court mediation service?**
>
> You have a responsibility to manage relationships between your tenants, and by providing a mediation service you are fulfilling that responsibility. There are a number of reasons why it is not appropriate for tenants to sue each other. This is likely to exacerbate disputes; it will involve tenants in expensive and frustrating proceedings; and any mediation service provided by the court is unlikely to have the expertise of the service you are currently using.

27.31   Many courts and tribunals now offer mediation services as an alternative and the government has published a tool kit to enable the expansion of this. It has also set up a National Mediation Helpline – 0845 60 27 809. The need to expand ADR is tackled in the government strategy paper, 'Proportionate Dispute Resolution'. The notion of proportionate dispute resolution underpinned the government's white paper, *Transforming Public Services: Complaints, Redress and Tribunals*, published in July 2004. We outline the principles underlying this paper below and speculate on its long-term implications.

Proportionate dispute resolution

27.32   The government's purpose is explained in the paper:

> Our strategy turns on its head the Department's traditional emphasis first on courts, judges and court procedure, and second on legal aid to pay mainly for litigation lawyers. It starts instead with the real world problems people face. The aim is to develop a range of policies and services that, so far as possible, will help people to avoid problems and legal disputes in the first place; and where they cannot, provides tailored solutions to resolve the dispute as quickly and cost effectively as possible.

27.33   This vision is to be operationalised through a variety of mechanisms, including:

- making the law simpler;
- making decision making by the state better;
- improving people's understandings of their rights and responsibilities;

- improving access to advice so that disputes can be avoided;
- tailored dispute resolution services to avoid recourse to courts and tribunals where not necessary.

27.34   This is clearly a long-term project and the exact implications have not yet been specified. Within the area of housing dispute resolution, the Law Commission Public Law team published an issues paper, 'Housing Proportionate Dispute Resolution', in April 2006 as part of its ongoing work to reform housing law. There is no doubt that possession proceedings and litigation connected with disrepair in housing forms a major proportion of the work carried out by the county courts, so attempts to reduce court action within housing could have a significant impact. It will be interesting to see the conclusions of the Law Commission exercise. In the short term, we can expect to see an increasing emphasis on ADR and increasing penalties for those who fail to make the most of the opportunities it represents. Whether this will be simply a cost-cutting exercise or whether it will provide increased access to justice in the broadest sense of the term will depend upon whether government is prepared to invest in quality ADR services which are accessible for all potential users.

Summary

27.35   Tribunals, ombudsman services and the less formal mechanisms of ADR and proportionate dispute resolution are likely to become increasingly significant in the resolution of disputes as the court system becomes more crowded. The RPTS already has a wide remit and is likely to increase its jurisdictions within residential property disputes. There is an increasing expectation from courts that parties to a dispute will have attempted to use other mechanisms to achieve its resolution prior to a formal mechanism. This can include service users complaining to outside bodies, for example, ombudsman services, where it is appropriate for them to do so. It is important, therefore, that you recognise how tribunals, ombudsman services, ADR and proportionate dispute resolution function and feel confident that you could use them to help solve relevant disputes. It would also be useful if more people who run supported housing services would put themselves forward to be lay members of the tribunal. In that way, providers could enhance the knowledge and expertise of the RPTS.

APPENDICES

Legislation: key provisions

Protection from Eviction Act 1977

Housing Act 1985 Schedule 2

Housing Act 1988 Section 13 and Schedule 2

PROTECTION FROM EVICTION ACT 1977

Part I: Unlawful Eviction and Harassment

Unlawful eviction and harassment of occupier

1. (1)   In this section 'residential occupier', in relation to any premises, means a person occupying the premises as a residence, whether under a contract or by virtue of any enactment or rule of law giving him the right to remain in occupation or restricting the right of any other person to recover possession of the premises.

(2)   If any person unlawfully deprives the residential occupier of any premises of his occupation of the premises or any part thereof, or attempts to do so, he shall be guilty of an offence unless he proves that he believed, and had reasonable cause to believe, that the residential occupier had ceased to reside in the premises.

(3)   If any person with intent to cause the residential occupier of any premises–

   (a)   to give up the occupation of the premises or any part thereof; or

   (b)   to refrain from exercising any right or pursuing any remedy in respect of the premises or part thereof;

does acts calculated to interfere with the peace or comfort of the residential occupier or members of his household, or persistently withdraws or withholds services reasonably required for the occupation of the premises as a residence, he shall be guilty of an offence.

(3A)   Subject to subsection (3B) below, the landlord of a residential occupier or an agent of the landlord shall be guilty of an offence if6

   (a)   he does acts likely to interfere with the peace or comfort of the residential occupier or members of his household, or

   (b)   he persistently withdraws or withholds services reasonably required for the occupation of the premises in question as a residence,

and (in either case) he knows, or has reasonable cause to believe, that that conduct is likely to cause the residential occupier to give up the occupation of the whole or part of the premises or to refrain from exercising any right or pursuing any remedy in respect of the whole or part of the premises.

(3B)   A person shall not be guilty of an offence under subsection (3A) above if he proves that he had reasonable grounds for doing the acts or withdrawing or withholding the services in question.

(3C)   In subsection (3A) above 'landlord', in relation to a residential occupier of any premises, means the person who, but for–

   (a)   the residential occupier's right to remain in occupation of the premises, or

   (b)   a restriction on the person's right to recover possession of the premises,

would be entitled to occupation of the premises and any superior landlord under whom that person derives title.

(4)   A person guilty of an offence under this section shall be liable–

(a)   on summary conviction, to a fine not exceeding £400 or to imprisonment for a term not exceeding 6 months or to both;

(b)   on conviction on indictment, to a fine or to imprisonment for a term not exceeding 2 years or to both.

(5)   Nothing in this section shall be taken to prejudice any liability or remedy to which a person guilty of an offence thereunder may be subject in civil proceedings.

(6)   Where an offence under this section committed by a body corporate is proved to have been committed with the consent or connivance of, or to be attributable to any neglect on the part of, any director, manager or secretary or other similar officer of the body corporate or any person who was purporting to act in any such capacity, he as well as the body corporate shall be guilty of that offence and shall be liable to be proceeded against and punished accordingly.

Restriction on re-entry without due process of law

2.   Where any premises are let as a dwelling on a lease which is subject to a right of re-entry or forfeiture it shall not be lawful to enforce that right otherwise than by proceedings in the court while any person is lawfully residing in the premises or part of them.

Prohibition of eviction without due process of law

3. (1)   Where any premises have been let as a dwelling under a tenancy which is neither a statutorily protected tenancy nor an excluded tenancy and–

(a)   the tenancy (in this section referred to as the former tenancy) has come to an end, but

(b)   the occupier continues to reside in the premises or part of them, it shall not be lawful for the owner to enforce against the occupier, otherwise than by proceedings in the court, his right to recover possession of the premises.

(2)   In this section 'the occupier', in relation to any premises, means any person lawfully residing in the premises or part of them at the termination of the former tenancy.

(2A)   Subsections (1) and (2) above apply in relation to any restricted contract (within the meaning of the Rent Act 1977) which–

(a)   creates a licence; and

(b)   is entered into after the commencement of section 69 of the Housing Act 1980;

as they apply in relation to a restricted contract which creates a tenancy.

(2B)   Subsections (1) and (2) above apply in relation to any premises occupied as a dwelling under a licence, other than an excluded licence, as they apply in relation to premises let as a dwelling under a tenancy, and in those subsections the expressions 'let' and 'tenancy' shall be construed accordingly.

(2C)   References in the preceding provisions of this section and section 4(2A) below to an excluded tenancy do not apply to–

(a)   a tenancy entered into before the date on which the Housing Act 1988 came into force, or

(b)   a tenancy entered into on or after that date but pursuant to a contract made before that date,

but, subject to that, 'excluded tenancy' and 'excluded licence' shall be construed in accordance with section 3A below.

(3)   This section shall, with the necessary modifications, apply where the owner's right to recover possession arises on the death of the tenant under a statutory tenancy within the meaning of the Rent Act 1977 or the Rent (Agriculture) Act 1976.

Excluded tenancies and licences

3A (1) Any reference in this Act to an excluded tenancy or an excluded licence is a reference to a tenancy or licence which is excluded by virtue of any of the following provisions of this section.

(2)   A tenancy or licence is excluded if–

(a)   under its terms the occupier shares any accommodation with the landlord or licensor; and

(b)   immediately before the tenancy or licence was granted and also at the time it comes to an end, the landlord or licensor occupied as his only or principal home premises of which the whole or part of the shared accommodation formed part.

(3)   A tenancy or licence is also excluded if–

(a)   under its terms the occupier shares any accommodation with a member of the family of the landlord or licensor;

(b)   immediately before the tenancy or licence was granted and also at the time it comes to an end, the member of the family of the landlord or licensor occupied as his only or principal home premises of which the whole or part of the shared accommodation formed part; and

(c)   immediately before the tenancy or licence was granted and also at the time it comes to an end, the landlord or licensor occupied as his only or principal home premises in the same building as the shared accommodation and that building is not a purpose-built block of flats.

(4)   For the purposes of subsections (2) and (3) above, an occupier shares accommodation with another person if he has the use of it in common with that person (whether or not also in common with others) and any reference in those subsections to shared accommodation shall be construed accordingly, and if, in relation to any tenancy or licence, there is at any time more than one person who is the landlord or licensor, any reference in those subsections to the landlord or licensor shall be construed as a reference to any one of those persons.

(5)   In subsections (2) to (4) above–

(a)   'accommodation' includes neither an area used for storage nor a staircase, passage, corridor or other means of access;

(b)   'occupier' means, in relation to a tenancy, the tenant and, in relation to a licence, the licensee; and

(c)   'purpose-built block of flats' has the same meaning as in Part III of Schedule 1 to the Housing Act 1988;

and section 113 of the Housing Act 1985 shall apply to determine whether a person who is for the purposes of subsection (3) above a member of another's family as it applies for the purposes of Part IV of that Act.

(6)   A tenancy or licence is excluded if it was granted as a temporary expedient to a person who entered the premises in question or any other premises as a trespasser (whether or not, before the beginning of that tenancy or licence, another tenancy or licence to occupy the premises or any other premises had been granted to him).

(7)   A tenancy or licence is excluded if–

(a)   it confers on the tenant or licensee the right to occupy the premises for a holiday only; or

(b)   it is granted otherwise than for money or money's worth.

(7A)   A tenancy or licence is excluded if it is granted in order to provide accommodation under Part VI of the Immigration and Asylum Act 1999.

(8)   A licence is excluded if it confers rights of occupation in a hostel, within the meaning of the Housing Act 1985, which is provided by–

(a)   the council of a county, county borough, district or London Borough, the Common Council of the City of London, the Council of the Isles of Scilly, the Inner London Education Authority, the London Fire and Emergency Planning Authority, a joint authority within the meaning of the Local Government Act 1985 or a residuary body within the meaning of that Act;

(b)   a development corporation within the meaning of the New Towns Act 1981;

(c)   the Commission for the New Towns;

(d)   an urban development corporation established by an order under section 135 of the Local Government, Planning and Land Act 1980;

(e)   a housing action trust established under Part III of the Housing Act 1988;

(f)   . . . .

(g)   the Housing Corporation. . .;

(ga)   the Secretary of State under section 89 of the Housing Associations Act 1985;

(h)   a housing trust (within the meaning of the Housing Associations Act 1985) which is a charity or a registered social landlord (within the meaning of the Housing Act 1985); or.

(i)   any other person who is, or who belongs to a class of person which is, specified in an order made by the Secretary of State.

(9)   The power to make an order under subsection (8)(i) above shall be exercisable by statutory instrument which shall be subject to annulment in pursuance of a resolution of either House of Parliament.

Special provisions for agricultural employees

4. (1)   [not reproduced.]

Part II: Notice to Quit

Validity of notices to quit

5. (1)   Subject to subsection (1B) below no notice by a landlord or a tenant to quit any premises let (whether before or after the commencement of this Act) as a dwelling shall be valid unless–

(a)   it is in writing and contains such information as may be prescribed, and

(b)   it is given not less than 4 weeks before the date on which it is to take effect.

(1A)   Subject to subsection (1B) below, no notice by a licensor or a licensee to determine a periodic licence to occupy premises as a dwelling (whether the licence was granted before or after the passing of this Act) shall be valid unless–

(a)   it is in writing and contains such information as may be prescribed, and

(b)   it is given not less than 4 weeks before the date on which it is to take effect.

(1B)   Nothing in subsection (1) or subsection (1A) above applies to–

(a)   premises let on an excluded tenancy which is entered into on or after the date on which the Housing Act 1988 came into force unless it is entered into pursuant to a contract made before that date; or

(b)   premises occupied under an excluded licence.

(2)   In this section 'prescribed' means prescribed by regulations made by the Secretary of State by statutory instrument, and a statutory instrument containing any such regulations shall be subject to annulment in pursuance of a resolution of either House of Parliament.

(3)   Regulations under this section may make different provision in relation to different descriptions of lettings and different circumstances.

Part III: Supplemental Provisions

Prosecution of offences

6.   Proceedings for an offence under this Act may be instituted by any of the following authorities:

(a)   councils of districts and London boroughs;

(aa)   councils of Welsh counties and county boroughs;

(b)   the Common Council of the City of London;

(c)   the Council of the Isles of Scilly.

Service of Notices

7. (1)   If for the purpose of any proceedings (whether civil or criminal) brought or intended to be brought under this Act, any person serves upon–

(a) any agent of the landlord named as such in the rent book or other similar document, or

(b) the person who receives the rent of the dwelling,

a notice in writing requiring the agent or other person to disclose to him the full name and place of abode or place of business of the landlord, that agent or other person shall forthwith comply with the notice.

(2) If any such agent or other person as is referred to in subsection (1) above fails or refuses forthwith to comply with a notice served on him under that subsection, he shall be liable on summary conviction to a fine not exceeding level 4 on the standard scale, unless he shows to the satisfaction of the court that he did not know, and could not with reasonable diligence have ascertained, such of the facts required by the notice to be disclosed as were not disclosed by him.

(3) In this section 'landlord' includes–

(a) any person from time to time deriving title under the original landlord,

(b) in relation to any dwelling-house, any person other than the tenant who is or, but for Part VII of the Rent Act 1977 would be, entitled to possession of the dwelling-house, and

(c) any person who, . . . grants to another the right to occupy the dwelling in question as a residence and any person directly or indirectly deriving title from the grantor.

Interpretation

8. (1) In this Act 'statutorily protected tenancy' means–

(a) a protected tenancy within the meaning of the Rent Act 1977 or a tenancy to which Part I of the Landlord and Tenant Act 1954 applies;

(b) a protected occupancy or statutory tenancy as defined in the Rent (Agriculture) Act 1976;

(c) a tenancy to which Part II of the Landlord and Tenant Act 1954 applies;

(d) a tenancy of an agricultural holding within the meaning of the Agricultural Holdings Act 1986 which is a tenancy in relation to which that act applies.

(e) an assured tenancy or assured agricultural occupancy under Part I of the Housing Act 1988

(f) a tenancy to which Schedule 10 to the Local Government and Housing Act 1989 applies.

(g) a farm business tenancy within the meaning of the Agricultural Tenancies Act 1995.

(2) For the purposes of Part I of this Act a person who, under the terms of his employment, had exclusive possession of any premises other than as a tenant shall be deemed to have been a tenant and the expressions 'let' and 'tenancy' shall be construed accordingly.

(3) In Part I of this Act 'the owner', in relation to any premises, means the person who, as against the occupier, is entitled to possession thereof.

(4)   In this Act 'excluded tenancy' and 'excluded licence' have the meaning assigned by section 3A of this Act.

(5)   If, on or after the date on which the Housing Act 1988 came into force, the terms of an excluded tenancy or excluded licence entered into before that date are varied, then–

    (a)   if the variation affects the amount of the rent which is payable under the tenancy or licence, the tenancy or licence shall be treated for the purposes of sections 3(2C) and 5(1B) above as a new tenancy or licence entered into at the time of the variation; and

    (b)   if the variation does not affect the amount of the rent which is so payable, nothing in this Act shall affect the determination of the question whether the variation is such as to give rise to a new tenancy or licence.

(6)   Any reference in subsection (5) above to a variation affecting the amount of the rent which is payable under a tenancy or licence does not include a reference to–

    (a)   a reduction or increase effected under Part III or Part VI of the Rent Act 1977 (rents under regulated tenancies and housing association tenancies), section 78 of that Act (power of rent tribunal in relation to restricted contracts) or sections 11 to 14 of the Rent (Agriculture) Act 1976; or

    (b)   a variation which is made by the parties and has the effect of making the rent expressed to be payable under the tenancy or licence the same as a rent for the dwelling which is entered in the register under Part IV or section 79 of the Rent Act 1977.

The court for purposes of Part I

9. (1)   The court for the purposes of Part I of this Act shall, subject to this section, be–

    (a)   the county court, in relation to premises with respect to which the county court has for the time being jurisdiction in actions for the recovery of land; and

    (b)   the High Court, in relation to other premises.

(2)   Any powers of a county court in proceedings for the recovery of possession of any premises in the circumstances mentioned in section 3(1) of this Act may be exercised with the leave of the judge by any registrar of the court, except in so far as rules of court otherwise provide.

(3)   Nothing in this Act shall affect the jurisdiction of the High Court in proceedings to enforce a lessor's right of re-entry or forfeiture or to enforce a mortgagee's right of possession in a case where the former tenancy was not binding on the mortgagee.

(4)   Nothing in this Act shall affect the operation of–

    (a)   section 59 of the Pluralities Act 1838;

    (b)   section 19 of the Defence Act 1842;

    (c)   section 6 of the Lecturers and Parish Clerks Act 1844;

    (d)   paragraph 3 of Schedule 1 to the Sexual Offences Act 1956; or

    (e)   section 13 of the Compulsory Purchase Act 1965.

Application to Crown

10. In so far as this Act requires the taking of proceedings in the court for the recovery of possession or confers any powers on the court it shall (except in the case of section 4(10)) be binding on the Crown.

Application to Isles of Scilly

11.(1) In its application to the Isles of Scilly, this Act (except in the case of section 5) shall have effect subject to such exceptions, adaptations and modifications as the Secretary of State may by order direct.

(2) The power to make an order under this section shall be exercisable by statutory instrument which shall be subject to annulment, in pursuance of a resolution of either House of Parliament.

(3) An order under this section may be varied or revoked by a subsequent order.

Consequential amendments, etc

12. (1) Schedule 1 to this Act contains amendments consequential on the provisions of this Act.

(2) Schedule 2 to this Act contains transitional provisions and savings.

(3) The enactments mentioned in Schedule 3 to this Act are hereby repealed to the extent specified in the third column of that Schedule.

(4) The inclusion in this Act of any express saving, transitional provision or amendment shall not be taken to affect the operation in relation to this Act of section 38 of the Interpretation Act 1889 (which relates to the effect of repeals).

Short title etc

13. (1) This Act may be cited as the Protection from Eviction Act 1977.

(2) This Act shall come into force on the expiry of the period of one month beginning with the date on which it is passed.

(3) This Act does not extend to Scotland or Northern Ireland.

(4) References in this Act to any enactment are references to that enactment as amended, and include references thereto as applied by any other enactment including, except where the context otherwise requires, this Act.

SCHEDULES

SCHEDULE 1: Consequential Amendments

Section 12

Reserve and Auxiliary Forces (Protection of Civil Interests) Act 1951

1. In section 22(1) of the Reserve and Auxiliary Forces (Protection of Civil Interests) Act 1951, for 'Part III of the Rent Act 1965' substitute 'Part I of the Protection from Eviction Act 1977'.

2. ....
    . . . . .

Caravan Sites Act 1968

3. In section 5(5) of the Caravan Sites Act 1968 (provisions of Part III of the Rent Act 1965 relating to protection against eviction etc. not to apply to caravans on protected sites) for the words 'Part III of the Rent Act 1965' substitute 'the Protection from Eviction Act 1977'.

Rent (Agriculture) Act 1976

4. In Schedule 5 to the Rent (Agriculture) Act 1976, in paragraph 10(2) for 'section 16 of the Rent Act 1957' substitute 'section 5 of the Protection from Eviction Act 1977'.

SCHEDULE 2: Transitional Provisions and Savings

1. (1) In so far as anything done under an enactment repealed by this Act could have been done under a corresponding provision of this Act, it shall not be invalidated by the repeal but shall have effect as if done under that provision.

   (2) Sub-paragraph (1) above applies, in particular, to any regulation, rule, notice or order.

2. The enactments mentioned in Schedule 6 to the Rent Act 1965 shall, notwithstanding the repeal of that Act by this Act, continue to have effect as they had effect immediately before the commencement of this Act.

SCHEDULE 3: Repeals

Section 12

Chapter	Short Title	Extent of Repeal
5 & 6 Eliz. 2. c. 25.	The Rent Act 1957.	Section 16.
1965 c. 75.	The Rent Act 1965.	The Whole Act, so far as unrepealed.
1968 c. 23.	The Rent Act 1968.	In section 108(2), the words 'or under Part III of the Rent Act 1965'.

		In section 109(3), the words 'or Part III of the Rent Act 1965 (protection against harassment)'.
		In Schedule 15, the entries relating to sections 32 and 34 of the Rent Act 1965.
1970 c. 40.	The Agriculture Act 1970.	Section 99.
1972 c. 47.	The Housing Finance Act 1972.	In Schedule 9, paragraph 12(2) and in paragraph 12(3) the words 'or to Part III of the Rent Act 1965'.
1972 c. 71	The Criminal Justice Act 1972.	Section 30.
1974 c. 44.	The Housing Act 1974.	Section 123.
1976 c. 80.	The Rent (Agriculture) Act 1976.	In Schedule 8, paragraphs 13, 14 and 15.

HOUSING ACT 1985

SCHEDULE 2

Section 84

Grounds for Possession of Dwelling-Houses Let under Secure Tenancies

Part I: Grounds on which Court may Order Possession if it Considers it Reasonable

Ground 1

Rent lawfully due from the tenant has not been paid or an obligation of the tenancy has been broken or not performed.

Ground 2

The tenant or a person residing in or visiting the dwelling-house–

(a) has been guilty of conduct causing or likely to cause a nuisance or annoyance to a person residing, visiting or otherwise engaging in a lawful activity in the locality, or

(b) has been convicted of–

    (i) using the dwelling-house or allowing it to be used for immoral or illegal purposes, or

    (ii) an arrestable offence committed in, or in the locality of, the dwelling-house.

Ground 2A

The dwelling-house was occupied (whether alone or with others) by a married couple or a couple living together as husband and wife and–

(a) one or both of the partners is a tenant of the dwelling-house,

(b) one partner has left because of violence or threats of violence by the other towards–

    (i) that partner, or

    (ii) a member of the family of that partner who was residing with that partner immediately before the partner left, and

(c) the court is satisfied that the partner who has left is unlikely to return.

Ground 3

The condition of the dwelling-house or of any of the common parts has deteriorated owing to acts of waste by, or the neglect or default of, the tenant or a person residing in the dwelling-house and, in the case of an act of waste by, or the neglect or default of, a person lodging with the tenant or a sub-tenant of his, the tenant has not taken such steps as he ought reasonably to have taken for the removal of the lodger or sub-tenant.

Ground 4

The condition of furniture provided by the landlord for use under the tenancy, or for use in the common parts, has deteriorated owing to ill-treatment by the tenant or a person residing in the dwelling-house and, in the case of ill-treatment by a person lodging with the tenant or a sub-tenant of his, the tenant has not taken such steps as he ought reasonably to have taken for the removal of the lodger or sub-tenant.

Ground 5

The tenant is the person, or one of the persons, to whom the tenancy was granted and the landlord was induced to grant the tenancy by a false statement made knowingly or recklessly by–

(a) the tenant, or

(b) a person acting at the tenant's instigation.

Ground 6

The tenancy was assigned to the tenant, or to a predecessor in title of his who is a member of his family and is residing in the dwelling-house, by an assignment made by virtue of section 92 (assignments by way of exchange) and a premium was paid either in conection with that assignment or the assignment which the tenant or predecessor himself made by virtue of that section.

In this paragraph 'premium' means any fine or other like sum and any other pecuniary consideration in addition to rent.

Ground 7

The dwelling-house forms part of, or is within the curtilage of, a building which, or so much of it as is held by the landlord, is held mainly for purposes other than housing purposes and consists mainly of accommodation other than housing accommodation, and–

(a) the dwelling-house was let to the tenant or a predecessor in title of his in consequence of the tenant or predecessor being in the employment of the landlord, or of–

a local authority,

a new town corporation,

a housing action trust

an urban development corporation,

. . . or

the governors of an aided school,

and

(b) the tenant or a person residing in the dwelling-house has been guilty of conduct such that, having regard to the purpose for which the building is used, it would not be right for him to continue in occupation of the dwelling-house.

Ground 8

The dwelling-house was made available for occupation by the tenant (or a predecessor in title of his) while works were carried out on the dwelling-house which he previously occupied as his only or principal home and–

(a) the tenant (or predecessor) was a secure tenant of the other dwelling-house at the time when he ceased to occupy it as his home,

(b)   the tenant (or predecessor) accepted the tenancy of the dwelling-house of which possession is sought on the understanding that he would give up occupation when, on completion of the works, the other dwelling-house was again available for occupation by him under a secure tenancy, and

(c)   the works have been completed and the other dwelling-house is so available.

Part II: Grounds on which the Court may Order Possession if Suitable Alternative Accommodation is Available

Ground 9
The dwelling-house is overcrowded, within the meaning of Part X, in such circumstances as to render the occupier guilty of an offence.

Ground 10
The landlord intends, within a reasonable time of obtaining possession of the dwelling-house–

(a)   to demolish or reconstruct the building or part of the building comprising the dwelling-house, or

(b)   to carry out work on that building or on land let together with, and thus treated as part of, the dwelling-house,

and cannot reasonably do so without obtaining possession of the dwelling-house.

Ground 10A
The dwelling-house is in an area which is the subject of a redevelopment scheme approved by the Secretary of State or the Housing Corporation or Scottish Homes in accordance with Part V of this Schedule and the landlord intends within a reasonable time of obtaining possession to dispose of the dwelling-house in accordance with the scheme.

or

Part of the dwelling-house is in such an area and the landlord intends within a reasonable time of obtaining possession to dispose of that part in accordance with the scheme and for that purpose reasonably requires possession of the dwelling-house.

Ground 11
The landlord is a charity and the tenant's continued occupation of the dwelling-house would conflict with the objects of the charity.

Part III: Grounds on which the Court may Order Possession if it Considers it Reasonable and Suitable Alternative Accommodation is Available

Ground 12
The dwelling-house forms part of, or is within the curtilage of, a building which, or so much of it as is held by the landlord, is held mainly for purposes other than housing purposes and consists mainly of accommodation other than housing accommodation, or is situated in a cemetery, and–

(a) the dwelling-house was let to the tenant or a predecessor in title of his in consequence of the tenant or predecessor being in the employment of the landlord or of–

a local authority,

a new town corporation,

a housing action trust

an urban development corporation,

. . . or

the governors of an aided school,

and that employment has ceased, and

(b) the landlord reasonably requires the dwelling-house for occupation as a residence for some person either engaged in the employment of the landlord, or of such a body, or with whom a contract for such employment has been entered into conditional on housing being provided.

Ground 13

The dwelling-house has features which are substantially different from those of ordinary dwelling-houses and which are designed to make it suitable for occupation by a physically disabled person who requires accommodation of a kind provided by the dwelling-house and–

(a) there is no longer such a person residing in the dwelling-house, and

(b) the landlord requires it for occupation (whether alone or with members of his family) by such a person.

Ground 14

The landlord is a housing association or housing trust which lets dwelling-houses only for occupation (whether alone or with others) by persons whose circumstances (other than merely financial circumstances) make it especially difficult for them to satisfy their need for housing, and–

(a) either there is no longer such a person residing in the dwelling-house or the tenant has received from a local housing authority an offer of accommodation in premises which are to be let as a separate dwelling under a secure tenancy, and

(b) the landlord requires the dwelling-house for occupation (whether alone or with members of his family) by such a person.

Ground 15

The dwelling-house is one of a group of dwelling-houses which it is the practice of the landlord to let for occupation by persons with special needs and–

(a) a social service or special facility is provided in close proximity to the group of dwelling-houses in order to assist persons with those special needs,

(b) there is no longer a person with those special needs residing in the dwelling-house, and

(c) the landlord requires the dwelling-house for occupation (whether alone or with members of his family) by a person who has those special needs.

Ground 16

The accommodation afforded by the dwelling-house is more extensive than is reasonably required by the tenant and–

(a)   the tenancy vested in the tenant by virtue of section 89 (succession to periodic tenancy), the tenant being qualified to succeed by virtue of section 87(b)(members of family other than spouse), and

(b)   notice of the proceedings for possession was served under section 83 more than six months but less than twelve months after the date of the previous tenant's death.

The matters to be taken into account by the court in determining whether it is reasonable to make an order on this ground include–

(a)   the age of the tenant,

(b)   the period during which the tenant has occupied the dwelling-house as his only or principal home, and

(c)   any financial or other support given by the tenant to the previous tenant.

Part IV: Suitability of Accommodation

1.   For the purposes of section 84(2)(b) and (c)(case in which court is not to make an order for possession unless satisfied that suitable accommodation will be available) accommodation is suitable if it consists of premises–

(a)   which are to be let as a separate dwelling under a secure tenancy, or

(b)   which are to be let as a separate dwelling under a protected tenancy, not being a tenancy under which the landlord might recover possession under one of the Cases in Part II of Schedule 15 to the Rent Act 1977 (cases where court must order possession), or

(c)   which are to be let as a separate dwelling under an assured tenancy which is neither an assured shorthold tenancy, within the meaning of Part I of the Housing Act 1988, nor a tenancy under which the landlord might recover possession under any of Grounds 1 to 5 in Schedule 2 to that Act and, in the opinion of the court, the accommodation is reasonably suitable to the needs of the tenant and his family.

2.   In determining whether the accommodation is reasonably suitable to the needs of the tenant and his family, regard shall be had to–

(a)   the nature of the accommodation which it is the practice of the landlord to allocate to persons with similar needs;

(b)   the distance of the accommodation available from the place of work or education of the tenant and of any members of his family;

(c)   its distance from the home of any member of the tenant's family if proximity to it is essential to that member's or the tenant's well-being;

(d)   the needs (as regards extent of accommodation) and means of the tenant and his family;

(e) the terms on which the accommodation is available and the terms of the secure tenancy;

(f) if furniture was provided by the landlord for use under the secure tenancy, whether furniture is to be provided for use in the other accommodation, and if so the nature of the furnitire to be provided.

3.   Where possession of a dwelling-house is sought on ground 9 (overcrowding such as to render occupier guilty of offence), other accommodation may be reasonably suitable to the needs of the tenant and his family notwithstanding that the permitted number of persons for that accommodation, as defined in section 326(3)(overcrowding: the space standard), is less than the number of persons living in the dwelling-house of which possession is sought.

4. (1) A certificate of the appropriate local housing authority that they will provide suitable accommodation for the tenant by a date specified in the certificate is conclusive evidence that suitable accommodation will be available for him by that date.

(2) The appropriate local housing authority is the authority for the district in which the dwelling-house of which possession is sought is situated.

(3) This paragraph does not apply where the landlord is a local housing authority.

Part V: Approval of Redevelopment Schemes for Purposes of Ground 10A

1. (1) The Secretary of State may, on the application of the landlord, approve for the purposes of ground 10A in Part II of this Schedule a scheme for the disposal and re-development of an area of land consisting of or including the whole or part of one or more dwelling-houses.

(2) For this purpose–

(a) 'disposal' means a disposal of any interest in the land (including the grant of an option), and

(b) 'redevelopment' means the demolition or reconstruction of buildings or the carrying out of other works to buildings or land;

and it is immaterial whether the disposal is to precede or follow the redevelopment.

(3) The Secretary of State may on the application of the landlord approve a variation of a scheme previously approved by him and may, in particular, approve a variation adding land to the area subject to the scheme.

2. (1) Where a landlord proposes to apply to the Secretary of State for the approval of a scheme or variation it shall serve a notice in writing on any secure tenant of a dwelling-house affected by the proposal stating–

(a) the main features of the proposed scheme or, as the case may be, the scheme as proposed to be varied,

(b) that the landlord proposes to apply to the Secretary of State for approval of the scheme or variation, and

(c) the effect of such approval, by virtue of section 84 and ground 10A in Part II of this Schedule, in relation to proceedings for possession of the dwelling-house, and informing the tenant that he may, within such period as the land-lord may allow (which shall be at least 28 days from service of the notice), make representations to the landlord about the proposal.

(2)   The landlord shall not apply to the Secretary of State until it has con-sidered any representations made to it within that period.

(3)   In the case of a landlord to which section 105 applies (consultation on matters of housing management) the provisions of this paragraph apply in place of the provisions of that section in relation to the approval or variation of a redevelopment scheme.

3. (1)   In considering whether to give his approval to a scheme or variation the Secretary of State shall take into account, in particular–

(a)   the effect of the scheme on the extent and character of housing accommodation in the neighbourhood,

(b)   over what period of time it is proposed that the disposal and rede-velopment will take place in accordance with the scheme, and

(c)   to what extent the scheme includes provision for housing pro-vided under the scheme to be sold or let to existing tenants or persons nominated by the landlord;

and he shall take into account any representations made to him and, so far as they are brought to his notice, any representations made to the landlord.

(2)   The landlord shall give to the Secretary of State such information as to the representations made to it, and other relevant matters, as the Secretary of State may require.

4.   The Secretary of State shall not approve a scheme or variation so as to include in the area subject to the scheme–

(a)   part only of one or more dwelling-houses, or

(b)   one or more dwelling-houses not themselves affected by the works involved in redevelopment but which are proposed to be disposed of along with other land which is so affected,

unless he is satisfied that the inclusion is justified in the circumstances.

5. (1)   Approval may be given subject to conditions and may be expressed to expire after a specified period.

(2)   The Secretary of State, on the application of the landlord or otherwise, may vary an approval so as to–

(a)   add, remove or vary conditions to which the approval is subject; or

(b)   extend or restrict the period after which the approval is to expire.

(3)   Where approval is given subject to conditions, the landlord may serve a notice under section 83 (notice of proceedings for possession) spec-ifying ground 10A notwithstanding that the conditions are not yet ful-filled but the court shall not make an order for possession on that ground unless satisfied that they are or will be fulfilled.

6.   Where the landlord is a social landlord registered in the register main-tained by the Housing Corporation under section 1 of the Housing Act 1996 or a housing association registered in the register maintained by Scottish Homes under section 3 of the Housing Associations Act

1985, the Housing Corporation, or Scottish Homes, (and not the Secretary of State) has the functions conferred by this Part of this Schedule.

7.   In this Part of this Schedule references to the landlord of a dwelling-house include any authority or body within section 80 (the landlord condition for secure tenancies) having an interest of any description in the dwelling-house.

HOUSING ACT 1988

Increases of rent under assured periodic tenancies

13. (1) This section applies to–

(a)   a statutory periodic tenancy other than one which, by virtue of paragraph 11 or paragraph 12 in Part I of Schedule 1 to this Act, cannot for the time being be an assured tenancy; and

(b)   any other periodic tenancy which is an assured tenancy, other than one in relation to which there is a provision, for the time being binding on the tenant, under which the rent for a particular period of the tenancy will or may be greater than the rent for an earlier period.

(2)   For the purpose of securing an increase in the rent under a tenancy to which this section applies, the landlord may serve on the tenant a notice in the prescribed form proposing a new rent to take effect at the beginning of a new period of the tenancy specified in the notice, being a period beginning not earlier than–

(a)   the minimum period after the date of the service of the notice; and

(b)   except in the case of a statutory periodic tenancy, the first anniversary of the date on which the first period of the tenancy began; and

(c)   if the rent under the tenancy has previously been increased by virtue of a notice under this subsection or a determination under section 14 below, the first anniversary of the date on which the increased rent took effect.

(3)   The minimum period referred to in subsection (2) above is–

(a)   in the case of a yearly tenancy, six months;

(b)   in the case of a tenancy where the period is less than a month, one month; and

(c)   in any other case, a period equal to the period of the tenancy.

(4)   Where a notice is served under subsection (2)   above, a new rent specified in the notice shall take effect as mentioned in the notice unless, before the beginning of the new period specified in the notice,–

(a)   the tenant by an application in the prescribed form refers the notice to a rent assessment committee; or

(b)   the landlord and the tenant agree on a variation of the rent which is different from that proposed in the notice or agree that the rent should not be varied.

(5)   Nothing in this section (or in section 14 below) affects the right of the landlord and the tenant under an assured tenancy to vary by agreement any term of the tenancy (including a term relating to rent).

* * *

SCHEDULE 2

Section 7

Grounds for Possession of Dwelling-houses let on Assured Tenancies

Part I: Grounds on which Court must order possession

Ground 1

Not later than the beginning of the tenancy the landlord gave notice in writing to the tenant that possession might be recovered on this ground or the court is of the opinion that it is just and equitable to dispense with the requirement of notice and (in either case)–

(a) at some time before the beginning of the tenancy, the landlord who is seeking possession or, in the case of joint landlords seeking possession, at least one of them occupied the dwelling-house as his only or principal home; or

(b) the landlord who is seeking possession or, in the case of joint landlords seeking possession, at least one of them requires the dwelling-house as his or his spouse's only or principal home and neither the landlord (or, in the case of joint landlords, any one of them) nor any other person who, as landlord, derived title under the landlord who gave the notice mentioned above acquired the reversion on the tenancy for money or money's worth.

Ground 2

The dwelling-house is subject to a mortgage granted before the beginning of the tenancy and–

(a) the mortgagee is entitled to exercise a power of sale conferred on him by the mortgage or by section 101 of the Law of Property Act 1925; and

(b) the mortgagee requires possession of the dwelling-house for the purpose of disposing of it with vacant possession in exercise of that power; and

(c) either notice was given as mentioned in Ground 1 above or the court is satisfied that it is just and equitable to dispense with the requirement of notice;

and for the purposes of this ground 'mortgage' includes a charge and 'mortgagee' shall be construed accordingly.

Ground 3

The tenancy is a fixed term tenancy for a term not exceeding eight months and–

(a) not later than the beginning of the tenancy the landlord gave notice in writing to the tenant that possession might be recovered on this ground; and

(b) at some time within the period of twelve months ending with the beginning of the tenancy, the dwelling-house was occupied under a right to occupy it for a holiday.

Ground 4

The tenancy is a fixed term tenancy for a term not exceeding twelve months and–

(a) not later than the beginning of the tenancy the landlord gave notice in writing to the tenant that possession might be recovered on this ground; and

(b) at some time within the period of twelve months ending with the beginning of the tenancy, the dwelling-house was let on a tenancy falling within paragraph 8 of Schedule 1 to this Act.

Ground 5

The dwelling-house is held for the purpose of being available for occupation by a minister of religion as a residence from which to perform the duties of his office and–

(a) not later than the beginning of the tenancy the landlord gave notice in writing to the tenant that possession might be recovered on this ground; and

(b) the court is satisfied that the dwelling-house is required for occupation by a minister of religion as such a residence.

Ground 6

The landlord who is seeking possession or, if that landlord is a registered social landlord or charitable housing trust, a superior landlord intends to demolish or reconstruct the whole or a substantial part of the dwelling-house or to carry out substantial works on the dwelling-house or any part thereof or any building of which it forms part and the following conditions are fulfilled–

(a) the intended work cannot reasonably be carried out without the tenant giving up possession of the dwelling-house because–

    (i) the tenant is not willing to agree to such a variation of the terms of the tenancy as would give such access and other facilities as would permit the intended work to be carried out, or

    (ii) the nature of the intended work is such that no such variation is practicable, or

    (iii) the tenant is not willing to accept an assured tenancy of such part only of the dwelling-house (in this sub-paragraph referred to as ìthe reduced partî) as would leave in the possession of his landlord so much of the dwelling-house as would be reasonable to enable the intended work to be carried out and, where appropriate, as would give such access and other facilities over the reduced part as would permit the intended work to be carried out, or

    (iv) the nature of the intended work is such that such a tenancy is not practicable; and

(b) either the landlord seeking possession acquired his interest in the dwelling-house before the grant of the tenancy or that interest was in existence at the time of that grant and neither that landlord (or, in the case of joint landlords, any of them) nor any other person who, alone or jointly with others, has acquired that interest since that time acquired it for money or money's worth; and

(c) the assured tenancy on which the dwelling-house is let did not come into being by virtue of any provision of Schedule 1 to the Rent Act 1977, as amended by Part I of Schedule 4 to this Act or, as the case may be, section 4 of the Rent (Agriculture) Act 1976, as amended by Part II of that Schedule.

For the purposes of this ground, if, immediately before the grant of the tenancy, the tenant to whom it was granted or, if it was granted to joint tenants, any of them was the tenant or one of the joint tenants of the dwelling-house concerned under an earlier assured tenancy or, as the case may be, under a tenancy to which Schedule 10 to the Local Government and Housing Act 1989 applied, any reference in paragraph (b) above to the grant of the tenancy is a reference to the grant of that earlier assured tenancy or, as the case may be, to the grant of the tenancy to which the said Schedule 10 applied.

For the purposes of this ground 'registered social landlord' has the same meaning as in the Housing Act 1985 (see section 5(4) and (5) of that Act) and 'charitable housing trust' means a housing trust, within the meaning of the Housing Associations Act 1985, which is a charity, within the meaning of the Charities Act 1993.

. . .

Ground 7

The tenancy is a periodic tenancy (including a statutory periodic tenancy) which has devolved under the will or intestacy of the former tenant and the proceedings for the recovery of possession are begun not later than twelve months after the death of the former tenant or, if the court so directs, after the date on which, in the opinion of the court, the landlord or, in the case of joint landlords, any one of them became aware of the former tenant's death.

For the purposes of this ground, the acceptance by the landlord of rent from a new tenant after the death of the former tenant shall not be regarded as creating a new periodic tenancy, unless the landlord agrees in writing to a change (as compared with the tenancy before the death) in the amount of the rent, the period of the tenancy, the premises which are let or any other term of the tenancy.

Ground 8

Both at the date of the service of the notice under section 8 of this Act relating to the proceedings for possession and at the date of the hearing–

(a) if rent is payable weekly or fortnightly, at least eight weeks' rent is unpaid;

(b) if rent is payable monthly, at least ' two months' rent is unpaid;

(c) if rent is payable quarterly, at least one quarter's rent is more than three months in arrears; and

(d)   if rent is payable yearly, at least three months' rent is more than three months in arrears;

and for the purpose of this ground ìrentì means rent lawfully due from the tenant.

Part II: Grounds on which Court may Order Possession

Ground 9

Suitable alternative accommodation is available for the tenant or will be available for him when the order for possession takes effect.

Ground 10

Some rent lawfully due from the tenant–
(a)   is unpaid on the date on which the proceedings for possession are begun; and
(b)   except where subsection (1)(b)of section 8 of this Act applies, was in arrears at the date of the service of the notice under that section relating to those proceedings.

Ground 11

Whether or not any rent is in arrears on the date on which proceedings for possession are begun, the tenant has persistently delayed paying rent which has become lawfully due.

Ground 12

Any obligation of the tenancy (other than one related to the payment of rent) has been broken or not performed.

Ground 13

The condition of the dwelling-house or any of the common parts has deteriorated owing to acts of waste by, or the neglect or default of, the tenant or any other person residing in the dwelling-house and, in the case of an act of waste by, or the neglect or default of, a person lodging with the tenant or a sub-tenant of his, the tenant has not taken such steps as he ought reasonably to have taken for the removal of the lodger or sub-tenant.

For the purposes of this ground, 'common parts' means any part of a building comprising the dwelling-house and any other premises which the tenant is entitled under the terms of the tenancy to use in common with the occupiers of other dwelling-houses in which the landlord has an estate or interest.

Ground 14

The tenant or a person residing in or visiting the dwelling-house–
(a)   has been guilty of conduct causing or likely to cause a nuisance or annoyance to a person residing, visiting or otherwise engaging in a lawful activity in the locality, or
(b)   has been convicted of–
    (i)   using the dwelling-house or allowing it to be used for immoral or illegal purposes, or

(ii)   an arrestable offence committed in, or in the locality of, the dwelling-house.

Ground 14A

The dwelling-house was occupied (whether alone or with others) by a married couple or a couple living together as husband and wife and–

(a)   one or both of the partners is a tenant of the dwelling-house,

(b)   the landlord who is seeking possession is a registered social landlord or a charitable housing trust,

(c)   one partner has left the dwelling-house because of violence or threats of violence by the other towards–

(i)   that partner, or

(ii)   a member of the family of that partner who was residing with that partner immediately before the partner left, and

(d)   the court is satisfied that the partner who has left is unlikely to return.

For the purposes of this ground 'registered social landlord' and 'member of the family' have the same meaning as in Part I of the Housing Act 1996 and 'charitable housing trust' means a housing trust, within the meaning of the Housing Associations Act 1985, which is a charity within the meaning of the Charities Act 1993.

Ground 15

The condition of any furniture provided for use under the tenancy has, in the opinion of the court, deteriorated owing to ill-treatment by the tenant or any other person residing in the dwelling-house and, in the case of ill-treatment by a person lodging with the tenant or by a sub-tenant of his, the tenant has not taken such steps as he ought reasonably to have taken for the removal of the lodger or sub-tenant.

Ground 16

The dwelling-house was let to the tenant in consequence of his employment by the landlord seeking possession or a previous landlord under the tenancy and the tenant has ceased to be in that employment.

For the purposes of this ground, at a time when the landlord is or was the Secretary of State, employment by a health service body, as defined in section 60(7) of the National Health Service and Community Care Act 1990, or by a Local Health Board, shall be regarded as employment by the Secretary of State.

Ground 17

The tenant is the person, or one of the persons, to whom the tenancy was granted and the landlord was induced to grant the tenancy by a false statement made knowingly or recklessly by–

(a)   the tenant, or

(b)   a person acting at the tenant's instigation.

Part III: Suitable Alternative Accommodation

1.   For the purposes of Ground 9 above, a certificate of the local housing authority for the district in which the dwelling-house in question is

situated, certifying that the authority will provide suitable alternative accommodation for the tenant by a date specified in the certificate, shall be conclusive evidence that suitable alternative accommodation will be available for him by that date.

2.   Where no such certificate as is mentioned in paragraph I above is produced to the court, accommodation shall be deemed to be suitable for the purposes of Ground 9 above if it consists of either–

(a)   premises which are to be let as a separate dwelling such that they will then be let on an assured tenancy, other than–

(i)   a tenancy in respect of which notice is given not later than the beginning of the tenancy that possession might be recovered on any of Grounds 1 to 5 above, or

(ii)   an assured shorthold tenancy, within the meaning of Chapter II of Part I of this Act, or

(b)   premises to be let as a separate dwelling on terms which will, in the opinion of the court, afford to the tenant security of tenure reasonably equivalent to the security afforded by Chapter I of Part I of this Act in the case of an assured tenancy of a kind mentioned in sub-paragraph (a) above,

and, in the opinion of the court, the accommodation fulfils the relevant conditions as defined in paragraph 3 below.

3. (1)   For the purposes of paragraph 2 above, the relevant conditions are that the accommodation is reasonably suitable to the needs of the tenant and his family as regards proximity to place of work, and either–

(a)   similar as regards rental and extent to the accommodation afforded by dwelling-houses provided in the neighbourhood by any local housing authority for persons whose needs as regards extent are, in the opinion of the court, similar to those of the tenant and of his family; or

(b)   reasonably suitable to the means of the tenant and to the needs of the tenant and his family as regards extent and character; and

that if any furniture was provided for use under the assured tenancy in question, furniture is provided for use in the accommodation which is either similar to that so provided or is reasonably suitable to the needs of the tenant and his family.

(2)   For the purposes of sub-paragraph (1) (a) above, a certificate of a local housing authority stating–

(a)   the extent of the accommodation afforded by dwelling-houses provided by the authority to meet the needs of tenants with families of such number as may be specified in the certificate, and

(b)   the amount of the rent charged by the authority for dwelling-houses affording accommodation of that extent,

shall be conclusive evidence of the facts so stated.

4.   Accommodation shall not be deemed to be suitable to the needs of the tenant and his family if the result of their occupation of the accommodation would be that it would be an overcrowded dwelling-house for the purposes of Part X of the Housing Act 1985.

5.   Any document purporting to be a certificate of a local housing authority named therein issued for the purposes of this Part of this Schedule and to be signed by the proper officer of that authority shall be received in evidence and, unless the contrary is shown, shall be deemed to be such a certificate without further proof.

6.   In this Part of this Schedule îlocal housing authorityî and îdistrictî, in relation to such an authority, have the same meaning as in the Housing Act 1985.

Part IV: Notices Relating to Recovery of Possession

7.   Any reference in Grounds 1 to 5 in Part I of this Schedule or in the following provisions of this Part to the landlord giving a notice in writing to the tenant is, in the case of joint landlords, a reference to at least one of the joint landlords giving such a notice.

8. (1) If, not later than the beginning of a tenancy (in this paragraph referred to as 'the earlier tenancy'), the landlord gives such a notice in writing to the tenant as is mentioned in any of Grounds 1 to 5 in Part I of this Schedule, then, for the purposes of the ground in question and any further application of this paragraph, that notice shall also have effect as if it had been given immediately before the beginning of any later tenancy falling within sub-paragraph (2) below.

(2)   Subject to sub-paragraph (3) below, sub-paragraph (1) above applies to a later tenancy–

   (a)   which takes effect immediately on the coming to an end of the earlier tenancy; and

   (b)   which is granted (or deemed to be granted) to the person who was the tenant under the earlier tenancy immediately before it came to an end; and

   (c)   which is of substantially the same dwelling-house as the earlier tenancy.

(3)   Sub-paragraph (1) above does not apply in relation to a later tenancy if, not later than the beginning of the tenancy, the landlord gave notice in writing to the tenant that the tenancy is not one in respect of which possession can be recovered on the ground in question.

9.   Where paragraph 8(1) above has effect in relation to a notice given as mentioned in Ground 1 in Part I of this Schedule, the reference in paragraph (b) of that ground to the reversion on the tenancy is a reference to the reversion on the earlier tenancy and on any later tenancy falling within paragraph 8(2) above.

10.   Where paragraph 8(1) above has effect in relation to a notice given as mentioned in Ground 3 or Ground 4 in Part I of this Schedule, any second or subsequent tenancy in relation to which the notice has effect shall be treated for the purpose of that ground as beginning at the beginning of the tenancy in respect of which the notice was actually given.

11.   Any reference in Grounds 1 to 5 in Part I of this Schedule to a notice being given not later than the beginning of the tenancy is a reference to its being given not later than the day on which the tenancy is entered into and, accordingly, section 45(2) of this Act shall not apply to any such reference.

Housing Corporation documents

The Housing Corporation's definitions of housing association supported housing for older people: Circular 03/04 (April 2004)

Tenancy management: eligibility and evictions: Circular 02/07 (April 2007)

THE HOUSING CORPORATION'S DEFINITIONS OF HOUSING ASSOCIATION SUPPORTED HOUSING AND HOUSING FOR OLDER PEOPLE

(HOUSING CORPORATION CIRCULAR 03/04)

1.0   Legislation, regulation and policy requirements

This circular applies to all housing associations excluding co-ownership societies. It should be read by all housing associations which own or manage supported housing, housing for older people or general needs housing for rent.

This circular replaces Circular R1-11/99 and provides new Housing Corporation definitions of supported housing and housing for older people.

The definitions are necessary for us to ensure appropriate regulation and funding of housing association stock. The definitions enable housing associations to categorise within the Housing Corporation's regulatory, data collection and investment systems their housing for rent as supported housing, housing for older people, or general needs housing.

This categorisation must be in full accordance with the guidance set out below. The Corporation may, by exception, require an association which has inappropriately classified its stock to re-designate it. However, please note 3.1 below regarding CORE in 2004/05.

2.0   Definitions

2.1   *Definition of supported housing*

There are two types of supported housing:

> Purpose designed supported housing; and
> Designated supported housing.

The term 'supported housing' applies to purpose designed or designated supported housing. The delivery of support under the Supporting People framework does not necessarily result in the categorisation of housing as supported if the property is not purpose designed or designated for a particular client group. In the absence of either of these two conditions, housing is general needs.

The design features which distinguish the two types of supported housing that interest the Housing Corporation are listed below.

2.1.1   **Purpose designed supported housing:**

Buildings that are purpose designed or remodelled to enable residents to adjust to independent living or to enable them to live independently and which require specific design features. There must be support services provided by the landlord or another organisation. At a minimum, a building or scheme must have the following:

Facilities: The scheme or main building must have basic facilities of a laundry for residents or washing machines in living units provided by the landlord. The scheme must also have a communal lounge.

Design features: The entrance area into the building, communal areas and some living units must be designed to wheelchair user standards.

2.1.2   **Designated supported housing:**
Buildings with some or no special design facilities and features but that are designated for a specific client group with support services in place to enable them to adjust to independent living or to enable them to live independently.

2.2   Definition of housing for older people
There are three types of housing for older people:

> Housing for older people (all special design features);
> Housing for older people (some special design features);
> Designated supported housing for older people

Properties should be described as housing for older people if they are intended for older people (regardless of the actual characteristics of each tenant) and they either incorporate the range of basic facilities and special design features set out below or are specially designated supported housing for older people. The distinctive design features should be over and above lifetime homes adaptations to general needs properties. The age of tenants actually resident is not a defining feature.

Tenants in housing for older people (**all** special design features) or housing for older people (**some** special design features) should have access to support services as need arises to enable them to live in the property for the rest of their lifetimes.

Access to support means that at a minimum, a process is in place to assist in accessing and/or signposting tenants to support services that they need. Except in the case of 'designated supported housing for older people', the delivery of or level of support is not a defining feature.

The three types of housing for older people are described below.

2.2.1   **Housing for older people (all special design features)**
Remodelled or purpose built grouped housing that has **all** the basic facilities and **all** special design features intended to enable people to live there for their lifetimes. **All** the following requirements have to be met:

Basic facilities: The scheme or main building must have basic facilities of a laundry for residents and/or washing machines in living units or provision for washing machines to be installed. The scheme must also have a communal lounge.

Special design features:

•   The whole scheme including entrances and the buildings that comprise it must be designed to wheelchair user standards;

- Living units must have walk in showers or bathrooms adapted for people with mobility problems or wheelchair users.
- Bathrooms in living units that are wheelchair standard must meet the criteria for adapted bathrooms;
- Living units must have kitchens that are designed to wheelchair standards;
- The scheme must have a bathroom with provision for assisted bathing;
- If there is more than one storey there must be a lift.

2.2.2 Housing for older people (some special design features)

Remodelled or purpose built grouped housing that has **all** the basic facilities and at least **one or more** of the special design features listed below. Residents must have access to support services to enable them to live there for their lifetimes. In addition, if there is more than one storey there must be a lift.

Basic Facilities: The scheme or main building must have basic facilities of a laundry for residents and/or washing machines in living units or provision for washing machines to be installed. The scheme must have a communal lounge.

Special design features:

- Living units have walk in showers or bathrooms adapted for people with mobility problems or wheelchair users.
- Bathrooms in wheelchair standard living units meet the criteria for adapted bathrooms;
- The living units, the entrance area into the building and communal areas are designed to wheelchair user standards.

2.2.3 Designated supported housing for older people:

Buildings with **none** of the special design facilities and features listed above but which provide accommodation designated for older people requiring support, with support services provided by the landlord or another organisation.

2.3 Further interpretation and clarification of the definitions

2.3.1 Care homes

Under the Care Standards Act 2000, the National Care Standards Commission defines care homes under service categories. In line with this the Corporation makes the following distinctions:

a) 'Care homes providing personal care' fall within the definition of social housing and are either purpose designed supported housing or housing for older people (all special design features).

b) 'Care homes providing nursing care' are excluded from the definition of social housing and are therefore outside the definitions of supported housing and housing for older people.

2.3.2 **Care or support services provided by other agencies**

The provision of care or support services to a resident such as domiciliary care is not in itself grounds for classifying the stock as supported housing or housing for older people. One of the above definitions must be met.

2.3.3 **Night shelters**

Night shelters which only provide accommodation overnight or a very short term resting place and give no written occupancy agreement are considered not to be social housing and therefore not supported housing. Those night shelters which constitute a home and provide a written occupancy agreement will be considered as social housing and, provided one of the above definitions is met, should be categorised as supported housing.

2.3.4 **Floating support and move-on accommodation**

The term 'supported housing' **excludes** floating or move-on support within general needs stock.

3.0 Corporation expectations

3.1 *Regulatory and other returns and regulatory implications*

Housing associations are required to report to the Corporation consistently on supported housing stock and housing for older people throughout their accounts, financial reports and plans (FV5 and FV3), Regulatory and Statistical Return and the CORE system.

Regulatory and Statistical Return and RSL accounts

Stock defined as supported housing or housing for older people will be treated together for the purpose of performance indicators.

CORE

Stock defined as housing for older people is considered a subset of supported housing within the CORE system.

IMPORTANT NOTE: The definitions set out in the 2004/05 CORE guidance are not consistent either with this Circular or with the RSR 2005 return. 'Designated supported housing for older people', will be classified as 'general needs' not 'supported' in CORE for 2004/05. This is a transition period until 1 April 2005 when CORE guidance will be amended.

3.2 *Investment implications*

The Housing Corporation will pay Social Housing Grant to capital fund supported housing and housing for older people. As with all capital funding, projects must meet the Regional Housing Strategies and follow the bids and allocations process for the whole capital funding programme.

4.0 Assessing compliance

Associations are expected to make their own assessment of compliance with our regulatory requirements and to report this to the

Corporation. We expect that this assessment will take account of:

a) any relevant issues identified in reviews or other work on which governing boards base their annual Statement on Internal Controls Assurance.

b) any relevant issues identified by an associations' external auditor during the preparation and audit of annual accounts

5.0 Enquiries about this circular

Please direct any enquiries about this circular to the regulation team at the appropriate regional office of the Housing Corporation.

TENANCY MANAGEMENT: ELIGIBILITY AND EVICTIONS

(HOUSING CORPORATION CIRCULAR 02/07)

Summary

This Circular sets out the Housing Corporation's expectations of housing associations when assessing the eligibility of applicants for a housing association home, and when working to prevent or respond to breaches of tenancy.

1   Introduction

Housing associations have a duty to co-operate (as is reasonable in the circumstances) with local authorities in offering accommodation to people with priority on the authority's register (or waiting list), and in assisting the local authority to discharge its housing functions, particularly to the homeless. These duties are set out in section 170 and section 213 of the Housing Act 1996.

Housing associations should act to prevent homelessness from occurring in the first instance. During the lifetime of a tenancy, housing associations should act to support and sustain, rather than terminate, a tenancy: early intervention is essential. Housing associations are often under pressure from tenants and communities to evict those accused of anti-social behaviour (ASB). Nevertheless, associations should pursue alternative interventions, retaining eviction as a last resort.

Applicants and tenants of different housing association landlords ought to receive reasonably consistent treatment. They ought to know what the consequences of breaches of their previous or current tenancy are and what action they can take to remedy the breach.

2   Corporation expectations: eligibility

The following guidance applies to both new and transfer applicants and nominations by the local authority:

Financial circumstances

Rent arrears

Rent arrears should not be an automatic barrier to access. Where applicants are deemed to be ineligible for housing because they owe rent for a previous tenancy, associations should actively encourage applicants to enter into agreements to pay their arrears. If such agreements are kept for a reasonable period, the application should be re-activated (see 'Suspensions' below). For transfer applicants, however, we recognise that a clean rent record is normally expected except for re-housing emergencies.

Non-housing debt

Debts arising from arrears of non-housing payments, such as council tax or hire purchase, should not have a bearing on eligibility.

Credit checks

If associations conduct checks on the credit status of applicants, the policy should be approved by the governing board, the applicant should be informed and shown a copy of the check without charge. Details of a household's financial position might help a landlord to identify vulnerability and to offer appropriate support, but should not have a bearing on eligibility.

Guarantors

Applicants for housing should not be asked to provide a guarantor for rent, as a condition of tenancy offer. The exception is tenancy offers to minors.

Deposits

Generally, deposits should not be taken from applicants for housing, whether as a bond for future behaviour or as a refundable administrative fee; a common exception to this rule is for furniture. However, after 6 April 2007, if a landlord takes a deposit of any kind from a tenant when offering an assured shorthold tenancy, the landlord will have to be a member of a statutory tenancy deposit scheme, as detailed in the Housing Act 2004.

Anti-social behaviour

Definition

The Anti-social Behaviour Act (ASB) 2003 describes anti-social behaviour for the purpose of seeking an injunction as 'conduct which is capable of causing nuisance or annoyance to any person and which directly or indirectly relates to or affects the housing management functions of a relevant landlord' (ASB 2003 s13(3)(1)).

Evidence

Ineligibility for housing on the ground of the applicant's anti-social behaviour should be based on evidence of the behaviour. Evidence might include the previous eviction of an applicant or a member of their household for ASB, or a previous injunction or Anti-social Behaviour Order (ASBO) taken out against the applicant or a member of their household. Previous tenancy enforcement action for ASB should not be taken into account if it occurred two or more years prior to the date of application and the tenant's household has conducted a tenancy satisfactorily in the intervening period (see 'Suspension period', below).

Previous convictions

Landlords may not ask an applicant about 'spent' convictions. A previous conviction is not an automatic barrier to access, especially for low-risk offenders. Eligibility should only be in question if there is reason to suppose that the ex-offender is likely to pose a risk to their household, neighbours and/or the wider community. Associations should be able to justify the exclusion of ex-offenders, with an accountable policy and procedures for considering cases.

Local issues

Local connection

Housing need should normally override any special consideration of local connection. No applicant should be excluded by an association because they do not have a local connection, except in the following circumstances: on rural exception sites; where section 106 agreements apply; if an offer of accommodation would conflict with the association's governing instrument; if a local lettings policy is in place. Local authorities may continue to select nominations from locally connected people.

Local lettings policies

Where associations operate local lettings policies, these should demonstrably and reasonably balance the competing demands of local authority nominations and pressing housing need, against policies promoting balanced communities.

Vulnerability

Support packages

Where assessments indicate vulnerability for whatever reason, housing associations should work with the local authority and other agencies to arrange appropriate support so that it is available at the beginning of a new tenancy. An applicant may be excluded if they will be unable to meet the conditions of tenancy without additional support and:

- the association, despite every effort, is unable to ensure that appropriate support is available; or
- the level of support required would seriously undermine the association's ability to support other residents in a scheme.

General

Blanket bans

Applicants should not be excluded automatically from housing if their circumstances 'fit' a defined category. Every case must be judged on its merits and efforts made to resolve any possible ineligibility.

Suspension period

The meaning and purpose of a suspension period, during which an application for housing is held inactive, should be clearly defined and should last no longer than two years. Suspension implies that the applicant is invited to apply to have their application re-activated at a specified time for a specified reason.

Appeals

All rejected applicants should have information about and access to an appeals process. The appeal should be heard by adjudicators who were not involved in the original decision to reject the housing application.

Advice
Rejected applicants should be referred to housing advice agencies.

Procedures and documentation
The process to be followed by association officers involved in assessing eligibility for housing forms part of an association's lettings policy. To achieve consistency, procedures should be clearly written; to achieve demonstrable fairness, decisions should be clearly documented and monitored.

3 Corporation expectations: Evictions

Financial circumstances

Housing Benefit
Possession proceedings for rent arrears should not be started against a tenant who can demonstrate that they have:

- a reasonable expectation of eligibility for housing benefit;
- provided the local authority with all the evidence required to process a housing benefit claim; and
- paid required personal contributions towards the charges.

Associations should make every effort to establish effective ongoing liaison with housing benefit departments and to make direct contact with them before taking enforcement action. A certificate should be obtained, if possible, to confirm that there are no outstanding benefit enquiries, according to the Department of Work and Pensions good practice guidance.

Holistic debt advice
Tenants with rent arrears often face multiple debts. Associations should refer tenants in arrears to holistic debt counselling services as soon as possible after the debt has arisen and should continue to do so during the recovery procedure. Possession action should not be taken where a tenant has maintained an agreement to pay the arrears.

Distress or distraint for rent
Distraint should not be used as a means of recovering rent arrears.

Mandatory grounds for possession (Ground 8).
Ground 8 of Schedule 2 to the Housing Act 1988 is a mandatory ground that can be used to seek possession of an assured tenancy where a tenant has arrears of more than eight weeks' rent. Before using Ground 8, associations should first pursue all other reasonable alternatives to recover the debt. Where the use of Ground 8 forms part of an arrears and eviction policy, tenants should have been consulted and governing board approval for the policy should have been given.

Other tenancy breaches

Anti-social behaviour

Section 12 of the Anti-social Behaviour Act 2003 places a statutory duty on housing associations to publish policies and procedures for tackling anti-social behaviour. These should show a commitment to using the full range of tools now available to tackle ASB. Eviction should be considered only when other interventions have failed to protect the wider community.

Gas safety tests

The Gas Safety (Installation and Use) Regulations 1998 place on landlords a statutory duty to carry out an annual test of gas appliances that they have fitted in tenants' homes. A failure to do so carries serious health and safety implications. Where tenants refuse to cooperate in allowing access to their home for safety tests, associations should consider alternative measures, such as injunctions, before seeking possession.

Sustainable tenancies

Prevention

At tenancy start-up, tenants should be offered advice and help with housing benefit claims and access to a benefits maximisation service.

Support for the vulnerable

Associations should make every effort at tenancy sign-up to identify the full range of the tenant's needs, and support packages provided as appropriate.

Starter and demoted tenancies

Associations that use assured shorthold tenancies as starter tenancies should do so as part of a managed strategy for dealing with ASB either:
• across their whole stock;
• across their stock in a local authority area; or
• in defined street areas or estates.

Section 14(2) of the Anti-social Behaviour Act 2003 requires associations to obtain a court order before demoting an assured tenancy.

4   Assessing compliance

The general standards of performance on approaches to applicant eligibility and evictions that housing associations are expected to meet

This Circular is issued as statutory housing management guidance under section 36 of the Housing Act 1996.

Our general expectations of housing associations are set out in the Regulatory Code and Guidance. The Code and Guidance identify, by means of paragraphs marked with an asterisk, which expectations are covered by section 36. The relevant sections are:

•   3.5, sets out how associations should deliver their services;

- 3.5.c, requires associations to repossess a property only as a last resort;
- 3.5.d, expects associations to have strategies to tackle anti-social behaviour;
- 3.6, sets out expectations deriving from associations' statutory duty to co-operate with local authorities;
- 3.6.d, expects local authorities to be consulted about rejection criteria;
- 3.6.e, explains the circumstances in which applicants can be excluded; and
- 3.6.f, seeks lettings policies that are responsive and fair.

Data returns

CORE lettings logs and the Regulatory and Statistical Return (RSR) record performance data on lettings to nominations and the homeless, and rejected nominations. The RSR also records performance data on the number of evictions carried out by associations, the reason for the eviction and the use of demoted tenancies. Associations' practice and performance in relation to eligibility and eviction policies may be subject to inspection by the Audit Commission.

How we will assess compliance

We will expect housing associations to certify that they have met the requirements of this Circular.

When undertaking a risk assessment, we will take account of and include any relevant findings from inspection reports. Where our risk assessment indicates an association might not be complying, we will undertake a more detailed review in accordance with our normal regulatory engagement.

We will consider and may act upon information brought to our attention by the Housing Ombudsman Service regarding non- compliance with this Circular.

Enquiries about this Circular

Please address enquiries about this circular to the appropriate Housing Corporation local field office.

Our offices

Maple House
149 Tottenham Court Road
London W1T 7BN

For enquiries, contact us at:

Tel: 0845 230 7000
Fax: 0113 233 7101
E-mail: enquiries@housingcorp.gsx.gov.uk
Internet: www.housingcorp.gov.uk

Central
Attenborough House
109/119 Charles Street
Leicester LE1 1FQ
31 Waterloo Road
Wolverhampton WV1 4DJ

Westbrook Centre
Block 1 Suite 1
Milton Road
Cambridge CB4 1YG

London
Maple House
149 Tottenham Court Road
London W1T 7BN

North
Fourth Floor
One Piccadilly Gardens
Manchester M1 1RG

1 Park Lane
Leeds LS3 1EP

St. George's House
Team Valley
Kingsway Trading Estate
Gateshead NE11 0NA

South East
Leon House
High Street
Croydon CR9 1UH

South West
Beaufort House
51 New North Road
Exeter EX4 4EP

Policies and procedures guidelines

Checklist for a code of conduct

Developing a confidentiality policy

Developing a health and safety policy

Developing a rent arrears policy and procedure

Developing your support planning

Developing an equal opportunities policy (EOP)

Developing a complaints policy

Developing an anti-social behaviour policy and procedure

CHECKLIST FOR A CODE OF CONDUCT

The aim of a Code of Conduct should be to leave no doubt as to what constitutes acceptable and unacceptable behaviour for staff, committee members and volunteers. The Code should cover the following:

Introduction
- ☐ Why professional boundaries are important.
- ☐ Link with values & mission statement of the organisation, ie conduct of employees will reflect the values.
- ☐ Responsibility to become familiar with Code of Conduct lies with employee.
- ☐ Consequences of not complying.

Relationships
- ☐ Declaring an interest (family, personal, commercial or social) in any organisation or individual with whom the organisation has dealings. How to declare and how conflicts of interest will be considered.
- ☐ Appropriate relationships: polite, caring, respectful, sensitive.
- ☐ Relationships of a business, social or personal nature. Limitations on with whom staff/volunteers can develop such relationship.
- ☐ Service users and ex-service users: how long a period needs to have elapsed before such a relationship is deemed appropriate?
- ☐ Service users of similar services, or individuals who experience similar issues as service users of the service (eg are in recovery from addiction).
- ☐ Social contact outside work.
- ☐ Appropriate conduct if you encounter service users or ex-service users in a social situation.
- ☐ Recording contact outside work.
- ☐ Correspondence.
- ☐ Giving out private contact details e.g. private addresses, phone numbers to service users.
- ☐ Confidentiality – at all times confined to the staff team and not to any individual member of staff.
- ☐ Lone working: ensure you are not in a position that could be construed as compromising.
- ☐ Clarity with service users: staff should ensure that professional boundaries are made clear when working with service users.
- ☐ Personal relationships between employees

Financial / gifts
- ☐ How to deal with gifts received and definition of acceptable gifts.
- ☐ Financial gifts are not acceptable.
- ☐ Gifts from staff to service users may be misconstrued and so should be avoided.
- ☐ Loans of money to service users and vice versa.

Specifics
- ☐ Alcohol and drugs whilst on duty (off-duty regulations?)/buying or accepting drinks for or from service users.
- ☐ Tobacco and cigarettes.
- ☐ 'Play fighting'.

DEVELOPING A CONFIDENTIALITY POLICY

The requirements *Supporting People* (interim contract) highlighted the need for a well thought out approach to confidentiality and data protection issues. A provider's review of their confidentiality policy could start by addressing these areas.

Aim of policy
Outline what it aims to do for staff, service users, other agencies, compliance with law.

Legislation
The procedure must comply with Data Protection Act 1998, Human Rights Act 1998 and Public Interest Disclosure Act 1998, plus any contractual requirements.

Who does it apply to?
You must ensure that everyone engaged in the support service that may have access to personal information understands their responsibilities and demonstrate evidence of compliance with their procedures. This includes employees, volunteers, self-employed sessional workers, consultants or contractors.

Record keeping
It should to cover accuracy and consistency of record keeping, security of data, information to service users, consent for disclosure requirements and identify responsible persons.

Being able to demonstrate compliance means keeping written records, eg a file note of the steps taken to check an enquirer's identity, a note of the information given, a signed confidentiality undertaking for a sessional or temporary worker, etc.

Contracts of employment, volunteering agreements, contracts with consultants and others should include a clause making explicit the person's responsibilities for confidentiality and data protection.

Disclosure of information
In order for the provider to plan and provide effective support, personal information may need to pass between them and other agencies. Information about when this may be appropriate should be set out in the agreement with the user.

Your policy should ensure that staff understand how to maintain confidentiality in the following situations:
- making phone calls on behalf of service users;
- responding to requests for information from other agencies;

- referring someone to another agency;
- typing records or letters;
- providing access to files which contain information about more than one person;
- storing records in public areas;
- deciding which information to pass on to other colleagues;
- where are they are obliged to pass on information even if the service user refuses consent.

Service users' consent

When service users first move into their home or accept a support service, they should be advised what type of information the service provider keeps on record, what can or must be disclosed without their consent, when their consent is needed for disclosure and their rights to see information recorded about them. This advice should be backed up with a section in a handbook or information pack in a language and form comprehensible to the user and accessible to their relative or advocate.

A service user should **not** be asked to sign a blanket, wide ranging consent to disclosure. A confidentiality agreement should set out areas where information will be shared and under what circumstances and serves as a record of their consent. In other cases, the user's consent must be obtained as the need arises.

Breaches of confidentiality

Your policy should cover what to do if a staff member breaches confidentiality by un-necessarily passing on information about a service user.

Further information is available from the Data Protection Commissioner at www.iso.gov.uk

DEVELOPING A HEALTH AND SAFETY POLICY

This checklist is intended to help providers develop or review a health and safety policy. Every organisation should have a clear policy for ensuring implementation and awareness of health and safety.

If you have more than five employees you will need a health and safety policy.

General statement of policy

- Statement of intention to provide healthy and safe living and working environments
- How the policy will be publicised
- The organisations commitment in writing must be dated and signed
- Responsibility for carrying out the statement of intent
- Name of the Director, secretary or manager responsible for implementing policy

- Names and responsibilities of key individuals responsible for day to day health and safety
- Arrangements and procedures
- Systems and procedures in place for health and safety
- Arrangements for joint consultation with a recognised trade union
- A list of the main health hazards identified from the assessment of the working arrangements and workplace. (What is the employer's duty with regard to dealing with accidents?)

Employer's duty with regard to dealing with accidents

- All accidents at the premise need to be recorded in the Accident book
- Three-day injury, death, disease and major incidents need to be reported to the local authority

Employer's duty in the provision of first aid

There must be at least one notice telling staff:

- Location of the first aid box
- Name of 'first -aider' or appointed person
- Location of 'first-aider' or appointed person

Contents of the first aid box should include the following

- one guidance card on first aid
- twenty individually wrapped sterile adhesive dressings in assorted sizes
- two sterile eye pads, with attachment
- four individually wrapped triangular bandages
- six safety pins
- six medium sized individually wrapped sterile unmedicated wound dressings
- two large sterile individually wrapped unmedicated wound dressings
- one pair of disposable gloves.

Employer's duty in conducting risk assessments

- Employers of five or more employees need to record significant findings of the assessment.
- To Identify each main work operation and summarise its associated hazards

Steps to conducting a risk assessment

- Identify potential harm
- Who might be harmed?
- Is the risk adequately controlled?
- What further action is necessary to control the risk?
- Review the risk assessment

What is the employer's duty in conducting a control of substances hazardous to Health (COSHH) assessment?

- Employers must ensure that every hazardous substance used or generated in the workplace and to adopt appropriate control and monitoring procedures
- Employers must ensure that they prevent their employees being exposed to hazardous substances by using less harmful substitutes or different methods of work to reduce the risk
- Employers must take steps to control any risk identified

Employer's duty with regards to manual handling

- Employers must assess the risk of injury from manual handling
- Employers must establish measures to avoid hazardous manual handling
- Employers must provide information and training on handling loads

Health and safety audits

- Set out who, when, how and of what safety checks will be carried out

Review of policy

- Identify how the compliance with the policy will be monitored
- Identify how often the policy will be reviewed

DEVELOPING YOUR SUPPORT PLANNING

Under *Supporting People* more emphasis is being placed on the quality of support planning and involving service users. The accurate assessment of need and individual planning are important steps to ensure service users receive a service that reflects their needs. The Quality Assessment Framework (QAF) places a lot of emphasis on this. Not only does needs assessment feature as a standalone objective of the QAF but it is also a means of achieving the requirements of the other standards. Participation of service users is a key element in demonstrating good practice. Services will need to provide evidence that service users are involved and their views and aspirations are taken into account in the needs assessment and support planning process.

Involving the service user

For support planning to work effectively mutual commitment from the service user and the support worker to work together is essential. With participation a person will take more ownership and responsibility for decisions that are made.

roviders often find it a difficult to encourage service users to become involved. In support planning some of the barriers to participation can be reduced by:

- Explaining the process clearly.
- Describing its purpose.

- Recognising users current situation, eg do they have needs around financial security or housing that need to be met before other aspects are considered?
- Awareness of cultural, social and racial issues for client.
- Overcoming any anxiety/tension that support planning is an institutional tool that the service user does not need.
- Avoiding jargon.
- Using acceptable language, eg some service users may prefer the term 'individual plan' to 'support plan'.
- Using other means to establish preferences and dislikes when a service user has communication difficulties, eg facilitated communication, video, audio, graphics.
- Describing any restrictions on choice and freedom (agreed with service user) imposed by a specialist programme.
- Meeting at a venue where the service user feels comfortable.
- Setting objectives that are SMART (specific, measurable, achievable, realistic and time-related).
- Giving the service user a copy of the plan.
- Reviewing the plan on a regular basis

Assessment	The assessment process will identify strengths, gaps in skills, issues or problems for the individual. It is a participative process and there may be others involved apart from the user and support worker. A formal risk assessment process should be included as part of the assessment process
Support Planning	Planning can be broken down into six steps: • what needs to be addressed? • what is the solution or goal • how can the solution or goal be reached • who will be involved • what is the time scale • when will it be reviewed
Implementation	This is the stage where the issues identified in the assessment and planning stages begin to be addressed. Implementation will depend very much on the issues identified but can involve practical help with life or social skills, accessing other services including leisure, employment activities, counselling or therapy. It is important to clarify who is responsible for doing what at this stage.
Monitoring of the plan	Procedures and pro-formas for recording and monitoring frequency and content of sessions.

| Review Plan | Review the progress of the plan. This can be done both informally through regular meetings between the tenant and worker and formal review. The purpose of the review is to look at what has been achieved, identify strategies which have not been effective, help prioritise and allow for changes in circumstances. |

DEVELOPING AN EQUAL OPPORTUNITIES POLICY

An equal opportunities policy (EOP) is about fairness. Most providers will, of course, be behaving fairly towards their service users, employees and others. But you will need to codify this in a formal procedure – and everyone will need to check that the procedure is actually working,

The contractual commitment

The interim *Supporting People* contracts oblige providers to, 'use all reasonable endeavours' to make sure that an equal opportunities policy complies with all statutory obligations to avoid discrimination on a wide range of grounds including gender, age, religion, race, disability and sexual orientation. This obligation covers both staffing and service delivery matters.

Employment

You must observe the Commission for Racial Equality (CRE) Code of Practice for Employment, and provide the Administering Authority (AA) for *Supporting People* with information to allow them to assess your compliance with it. You must inform the AA if it is found you have unlawfully discriminated against any person in the provision of the support services. You will also have to inform the AA of your action plan to remedy the situation.

Services

You must give 'appropriate consideration' to each service user's race, nationality, cultural or ethnic background, marital status, age, gender, religion, sexual orientation and disabilities.

You need to adopt a written EOP policy and procedure that must address the points in the table below.

| Aims and public commitment | The policy should outline who complaints should be directed to, ie the person the complaint is about, their line manager or the member of staff responsible for a particular aspect of service provision. |
| | Any barriers which deter or prevent people from making complaints need to be identified and steps taken to remove them. |

	For instance by allowing advocates or other parties who are acting on behalf of the service user (with their permission) to make a complaint.
Responsible persons	State who is responsible for implementing and monitoring the policy and practices.
	Example: The Averill House project manager is responsible for implementing and monitoring our policy.
Information	Set out how the policy will be developed to take account of the needs and interests of all sections of the community.
	State how policy will be publicised to existing and potential staff, volunteers, service users.
	Example: We will consult with the local authority, local organisations representing discriminated against groups (inc CRE, others, list) in drafting our policy A copy of our policy will be issued to all users, staff and relatives or carers.
Action planning	Identify the project's present position on engagement of workers and contractors and applications from service users from discriminated against groups.
	Set out where the project should be in the future and what short and long term action is needed if the position needs to be changed.
	Example: Averill House currently employs X and accommodates X. Compared to the general population/needs of the area as identified in the SP strategy, X group is under-represented among employees/residents.
	Our action plan for 2007/08 is to: (include image, working practices, any other identified barriers to joining, train staff, develop links with communities)
Monitoring	Set out here how you will monitor the employment, promotion and access to training and development of those you engage to provide your services.
	Set out how you will monitor the applications and acceptances of those wishing to use the projects support services.

	Set out how you will monitor harassment or discrimination against workers or service users.
	Example: Averill House (named Post) will record the characteristics (list sources of discrimin-ation) of all applicants for housing at the project and of all those accepted as residents on the (equivalent to the CORE form) attached.
Review	Make a commitment to review practices regularly to see if delivering outcomes required by action plan
	Set out who will do this and how often
	Example: the monitoring information described above will be compiled and monitored by [named post], compared to the current action plan targets and reported to the owner/committee/SP team) each quarter/year

DEVELOPING A COMPLAINTS PROCEDURE

A person's right to complain should be recognised and supported at all levels of the service. A clearly understandable complaints policy that all service users and staff are familiar with will contribute to this. All service users and staff should have the policy and their responsibilities explained at their induction to the service.

You may be expected to at the reasonable request of funders to supply a copy of your records relating to complaints made in relation to the services and your response.

A complaints procedure should follow a staged process with the aim to resolve the issue as early as possible, before it escalates. It is useful to allow more informal complaints to be resolved quickly without the need for a long drawn out investigation. Where it is not possible to sort them out at this stage then a more comprehensive process can be instigated.

Checklist

In summary a complaints procedure should at least cover the following points:

CHECKLIST	GOOD PRACTICE
Identify the purpose of the policy	Outline what it aims to do and who it is for:staff, service users etc.
Separate procedure for informal	The policy should define the difference between an informal, often verbal, complaint, and a

complaints and formal complaint	formal, often written, complaint. In all cases a person who makes a complaint needs to feel their concern is being listened to.
Identify to whom complaints should be directed – may depend on who or what the complaint is about	The policy should outline who complaints should be directed to, ie the person the complaint is about or their line manager, the member of staff responsible for a particular aspect of service provision etc. Any barriers which deter or prevent people from making complaints need to be identified and steps taken to remove them. For instance allowing advocates or other parties who are acting on behalf of the service user (with their permission) to make a complaint.
	Issues of confidentiality need to be addressed. Service users need to have confidence that they will not suffer detriment as a result of making a complaint.
How should the complaint be made – verbally or in writing?	Flexibility is important so that individuals are not discouraged from complaining but informal complaints are usually made verbally and formal complaints are made in writing. The policy should outline what information should be included in the complaint i.e. enough detail for the complaint to be fully investigated, and suggestions for how the complaint might be resolved. Complainants may need support.
What will you do when a complaint is made?	The policy should outline what response a complainant can expect and what action will be taken, ie how you will investigate the complaint, what action you will take.
	All complaints should be dealt with promptly and investigated impartially.
How quickly will you acknowledge and respond?	It should state the time limits for responses, eg to acknowledge, investigate and provide a full response to complaint. The complainant (or person acting for them) should be informed of the progress and result of the investigation, if there are any delays in response and the reason for the delay.
Will you respond in writing or verbally?	Informal complaints may be responded to verbally, but formal complaints must be responded to in writing within the time scales outlined in the policy. It is good practice to also respond to informal complaints in writing.

What will you say?	The policy should outline the limitations of a response to a complaint, ie where confidentiality must be maintained. Policies should also outline that responses will include the organisation's View/understanding of the complaint and what action it proposes to take.
What should people do if they are not satisfied with your response?	If a complainant is not satisfied with the response there should be a specified process for appealing the decision. Details of relevant external bodies should be included in the policy.

DEVELOPING AN ANTI-SOCIAL BEHAVIOUR POLICY AND PROCEDURE

Content of policy

The policy statement should include a description of the conduct that can amount to anti-social behaviour (ASB) including examples of what this means in practice, eg noise nuisance or dealing drugs. It should set out the provider's general approach, and the range of services offered to tackle ASB. The standards of behaviour expected of tenants, household or visitors should be clear with reference to clauses in the tenancy agreement.

Specific policies dealing with ASB should be outlined in detail in the statement. These may include

- Support of complainants
- Racial and other harassment polices
- Domestic violence policy
- Prevention of ASB
- Supporting witnesses
- Professional witness schemes
- Data protection and information exchange
- Confidentiality
- Cross-tenure issues
- Training of staff
- Multi-agency partnerships

Support

Providers should consider the positive effects that support might have on perpetrators. The impact of case law on nuisance and disability is making itself felt as providers are expected to ensure that those who may already feel stigmatised (eg those with mental health problems) are treated equitably where allegations of ASB are made.

Managing agents

Where managing agents manage Registered Social Landlords (RSLs) stock they should be involved in the preparation of policies and procedures as these affect the delivery of their housing management responsibilities. RSLs must ensure managing agents understand their role and responsibilities under the policy statement and that robust working arrangements are in place covering information sharing, handling and monitoring complaints and dealing with perpetrators. Managing agents can either adopt the RSL's policy or develop their own.

Content of procedures

The statement should include the operational procedures introduced to implement polices on ASB including:

- How and to whom the initial complaint should be made and give contact details.
- How the complaint will be processed and how complainants are kept informed of progress.
- How complainants support needs will be met
- The options available to the provider to tackle the ASB from mediation to possession or demotion of tenancy.
- How ASB and the services for tackling ASB will be monitored

Developing an anti-social behaviour strategy

Providers who are RSLs not only need policies and procedures dealing with types of ASB eg racial harassment, domestic violence, but also an overall strategy that includes their range of approaches in tackling ASB. This is good practice for other providers of supported housing. The following guidelines have been drawn up from some of the recommendations in the Housing Corporation briefing on anti-social behaviour.

Planning

- Your strategy should be based on current research on the types of ASB service users experience and the scope of the problem. It should define what you consider to be ASB so users know what behaviour should be reported.
- Your service users should be involved in drawing up the strategy and developing targets.
- Your strategy should be clearly understood by both staff and service users; this will prevent inconsistencies in staff approach to ASB.
- The policies and procedures should be based on your service users needs, transparent and fair to both complainants and alleged perpetrators. It is crucial that service users feel they can report ASB without fear of intimidation.
- You consider crime prevention as key to all existing services and development of new services eg is your office located in an area covered by CCTV

Service delivery

- The service users' occupancy or support contracts/agreements need to contain clear clauses regarding ASB and the sanctions you will use e.g. withdrawing services or eviction in extreme cases.

- Your service users handbook should give information on addressing ASB and what support is available
- Your procedure needs to tackle ASB at an early stage, and consideration given to the tools available, acceptable behaviour contracts, injunctions, ASB orders etc. Procedures should ensure that complainants are kept informed of progress and it is clear when and how the case is closed.
- Staff should be trained to handle both causes and effects of ASB and be aware of and able to involve other service providers e.g. the police or social services. You should have information sharing protocols with other agencies.
- You should have procedures in place to ensure that your strategy reflects current legislation, policy and good practice. Smaller providers may want to give a member of staff specific responsibility for ASB to ensure all cases are dealt with consistently and the organisation keeps up to date.

Consultation, monitoring and review

- All your stakeholders should be involved in reviewing your strategy. The local crime and disorder reduction partnership is a good forum to identifying local problems and agencies involved in strategic and practical management of ASB in your area. You may want to become involved in local initiatives such as mentoring schemes with children focussing on the effects of ASB.
- Publicise your strategy making sure it is plain English so all staff, users, stakeholders and the community know of its existence and are able to use it.
- Complaints, satisfaction surveys and your methods of user participation should be used to find out if users are satisfied with the way that you manage ASB.
- Contact other groups in your area to compare your performance and share good practice – don't reinvent the wheel.
- Have effective methods of monitoring so you can assess whether your approach is working and how it can be improved. Reports should be made regularly to the governing board that approve the strategy to ensure the whole organisation is seeking continuous improvement.

Specimen documents

Rent Increase Notice (HA 1988 s13(2))

Equitable tenancy agreement

Notice of Seeking Possession (NOSP) for Secure tenancy (HA 1998 s83)

Notice of Seeking Possession (NOSP) for Assured tenancy (HA 1988 s21)

Section 21 Notice requiring possession

Notice to Quit

Notice termination of licence to occupy

Statement of service

RENT INCREASE NOTICE (HA 1988 s13(2))

Oyez Form No. 4B of the Assured
Tenancies and Agricultural Occupancies
(Forms) (Amendment) (England) Regulations 2003

HOUSING ACT 1988

Section 13(2), as amended by the Regulatory Reform (Assured Periodic Tenancies) (Rent Increases) Order 2003

Landlord's Notice Proposing a New Rent Under an Assured Periodic Tenancy of Premises Situated in England

The notes over the page give guidance to both landlords and tenants about this notice.

(1) Insert the tenant(s).

To(^{1}):

(2) Insert the address of the premises subject to the tenancy.

of(^{2}):

(3) Insert an address for correspondence and a contact telephone number.

From(^{3}):

[Landlord(s)][Landlord's Agent](^{4})

(4) Delete as appropriate.

1. **This notice affects the amount of rent you pay.** Please read it carefully.

2. The landlord is proposing a new rent of £   **per [week][month][year]**(^{4}), in place of the existing one of £   per [week][month][year](^{4})

(5) See note 10 over the page.

3. The first rent increase date after 11th February 2003 is (^{5})

(6) See notes 13-17 over the page.

4. The starting date for the new rent will be (^{6})

(7) See note 11 over the page.

5. Certain charges may be included and separately identified in your rent(^{7}).The amounts of the charges (if any) are:

Charges	Amount included and separately identified *(enter "nil" if appropriate)*	
	In the existing rent	In the proposed new rent
Council tax	£	£
Water charges	£	£
Fixed service charges	£	£

6. If you accept the proposed new rent, you should make arrangements to pay it. If you do not accept it, there are steps you should take before the starting date in paragraph 4 above. **Please see the notes over the page for what to do next.**

(8) See note 12 over the page.

Signed: [Landlord(s)][Landlord's Agent](^{4})(^{8})

Date: 20th August 2007

[P.T.O.

Please read these notes carefully.

Guidance notes for tenants

What you must do now

1. This notice proposes that you should pay a new rent from the date in paragraph 4 of the notice. **If you are in any doubt or need advice about any aspect of this notice, you should immediately either discuss it with your landlord or take it to a citizens' advice bureau, a housing advice centre, a law centre or a solicitor.**

2. If you accept the proposed new rent, please make arrangements to pay it. If you pay by standing order through your bank, you should inform them that the amount has changed. You should also notify your Housing Benefit office if you are claiming benefit. If you are worried that you might not be able to pay your rent, you should seek advice from a citizens' advice bureau or housing advice centre.

3. If you do **not** accept the proposed new rent, and do not wish to discuss it with your landlord, you can refer this notice to your local rent assessment committee. **You must do this before the starting date of the proposed new rent in paragraph 4 of the notice.** You should notify your landlord that you are doing so, otherwise he or she may assume that you have agreed to pay the proposed new rent.

4. To refer the notice to the local rent assessment committee, you must use the form *Application Referring a Notice Proposing a New Rent under an Assured Periodic Tenancy or Agricultural Occupancy to a Rent Assessment Committee.* You can obtain this from a rent assessment panel, housing advice centre or legal stationer (Oyez form HA34) (details can be found in the telephone directory).

5. The rent assessment committee will consider your application and decide what the maximum rent for your home should be. In setting a rent, the committee must decide what rent the landlord could reasonably expect for the property if it were let on the open market under a new tenancy on the same terms. The committee may therefore set a rent that is higher, lower or the same as the proposed new rent.

Guidance notes for landlords on how to complete the notice

6. You can complete this notice in ink or arrange for it to be printed.

7. This notice should be used when proposing a new rent under an **assured periodic tenancy (including an assured shorthold periodic tenancy) of premises situated in England.** There is a different notice (Form No. 4C - *Landlord's or Licensor's Notice Proposing a New Rent or Licence Fee under an Assured Agricultural Occupancy of Premises Situated in England*) (Oyez form HA33C) for proposing a new rent or licence fee for an assured agricultural occupancy of premises situated in England.

8. Do not use this notice if the tenancy agreement contains a term allowing rent increases, or there is some other basis such as a separate agreement with the tenant for raising the rent. Any provision you rely on needs to be binding on the tenant. Legal advice should be sought if there is any doubt on this score.

9. You need to use a different form to propose a rent increase for a statutory periodic tenancy (the first exception mentioned in note 16) if you are seeking to adjust rent solely because of a proposed change of terms under section 6(2) of the Housing Act 1988. Seek legal advice if you think this may apply to you. You can obtain the form headed *Notice Proposing Different Terms for a Statutory Periodic Tenancy* from a rent assessment panel or a legal stationer (Oyez form HA30).

10. Unless the tenancy is a new one, or one of the exceptions mentioned in note 16 applies, you must insert in paragraph 3 of the notice the first date after 11th February 2003, on which rent is proposed to be, or was, increased under this statutory notice procedure. That date determines the date that you can specify in paragraph 4 of the notice. See also note 15.

11. You should enter in each of the boxes in the second and third columns of the table in paragraph 5 either "nil" or the amount of the existing or proposed charge. You should only enter amounts for council tax and water charges where the tenant does not pay these charges directly. You should only enter fixed service charges which are payable by the tenant in accordance with a term or condition which specifies that these charges will be included in the rent for the tenancy. Only enter an amount for service charges where the tenant has agreed to pay a **fixed** sum. Do **not** include in the table any **variable** service charge, ie a service charge within the meaning of section 18 of the Landlord and Tenant Act 1985, where the whole or part of the sum payable by the tenant varies or may vary according to **costs**.

12. You or your agent (someone acting on your behalf) must sign and date this notice. If there are joint landlords, each landlord must sign unless one signs on behalf of the rest with their agreement. The signature does not have to be hand-written if, for instance, the form is being printed or if you wish to use a laser or autosignature.

When the proposed new rent can start

13. The date in paragraph 4 of the notice must comply with the three requirements of section 13(2) of the Housing Act 1988, as amended by the Regulatory Reform (Assured Periodic Tenancies) (Rent Increases) Order 2003.

14. The **first requirement**, which applies in **all** cases, is that a minimum period of notice must be given before the proposed new rent can take effect. That period is:

- one month for a tenancy which is monthly or for a lesser period, for instance weekly or fortnightly;
- six months for a yearly tenancy;
- in all other cases, a period equal to the length of the period of the tenancy - for example, three months in the case of a quarterly tenancy.

15. The **second requirement** applies in **most** cases (but see note 16 for two exceptions):

(a) the starting date for the proposed new rent must not be earlier than 52 weeks after the date on which the rent was last increased using this statutory notice procedure or, if the tenancy is new, the date on which it started, **unless**

(b) that would result in an increase date falling one week or more before the anniversary of the date in paragraph 3 of the notice, in which case the starting date must not be earlier than 53 weeks from the date on which the rent was last increased.

This allows rent increases to take effect on a fixed day each year where the period of a tenancy is less than one month. For example, the rent for a weekly tenancy could be increased on, say, the first Monday in April. Where the period of a tenancy is monthly, quarterly, six monthly or yearly, rent increases can take effect on a fixed date, for example, 1st April.

16. The two exceptions to the second requirement, which apply where a statutory tenancy has followed on from an earlier tenancy, are:

- where the tenancy was originally for a fixed term (for instance, 6 months), but continues on a periodic basis (for instance, monthly) after the term ends; and
- where the tenancy came into existence on the death of the previous tenant who had a regulated tenancy under the Rent Act 1977.

In these cases the landlord may propose a new rent at once. However, the first and third requirements referred to in notes 14 and 17 must still be observed.

17. The **third requirement**, which applies in **all** cases, is that the proposed new rent must start at the beginning of a period of the tenancy. For instance, if the tenancy is monthly, and started on the 20th of the month, rent will be payable on that day of the month, and a new rent must begin then, not on any other day of the month. If the tenancy is weekly, and started, for instance, on a Monday, the new rent must begin on a Monday.

AGREEMENT FOR TENANCY

This agreement for a tenancy is between

Name and address of the *Landlord/Housing Association:*

_____

_____

(acting through its agent [*name and address of agent*]
and

_____

Name and address of the tenant

_____

_____

in respect of
[Address of premises including room number for shared]

_____

_____

The tenancy begins on the   2007
the terms of the tenancy are set out in the attached agreement.

It is agreed as follows:

1)   The [name of Landlord Housing Association] agrees:

a)   To grant the tenant an Assured (*Shorthold*) Tenancy of the Premises in the form of the attached Tenancy Agreement on the .... day of .... 200 . (the date on which the tenant reaches their 18th birthday);

b)   To observe and perform the obligations of the *Landlord/Housing Association* contained in the attached Tenancy Agreement from the date of this agreement.

c)   The *Landlord/Housing Association* shall not be obliged to grant the Tenancy to any person other than the tenant.

d)   The *Landlord/Housing Association* considers 28 days a reasonable time for the tenant to renounce this Agreement and the tenancy on attaining the age of 18. If the Agreement and the tenancy is renounced, the tenant will still be liable to pay for the time the tenant had the Agreement and will be liable for any breaches of terms committed whilst in occupation and the tenant will not in any circumstances be able to reclaim any money paid.

2)   The tenant agrees:

a)   To sign a counterpart of the tenancy;

b)   To accept an Assured (*Shorthold*) Tenancy on reaching their 18th birthday;

c) To observe and perform the obligations of the tenant contained in the attached Tenancy Agreement from the date of this agreement;

d) Not to assign or underlet this Agreement in whole or in part to any other person.

e) If the tenancy is to be held by more than one person, each of those persons shall be responsible in full for the tenant's obligations and liabilities under this agreement.

3) Termination of the Agreement

a) If there is a breach of the terms of this Agreement (including the terms of the attached Tenancy agreement) by the tenant, this Agreement may be ended by the *Landlord/Housing Association* serving written notice on the tenant in accordance with the terms of clauses........................... and .... of the attached Tenancy Agreement and when the notice period expires, this Agreement will end and be null and void.

b) Ending the Agreement in this way will not affect the rights of the *Landlord/Housing Association* against the tenant in respect of any breach of any of the provisions of this Agreement by the tenant prior to the Agreement being ended.

c) In the event that the tenant does not reach his/her 18th birthday this Agreement will end and have no further effect.

4) Signature of the parties

Signed on behalf of the *Landlord/Housing Association*

_____ (Name)

_____ (Position)

_____ (Date)

Signed by the tenant

_____ (Name)

_____ (Date)

NOTICE OF SEEKING POSSESSION: HOUSING ACT 1985 s83

THIS NOTICE IS THE FIRST STEP TOWARDS REQUIRING YOU TO GIVE UP POSSESSION OF YOUR DWELLING.

YOU SHOULD READ IT VERY CAREFULLY.

1) **To [secure tenants]**

_____

- If you need advice about this notice and what you should do about it, take it as quickly as possible to a Citizen's advice Bureau, a Housing Aid Centre, or a Law Centre, or to a Solicitor. You may be able to receive Legal Aid but this will depend on your personal circumstances.

2) **[landlord's name]**

_____

Intends to apply to the Court for an order requiring you to give up possession of:

[address of property]

_____

- If you are a secure tenant under the Housing Act 1985, you can only be required to leave your dwelling if your landlord obtains an order for possession from the Court. The order must be based on one or more of the Grounds which are set out in the 1985 Act (see paragraphs 3 and 4 below).

If you are willing to give up possession without a court order, you should notify the person who signed the notice as soon as possible and say when you would leave.

3) **POSSESSION WILL BE SOUGHT ON GROUND(S) OF SCHEDULE 2 TO THE HOUSING ACT 1985 WHICH READS**

Grounds:

_____

* Whatever grounds for possession are set out in paragraph 3 of this notice, the Court may allow any of the other grounds to be added at a later stage. If this is done, you will be told about it so you can argue at the hearing in Court about the new ground, as well as the grounds set out in paragraph 3, if you want to.

4) PARTICULARS OF EACH GROUND ARE AS FOLLOWS:

_____

_____

_____

_____

_____

_____

- Before the Court grants an order on any of the Grounds 1 to 8 or 12 to 16 it must be satisfied that it is reasonable to require you to leave. This means that, if one of these Grounds is set out in paragraph 3 of this notice, you will be able to argue at the hearing in Court that it is not reasonable that you should have to leave, even if you accept the Ground applies.
- Before the court grants an order on any of the Grounds 9 to 16 it must be satisfied that there will be suitable alternative accommodation for you when you have to leave. This means that the court will have to decide that, in its opinion, there will be other accommodation which is reasonably suitable for the needs of you and your family, taking into account various factors such as the nearness of your place of work, and the sort of housing that other people with similar needs are offered. Your new home will have to be let to you on another secure tenancy or a private tenancy under the Rent Act of a kind that will give you similar security. There is no requirement for suitable alternative accommodation where Grounds 1 to 8 apply.

If your landlord is not the local authority, and the local authority gives a certificate that they will provide you with suitable alternative accommodation, the court has to accept the certificate.

One of the requirements of ground 10A is that the landlord must have approval for the redevelopment scheme from the Secretary of State (or, in the case of a housing association landlord, the Housing Corporation). The landlord must have consulted all secure tenants affected by the proposed redevelopment scheme.

Cross out this paragraph if possession *is* being sought on Ground 2 of Schedule 2 of the Housing Act 1985 (whether or not possession is also sought on another Ground)

5) THE COURT PROCEEDINGS WILL NOT BE BEGUN UNTIL AFTER

- Court proceedings cannot be begun until after this date,which cannot be earlier than the date when your tenancy or licence could have been brought to an end. This means that if you have a weekly or fortnightly tenancy, there should be at least 4 weeks between the date this notice is given and the date in this paragraph.
- After this date, court proceedings may be begun at once or at any time during the following twelve months. Once the twelve months are up this notice will lapse and a new notice must be served before possession can be sought.

Cross out this paragraph if possession *not* being sought on Ground 2 of Schedule 2 of the Housing Act 1985

5) COURT PROCEEDINGS FOR POSSESSION OF THE DWELLING-HOUSE CAN BE BEGUN IMMEDIATELY. THE DATE BY WHICH THE TENANT IS TO GIVE UP POSSESSION OF THE DWELLING-HOUSE IS

- Court proceedings may be begun at once or at any time during the following twelve months. Once the twelve months are up, this Notice will lapse and a new Notice must be served before possession can be sought.
- Possession of your dwelling-house cannot be obtained until after this date, which cannot be earlier than the date when your tenancy or licence could have been brought to an end. This means that if you have a weekly or fortnightly tenancy, there should be at least four weeks between the date this Notice is given and the date possession is ordered.

Signed:

---

on behalf of *

---

whose address is *

_____

_____

_____

_____

Date:

_____

LANDLORD AND TENANT ACT 1987 s48
* This is the address of the Landlord at which notices (including notices in proceedings) may be served

The original of which this notice is a copy was served:

On (date) at approximately (time)

_____

Method of service:

_____

Signed:

_____

Witness:

_____

NOTICE SEEKING POSSESSION OF A PROPERTY LET ON AN ASSURED TENANCY OR AN ASSURED AGRICULTURAL OCCUPANCY

- Please write clearly in black ink
- Please tick boxes where appropriate and cross out text marked with an asterisk (*) that does not apply
- This form should be used where possession of accommodation let under an assured tenancy, an assured agricultural occupancy or an assured shorthold tenancy is sought on one of the grounds in Schedule 2 to the Housing Act 1988
- Do not use this form if possession is sought on the ?shorthold? ground under section 21 of the Housing Act 1988 from an assured shorthold tenant where the fixed term has come to an end or, for assured shorthold tenancies with no fixed term which started on or after 28 February 1997, after six months has elapsed.

  There is no prescribed form for these cases, but you must give notice in writing.

1) To: *Name(s) of tenant(s) / licensee(s)**

   _____

   _____

   _____

   _____

- **Tenants full name including change of name or street name**

   _____

   _____

2) Your landlord / licensor * **Housing Association/Trust/Group** intends to apply to the court for an order requiring you to give up possession of:

   _____

   _____

   _____

   _____

Full address including room/flat number and any shared communal areas

   _____

   _____

   _____

   _____

3) Your landlord / licensor* intends to seek possession on ground(s)

? in Schedule 2 to the Housing Act 1988, as amended by the Housing Act 1996, which reads:

FULL TEXT OF GROUNDS RELIED ON FROM SCHEDULE 2 OF THE 1988 HOUSING ACT AS AMENDED BY THE 1996 HOUSING ACT. THE GROUNDS RELIED ON MUST BE IDENTIFIED IN THE TENANCY AGREEMENT.

_____

_____

_____

_____

_____

Give the full text (as set out in the Housing Act 1988, as amended by the Housing Act 1996) of each ground which is being relied on. Continue on a separate sheet if necessary.

4)   Give a full explanation of why each ground is being relied on:

THERE MUST BE A FULL EXPLANATION OF THE REASON WHY EACH GROUND HAS BEEN CITED.

THE NOSP SERVES 3 PURPOSES
1)   **TO DEMONSTRATE TO THE TENANT HOW THEY HAVE BREACHED THE AGREEMENT**
2)   **TO INFORM THEM WHAT THEY HAVE TO DO TO REMEDY THE BREACH AND**
3)   **TO ALLOW THEM TO PREPARE A DEFENCE.**

IN RENT ARREARS MATTERS THIS IS USUALLY STRAIGHT-FORWARD HOWEVER IN NUISANCE MATTERS A LENGTHY EXPLANATION WILL BE REQUIRED. SPECIFIC DETAIL MUST BE INCLUDED THAT IS DATES TIMES AND INCIDENTS.

_____

_____

_____

_____

5)   The court proceedings will not begin until after **STATUTORY**

NOTICE PERIOD OR CONTRACTUAL NOTICE PERIOD. NOTICE PERIOD MUST START ON THE BEGINNING OF A PERIOD AND END ON THE LAST DAY OF A TENANCY PERIOD USUALLY FOLLOWS RENT PERIOD MONDAY TO SUNDAY

- Where the landlord is seeking possession under grounds 1, 2, 5 to 7, 9 or 16, court proceedings cannot begin earlier than 2 months from the date this notice is served on you (even where one of grounds 3, 4, 8, 10 to 13, 14A, 15 or 17 is specified) and not before the date on which the tenancy (had it not been assured) could have been brought to an end by a notice to quit served at the same time as this notice.
- Where the landlord is seeking possession on grounds 3, 4, 8 or 10 to 13, 14A, 15 or 17, Court proceedings cannot begin until 2 weeks after the date this notice is served (unless one of grounds 1, 2, 5 to 7, 9 or 16 is also specified in which case they cannot begin earlier than two months from the date this notice is served).
- Where the landlord is seeking possession on ground 14 (with or without other grounds), court proceedings cannot begin before the date this notice is served.
- Where the landlord is seeking possession on ground 14A, court proceedings cannot begin unless the landlord has served, or has taken all reasonable steps to serve, a copy of this notice on the partner who has left the property.
- After the date shown in paragraph 5, Court proceedings may be begun at once but not later than 12 months from the date this notice is served. After this time the notice will lapse and a new notice must be served before possession can be sought.

6)   Name and address of landlord / licensor *.

_____

_____

_____

Signed   Date

_____

Please specify whether: landlord [ ] licensor [ ] joint landlords [ ] landlords agent [ ]

Name(s)
(Block Capitals)

_____

Address

_____

_____

_____

_____

Telephone: Daytime: Evening:

_____

What to do if this notice is served on you

* This notice is the first step towards requiring you to give up possession of your home. You should read it very carefully.

* Your landlord cannot make you leave your home without an order for possession issued by a court. By issuing this notice your landlord is informing you that he intends to seek such an order. If you are willing to give up possession without a court order, you should tell the person who signed this notice as soon as possible and say when you are prepared to leave.

* Whichever grounds are set out in section 3 of this form, the court may allow any of the other grounds to be added at a later date. If this is done, you will be told about it so you can discuss the additional grounds at the court hearing as well as the grounds set out in section 3.

* If you need advice about this notice, and what you should do about it, take it immediately to a citizens advice bureau, a housing advice centre, a law centre or a solicitor.

LANDLORD AND TENANT ACT 1987 s48: Notices (including notices in proceedings) may be served on the landlord at the address shown in this notice.

The original of which this notice is a copy was served:

_____

On (date)   *at approximately (time)*

_____

Method of service:

_____

Signed: *Witness:*

_____

NOTICE REQUIRING POSSESSION – HOUSING ACT 1988 s21 AS AMENDED BY HOUSING ACT 1996

To (tenant's name):   [tenant(s) names(s) including change of name or street name]

_____

_____

_____

I/We (your landlords) [**Name of landlord**]

_____

_____

_____

Hereby give you Notice pursuant to section 21 of the Housing Act 1988, as amended by the Housing Act 1996, that possession of the premises at:

_____

_____

_____

(address) [**The address of the premises, including room/flat number (and communal areas if sharing) as stated on Tenancy Agreement**]

_____

_____

_____

Will be required on the: > **Always calculate the notice period to start from the Monday following the issue. If section 21 is served on a Monday, that day is discounted for calculating the period. The period should then be calculated from the following Monday.**
> **Section 21, requires two full calendar months notice from the Monday following service of the Notice, therefore if you serve a Notice on a Thursday calculate two months from the next Monday and ensure that it ends on a Sunday.**

(date)

_____

Or if your tenancy has already expired, at the end of the period of your tenancy expiring next after two months from the date this Notice is given to you, if that is later than the date shown above.

Date of Notice: **[Insert date served]**

Signed: **[The person signing should sign here]**

Landlord's name *: **[Insert RSL's name]**

Landlord's address*: **[Insert RSL's address]**

*Landlord and Tenant Act 1987 s48
The name and address of the Landlord at which notices (including notices in proceedings) may be served is that shown against 'Landlord's name' and 'Landlord's address' above.

The original of which this notice is a copy was served on:

(date):   *At approximately (time):*

Method of service:

Signed: *Witness (optional):*

NOTICE TO QUIT

NOTICE TO QUIT

(BY LANDLORD OF PREMISES LET AS A DWELLING)

Name and Address of Tenant.	To of
Name and Address of Landlord.	[I] [We] [as] [on behalf of] your landlord[s], of
*Me/them or as appropriate. †Address of premises. ‡ Date for possession.	give you **NOTICE TO QUIT** and deliver up possession to* of† on‡ , or the day on which a complete period of your tenancy expires next after the end of four weeks from the service of this notice.
Date of notice.	Dated 22nd August 2007 Signed _____
Name and Address of Agent if Agent serves notice.	

INFORMATION FOR TENANT
(See Note 2 overleaf)

1.   If the tenant or licensee does not leave the dwelling, the landlord or licensor must get an order for possession from the court before the tenant or licensee can lawfully be evicted. The landlord or licensor cannot apply for such an order before the notice to quit or notice to determine has run out.

2.   A tenant or licensee who does not know if he has any right to remain in possession after a notice to quit or a notice to determine runs out can obtain advice from a solicitor. Help with all or part of the cost of legal advice and assistance may be available under the Legal Aid Scheme. He should also be able to obtain information from a Citizens' Advice Bureau, a Housing Aid Centre or a Rent Officer.

[P.T.O.

NOTES

1. Notice to quit premises let as a dwelling must be given at least four weeks before it takes effect, and it must be in writing (Protection from Eviction Act 1977, s. 5 as amended).

2. Where a notice to quit is given by a landlord to determine a tenancy of any premises let as a dwelling, the notice must contain this information (The Notices to Quit etc. (Prescribed Information) Regulations 1988).

3. Some tenancies are excluded from this protection: see Protection from Eviction Act 1977, ss. 3A and 5(1B).

L&T61/2

NOTICE OF TERMINATION OF LICENCE TO OCCUPY

(EXCLUDED LICENCE)

[Name of RSL]

To: *(Name of Resident)*

_____

Of: *(Address of Property)*

_____
_____
_____
_____

I *(Name of Person issuing the Notice),*

_____

being a *(job title)*

_____

for the *(name of managing agent)*

_____

a managing agency on behalf of: *(name of RSL)*

Of : *(Address of RSL)*

_____
_____
_____
_____

hereby give you Notice to Quit *(room number and address)*

_____
_____
_____
_____

In accordance with your licence agreement you are given hours/days to vacate the property from the date of service of this notice.
The reason why your Licence has been terminated is as follows:

_____
_____
_____
_____

_____

_____

_____

Date:

_____

Signed:

_____

FOR: *(name of managing agent/landlord)*

_____

Date/Time served:

_____

You must ensure that all of your personal belongings are also removed. If you fail to do so your possessions will be removed and stored at your expense. If they are not claimed they will be disposed of after 28 days.

STATEMENT OF SERVICE

Standard Wording of Statement

CLAIM NO:

IN THE [NAME]

COUNTY COURT

BETWEEN:

Name of housing trust/group(and managing agent)

Claimant

and

Name of tenant

Defendant

STATEMENT OF [job title of staff member]

I, [*name of staff member*], a Housing Officer with [name] of Housing Trust/Group (Managing Agents on behalf of Housing Trust/Group), am duly authorised to sign the following statement on behalf of the Trust.

I confirm that I served [*type of notice for example notice to quit*] on the Defendant at [*address of property including flat/room number*] on [*date and time notice was served*] by [*method of service e.g. pushing under the door of flat C*].

Signed:

Dated:

Name of Housing Trust/Group

_____

_____

Address of Regional Office

_____

_____

_____

_____

Address of Area/managing agents office

_____

_____

_____

_____

Index

Sitra training and consultancy

Sitra is the leading umbrella organisation for the housing with care and support sector. We have over 20 years' experience of delivering high calibre and cost-effective services making us the preferred choice for many organisations. Our experts offer policy advice and guidance, training and consultancy services, all tailored to your unique needs.

Sitra specialises in:

► Business development – helping you to compete in the new market place
► Leadership and management – implementing structural and cultural change
► Personal and professional development – building the capacity of your workforce
► Policy and regulation – making sense of the changing political environment
► Involving service users – helping you to put your clients at the heart of what you do
► Delivering front line services – making sure your working practices are 'fit for purpose'

Our specialist trainers can offer cost-effective, bespoke in-house training courses or you can attend a course on our open programme training. **Call the Inspire Team on 020 7793 4713 to arrange your training package or visit www.sitra.org.uk.**

Sitra is committed to delivering quality, dynamic solutions inspiring you to shape the services your organisation needs to succeed.

sitra

policy, training & consultancy
for housing with care and support

lag.org.uk

- Read sample chapters of our titles.

- Access the *Legal Action* editorial archive.

- Read the news stories from the latest issue of *Legal Action*.

- Register your interests to receive free e-mail bulletins on relevant LAG products and policy.

- Find out more details on our full range of training courses.

- Use the new simplified ordering process for secure online purchases of our products.

- Find out more about the LAG membership scheme and donate money to help fund our campaigns.

- Get access to our full policy archives: discussion papers, press releases, consultation responses and parliamentary briefings.

Legal Action Group | working with lawyers and advisers to promote equal access to justice

The Adviser's Toolkit
giving legal advice

Elaine Heslop

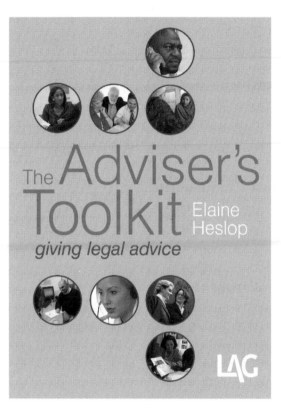

The Adviser's Toolkit: giving legal advice supports advisers by providing guidance on the skills and processes of advice-giving against a background of the key areas of social welfare law. It clearly illustrates each topic through the use of case studies, flow charts, examples of letters and documents. This is a highly practical resource for advisers working in both the voluntary and statutory sectors. It provides expert guidance from an experienced practitioner and adviser on the core advice-giving skills.

Pb 978 1 903307 49 6 c350pp October 2007 c£22

www.lag.org.uk/books

LAG

Legal**Action**

The only independent magazine to cover areas of interest to legal aid
practitioners, advisers and local authority staff.

Each month Legal Action includes:

editorial
Legal Action's editorials are renowned and
respected for their challenging and thought-
provoking approach to recent events.

news and features
The news and features pages give the latest
information and critical opinion on a broad
range of subjects.

noticeboard
Legal Action also gives you access to information
on courses, meetings, conferences, seminars,
and training contracts.

law and practice
Legal Action's authoritative law and practice
pages are written by a team of expert solicitors,
barristers and advisers. These pages will keep
you up to date with the law, practice and
procedure that affect your area of work.

ISSN 0306 7963

For more information on subscription rates visit:
www.lag.org.uk/magazine